Guide to Musical America

GUIDE TO
MUSICAL AMERICA

By Lynne Gusikoff

Facts On File Publications
New York, New York ● Bicester, England

Guide to Musical America

Library of Congress Cataloging in Publication Data

Gusikoff, Lynne.
  Guide to musical America.

  Bibliography: p.
  Includes index.
  1. Music—United States—History and criticism.
I. Title.
ML200.G95 1983   781.773   82-7377
ISBN 0-87196-701-4

Maps by Eric Elias

Printed in the United States of America

10 9 8 7 6 5 4 3 2 1

To the memory of my father,
Isadore Gusikoff

And to my mother,
Alice Gusikoff

CONTENTS

WEST

WEST COAST

ACKNOWLEDGEMENTS

Expert and congenial help in preparing this book was provided by a number of people and organizations, to whom I would like to offer thanks and appreciation.

First, special thanks to Andrea Salop Terdiman for her research and for writing two chapters on the South—"Ragtime, Blues, Jazz" and "Opera, Symphonic Music, Dance". Andrea, granddaughter of the late Isadore Gusikoff, is an exquisitely sensitive, gifted young woman, in whose life the love of music occupies a central role. She has added her personal touch to the *Guide*.

Thanks go also to Helen Gusikoff Price for her firsthand observations of Preservation Hall in New Orleans, and to John Sinor for his competent guidance around San Diego. Mary Racette, faithful typist as always, has come through with a thoroughly professional job. And Gene R. Hawes was encouraging, supportive and infinitely helpful in his singularly reliable manner.

The following organizations, institutions and associates contributed significantly; if I have forgotten anyone, I ask forgiveness—the sin is omission rather than commission:

The Louisiana State Museum; Don Wick at the Tennessee Tourist Development Bureau in Nashville; Betty Martin at Charlie's Georgetown in Washington DC; Variety Artists International in Minneapolis; Maxine Makas of the Eglevsky Ballet; Gayle R. McIntosh, member of the St. Louis Symphony Orchestra; the great New York Philharmonic; Herbert Breslin, Inc.; The Arkansas Department of Tourism; Phyllis Torstrick at the Kentucky Opera Association; the Wichita Symphony Orchestra; Marilyn Foss, Orchestra of Santa Fe; the Cleveland Ballet; the San Francisco Symphony Orchestra; Marilyn Pred, Omaha Symphony; Kathy Hotchkin at the Seattle Opera Association; Robyn Carey Wilson, of the Cincinnati Opera Association, Jutta Visnick at the Portland Opera Association; Henry Fogel, National Symphony, Washington, DC; the Philadelphia Orchestra; Jennifer Wada at Carnegie Hall; Dover Publications in New York City; Dana A. Blanchard at the Vermont Travel Division; Martha Steger with Virginia State Travel; Gary L. Smith at the Visitors' Bureau, Winston-Salem, NC; Mack

Miles of the Department of Culture and History in West Virginia; Joan Wingerson, with the Kansas Arts Commission; Stuart Bernstein of Ohio Travel and Tourism; Kathy Bugman at the Indiana State Library; the Chicago Symphony Orchestra; Nevada Department of Economic Development; Susan Edwards of the South Dakota Department of Tourism; the Travel Bureau of Austin, TX; Linda Barragen at the Los Angeles Visitors' Bureau; Washington State Commerce and Economic Development Bureau; the Library of Congress; the New York Public Library; Lincoln Center Library for the Performing Arts; the Library for the Performing Arts at SUNY Purchase; the Atlanta Ballet; and the North Carolina Dance Theater.

A fine copyediting job was done by Ellen Mendelsohn. Finally, thanks to my editors, Eleanora Schoenebaum and Phil Saltz who worked with me knowledgeably and cheerfully to develop and complete the book.

INTRODUCTION

The intention of this book is twofold: to present historic highlights of different styles of music as they developed in particular regions of the United States at various times; and to specify certain geographic locations where one may hear different styles of music today. Thus, the armchair reader at home, as well as the music-loving traveler, can journey through the world of music, caught up in the sense of place and also of time. To my knowledge, this book is the first endeavor of such scope.

The *Guide* is organized according to five geographical regions: the Northeast; the South; the Midwest; the West; and the West Coast. Within a region, each of several chapters discusses a particular musical style. At the end of each regional section, a general map of that region as well as several maps of its large cities are annotated to show places significant for music. Although the city maps show many major streets and intersections, they are not meant to be complete street maps, such as may be obtained from chambers of commerce or tourist bureaus. The reader is urged to explore an area further after becoming generally familiar with what is available in terms of music.

I have been selective while journeying through music history, emphasizing significant developments relating to place and time: for example, jazz in the South in the early 1900s; psalmody in New England in the 17th and 18th centuries; symphonic music in the Northeast in the mid-1800s. Information was gathered from correspondence with major symphony orchestras, opera and ballet companies, tourist and travel bureaus, music agents and managers and public relations people; from general guidebooks; from extensive library research; and from my own continuing personal travels and experiences.

One observes that musical styles overlap today. Although the chapters in this book deal with specific styles, such as rock, jazz, country, etc., listening to music demonstrates clearly that styles have interacted, fused, and either diluted or added to each other's essence. Purity in form has yielded to the eclectic, and we now hear country-rock, folk-pop, and other modern hybrids. Nevertheless, I feel it is important to know how it all started and where, in order to listen to music knowledgeably and with enhanced pleasure.

Throughout the nation is a plethora of regional music fairs and festivals; numerous colleges and universities with active music departments and programs; and an inordinately large number of hotels, nightclubs, and museums all offer musical fare. It was an overwhelming task to decide which ones to list. Limits of space and my own judgment were solely responsible for the choices. I trust that any omissions will not be interpreted as being unimportant or unworthy.

A word of advice. Before contemplating a visit to a musical event, always check with the sponsors in advance to verify dates and addresses—which frequently are changed. Entertainment sections in local newspapers are helpful too for checking.

I earnestly hope readers will derive as much enjoyment in reading about and attending events as I did in writing about and attending them. We are fortunate indeed that the United States is richly varied in its musical offerings. Wherever we look, whatever our preferences, we find that the beat goes on.

N·O·R·T·H-
E·A·S·T

INTRODUCTION

In 1620 the Mayflower carried 103 men, women, and children across the stormy seas to a narrow strip of land extending westward from the Atlantic Ocean. The place was Massachusetts, the sixth of the original thirteen colonies. It was here that the settlers found shelter, peace, and hope for a productive life. And it was here that American music began to develop. These weary settlers had brought with them their musical expression in the psalmody that they sang regularly. Psalmody took firm root in conservative New England and throughout many of the New World colonies in the seventeenth and eighteenth centuries. Psalmody was practiced in churches and meeting halls. It vocally defined the society's taste for solemnity, simplicity, and morality.

In the eighteenth and nineteenth centuries growing numbers of European emigrants settled in the large cities of New York, Boston, and Philadelphia. These cities thus grew rapidly and became "melting pots" of the Northeast. The heritage of Bach, Handel, Haydn, and Beethoven, and then Brahms, Tchaikovsky, and Wagner spread through the region. There were enough musically aware citizens to create a demand for large concert halls for the performance of symphonic music, opera, and dance.

The Europeans also brought their folk music. And the Africans brought their music, which was to become part of the foundation of that American art form called jazz. Cultural diversity assimilated with developing American experience and resulted in the development of several genres of popular music. The different kinds of music interacted, changed, and grew, reflecting the interaction, change, and growth of the people of the United States.

PSALMODY IN NEW ENGLAND: OUR COLONIAL BEGINNINGS

Austere Life, Austere Music

The Pilgrims who arrived in Massachusetts in 1620 were plain people. A Separatist sect of Puritans from England and Holland, they were strict of mind and sturdy of character. Their arduous struggle for physical survival in the New World paralleled in rigor their struggle to keep a demanding faith. Hard work, austerity, and a conservative vision constituted the Protestant Ethic. An intense, all-pervasive ongoing religious experience was sought by the Pilgrims. Leisure and luxury were viewed as sinful. This prescribed manner of living was reinforced in their music, colonial psalmody. Moreover, any other music was considered evil and improper.

In Salem, a woman complained to authorities that she saw the master of the house "dancing and drinking." The Reverend John Cotton proclaimed from his pulpit, "Wanton dancing to lascivious music with amorous gestures should be frowned upon." Indeed, plain services, plain meeting houses, and plain music describes the Pilgrims' way of life.

Psalms

A psalm is a sacred song or hymn, usually one of the hymns from the Old Testament *Book of Psalms*. The name comes from the Greek, meaning "a song sung to the playing of a harp." In Hebrew, *tehillim* is the word for "songs of praise," or psalms. The *Book of Psalms*, also called the *Psalter*, is a great resource for Jewish and Christian liturgies. Musically, the meters of the psalms in English translation vary widely, with inconsistent line syllabification and accents. This fact was responsible for much of the music history associated with New England psalmody.

3

Ainsworth's Psalter

The Pilgrims brought with them Henry Ainsworth's *Psalter,* or *Book of Psalmes.* It was printed in Holland in 1612 for the Separatists who had fled from England to Holland. It contained thirty-nine psalm-tunes translated into English from the original Hebrew and was described in the later *Bay Psalm Book* thus:

> *Psalmes of David in Englishe Metre, by Thos. Sternhold and others. . . . Very mete to be used of all sorts of people privately for their godly solace and comfort, laying aparte all ungodly songes and ballades, which tende only to the nourishing of vice, and corruption of youth.*

Some of the widely sung songs from Ainsworth's *Psalter* were "I Laid Me Down and Slept," "Confess Jehovah," and "Old Hundredth." The last song survives as the familiar modern hymn, "Praise God from Whom All Blessings Flow." Written in five, six, eight, or twelve lines, each line of a typical psalm might express a different rhythm and seem to be independent of the other lines. The melodies, written with one note to a syllable, were designed for a single musical part to be sung in unison and unaccompanied. Although few could read music, the music was nevertheless notated. The music notation was in the form of diamond-shaped notes without bar lines on the staff. A tune from the Ainsworth *Psalter* was the following, Psalm 7.

Pfalm 7

Jehovah mine almıghtie — God, I hope

Musical notation from the Ainsworth Psalter (Amsterdam, 1612)

In the nineteenth century Henry Wadsworth Longfellow immortalized Ainsworth's *Psalter* in his poem, "The Courtship of Miles Standish," in which he describes Priscilla singing:

Open wide in her lap lay the well-worn psalm book of Ainsworth,
Printed in Amsterdam, the words and the music together.
Rough-hewn, angular notes, like stones in the wall of a churchyard,
Darkened and overhung by the running vine of the verses.

"Old Style Singing"
The style of singing in unison in church was called "old style singing" or "common singing." Not only was it a slow and tedious manner of singing, but it lent itself to musical chaos. Tempo and pitch varied among the singers in a group, singers did not always keep in time with each other, and grace notes and trills were introduced gratuitously. Everyone sang more or less as he or she pleased. Frequently, one person, most likely the presiding clergyman might "lead" by modulating his voice (raising or lowering the pitch accordingly), hoping to encourage group members to follow. The results were not always musical. And repertoire probably consisted of no more than half a dozen songs sung over and over.

Psalmody Spreads Throughout New England

Beginning in 1630 congregations expanded to include non-Separatist Puritans who had sailed to America from all parts of the British Isles. These Puritans settled in the Massachusetts Bay Colony (encompassing Boston, Medford, Lynn, and Charlestown), Dorchester (now in New Hampshire), Watertown (now in Connecticut), and Roxbury (now in Maine).

Later Puritan arrivals founded the New Haven Colony in 1638, as well as the towns of Hartford, Wethersfield, and Windsor along the Connecticut River. These towns formed the nucleus of what would later become Connecticut. Roger Williams, remembered as a pioneer of religious freedom, founded Rhode Island in 1636. New Hampshire was formed in 1689, and Vermont and Maine became states in 1791 and 1820 respectively. Puritans and Pilgrims mixed.

The more educated and sophisticated citizens, especially those from the Massachusetts Bay Colony, severely criticized those who took part in "common singing." They thought it akin to crude, uneducated, and even disgraceful singing. In spite of this, Ainsworth's *Psalter* and "old style singing" prevailed until 1692, when Plymouth merged with the Massachusetts Bay Colony and its people began to use the *Bay Psalm Book*.

The *Bay Psalm Book*

The *Bay Psalm Book* was the first book to be printed by the English colonists in North America. Matthew Daye printed it in 1640 in Cambridge. It contained fifty English hymn tunes and several reforms in the singing of hymns. In response to cries for more orderly singing the use of the four-line ballad stanza, called the common meter, was incorporated into the *Bay Psalm Book*. In common meter lines alternated between eight and six syllables. An example of this can be found in the famous Twenty-Third Psalm from the *Bay Psalm Book:*

> *The Lord to mee a shepeard is,*
> *Want therefore shall not I*
> *He in the folds of tender grasse,*
> *Doth cause me downe to lie.*

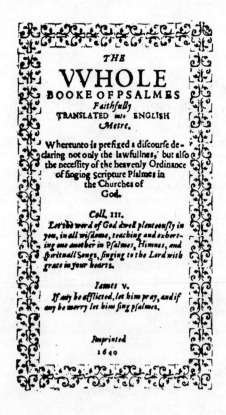

Title page from the first edition of the *Bay Psalm Book* (Cambridge, 1640)

The use of the common meter resulted in a more orderly, regular, standardized sound.

Directions for Singing

The *Bay Psalm Book* contained no music, but in its "Admonition to the Reader" there were detailed instructions regarding the melodies to which psalms in different meters might be sung.

> *The verses of these psalmes may be reduced to six kinds, the first whereof may be sung in very neere fourty common tunes; as they are collected out of our chief musicians by Thos. Ravenscroft.*

The reference was to Thomas Ravenscroft's *Psalter* or *The Whole Booke of Psalmes*, published in London in 1621, in which the "chief musicians"

Low Dutch Tune from the *Bay Psalm Book* (Boston, 1698)

were English composers, namely Ravenscroft himself, Thomas Morley, John Dowland, and Richard Allison, among others. Some of the well-known forty tunes were identified by the abbreviated titles, "Oxford," "Windsor," "St. David's," and "Martyrs." In the back of the book music notation was written in solmization, a system that used syllables (do, re, mi, fa, sol, la, ti, do) to indicate the different tones of the scale.

Another reform ushered in with the *Bay Psalm Book* was the change to "regular singing" or "singing by note," a departure from the haphazard "common singing" that critics had charged was rural and backward. Notes were now to be sung exactly as designated—in correct time, with correct pitch, and without spontaneous individual embellishment. A lively tempo replaced the slow, tedious tempo of "old singing." Many leaders fought vigorously for "regular singing," especially the Reverends Cotton Mather of Boston, Thomas Walter of Roxbury, and Nathaniel Chauncey of Durham, Connecticut. Walter wrote a pamphlet, printed in New London in 1728 entitled *Regular Singing Defended and Proved to be the Only True Way of Singing the Songes of the Lord.*

Lining Out

Reform continued with the attempt to abolish the practice of "lining out." Lining out was an old Scottish tradition that conferred upon the leader or deacon the task of setting the tune by reading the psalm line by line (primarily for those unable to read), then singing it, and finally pausing for the congregation to sing the line. The results were often more solemn and monotonous than melodious:

> *Low-voiced deacon reading: "Shout to Jehovah, al the earth"*
> *Low-voiced deacon singing: "Shout to Jehovah, al the earth"*
> *Mixed-voice congregants singing: "Shout to Jehoval, al the earth"*

For more than sixty years the use of the *Bay Psalm Book* prevailed. It was revised many times, passing through numerous editions. Among the most widely used were those of Sternhold and Hopkins (1562), Tate and Brady (1696), and Watts (1711). The ninth edition (1698) contained the first music to be printed in the colonies. Thirteen tunes were inserted in the back of the book with solemn directions for singing "without squeaking above or grumbling below." By the time this edition was printed the literary quality of the translation had begun to improve, and instead of importing their melodies, the colonists had started to compose their own, which must have sounded fresher and more pleasing to them.

Singing Instruction and Singing Schools

In 1721, the Reverend John Tufts of Newburyport, Massachusetts, wrote the first instruction book on singing published in America, *A very plain and easy introduction to the whole Art of Singing Psalm Tunes.* Instead of using notes, Tufts used letters based on the system of solmization (see page eight). He indicated tempo by marking or not marking dots to the right of the letter. A letter standing alone (F, for Fa) equaled a quarter note or one beat in 4/4 time, one dot to the right of the

Page from *An Introduction to the Singing of Psalm Tunes* by John Tufts (Boston, 1721)

letter (F.) signified a half note or two beats in 4/4 time, and two dots meant a whole note or four beats in 4/4 time (F:).

Tufts included thirty-seven tunes set in three voice parts, with further singing instructions adapted from London's Ravenscroft.

In 1721 the Reverend Thomas Walter of Roxbury, Massachusetts, introduced his own book for "singing by note." He included rules for tuning the voice by diligent practice. His *The Grounds and Rules of Musick Explained: Introduction to the Art of Singing By Note* had music notes with bars on the staff.

A page from *The Grounds and Rules of Musick Explained* by Thomas Walter (Boston, 1721)

The Growth of Singing Societies

The second half of the seventeenth century witnessed the growth of singing societies. Singers demanded music books, which resulted in the growth of the music business as well. Churches reserved first rows for their best singers, who led in singing psalms; thus, the church choir was born. Church choirs were first seen (and heard) in the Brattle Street Church and Old South Church in Boston. "Regular Singing" created the need for singing schools. Under the influence of such schools, different forms of music, such as hymns, spirituals, and anthems, and even the technique of counterpoint were added to the psalm repertoire. In Boston the first singing school was established in 1720 in the schoolhouse of Dr. Cotton Mather. Its success gave rise to the development of other singing schools throughout the colonies. Singing schools prepared the way for the formation of the Handel and Haydn Society in 1815, in Boston again. This choral society emphasized the classical music of the German composers. Thus, a trend began toward a more cosmopolitan taste in music.

Instruments

Not only was the playing of instrumental music forbidden at first in Puritan churches, but the pursuit of music as a vocation was prohibited in the colonies. However, the rigidity of the seventeenth century eventually began to thaw, and by 1711 Mr. Thomas Brattle of Boston had imported the first organ from England. It is said to have remained untouched in its crate for several months, which suggests a lingering reluctance to risk profaning holy singing. Brattle finally unpacked it and played on it. The Reverend Joseph Green wrote an entry in his diary: "I was at Mr. Thos. Brattle's; heard ye organ. . . . " Unfortunately, Brattle's organ experience was short-lived. He died two years later, having bequeathed the organ to the Brattle Square Church (no longer in existence). From there it went to King's Chapel where it was eventually replaced by another organ that can be seen today in St. John's Church in Portsmouth, New Hampshire.

Conservatives remained hesitant to accept innovation and organists were hard to find; nonetheless the first organ in the colonies was built in the 1740s by Edward Bromfield, a Harvard graduate from Boston. Interest heightened and importation accelerated. By the end of the eighteenth century some twenty organs could be found, most of them in Anglican or Episcopal churches and a few in homes. William Libby of Boston was the organist of the day.

With attitudes relaxing, other instruments were imported for the performance of both sacred and secular music, the latter of which was gaining in use. Some of these instruments were the jew's harp, the virginal, the drum, and the trumpet. Trumpets were simple, flared tubes of different lengths. Not until the early nineteenth century were finger valves added. With the added valves the instrument began to approach the tone of the cornet.

There followed the flute, the oboe (then called haut-boy), along with the viol (violin), the bass viol (viola), the guitar, the harpsichord, and later the violoncello. In all this activity we can see the seed of the later symphony orchestra with its developing string, brass, woodwind, and percussion sections.

Moravian Music

During the mid-eighteenth century another religious sect existed whose musical life, like that of the Puritans, occupied a central role. This sect was the *Unitas Fratrum* or Moravian Brotherhood. A Christian missionary group originally from Bohemia, the sect founded colonies in Bethlehem, Pennsylvania in 1732, and in Winston-Salem, North Carolina in 1753.

Moravian music, although similar to the ascetic music of the Puritans, had more emotional appeal. The form, harmony, and melody of the Moravian hymn were modeled after pre-classical and classical European music, with elaborate arias and choruses, some in four parts, and with instrumental accompaniment for use in church. Unlike the Puritans, the Brotherhood encouraged the study of music among its members. Two prolific composers in Bethlehem were Count Zinzendorff (a leader in establishing the colony), who is credited with writing several hundred hymns, and John Frederick Peter, an organist from Holland, who joined the colony as its music director. By composing six string quintets patterned after the classical style of Haydn, Peter helped establish a classical music tradition among the settlers.

Moravians embraced secular music along with church music and in general espoused an international outlook in living. This was indeed a stark contrast with the provincialism of the Puritans. The Bethlehem colony supported a small orchestra that consisted of an organ, violins, viola da gamba, flutes, haut-boys, French horns, trombones, and a spinet. Concerts were performed here as early as 1734. Benjamin Franklin, displaying a marked interest in music, attended one and remarked: "I was at their [Moravian] church where I was entertained with good musick, the organ being accompanied with violins, haut-boys, flutes, and trombones."

In 1744, the Moravians formed a musical society, Collegium Musicum, dedicated to offering symphonic and choral works of the German masters (Bach, Handel, Haydn, and Mozart). Collegium Musicum created a choir for the performance of oratorios and presented American premières of such choral works as Karl Philipp Emanuel Bach's "The Israelites in the Desert" and Handel's "Messiah." The choir survives today as the renowned Bach Choir in Bethlehem and its performances have become tradition. It attracts thousands each May at the annual Bach event given in Packer Memorial Chapel at Lehigh University. There are some two hundred local singers of diverse backgrounds in the choir and eleven hundred seats in the chapel in which to hear them. Several years ago the choir traveled to Leipzig, Germany, to sing in Bach's own church.

Moravian music may be heard in the Central Moravian Church (built in 1806) on Main and West Church Streets in Bethlehem. A trombone choir performs during Easter and other religious holidays. To celebrate Christmas there is a special treat on South Mountain on Main Street, just over the Lehigh River. Moravian Christmas songs mingle with the music of Handel and Mozart. A star of Bethlehem is carefully lit atop South Mountain, adding to the beauty of the music.

Another Moravian community is in Winston-Salem, North Carolina. It boasts a great deal of original music, particularly religious compositions for brass bands and pipe organs. Many manuscripts can be seen at the Moravian Music Foundation, at 20 Cascade Avenue.

Provincialism Wanes

In the early nineteenth century, following the end of the colonial period, provincial taste yielded steadily to the acceptance of more diversified forms of musical expression. The lyrical folk ballads, brought to America by the English, Scotch, and Irish immigrants more than a century earlier, were widely sung. Professional European musicians, trained in classical and romantic traditions, added the music of Vivaldi, Corelli, Mozart, and Beethoven to the already familiar music of Handel and Haydn. In 1881 Boston founded a major symphony orchestra, joining ranks with other leading northeastern cities which had their own orchestras. African music, infused with rhythm and spontaneity, was brought here by Black slaves. It gave rise to the development of "popular" music and jazz. Native American composers began to write, and are still writing, music rooted in the growing American experience.

New England Psalmody and Churches Today

Scenes of New England psalmody have, of course, all but vanished with time. But the music has not been lost; it has found its way into hymnody not only in New England but throughout the nation.

There are church buildings standing today in the New England area that are the original foundations or restored sites of historical Pilgrim and Puritan worship. While visiting these sites, one is keenly aware of the awesome force that drove the early settlers to build their churches— the quest for religious freedom in the New World. The churches have exemplified the spiritual values and worthy aspirations of their citizens for four centuries.

Pleasant, relaxed visits today contrast vividly with the grim, austere Sundays of yesteryear. Today there is no more required all-day attendance at long, unrelieved services, and there are no more fiery sermons delivered by intimidating deacons in black. Sessions of intense psalmody to be endured in unheated churches during bitterly cold New England winters are memories only. Unaccompanied "old-style singing" in unison of "Confess Jehovah" (with its emphasis on the theme of individual salvation) has evolved into richly textured polyphonic singing, accompanied frequently by an electric organ and sometimes by a trumpet. Below is an example of a hymn likely to be heard today. It stresses the brotherhood of man; it is found in a twentieth-century book of hymns called *Songs of the Spirit*, written by Reverend Marion Franklin Ham:

> *As tranquil streams that meet and merge . . .*
> *Our kindred fellowships unite*
> *To build a church that shall be free.*

Lining out "Shout to Jehovah, al the earth," for the benefit of those unable to read, has long since been replaced by trained choir voices singing, among other hymns, one written by the twentieth-century clergyman Reverend M.D. Babcock. This is from *Thoughts for Every-day Living:*

> *This is my Father's world . . .*
> *Of rocks and trees, of skies and seas;*
> *His hand the wonders wrought.*

A visitor to these churches can feel the presence of Puritan values—the solemnity; the harsh discipline; the fear-ridden morality; the hopes expressed through psalmody. The following is a list of places where psalmody flourished.

CONNECTICUT

Brooklyn
Old Trinity Church (1771), off Route 6.
It is used occasionally for worship. Its "hip" roof (projecting angle at the junction of a sloping side and a sloping end) is a feature typical of colonial architecture. Adjacent to the church is an old burial ground.
Hartford
Center Church (1638), 60 Gold Street.
It is a monument to the city's Puritan founding fathers. There are many

historic graves in its adjoining cemetery, including that of the Reverend Thomas Hooker, who espoused the separation of church and state.

New Haven

Trinity Church, (1752), on the green on Church Street.

It was restored in 1816. An Aeolian Skinner organ and Tiffany stained glass windows are among the stone church's impressive features.

Wethersfield

First Church of Christ Congregational (1685), at Main and March Streets.

It is known as the "onion church" because when it was being reconstructed in 1761 as a brick building, the cost of construction was so high that the town fathers voted to accept payment in onions instead of money. The interior seating arrangement is semicircular. The church may be visited by appointment only.

Windsor

United Church of Christ Congregational, 75 Palisade Avenue.

It has a small colonial cemetery with graves dating back to 1644.

MAINE

Kennebunk

First Parish Church (1773), on the corner of Main Street and Portland Road.

The original bell cast by Paul Revere still chimes. Tours are given in July and August.

Kittery Point

First Congregational Church (1659), on Pepperrell Road.

It contains the original pulpit and two original box pews. One box pew holds the church organ; the other was the box occupied by Sir William Pepperrell, psalm singer and founder of the church. The silver christening bowl given to the church by Sir William is still in use.

Castine

First Parish Church Meeting House.

It was the site of civil and criminal trials as well as a house of Puritan worship in the eighteenth century.

Roxbury

It was here in 1721 that the Reverend Thomas Walter published his book of instruction, "Singing by Note."

MASSACHUSETTS

Boston

King's Chapel (1686), at Tremont and School Streets.

A large granite building with a triple-tiered pulpit, King's Chapel is a Registered National Historic Landmark. It housed Thomas Brattle's imported-from-England organ for a time. One can visit during the week or attend a Sunday morning service.

Old South Meeting House (1729), at Washington and Milk Streets.
This is where Dr. Mather preached and led in the singing of psalms. It now houses colonial exhibits. It is open to visitors from the spring through the fall.

Old North Church (1723), 193 Salem Street at the foot of Hull Street.
This is the oldest church building in Boston where psalmody rang out. Now a historic site, it is open daily. A restored organ and an early peal (set) of bells are among its artifacts. This is the church from whose steeple lanterns were displayed, signaling the message carried by Paul Revere.

Cambridge
Christ Church (1761), on Garden Street at the common.

Hingham
Old Ship Church (1681), 90 Main Street.
An Elizabethan Gothic wooden building, the church has been in continuous use since it was built. The roof is similar in construction to old wooden ship hulls. The bell tower ceiling is attractively decorated with rosettes, as is the pulpit sounding board. There are guided tours in the summer and by appointment during the rest of the year.

Plymouth
First Parish in Plymouth and Church of the Pilgrimage, both on Leyden Street (originally First Street).
The churches stand in front of historic Burial Hill where Pilgrims worshipped at a fort, which was erected on the crest of the hill in 1622. A semi-annual event in Plymouth is "Pilgrim's Progress," a re-enactment of the Pilgrims' church-going and psalm-singing. The event captures the true spiritual flavor of the past.

Salem
First Church of Salem, 316 Essex Street.
It stands on the site of the first meeting house, erected in 1634. In 1629 a prayerbook service was held here for the first time in New England. Roger Williams taught here in 1631; he preached separation of church and state. Along with the sermon there was, of course, psalm singing. The church is an attractive brick building, beautifully landscaped.

Stockbridge
Mission House (1739), on Main and Sergeant Streets.
It is now a museum of colonial life, a popular school trip. Visitors to the Mission House are quickly transported into the days of the dramatic sermons preached by John Sergeant or Jonathan Edwards and the accompanying vigorous psalmody of the congregants. May through October is the best time to visit.

NEW HAMPSHIRE
Portsmouth
St. John's Church (1732), 101 Chapel Street.
This colonial brick church houses old citizen Brattle's successor organ, its own eighteenth-century pipe organ, plus a few original grayish-yellow colonial prayerbooks. It also possesses one of four copies of the *Vinegar Bible*, printed in 1717. In this edition the word *vineyard* is printed *vinegar*. The church is open daily and is well worth a visit for its connections with the past.
Westmoreland
Park Hill Meeting House (1764).
It has an original Paul Revere bell in its steeple. Four great columns, thirty feet tall and twenty inches in diameter, grace the building's exterior. Inside is a lovely set of pewter for Communion services.

RHODE ISLAND
Newport
Trinity Church (1698), at Church and Spring Streets.
This is the oldest Anglican church in the state. George Washington worshipped here and sang psalms from the *Bay Psalm Book* with other congregants. This early colonial wooden structure has been well preserved and proudly displays an original silver baptismal font, a bell tower with possibly the first church bell rung in New England, and several dozen books from England received in 1701 to create the first church library in Rhode Island.
North Kingston
Smith's Castle (1678), on Post Road.
Rhode Island is rich in its colonial music heritage; Smith's Castle is but one example. Roger Williams preached here, while accompanied by loud psalmody. It is open from the spring to the fall.
Providence
First Baptist Church (1638) on Main Street.
Founded by Roger Williams of Salem, Massachusetts, the church represented the first significant break from the colonial church/state concept and established the foundations of the Baptist denomination. Psalmody was sung in this church.
Beneficent Congregational Church (1744), on Weybosset Street.
This church was originally organized as the First Congregational Church, with the Reverend Josiah Cotton as minister. Early parishioners cut logs and erected a crude building that later gave way to early Greek Revival style of architecture.
Wickford
St. Paul's Church (1707), 55 Main Street.
It is a two-story wooden building with arched windows. A silver Com-

munion service, given to the church by Queen Anne in 1710, is still in use.

VERMONT
Arlington
St. James Church (1764).
The church was originally organized as Bethel Church and was renamed in the nineteenth century. The building is a Gothic structure of wood and gray granite with an adjoining cemetery.
Bennington
First Church (1762), on Monument Avenue.
This building is now Vermont's official colonial shrine. The interior has a high pulpit, pewter candle holders in box pews, and a three-sided gallery displaying various state figures. Poet Robert Frost lies buried in the graveyard.

A Sprinkling of Psalmody Revival
How rare it is to find a psalmody revival! Don't expect to see pious Puritans, or deacons in black robes, but, between Bennington, Vermont, and Troy, New York, on the Vermont/New York border, is Petersburg, New York, where a revival of sorts has begun. It is an annual August Festival of "Traditional Music in the Woods" at Fox Hollow. Psaltery is presented to interested audiences, with psalm singing accompanied by an ancient stringed instrument akin to the zither.

Every now and then a contemporary composer attempts to revive a link with seventeenth- and eighteenth-century psalmody. A New York premiere of *Psalms*, by the Canadian composer Srul Glick, was presented at Carnegie Hall with Andrew Davis and the Toronto Symphony in March of 1982. Glick described his piece as "a progression of quiet ecstasy to a joyful dance." He used different Hasidic tunes, however, rather than formal psalm tunes at the beginning and end of the piece in contrasting moods.

Steve Reich's "Tehillim" (1981) premiered at the Metropolitan Museum of Art in chamber version. The piece, consisting of four psalms, is scored for seventeen instruments and four singers, all sopranos. The tempos vary, following the rhythm of the Hebrew texts. In this work there is much hand clapping and shaking of maracas to illustrate primitive settings. The composer's aim was to emulate vocal music before 1750. "Tehillim" was played again at a New York Philharmonic concert in 1982 in its full orchestral version under the baton of Zubin Mehta.

EARLY HYMNS AND EARLY PATRIOTIC MUSIC

Early American Composers

Francis Hopkinson (1737–1791), born in Philadelphia and later a resident of Bordentown, New Jersey, seems to have been our first American composer, according to surviving accounts. With his quill pen, he composed hymn tunes that enlarged upon the biblical scope of psalmody, reflecting a new growing America. He enjoyed popularity throughout the Northeast.

A harpsichordist and organist, Hopkinson played and taught singing in church. His songs were written in two parts, treble and bass, and the harpsichordist improvised connecting harmonies when needed. People loved to sing his "With Pleasure Have I Passed My Days," and "My Days Have Been so Wondrous Free." Many of his early works are available for perusing in a manuscript book of songs in the Library of Congress. After the Revolution, he dedicated his most important work, *Seven Songs for Harpsichord*, to George Washington, who was then about to assume the presidency, in 1788. (Washington himself was interested in music, and at Mount Vernon the harpsichord he bought for his step-granddaughter, Nelly Custis, is still preserved.)

As noted before, by the end of the eighteenth century, Philadelphians, New Yorkers, and New Englanders, in addition to singing hymns in church, began to enjoy a musical life outside the church. Northeasterners broadened their musical taste with soirées devoted to playing and listening to European music in homes and in halls. The Assembly House at 138 Federal Street in Salem, Massachusetts, was built in 1782 specifically to accommodate such concerts and social gatherings. The building is still standing today, although it has been remodeled for use as a private residence.

Andrew Law (1748–1821) of Hartford, Connecticut, James Lyon (1735–1794) of Mathias, Maine, and William Billings (1746–1800) of Boston, Massachusetts, were popular composers during this post-psalmody period. Law used a system of musical notation called "shape notation" that employed notes of different shapes to represent the syllables of solmization. A triangular note represented *fa;* a round note, *sol;* a

19

**William Little's shape notation from *The Easy Instructor* (1802) and
Andrew Law's shape notation from *The Art of Singing*, 4th ed. (1803)**
(Courtesy Library of Congress)

square note, *la;* a diamond note, *mi.* Shape notation was written with
no staff lines.

An interesting petition from Law to the Connecticut Legisla-
ture requesting copyright of his works can be seen in the Connecticut
Archives, which are in the Public Library on Main Street in Hartford.

Lyon, a Presbyterian minister, produced and wrote six works
for a famous hymn collection, *Urania*, in 1761. *Urania* also included the
tune for the well-known "America" ("My Country 'Tis of Thee").
Interesting singing instructions appear in *Urania:*

1. *In learning the 8 (eighth) notes, get the assistance of some person
   well-acquainted with the Tones and Semitones.*
2. *Choose the part which you can sing with the greatest ease, and
   make yourself Master of that first.*
3. *Sound all high Notes as soft as possible; but low ones hard and
   full.*
4. *Pitch your Tune so that the highest and lowest Notes may be
   sounded distinctly.*

Reading over these specific and professional instructions of Lyon's, it is
not difficult to understand why his music was often performed on the
same program as Handel's.

Lyon's *Urania* (1761), engraved by Henry Dawkins (Courtesy Library of Congress)

William Billings of Boston was known for the innovations he brought to psalmody. After elevating psalmody to its highest form, he began to change it. The Brattle Square Church, no longer in existence, and the Old South Street Church, on Washington and Milk Streets, were the sites where Billings established the original American church choirs. He taught singers to read music. Using a pitch pipe for tuning the voice and introducing the cello into church services were among his then daring innovations. In 1774 he formed a singing class in Stoughton, Massachusetts. After his death in 1800, it became the first American musical performance organization. It was first called the Stoughton Musical Society, and later, the Handel and Haydn Society. It remains in its original location, 158 Newbury Street.

Billings inaugurated polyphonic singing, a bold action in contrast to old style unison singing. His compositions heralded a new age in religious music. An example of his work is the four-part chorus in *The Singing Master's Collection* or *The Psalm Singer's Amusement*. Defying convention this singing master wrote music with a freer feeling. Fast tempos, contrapuntal harmony, and rhythm in the bass line are characteristic of his fuguing tunes, such as "The Lord is Risen," "When Jesus Wept," and "Be Glad Then America." Occasionally, he even adapted the rhythms of popular folk tunes (tunes then with English, Scottish, and Irish roots).

Pre-Revolutionary War days produced in the colonists a fiery new patriotism for their land. Billings's most famous song, "Chester," highlighted the emotions generated by the Revolution, and is occasionally still sung in rural New England congregations. It has a rapid tempo:

Let tyrants shake their iron rod
And slav'ry clank her galling chains
We fear them not, we trust in God,
New England's God forever reigns.

Sadly, Billings died a pauper. He lies in an unmarked grave amid other unmarked graves in the little graveyard on the Boston Common.

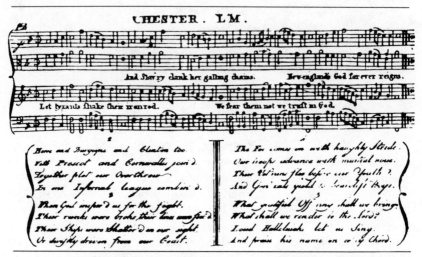

"Chester" by William Billings from the *The Singing Master's Assistant* (Boston, 1778)

"Broadsides" and Patriotic Music

"Chester," a Revolutionary War song, was essentially a patriotic hymn written to be sung in church. Its patriotic quality, however, carried the song beyond the church walls into the streets. Nationalistic feelings ran high with a demand for more patriotic songs. One such song was "Yankee Doodle," which came on the scene in the late eighteenth century. Its words and melody were made widely available in broadsides, the first examples of sheet music, printed in the major American cities. Broadsides were sold on street corners for a penny a sheet.

"Yankee Doodle" was tremendously popular when it appeared in print. Its origins are unknown, but various speculations attribute the song to English or Dutch roots. Other versions classify it as German,

Hungarian, or Spanish. Still another account tells of a British surgeon writing the lyrics in an eighteenth-century Dutch house near Albany, New York. You can see this house today. It has become the Fort Crollo State Historic Site at 9½ Riverside Avenue in Rensselaer and is open to the public.

Whatever the true origin, the British sang "Yankee Doodle" to taunt the Yankees, and the Yankees sang their version to rally against the British. On Patriot's Day, April 19, a celebration called "Fife and Drum" takes place in Concord and Lexington, Massachusetts, and in Hatch Shell on the Esplanade in Boston."Yankee Doodle" rings out in patriotic, revolutionary style. Some other places where one can hear fife-and-drum music on Independence Day listed below are:

Connecticut
Deep River, on Main Street
Norwalk, at Veterans Memorial Park
New Haven, the Green
Westbrook, at the recreation field

Maryland
Indian Head, on the Village Green

Pennsylvania
Philadelphia, at Independence Mall

New York
Niagara Falls, at Art Park

Washington, D.C., in all parts of the city

Rhode Island
New Kingston, on Main Street in Wickford Village

Vermont
Burlington, in Battery Park

New Hampshire
Portsmouth, at Prescott Park
Laconia, on Weirs Beach (on US 3)

Maine
Bangor, at Paul Bunyan Park
Bar Harbor, on the Village Green

"Hail Columbia"

Joseph Hopkinson, the son of Francis Hopkinson, wrote the words to "Hail Columbia" in 1798, inspired by his concern over unrest between America and France. Gilbert Fox, an actor and singer in Philadelphia, sang it at the New Theater, and brought down the house. The New Theater no longer exists, but during the summer, at the National Drum and Bugle Corps in Philadelphia, and at a "Philly" Pops concert at Independence Mall, "Hail Columbia" comes alive again.

"The Star-Spangled Banner"

Francis Scott Key (1779–1843) was a Washington, D.C., lawyer sent to rescue a friend held by the British fleet in Chesapeake Bay, Maryland, in 1814. Key was on board ship at night watching the shelling of Fort McHenry by the British. The next morning his astonishment was so great at finding the American flag still flying over the fortress after the bombardment, that he was inspired to write a poem. The work appeared immediately in broadside as "Defence of Fort McHenry" and in Baltimore newspapers as "The Star-Spangled Banner." Then, set to the tune of the English drinking song, "To Anacreon in Heaven," it became popular throughout the nation following the War of 1812. However, it was not until 1931 that President Herbert Hoover proclaimed it our national anthem.

The first copy of the words that Key wrote is in the Walters Art Gallery in Baltimore at Charles and Center Streets. Star-Spangled Banner House, at 844 East Pratt Street in Baltimore, is open to the public. It contains memorabilia of the event and a replica of the banner with the fifteen stars and stripes that Key saw "by the dawn's early light."

"America"

My country 'tis of thee
Sweet land of liberty

"America" is a hymn associated with no wars or strife. The tune is that of the English national anthem, "God Save the King." The words to "America" were written in 1831 by Reverend Samuel Smith of Boston (1808–1895). Today "America" rings out at the Park Street Church, 1 Park Street, in Boston, every July 4, as it did at its premiere performance on July 4, 1831.

Lowell Mason

Mid-nineteenth-century music continued to develop in the

form of hymns. A dominant figure at this time was Lowell Mason (1792–1872) of Boston. Active in the Handel and Haydn Society, Mason and his contemporaries published large volumes of hymns, many of which are sung at the present time in Protestant churches all over the nation. Among the best-known are "My Faith Looks Up to Thee," "Nearer My God to Thee," and "From Greenland's Icy Mountains." He established teacher-training institutes, introduced singing classes into the public schools, and introduced the study of music into colleges. Thanks to Lowell Mason, one can major in music in college.

Together with contemporaries Samuel Eliot, George Webb, and others, Mason founded the Boston Academy of Music in 1832 (precursor of the present day New England Conservatory of Music at 290 Huntington Avenue). Classes were held originally at the Bowdoin Street Church (no longer in existence), and tuition was free to those pupils who attended classes for a full year. Fifteen-hundred pupils studied at the Academy during its first year.

Mason's son William was a concert pianist and teacher, and William's son Henry was a co-founder of the Mason & Hamlin Organ Company, manufacturer first of organs and then pianofortes.

Two Significant Songs of the Civil War

The early 1860s, during the pre–Civil War period, produced two memorable songs: "Dixie," and "Battle Hymn of the Republic." "Dixie," oddly enough, was written by a northerner, Daniel Decatur Emmett (1815–1904) of Mt. Vernon, Ohio, who, with Stephen Foster, composed tunes for the increasingly popular minstrel shows. (Foster himself was a native of Pittsburgh, Pennsylvania.) The word "Dixie" may have been taken from "Mason and Dixon Line," and was used by Emmett to indicate a place in which people might live with pride. Dixie became the symbol of the Confederacy, and although the associations were Southern, "Dixie" came to represent a truly American song.

The tune for "Battle Hymn of the Republic" was composed by a Sunday School teacher, William Steffe, in Charleston, South Carolina. The music was lively (a good marching song) and was taken up enthusiastically by many army regiments before and during the Civil War. Several verses were written, but the one remaining today is the verse written in 1861 by author and educator Julia Ward Howe (1819–1910).

Mine eyes have seen the glory of the coming of the Lord . . .
His truth is marching on.

Some Early Twentieth-Century Hymns and Composers

We have seen that the first psalmodists and hymn writers were succeeded by people with further training and education, and that the early Boston singing school tradition created a demand for more music. The early twentieth century produced some church composers (Hamilton MacDougall, Charles Whitney Coombs, Harry Rowe Shelley, among others) who carried on the hymn tradition in tunes still sung today.

Hamilton MacDougall (1858–1945) was organist, choirmaster, and professor of music at Wellesley College in Wellesley, Massachusetts for three decades. "Onward Christian Soldiers" is his greatest contribution to hymnody. In addition, MacDougall wrote music for the traditional Masonic ritual.

Charles Whitney Coombs (1859–1940), born in Buckport, Maine, came to New York as organist of the Church of the Holy Communion, 209 East Sixteenth Street, and then of St. Luke's Church, 308 West Forty-sixth Street. Coombs utilized the cantata form and mixed quartet in "The Vision of St. John," "Light Eternal," and "Sorrows of Death."

Harry Rowe Shelley (1858–1947) began his career as organist of Center Church on Temple Street in New Haven, Connecticut. From there he went to two of Brooklyn's leading twentieth-century churches, Plymouth Church on East Ninety-sixth Street, and Church of the Pilgrims, 24 Arlington Place. All three churches can be visited today; the latter two churches are colonial in style. Shelley composed cantatas ("Death and Life" and "The Inheritance Divine") as well as two symphonies, anthems, and a violin concerto.

Today, at any Protestant church, one can hear some representative hymns of the early twentieth century.

Religious music would take a back seat now, while other forms rose to occupy the musical scene.

FOLK MUSIC: ARRIVAL AND REVIVAL

Development of the American Folk Song and Folk Singers

America, of course, is a nation of immigrants. The English and Scotch arrived from the British Isles, beginning in the seventeenth century, bringing with them the music and instruments of their homelands. Bagpipes, fiddles, and dulcimers are some of the instruments they brought. The British ballad "Barbara Allen," which narrates a simple story, is a typical example of their folk music. Such ballads were central to the development of the American folk song.

> In Scarlet Town where I was born
> There was a fair maid dwelling,
> Made many a youth cry well a-day,
> Her name was Barb'ra Allen.

The Anglo-Scotch tradition was the main influence on American folk music for almost two centuries. In the late eighteenth and nineteenth centuries our folk music was enriched and broadened by the influx of people from all corners of the world (Italians, and Germans; Eastern Europeans, Russians, Irish, and Asians). The wave was completed in the early twentieth century as large numbers of new Americans settled in the big cities of New York, Philadelphia, and Boston.

Folk songs express feelings and experiences of the people, and the growing American experience became the focus of expression in folk song.

Special to the Northeast was the development of protest songs. These kinds of songs came to characterize and perhaps distinguish the folk music of this region. Laborers sang "Factory Girl" to expose the hardships and discontent of workers in the early 1900s:

> Yonder stands that spinning room boss . . .
> Pity me all day, pity me I pray,
> Pity me my darling, and take me far away.

27

In 1912, "Bread and Roses" was sung by workers who protested pay cuts in a large woolen mill in Lawrence, Massachusetts.

Yes, it is bread we fight for
But we fight for roses, too.

In the 1930s the spotlight of northern folk music activity, especially in New York City, centered around left-wing intellectuals and trade unions. Songs of protest accompanied labor struggles. The Industrial Workers of the World (commonly called the IWW, or Wobblies) glorified their songwriter Joe Hill, who wrote "Casey Jones—the Union Scab" and "Pie in the Sky," along with other grievance songs, compiled in "The Little Red Songbook," published in 1909. These songs were sung at union rallies, on picket lines, in jail, at any time or any place throughout the country deemed appropriate to convince others of some social or economic or political injustice. The area of 14th Street and Union Square was a sympathetic place for such events, since most of the neighborhood population consisted of poor immigrants. The songs sung were both traditional and radical.

One radical folk singer in the 1930s was Molly Jackson, who grew up in a coal-mining area of Harlan County in Kentucky. She tried through her songs to persuade people of the need to improve the quality of working life for coal miners, as in "Only a Miner."

He's only a miner . . .
Killed by an accident . . .
His mining days are over, poor miner farewell.

Jackson's songs have been recorded for the Library of Congress in Washington, as have those of many other folk performers.

One of the most beloved of American folk singers was Woody Guthrie, a drifter born in Oklahoma who came to New York in 1940, singing and playing the guitar. He had already written the tune "So Long, It's Been Good to Know Yuh," and was sympathetic to radical causes. In New York that year he met Pete Seeger, who played the five-stringed banjo and sang folk tunes. The two men teamed up for a while and toured the West. The following year, back in New York, Guthrie, Seeger, Lee Hays, a former college teacher, and Millard Lampell, a writer, formed a folk group, the Almanac Singers, based in Greenwich Village. The group soon became the nucleus for urban song activity and, in addition, offered performing experience for neophyte folk singers during the forties and early fifties. Their purpose, as was that of the Wobblies earlier, was to utilize songs to help reform society.

Some of the other musicians who joined the Almanac Singers were Bess Lomax, Cisco Houston, and Earl Robinson, who sang "Tarrier

Song"). Burl Ives, Josh White, and Oscar Brand sang and played with the group from time to time. (Brand has had a radio program, the "Folk Song Festival," on WNYC in New York for many years.) The Almanacs popularized the term "hootenanny," meaning a gathering of folk singers. Hootenannies took place in bars, restaurants, and informal places such as Washington Square and throughout Greenwich Village, with its small-town atmosphere.

Shabby saloons abounded in Greenwich Village's crooked streets. Some of the bars around Sheridan Square, looking toward 6th Avenue and north, were the Jericho, Village Square Bar & Grill, the Belmar, Goody's, and Rochambeau.

The oldest saloon in New York City and representative of the corner saloon of the day was McSorley's at 15 7th St., off Cooper Square. Ale was five cents a mug, free lunches of crackers and cheese were available and no ladies were served. Artists, writers, and musicians gathered there to proclaim new visions of life. The bar had gas lamps that cast shadows on the cobwebbed ceiling. No cash registers were evident; rather, coins rested in bowls and bills were kept in a cash box.

Photos of horses, steamboats, political bosses, singers, and actors filled the walls alongside three clocks, each showing a different time. Woody Gutherie sang songs here, indulging occasionally in provocative behavior, such as throwing bottles, kicking furniture, and stopping in the middle of a song and walking out.

In contrast to this seedy atmosphere was the Rainbow Room, atop Rockefeller Center, much further uptown. The Rainbow Room played host to Woody Guthrie, who sang:

The Rainbow Room is mighty high
You can see John D. a-flyin' by.

In the forties the group sang union songs like "Talking Union," and antiwar songs, including "Round and Round Hitler's Grave." In the McCarthy era of the early fifties, they were blacklisted, at which time they disbanded. Guthrie became ill and was hospitalized frequently up until the time of his death in 1967. He wrote more than a thousand songs, including "Pretty Boy Floyd," "Pastures of Plenty," "New York Town," "This Train is Bound for Glory," and "This Land is Your Land."

Pete Seeger and Lee Hays went on to form the Weavers Quartet with guitarist Fred Hellerman and singer Ronnie Gilbert. They performed frequently at the Village Vanguard (see listings) and went on to record hits such as "Good Night Irene" and "Wimoweh," an old Indian melody. The Weavers were innovative in their encouragement of audiences to join them in song, which added a new dimension to their popularity. Their old protest songs were toned down slightly now, and folk music for a time was performed much in the style of popular music.

An artist of legendary fame in the forties, often grouped justi-fiably with folk singers, was Paul Robeson, a black concert singer with a powerful voice. Robeson immortalized "Ballad for Americans." How-ever, in 1949 he appeared at a concert on the shores of the Hudson River in Peekskill, New York, where social and political race tensions erupted into a rock-throwing fiasco. Unfortunately, the incident did much to reduce Robeson's status, and afterward he began to fade from the folk scene.

The Folk Revival of the 1960s and Its Artists

Unlike the movement in the 1930s, the folk resurgence in the sixties came about through the interest and efforts of college students rather than through union workers. Students and "counterculture" sym-pathizers sang at rallies, workshops, sit-ins, and demonstrations out of a need for new values and for personal identity. Drawn to the causes of civil rights and the protesting of the Vietnam War, young people searched for some emotional fulfillment in songs such as "No More Segregation," and "I Ain't Marchin' Anymore."

New names like Doc Watson, Tom Paxton, Sonny Terry, Jean Ritchie, and Janis Ian (known for "God Bless the Child") appeared on the folk scene. The Kingston Trio and Brothers Four began their careers on the West Coast and toured the Northeast. Pete Seeger, still going strong, did a rewrite with others of an old tune and produced "We Shall Over-come." Seeger was instrumental in creating the famous Newport Folk Festival in Newport, Rhode Island, that lasted for a decade until 1969. It was the largest of the urban folk festivals and welcomed 80,000 listeners. Unforgettable folk songs of the era include "Where Have All the Flowers Gone," "Turn, Turn, Turn," and "If I Had a Hammer."

The 1960s protest created freedom songs, whose spokespeople included Peter, Paul, and Mary, Buffy Sainte-Marie, Judy Collins, and Joan Baez. Baez attained great heights as a singer in the sixties after coming to New York from Boston, where she had sung in restaurants and cafés. She was one of numerous stars at the Newport Folk Festival for many years. Baez was arrested after one performance for inciting disturbances. Sometimes disturbances were incited; more often these performers succeeded in uniting people for or against issues of the day.

An all-time favorite, Bob Dylan, started as a country music singer, whose idol was Hank Williams of Nashville. Dylan became in-terested in urban folk music mainly because of Woody Guthrie, whom he came to admire even more than Williams. Dylan wrote numerous songs and performed at Folk City in Greenwich Village (see listings) as well as in bars, restaurants, and hootenannies throughout the Northeast. Dylan entertained in Harvard Square in Cambridge, which is similar to Greenwich Village with its many informal spots for folk entertainment. His first recorded album included "Song to Woody" and "Talkin' New York." His protest songs inveighed against nuclear weapons, the John Birch Society, and the waste of natural resources. "Blowin' in the Wind" is perhaps his smashing success.

The Newport Folk Festival of 1965

Mentioned earlier was the Newport Folk Festival founded by Pete Seeger. The Festival of 1965 was a memorable event in which Bob Dylan almost destroyed the pure folk idiom by combining it with rock.

Dylan appeared on the giant stage wearing a black leather jacket and high-heeled boots. He sported an electric guitar and was accompanied by members of a small rock group. They proceeded to play a hard-driving song, "Like a Rolling Stone," with a great deal of amplification.

The audience, feeling betrayed by its hero, was incensed, and booed wildly. They took over the stage in frenzied upheaval. Dylan walked off the stage, to return after a few moments, tears in his eyes, singing, "It's All Over Now, Baby Blue" using his regular guitar. With this demarcation between the old and the new, Bob Dylan abandoned the folk movement.

The following cities offer opportunities to hear folk music in the Northeast.

CONNECTICUT
Hartford
The New England Fiddle contest, at Bushnell Park in May.
Peace Train concerts, at Bushnell Park during the summer months. These concerts offer traditional folk music and folk-rock.
Mystic
Festival of the Sea, at Mystic Seaport during June. The festival features sea chanties.
New Haven
Peace Train concerts, on the green during the summer.
New London
International Festival, at Captains' Walk in downtown New London in July.

Bluegrass Festival, at Ocean Beach Park in August.

New Preston

Old-time Yankee Jamboree, at the Inn on Lake Waramug in July.

Bagpipe concert and Scottish Dancing Day in August.

Norwalk

Scottish games and bagpipe music, at Central High School, exit 36 off the Merrit Parkway, in the spring.

Preston

Country-Western Jamboree, at Strawberry Park campgrounds on Pierce Road in the summer.

Bluegrass Festival, in late June.

DELAWARE

Harrington

The Delaware State Fair, at the Grand Opera House at Wilmington Square in the downtown mall.

Wilmington

Brandywine Arts Festival, at Josephine Gardens in September. This festival includes folk as well as other music.

DISTRICT OF COLUMBIA

Situated between the regions of the South and the Northeast, Washington has an abundance of folk music:

Festival of American Folklife, at the Washington Monument grounds at Fourteenth Street and Constitution Avenue, in June and October. The festival offers gospel music, folk music, and country music from Appalachia.

Outdoor concert series, in Neptune Plaza, Library of Congress, in spring and summer.

Concerts at the American Folklife Center, in the Thomas Jefferson Building, First Street and Independence Avenue SE. Concerts are given four times a year.

Folk presentations, at the Warner Theater, 513 Thirteenth Street NW.

Folk presentations, at Hearst Hall in the Washington Waldorf School, Wisconsin Avenue and Woodley Road NW.

Folk Festival, at Rock Creek Park, in June. This festival offers traditional and ethnic music.

Folk music events, at Rock Creek Park, in September.

Many kinds of music programs can be found at the Kennedy Center.

Several nightspots offer folk music.

The Cellar Door, 1201 Thirty-fourth Street NW.

Gallagher's, 3319 Connecticut Avenue NW.

Childe Harolde, 1610 Twentieth Street NW. This converted townhouse features bluegrass music.

MAINE
Bar Harbor
The Downeast Dulcimer Festival, on Mt. Desert Island. Acadia National Park, and in Village Green Park on Main Street, in July. The festival offers entertainment as well as workshops for those who wish to bring instruments.
Cambridge
New England Salty Dogs Bluegrass Celebration, in July.
Central Maine Bluegrass Festival, in August.
Old Town
The remaining few hundred Indians of the Abenaki Tribe, descendants of the Algonquin Federation, live on Penobscot Reservation, an island in the river, north of town. Indian songs and dances, precursors of American folk music, go on throughout the year.
Windsor
The Common Ground Country Fair, in September. Maine's favorite fair, it offers fiddle contests, square dancing, and country music.

MARYLAND
Annapolis
Folk programs, at the Maryland Hall for Creative Arts, Chase and Smith Avenues.
Baltimore
Many different kinds of music are performed at the Baltimore Civic Center, 210 West Baltimore Street.
Pride of Baltimore Festival, at the inner harbor area, in May.
Maryland All-American Square Dance Festival, at the Hunt Valley Inn, in November. This festival features well-known groups, such as the Clog Dancers.
Bel Air
Bluegrass and Fiddler's Conventions, at Heavenly Waters Park.
Bowie
A variety of musical events takes place at the Bowie Performing Arts Center at Whitemarsh Park.
Chestertown
Cloggers, square dancers, and folk and country music artists get together in May.
Columbia
Maryland Renaissance Festival, at Symphony Woods, during September and October. This festival attracts hundreds of entertainers.

Frederick

A number of programs take place at the Weinberg Center for the Arts, 20 West Patrick Street. Brunswick-Potomac River Festival, in August.

Gaithersburg

Shady Grove Music Fair, fifteen miles north on MD-355, in the summer.

Grantsville

Springs Folk Festival, in Springs Museum, off MD-669, from May through October.

Hagerstown

A variety of folk music is offered at the City Park Bandstand at the Hagerstown City Park on Virginia Avenue.

Thurmont

Folk Festival, on a spur of the Blue Ridge Mountains in Catoctin Mountain Park, in the summer.

Westminster

Fiddler's Convention, at the Carroll County Farm Museum, just north of Baltimore, in August. Although it's a fiddler's convention, it also includes banjos, guitars, and mandolins.

MASSACHUSETTS

Berkshire Area

International folk dancers perform at Becket, Jacob's Pillow, in the summer.

Berkshire County Fair, on the fairgrounds in Great Barrington, Route 7, in the summer.

Great Barrington Fair, on the fairgrounds in Great Barrington, in September, after the Berkshire County Fair ends.

Lenox is the home of Tanglewood, where there are occasional folk concerts.

Pittsfield Arts Festival, throughout the center of the city of Pittsfield, in July.

Boston

The following nightspots offer folk music:

The Black Rose, 160 State Street, for Irish folk music. Passim, 47 Palmer Street. Musicians such as Orrin Star and Gary Mehalick perform here. Cantab Lounge, 738 Massachusetts Avenue, for bluegrass music. Ryles, 212 Hampshire in Inman Square, for bluegrass music.

North Dartmouth

Eisteddfod Festival of Music, at Southeastern Massachusetts University, in September. Tunes of English and Scottish origin are played with bagpipes, dulcimers, guitars, and fiddles.

Salem

Heritage Days, in the center of town, a week-long celebration in August.

NEW HAMPSHIRE

County fairs abound from July to October in the following cities: Cornish, Deerfield, Keene, Laconia, Lancaster, New Boston, North Haverhill, and Stratham.

Square dancing is a large part of entertainment throughout the year in the following cities: Claremont, in the Junior Sports League Building; Concord, in the Community Center, 39 Green Street.

Fitzwilliam, in Town Hall.

Littleton, in the Opera House, on Main Street.

Franconia

Bluegrass Festival and Square Dance, Muster Field, Franconia Village, in July.

Laconia

Folk and gospel groups perform at the South Baptist Church, 85 Court Street, during the summer.

Lincoln

The Gathering of the Scottish Clans, at the Loon Mountain Recreation Area, in September. Bagpipe music can be heard.

Manchester

Folk music concerts are featured at the Manchester Institute of Arts and Sciences, 148 Concord Street.

Portsmouth

Arts festival, on Marcy Street in Prescott Park, in the summer. All types of music can be heard.

Market Square Day, in June.

Weirs Beach

Indian Village, on Route 3, in July and August. Sioux, Pima, and Kickapoo Tribes are involved in Indian folk dancing at their campsite. Such leaders as Chief Red Dawn and Blue Eagle have been featured.

NEW JERSEY

Bayonne

Veterans Memorial Stadium, 267 F Street, offers music galore.

Branchville

Folk and country music, at the fair in Peters Valley Village, off US-206, in July.

Clinton

Bluegrass concerts, at the Historical Museum.

"Center Stage," at the Hunterdon Art Center, 7 Center Street.

East Rutherford

The Brendan Byrne Arena, exit 20 off NJ 50, welcomes such artists as John Denver.

Hoboken

Folk dance programs, at the Urban Dance Center, 400 Washington Street.

35

Holmdel
Folk Heritage events of all types can be found at the Garden State Arts Center, Telegraph Hill Park.

Newark
There are many different kinds of programs, including gospel, at Symphony Hall.

The Ferry Street area is known as "Portuguese Newark" and claims ethnic music at Sol-Mar; O. Campino, 70 Jahez Street; and Mediterranean Manor, 255 Jefferson Street.

New Brunswick
George Street Folk Festival, on George Street, in September.

Stanhope
Concert series by the Waterloo Festival Orchestra include many types of music, including folk.

Willingboro
Folk music programs often take place at the Theater of Performing Arts, Mt. Holly Community Center.

NEW YORK

Buffalo
Many stars of folk music and country music perform at Fantasy Island, 2400 Grand Island Boulevard in Grand Island, from June until September.

Croton-on-Hudson
In June in recent years, a 106-foot sloop, the *Clearwater*, a replica of the extinct sloop, *Hudson River*, drops anchor in Croton, along with the ferry sloop, *Woody Guthrie*. A weekend is devoted to traditional and contemporary folk, ethnic, country, gospel, and jazz. Ecology is the theme of this musical weekend, and the money earned is earmarked to restore clean water to the Hudson River. There are five separate stages that have attracted fifteen-thousand people in past years. Pete Seeger was instrumental in creating this *Clearwater Revival*. Such stars as Tom Paxton, Arlo Guthrie, and Emmylou Harris have appeared.

Hunter
In summer, a country music weekend attracts top name performers.

There is a National Polka Event at Hunter Mountain with several polka bands under a large tent, and a German Alps Celebration as well.

New York City
There are so many places to hear folk music in New York City that we will have to confine the discussion to Manhattan, leaving the other boroughs for your further exploration.

Avery Fisher Hall at Lincoln Center, Broadway at Sixty-fifth Street, has had Nana Mouskouri on stage.

Carnegie Hall, Fifty-seventh Street and Seventh Avenue, has hosted Ravi Shankar, and Peter, Paul, and Mary.

Abraham Goodman House, 129 West Sixty-seventh Street, frequently features folk trios.

The Ninety-second Street Y at Ninety-second Street and Lexington Avenue has billed Theodore Bikel in past years.

Hunter College Auditorium, 695 Park Avenue, attracts such folk singers as Miriam Makeba.

Madison Square Garden, Thirty-third Street and Seventh Avenue, has occasional folk concerts.

Sundown, 227 East Fifty-sixth Street, hosted John Anderson recently.

In Greenwich Village there is a heavy concentration of folk music. Here are a few places that feature folk music:

Folk City, 130 West Third Street. Opened in 1960, it has attracted name entertainers such as Bob Dylan, John Baez, Judy Collins, Taj Mahal, and Danny Kalb.

The Bottom Line, 15 West Fourth Street, goes all out with gospel groups doing spirituals, political songs and protest songs. Sweet Honey in the Rock performed here recently. On Sundays, professionals and amateurs get together for fun with hootenannies.

Third Street Club on Eleventh Street welcomed folk composer David Amram in the past, who performed original compositions of many cultures on authentic instruments.

The Palladium, on Fourteenth Street between Third and Fourth Avenues, is where Joan Armatrading and others receive enthusiastic responses from audiences.

Cooper Union, at Third Avenue and Seventh Street, is a favorite spot for Oscar Brand.

D.B.'s, 119 East Eleventh Street,

City Limits, Tenth Street and Seventh Avenue, features country music and dancing. A landmark is the Village Vanguard, at 178 Seventh Avenue South.

Speakeasy, 107 MacDougal Street.

The Ethnic Arts Folk Center, 179 Varick Street, holds classes in folk dancing.

McBurney YMCA, 215 West Twenty-third Street, holds classes in folk dancing and Indian Pow Wows here are a special treat.

Old Forge

State Fiddler's Contest at the Enchanted Forest, a thirty-seven-acre park, off NY 28, in June.

Petersburg

The Fox Hollow Festival of Traditional Music, held in the woods (mentioned in Chapter 1, Psalmody), also has folk, bluegrass, and ethnic music with bagpipes and fiddles.

37

PENNSYLVANIA

Altoona

Keystone Country Festival at Lakemont Park on PA-36, in September. Folk music is featured at this festival.

Bedford

The Northern Appalachian Festival, in downtown Bedford, in May. The festival includes square dancing and a folk celebration.

The Fall Foliage Festival, in October.

Kutztown

The renowned Pennsylvania Dutch Folk Festival at the Fairgrounds in July is a musical delight.

Ligonier

Ligonian Highland Games, at Idlewild Park on US-30 from May through September. Pipe bands and Highland dancing are featured.

Philadelphia

Musical instruments are displayed at the Chinese Cultural and Community Center, at 125 North Tenth Street.

Freedom week is proclaimed in July to re-create historic events with folk music at such places as the Civic Center, Independence Mall and the Mann Music Center.

Pittsburgh

Although Stephen Foster's music is placed in the South, he was born in Lawrenceville, near Pittsburgh in 1826. One can see his memorial at the University of Pittsburgh, on Fifth Avenue and Bigelow Boulevard, which contains a splendid collection of his music and memorabilia. It is the most elaborate memorial ever built to a composer. Foster wrote 235 songs and each January, a special musical program devoted to them is presented in Heinz Chapel in the Oakland section of Pittsburgh.

The Three Rivers Arts Festival at Gateway Center, a tree-lined area, features all types of music. It is a gala event.

Smoky City Folk Festival, throughout the summer.

Schwenksville

The Philadelphia Folk Festival on a large campsite at Poole Farm, in August. The festival consists of concerts, workshops, and hootenannies. Past performers have included Tom Paxton, Tom Rush, Jim Couza (playing the dulcimer), Woody Guthrie, and Pete Seeger. This is an important event.

Uniontown

State Fiddler's Championship, at the Fayette Country Fall Foliage Festival, in October. They stomp up a storm.

RHODE ISLAND

Bristol

Square dancing and folk music are available at the Festival in June-July.

Providence
Folk music events take place from time to time at the Providence Civic Center at LaSalle Square.

VERMONT

Barre
Old-Time Fiddler's Contest, at the Barre Auditorium.
Annual Ethnic Heritage Festival, in July.

Brattleboro
The Green Street School runs a Folk Dance Series, complete with callers and fiddlers.

Craftsbury Common
This town has its own Northeast Fiddler's Celebration in July and Banjo Contest in September.

Stowe
The October Festival features country music and folk dancing.

Swanton
Swanton Summer Festival, on the Village Green, in July.
Other country-Western dancing takes place in Barre, East Burke, Randolph Center, Springfield, Townshend, and Vergennes, in the spring.

It seems that with the pressing economic, social, and political problems in the Northeast in the 1980s, once again there is widespread interest in folk music that comes from and reaches the hearts of the people.

OPERA, SYMPHONIC MUSIC, AND DANCE

Opera in Early Eighteenth-Century America

Opera, with its ornate costumes, splendid jewels, and elaborate sets, was to colonial Americans an entertainment form representative of former upper-class European affluence, available to the few, and with scant significance for the rigorous life of the New World. Not until the steady growth of cities along the eastern seaboard in the early eighteenth century did the first theaters appear, housing some opera and thus cultivating interest in the art form.

The Beggar's Opera by John Gay, and Flora patterned after ballad-style pieces from England, were performed as early as 1735 in Baltimore, Philadelphia, New York, and Boston. Only in 1752 was an informal orchestra introduced for instrumental accompaniment to Beggar's Opera in a theater in Upper Marlboro, Maryland. More than half a century later, in 1810, Gottlieb Graupner initiated the first formal United States orchestra, the Philharmonic Society in Boston. The orchestra became an integral part of opera.

Early ballad operas, produced mostly by traveling companies, reflected issues of the day: Tammany (by James Hewitt in 1794), Indian Chief, Columbus, and Fourth of July. New Yorkers traveled to the Nassau Street Theater, Bostonians frequented the Federal Street Theater to hear the Charles Powell Company perform, although conservative Boston preferred the oratorios of Handel and Haydn.

New York's John Street Theater presented The Temple of Minerva, a political oratorio written by Francis Hopkinson of early hymnal fame (See Section I, Chapter 3.) Friend George Washington is said to have been in the audience in 1781 enjoying the music.

Centers of Music in the Nineteenth Century
New York became the leading center of music in the early nineteenth century. Beginning in 1825 the Park Theater welcomed European touring groups, who brought European opera (mostly Italian, and some French and German). Manuel Garcia, a tenor and composer, titil-

lated New Yorkers with a small-scale production of *The Barber of Seville* by Rossini. Garcia's daughter, Maria Malibran, later became a famous opera star. The Park Theater also hosted Carl Maria von Weber's *Der Freischutz* in 1825, complete with costumes and modest scenic effects. *Der Freischutz* was billed at Philadelphia's Chestnut Street Theater later that same year.

A short time after that, in 1833, the Italian Opera House was erected on Church and Leonard Streets in New York City. This was the first building in America earmarked exclusively for opera. Opening night featured Rossini's little-known *La Gazza Ladra*. Palmo's Opera House on Chamber Street came into existence in 1844 with the Italian Da Ponte Opera Company presenting *I Puritani* of Bellini. Lorenzo da Ponte, for whom the opera company was named, was the librettist of Mozart's *Cosi fan Tutte* and *Don Giovanni*.

Three other theaters were busily engaged with productions: Richmond Hill, which emphasized Italian repertory; Niblo's Gardens, specializing in English light opera, and later German opera; and Castle Garden, where, in 1850, Jenny Lind, the world-famous coloratura soprano, known as the "Swedish Nightingale," managed by American

Jenny Lind, the "Swedish Nightingale" (Courtesy Dover Pictorial Archive Series, 1980)

showman, P.T. Barnum, sang arias from Bellini's *Norma* to an audience of six-thousand wildly cheering listeners.

Aided by European singers, opera, was gradually "catching on." The Astor Place Opera was built in 1847 and the Academy of Music opened in 1854 on Fourteenth Street and Irving Place. The Academy was the forerunner of the current Metropolitan Opera House. It remained the leading musical edifice for high society until the first Metropolitan Opera House was established in 1883.

Philadelphia built its own Academy of Music in 1857, embracing Italian, French, and German opera. President Lincoln is said to have taken pleasure in a box seat there for several performances.

The Boston Theater opened around this time, seating three thousand in its auditorium. The theater still tended toward conservative taste, banning from its stage *Rigoletto* by Verdi and *Salome* by Richard Strauss.

The First Metropolitan Opera House in New York in 1883

The Academy of Music on Fourteenth Street in New York was a fashionable place. Among its boxholders were such names as Astor, Vanderbilt, Roosevelt, and Morgan, carrying forward a tradition of wealth and elegance. The Academy continued to accommodate the elite until it could no longer comfortably house the increasing numbers who demanded opera. These notables decided to contribute impressive sums of money to build a new and larger opera house, the Metropolitan Opera House, at 1423 Broadway, a site extending from Thirty-ninth to Fortieth Streets between Broadway and Seventh Avenue.

The new building's exterior was large, designed in early Italian Renaissance style. The interior was majestically decorated in colors of red, cream, and gold, with sparkling lights illuminating stately parterre boxes, and a curving horseshoe pattern of seating, reminiscent of the center box from which former European nobility held court.

Monday night was fashionable night at the "Old Met." It was the place to be seen and to socialize. Indeed, much upper-class social life revolved around the opera. Stockholders owned boxes and renters paid a fee to frequent this large brown brick, gaslit building. Renters were looked down on, but if you owned, you were "in."

Choice seating was in the Diamond Horseshoe, filled with splendidly-gowned, bejewelled women, and men in tails, white ties, and white gloves. The walls of the anteroom leading to the boxes were usually bedecked with colorful flowers. According to custom, the social leader, Mrs. Astor, for example, would appear ostentatiously at about nine, and during intermission, would receive friends in her box. Social snobbery ran high since the Met was essentially a club with assessments to keep it going. In 1965, the Old Met was torn down. Larger quarters at Lincoln Center were built.

The Metropolitan Opera, when housed at the former Metropolitan Opera House (known now as the Old Met), served as a repertory company and presented a different opera each night during brief seasons. Opening night in 1883 featured *Faust* by Gounod, in Italian, with singers Christine Nilsson and Italo Campanini. Italian opera, characteristically melodious and lively, employing colorful costumes and stage settings, and expensive to produce originally dominated the Met. Typical examples of such operas are *The Barber of Seville* by Rossini, *Il Trovatore* by Verdi, and *Tosca* by Puccini. Due largely to the influence of conductor Leopold Damrosch (and later, his son Walter), German opera found a place at the Met. Damrosch introduced Wagner to American audiences toward the late nineteenth century. *Tannhauser* was presented with singers Auguste Kraus, Anton Schott, and Adolf Robinson. Between the senior Damrosch's term as conductor of the Met's Orchestra and that of son Walter's, Anton Seidl, Wagner's own personal assistant at Bayreuth, Germany, took up the baton, beginning with *Lohengrin* in 1885, and ending the German reign seven seasons later in 1891. Compared to Italian opera, German opera is somber, more modest in setting, less costly to produce, and elevates the orchestra to a major role in creating mood for the text, as evidenced in Wagner's *Ring* of four operas.

The Oratorio Society of New York, for which Andrew Carnegie built Carnegie Hall, was founded in 1873 by Leopold Damrosch and has been active since then. Damrosch also founded the New York Symphony Society, which later merged with the New York Philharmonic Society.

Walter Damrosch composed *Scarlet Letter* in 1896, based on Nathaniel Hawthorne's story. It was performed first at the Boston Opera House then at the Met. Damrosch was innovative, taking the Company "on the road." In addition to conducting and importing German singers, he utilized radio in the early twentieth century to aid in teaching music appreciation. A second opera of his, *Man Without a Country*, was performed at the Met in 1937 with Arthur Carron and Helen Traubel among the cast of singers.

The Met in the Early Twentieth Century

The year 1908 was a significant one for the Met because it was the beginning of Giulio Gatti-Casazza's reign as general manager. For more than a quarter century, Gatti-Casazza enriched the opera's artistic accomplishments. Under his aegis such names as Arturo Toscanini, Enrico Caruso, Geraldine Farrar, and Nellie Melba attained great musical heights and fame that became legendary.

A few memorable highlights from Gatti-Casazza's reign were

Melba in *Lucia di Lammermoor* by Donizetti, and Caruso singing in both *Rigoletto* and *Aida* by Verdi and in *I Pagliacci* by Leoncavallo. Caruso sang for eighteen seasons, 607 times in thirty-seven operas. His voice, a mellow, lyric tenor, set high standards for future tenors all over the world. Arturo Toscanini, conductor and musician par excellence, brought to America conventional Italian repertory and some German operas. His reign opened with a new production of *Aida*. The remarkable quality of the Maestro was his facility in memorizing complete scores. He never needed the score when he conducted a performance. He was unrelenting in his demand for perfect performances from his artists. Tempers flared frequently, insults were hurled, but the excellent musical results were worth it. After conducting at the Met for seven seasons Toscanini left, returning to New York in 1926 to conduct the Philharmonic Orchestra. Bruno Walter, Fritz Reiner, and Leopold Stokowski were some of the conductors who succeeded Toscanini at the Met.

Two other personalities whose names became legend during Gatti-Casazza's leadership were Rosa Ponselle, best remembered for her role in *La Forza del Destino* by Verdi and in *La Gioconda* by Ponchielli, and Ezio Pinza, who made his debut in 1926 in Spontini's *La Vestale*. Pinza displayed remarkable voice range and flexibility, shown especially in Mozart's *Don Giovanni*.

When Gatti-Casazza retired from the Met in 1934, tickets were selling at $8.25 a seat and the season expanded to twenty-four weeks.

Other Sites for Opera in the Early Twentieth Century

Other places that were involved in operatic productions in the early twentieth century were the Manhattan Opera House (where Oscar Hammerstein, Sr. produced Debussy's *Pelleas and Melisande*), the New Theater at Central Park West and Sixty-first Street, the Brooklyn Academy of Music, the Philadelphia Academy of Music, and the Lyric Theater in Baltimore.

Some American Operas and American Composers

Although Italian and German opera remained prevalent in the United States, as the country grew, Americans composed some operas, blending the American musical idiom with American history in the text.

In 1910, *The Pipe of Desire* by Frederick Converse was the first American opera to be presented at the Met. Charles W. Cadman's *Shanewis* (an opera with an Indian theme) followed in 1918. *Cleopatra's Night* was written in 1921 by Henry Hadley, the man who founded the Berkshire Music Festival in Massachusetts. Deems Taylor wrote *The King's Henchman*, commissioned by the Met in 1927, with Lawrence Tibbett, Edward Johnson, and Florence Easton singing the text of Edna

St. Vincent Millay. Louis Gruenberg used Eugene O'Neill's play as the basis for *The Emperor Jones* in 1933. Howard Hanson is remembered for *Merry Mount* in 1934, inspired by Hawthorne's tale "The May-Pole of Merry Mount."

In the 1940s and 1950s Leonard Bernstein composed *Trouble in Tahiti*, and Samuel Barber created *Vanessa*. Virgil Thomson collaborated with Gertrude Stein on *Four Saints in Three Acts* and *The Mother of Us All*. Versatile Aaron Copland composed *The Tender Land*, and the Italian-American composer, Gian-Carlo Menotti, did a great deal for American opera with *The Telephone*, *The Medium*, *The Saint of Bleecker Street*, and *Amahl and the Night Visitors*.

Other American composers who contributed operas were Alex Wilder (*Lowland Sea*), Lukas Foss (*The Jumping Frog of Calaveras County*), and Douglas Moore (*The Devil and Daniel Webster* and *The Ballad of Baby Doe*). In a lighter vein, folk opera and light opera were popularized by George Gershwin in *Porgy and Bess* and by the many works of Gilbert and Sullivan.

Opera Expands

Modern-day opera has changed its course from representing luxury for the affluent few to representing culture for the many. Most opera houses in the major northeastern cities have full subscription seasons running eight months a year.

The Metropolitan Opera Guild, whose purpose is to increase public knowledge and appreciation of opera by promoting lectures, tours, and exhibitions, helps make still-glamorous opera widely available to a broader base of people than ever before.

The Met Moves to a New Home in 1966

Time to move again. Nineteen sixty-six saw the Metropolitan Opera move into new, more luxurious quarters at Lincoln Center, Broadway and Sixty-fifth Street in New York City, under the management of Rudolf Bing. The new home for the Met is an attractive building in the Lincoln Center Complex between Avery Fisher Hall and the New York State Theater, with water fountains and sculpture adding attractive touches outside. The interior is tastefully decorated in gold leaf design with brilliant glass chandeliers, plush seats, and sumptuous accessories, including Chagall murals. Opening night in 1966 welcomed an American work by Samuel Barber, *Antony and Cleopatra*.

Some of the artists who have appeared on stage since then have been Leontyne Price, Renata Tebaldi, Placido Domingo, Marilyn Horne, and Luciano Pavarotti.

Other Opera Companies

The New York City Opera came into existence in 1944. Originally part of the City Center for Music and Drama, the company performs today at the New York State Theater at Lincoln Center under the management of Beverly Sills, former opera star. The New York City Opera periodically presents American opera.

Sarah Caldwell, Artistic Director of the Opera Company of Boston, has been responsible for introducing such U.S. premieres as Bernd Zimmermann's *Die Soldaten* in Boston at the Savoy Theater.

There are opera houses and places for opera performance throughout the Northeast. Verdi and Wagner share the stage with Barber and Berg. Millions listen to radio broadcasts of opera each week but admit that a night spent at the opera is a memorable one.

Symphonic Music

As the first American symphony orchestras began to develop in the mid-nineteenth century, they were staffed with artistic emigrés, who brought with them their European cultural heritage. Symphonic music in America until the end of the first World War was predominantly Austro-German, with an occasional addition of Italian, French, Russian, Hungarian, and Czechoslovakian repertory. American musicians knew that they had to travel to Berlin, Leipzig, and Vienna to study classical music.

The Major Orchestras in the Northeast

The Northeast boasts three major symphony orchestras, as noted earlier: The New York Philharmonic, the Boston Symphony, and the Philadelphia Orchestra.

The New York Philharmonic
The beginnings of opera, brought from Europe to America in the eighteenth and mid-nineteenth centuries, prodded opera companies to look for native American orchestral musicians, in addition to European musicians for musical accompaniment. Since New York was home territory for large numbers of artists, attempts were made to establish an independent orchestra exclusively for symphonic enjoyment.

In 1842, a group of New York musicians founded the first permanent, although part-time, symphony orchestra in the United States, The New York Philharmonic Society of New York. This new group made its début at the Apollo Rooms on Lower Broadway between Walker and Lispenard Streets. The performance was attended by an audience of 600, who sat on wooden benches to listen to Ureli Corelli Hill conduct Beethoven's Fifth Symphony. During the Society's early years the repertory was mostly German (including the premieres of two symphonies by Beethoven) with an occasional Russian or French work included. Subscribers to the first season paid $10.00 for a series of three concerts which took place in late fall, winter, and early spring.

Some other important non-German works premiered by the Society in the years that followed were: Dvorak's New World Symphony, Ives's Symphony No. 2, and Stravinsky's Symphony in Three Movements.

Some Early Conductors

The first regular conductor of the Philharmonic Society was Theodore Eisfeld, contracted in 1852. He was followed by Leopold Damrosch. And Damrosch was succeeded by Theodore Thomas, the first American-trained conductor and violinist in the Society. Thomas was a formidable and hard-driving disciplinarian, who had previously created and conducted his own Theodore Thomas Orchestra in 1864, with repertory of Brahms, Wagner, and Richard Strauss. After Thomas came Anton Seidl of Wagner fame wielding the baton.

New York enjoyed a musical heyday toward the end of the nineteenth century. Thomas raised the artistic standards of the orchestra and, through touring, expanded the availability of symphonic music and attracted many more audiences. He also further increased repertory to include works by Berlioz, Tchaikovsky, and Sibelius. In later years, Thomas left the Philharmonic Society to found the Chicago Symphony Orchestra and to help erect its Orchestra Hall. (See Section III, Chapter 2.)

Anton Seidl, too, worked to enlarge audiences by conducting concerts throughout Manhattan, at Coney Island, and at the Brooklyn Academy of Music. Seidl's term as conductor was followed by such notables as Walter Damrosch, Gustav Mahler, and Willem Mengelberg in the early twentieth century.

In addition to their musical distinctions, the Damrosch family had the social distinction of being good friends with music lovers Mr. and Mrs. Andrew Carnegie. Andrew Carnegie financed the building of the world-famous Carnegie Hall on Fifty-seventh Street and Seventh Avenue in 1891. Originally called The Music Hall, Carnegie Hall opened with a five-day music festival in which Tchaikovsky, himself conducted along with Walter Damrosch. This landmark institution with exceptionally fine acoustics housed the Philharmonic Society/Orchestra for more

Mrs. Andrew Carnegie lays the cornerstone for Carnegie Hall on May 15, 1890. (Courtesy Carnegie Hall)

than 70 years until it moved into Philharmonic Hall (now Avery Fisher Hall) at Lincoln Center.

The year 1928 marked the merger of the Philharmonic Society and the New York Symphony (founded by Leopold Damrosch) into the New York Philharmonic. The following year Arturo Toscanini was imported from Italy's La Scala Opera House in Milan to assume principal conductorship. In his conducting Toscanini aimed for clarity, precision, objectivity, and fidelity of interpretation, as he revered the composer as omnipotent. Repertory was still heavily German. He demanded musical perfection and, with his artistic temperament, he never allowed his musicians to deviate from this goal. Colleagues both respected and feared him, and true to those feelings, they nicknamed him "The Old Man."

This author's father, Isadore Gusikoff, played first cello under Toscanini at the NBC Symphony in the 1940s and has recounted tales of "The Old Man" screaming, shrieking, and cursing in Italian during rehearsals in studio 8H, tearing his Florentine gold watch from his wrist, throwing it on the floor, stamping on it with his foot, smashing it to smithereens, and then asking, "Now will you give me what I want?"

Other Conductors

From the 1940s through the 1970s Sir John Barbirolli, Artur Rodzinsky, and Leonard Bernstein were some of the conductors who followed Toscanini on the Philharmonic podium. Many composers have conducted their own works at Philharmonic concerts: Anton Rubinstein, Richard Strauss, Igor Stravinsky, Sergei Rachmaninoff, Gustav Mahler, Bela Bartok, and, more recently, Leonard Bernstein, Aaron Copland, and Pierre Boulez.

Zubin Mehta became the principal conductor in 1979 and under his leadership, a number of soloists have appeared with the orchestra, such as Isaac Stern, Itzhak Perlman, and Jean-Pierre Rampal. The Juilliard School of Music at Lincoln Center frequently supports the Philharmonic musically in its artistic endeavors.

Summer Concerts

The idea for summer symphonic music in New York City (the regular season runs from the fall through the spring) was inaugurated in 1922 when a series of low-priced summer concerts was held at Lewisohn Stadium on 135th Street and Convent Avenue, next to City College of NY (CCNY). Lewisohn Stadium was located in Harlem, which made for an interesting contrast.These concerts were enormously popular and continued for many years. Today the Stadium is a musical memory, but outdoor park concerts developed large audiences in the 1960s and since then have been given throughout New York's five boroughs, and in Nassau and Suffolk Counties. Damrosch Park, adjacent to Lincoln Center, is a particularly attractive site for bandshell performances. So is Central Park.

Indoors at Avery Fisher Hall, the "Mostly Mozart" Summer Festival is an annual occurrence. The presiding chamber orchestra has set a high standard emulated in many parts of the nation. Guest conductors appear frequently, as they do with all major orchestras.

The Boston Symphony Orchestra

The foundations for orchestral performances in Boston were laid in the early 1800s with the Handel and Haydn Society and the Philharmonic Society of Boston. The Boston Academy of Music, some years later, produced little in the way of successful symphonic endeavors. Following the Academy's disappointing results, the Harvard Musical Association was established and a clamor for a formal orchestra was heard. It was acted upon by Henry Higginson, who, in 1881, created the Boston Symphony Orchestra.

The orchestra's first program took place in the old Music Hall in downtown Boston, said to be acoustically wanting, drafty, and uncomfortable. Works by Beethoven, Gluck, Haydn, and Bruch (standard fare of the day) were conducted by George Henshel. Shortly thereafter, in 1900, the Orchestra moved to Symphony Hall, which was more luxurious and acoustically superior. The Orchestra performs there today. Under Higginson's management, Symphony Hall became Boston's top musical institution.

It was Higginson's decision to further extend the season by adding several weeks of popular and semi-classical programs to the schedule. The Boston "Pops" had immense appeal under the baton of Arthur Fiedler for decades. After Fiedler's death, John Williams assumed musical directorship.

Major Conductors

Pierre Monteux conducted in 1920. A short, rotund, charming Frenchman, he covered music from Beethoven to the day's "modern" composers: Honegger, Respighi, and Vaughan Williams. He introduced Ravel's "Daphnis and Chloe" to American audiences. Unlike Theodore Thomas or Toscanini, men with intense, driving personalities, Monteux was courteous, elegant, low-keyed, and somewhat poetic in his musical interpretation.

The Frenchman left in 1924 and was replaced by Serge Koussevitsky, a musical giant equal in artistic depth to Toscanini. At his debut with the Boston Symphony, Koussevitsky conducted Vivaldi's *Concerto Grosso in D*, Scriabin's *Poem of Ecstasy*, Berlioz's *Roman Carnival Overture*, and Brahms's *Haydn Variations*. Koussevitsky felt deeply for the music of Rachmaninoff, Shostakovich, and Prokofieff, but gave the music of Copland, Barber, Hanson, Milhaud, and Ravel opportunities to be heard. Koussevitsky's personality, like Toscanini's, was emotional and dramatic as he led his musicians in pursuit of musical excellence. He assumed leadership of the Berkshire Music Festival, organized originally by Henry Hadley in 1933. The Berkshire Music Festival takes place at Tanglewood in the green, rolling Berkshire foothills in Lenox, Massachusetts. In 1940 Koussevitsky established the Berkshire Music Center, one of the nation's most prestigious music schools, among whose gifted students was a pianist named Leonard Bernstein.

Erich Leinsdorf was appointed musical director of the Boston Symphony in 1962 and immediately modified the Franco-Russian emphasis. A demanding, detail-oriented, technically proficient interpreter, he changed the romantic approach to a style of logic and order.

The conductor of the Boston Symphony in 1983 is Japanese-born Seiji Ozawa, who is also co-director of the Tanglewood School, at the Berkshire Music Center.

The Philadelphia Orchestra

Philadelphia had its Musical Fund Society as early as 1820 for purposes of organizing instrumental performances. The Academy of Music was built in 1857. This is where the Philadelphia Orchestra, since its founding in 1900, has performed. Music-lovers proclaim its acoustics to be among the finest in the world.

The high quality of the Philadelphia Orchestra is due largely to the influence of one of its early conductors, Leopold Stokowski, an ex-

Interior of the Academy of Music, Philadelphia (Photo by Adrian Siegal, courtesy Philadelphia Orchestra)

traordinary showman and personality who served from 1912 until 1938. Also, the Curtis Institute of Music, renowned teaching institution, has supported the Orchestra artistically and financially for many years, helping it to attain and maintain its high standards.

Stokowski's repertory was large and varied, including traditional Russian and French music, Bach and Brahms, and "moderns," such as Mahler and Stravinsky. This author's father served as first cellist under the Maestro for almost two decades in the 1920s and 1930s and recounted the following tale indicating "Stoki's" dedication to playing modern works at that time:

The Orchestra began its program at the Academy of Music in the 1930s with "Le Sacre du Printemps" by Stravinsky. The music is basically anti-romantic and polyrhythmic, with little melody and much discord. After ten minutes or so, many people in the audience stirred uncomfortably, rose from their seats, and proceeded to leave the Hall in disenchantment. Stoki, who rarely used a baton, motioned angrily with his hands for the musicians to stop playing during the exodus. When the interruption ended after about four minutes, he beckoned for playing to resume from the *beginning* of the piece, thus the remaining listeners were treated doubly to the first part of the work. Stokowski considered this a lesson in music appreciation.

Mahler's Eighth Symphony, with its extensive and dramatic use of chorus and orchestra, was introduced to the public by Stokowski. The music of Hindemith, Schoenberg, and Ives received equal exposure in Philadelphia and on tours. Stravinsky and Rachmaninoff themselves were frequent visitors to the orchestra when their works were rehearsed and performed.

In contrast to Toscanini, who labored to interpret the composers faithfully, Stokowski was intent upon creating a unique and memorable sound. This he did regularly by adding his own touches to the scores, especially in Bach's D Minor Toccata and Fugue.

Stokowski left Philadelphia in 1938. In later years he established the American Symphony Orchestra in New York. Carnegie Hall paid tribute to this artist in early 1982 on the date that would have been his 100th birthday. Sergiu Comissiona, current music advisor of the American Symphony, laid down his baton, and in deference to Stoki, conducted the Bach D Minor Toccata and Fugue with his hands.

Eugene Ormandy took the reins of the Philadelphia Orchestra next, and held them for about forty years. Ormandy preferred the late romantic school of Tchaikovsky and the early modern era of Debussy. Recently retired, he has chosen Ricardo Muti to succeed him.

Summer concerts are popular at the Mann Music Center, formerly the Robin Hood Dell. The orchestra travels to Saratoga each summer to entertain at the Performing Arts Center.

Some Twentieth-Century American Composers and Conductors

The period after World War I, for several decades, witnessed the rise of some American musicians composing with nationalistic feeling.

Charles Ives

Ives's music, like Stravinsky's, tends to be discordant, employing fragmented melodies and thwarting expectations. His Second Symphony, composed in 1901, incorporates bits and pieces of folk music from "Columbia, the Gem of the Ocean" and "Old Black Joe." The Third and Fourth Symphonies quote old American hymns, but in a broken musical train of exposition. "Three Places in New England" is based on American history and geography. Ives is intellectual rather than emotional in his artistic expression.

Samuel Barber

Barber studied at the Curtis Institute in Philadelphia and, like Ives, was interested in polytonal and polyrhythmic combinations. His Adagio for Strings and Essay No. I were the first American works to be performed by Toscanini and the NBC Symphony Orchestra in 1938. The Boston Symphony played his Symphony No. 2 in 1944 in Boston and his Piano Concerto in 1962 in New York as a visiting orchestra at Lincoln Center. Barber has also written operas (*Vanessa* and *Antony and Cleopatra*) which are performed every now and again.

Aaron Copland

A prolific composer in the American idiom, Copland combines folk, and serious music. His Concerto for Piano and Orchestra was premiered by Koussevitsky and the Boston Symphony in 1927, with Copland as pianist. He has written an opera (*The Tender Land*) and ballets. *Appalachian Spring*, one of his most well-known ballets, has a great deal of American folk music in it, including square dances, fiddle tunes, revivalist hymns, and a Shaker tune (*Simple Gifts*).

Leonard Bernstein

A talented pianist who studied at Koussevitsky's Music School at Tanglewood, Bernstein is a multi-talented American musician/composer/conductor. He was the New York Philharmonic's musical director from 1958 to 1969 and guest conductor with other orchestras as well. A charismatic man who opened up channels between Mahler and audiences and Beethoven and audiences, Bernstein also composed music for the theater and ballet (*On the Town*, *Fancy Free*, and *West Side Story*).

John Cage

A true late twentieth-century, ultra-modernist, Cage is considered by some still to be avant-garde. His use of electronics and startling sound textures is highly innovative. *Williams Mix*, composed in 1952, offers sounds on magnetic tape made by the wind and on the streets. *Water Music* creates sounds produced by pouring water from a full paper container into an empty one. An extreme touch in Concerto for Piano and Orchestra, written in 1958, calls for the pianist to thump with his fists on the undersurface of the piano.

Chamber, Groups and Chamber Music

One hundred or more players make up a full modern orchestra, which is divided into four instrumental sections: string (the largest section), woodwind, brass, and percussion. Although augmentation is possible, generally here is what they contain:

Strings — violins, violas, cellos, basses, piano, harps
Woodwinds — flutes, piccolos, oboes, bassoons, clarinets
Brass — trumpets, trombones, English Horns, French Horns, tubas
Percussion — tympani, chimes, bells, chimes, etc.

Very appealing today are the chamber orchestra, a small orchestra consisting of about twenty-five players, and chamber groups, instrumental ensembles in which there is one player to a part. Two examples of chamber group classifications are: piano trio, consisting of violin, cello, and piano (the Borodin Trio); string quartet, consisting of two violins, viola, and cello (the Emerson String Quartet).

Some Major Symphonic Festivals in the Northeast

There are numerous festivals offered throughout the Northeast that are listed at the end of this chapter. Here, though, are mention of several major ones.

Mostly Mozart Festival at Lincoln Center in New York City

This festival of concerts is held during July and August in Avery Fisher Hall with the Mostly Mozart Chamber Orchestra. The music of other composers, such as Handel, Haydn, Schubert, is also played.

Mostly Mozart Festival in Vermont

Concerts are given in many parts of the state including Burlington, Barre, Middlebury, Bolton, and Waitsfield; in barns, churches, and museums; on farms and ferryboats. There are also workshops and seminars with the Emerson Quartet, among others, in residence.

Tanglewood Festival at Lenox, Massachusetts

An estate of 210 acres in the Berkshire Mountains is the site of the world-famous Tanglewood, the summer home of the Boston Symphony and the home of the Berkshire Music Center and Festival. Seating is under a roofed area and on the lawn. Musical activities continue all summer, including morning rehearsals which are open to the public.

Marlboro Music School and Festival in Vermont

Another fine music school that holds classes, workshops, and festivals for musically gifted people is at Marlboro. Directed by the pianist, Rudolph Serkin, it is located in the foothills of the Green Mountains in southern Vermont. In its auditorium and on its attractive lawn are held chamber music concerts in August with guest artists. The cellist, Pablo Casals, taught here in past years. The year 1982 marked its 50th season.

Dance—From Popular to Ballet and Modern Dance

Popular dance in the eighteenth and nineteenth centuries consisted in large part of rhythmic steps of blacks, characterized by shuffling, wiggling, and yelping, and of jigs, reels, and clog dances brought here by the Irish. Mix these steps with the European waltz and you have a blend producing the one-step, the two-step, the Charleston, the Black Bottom, the Varsity Drag, the Shag, the Big Apple, and the Susie-Q, popular in the late nineteenth and early twentieth century.

Joseph Smith devised the Turkey Trot and Bunny Hug from watching blacks and their body movements during work. Smith, together with Vernon and Irene Castle, invented new steps in ballroom dancing in the early twentieth century that were enormously appealing: the Fox Trot, the Castle Walk, and an improved Latin American Tango. Veloz and Yolanda, and Fred and Adele Astaire were among those artists who introduced the idea of dancing schools, both as recreation and to improve social skills.

Beginnings of Ballet

Ballet, a European dance form employing classical, traditional, precise steps, points (on the toes), lifts, and finger turns, received slight interest in mid-nineteenth-century America. The little that existed took place in second-rate theaters, barrooms, and cafés, mixed with popular entertainment of tap dancing and jazz. With the growth of cities, English musicians and dancing teachers arrived. They settled largely in New York, Philadelphia, and Boston, eagerly seeking pupils to teach. George Washington Smith (the father of Joseph Smith), Mary Ann Lee, and Julia Turnbull were among those pupils associated with the beginnings of American ballet.

George Washington Smith, our first *danseur noble,* made his debut in 1838 before a modest audience at the Chestnut Street Theater in Philadelphia. In 1840, Fanny Elssler, a Viennese ballerina visiting the United States, joined him in dance at the Park Theater in New York, performing *La Tarentule* and *La Cracovienne.* Before Elssler returned to Europe in 1842, her *La Fille Mal Gardée* by Jean Dauberval left a spark in the hearts of her viewers. Several years later, in 1846, Smith and partner Mary Ann Lee performed *Giselle* with music by Adolphe Adam at the Howard Atheneum in Boston.

Some impetus clearly was under way and small ballet companies began to develop in the New York/Philadelphia/Boston/Baltimore area. The Park Theater in New York imported many European dancers as did the National and Bowery Theaters. In 1854, the Academy of Music opened on Fourteenth Street in New York City and introduced Beethoven, Donizetti, and Meyerbeer with the dance form.

Anna Pavlova in the Northeast

Although the illustrious Metropolitan Opera House opened in New York in 1883, it rarely welcomed ballet until 1910, when the renowned Russian ballerina, Anna Pavlova, graced its stage. Pavlova was an artist from the traditional European school, upholding balance, grace, purity of line, nobility, and order. Her style imparted beautiful lyricism, flowing sequence of step, and continuity of pattern. Her role of Swanhilda in Delibes' *Coppelia* was said to have been memorable, as was her role in *Hungary* by Alexander Glazounov.

Pavlova toured the Northeast between 1916 and 1926, dancing *The Seasons* and *La Mort du Cygne,* choreographed by Michel Fokine of Diaghilev's Ballets Russes in Russia. She established a mind set in preparing the American public for dance.

With her came Russian dancers, Adolph Bolm, Mikhail Mordkin, Alexandre Volinine, and Pierre Vladimiroff, appearing in New York at the Hippodrome on Sixth Avenue, and at the Manhattan Opera House. At this time Pavlova met the impresario, Sol Hurok, and together they are credited with creating audiences for ballet and bringing ballet to the masses.

Ballets Russes

The year 1916 also witnessed the first American appearance of Diaghilev's Ballets Russes at the Century Theater in New York, with principal dancers Adolph Bolm, Leonide Massine, Federova, Sololova, and Cecchetti. In addition, Vaslav Nijinsky came to New York to dance *Le Spectre de la Rose* and *Petrouchka* at the Metropolitan Opera House. Nijinsky, by reputation, was the greatest jumper of all time, capable of doing six entrechat douze (crossings of the legs in mid-air) with instants remaining before he descended.

Philadelphia's Metropolitan Opera House at Broad and Poplar Streets also hosted the Ballets Russes, with Michel and Vera Fokine, the former, master choreographer as well as dancer. They danced at the Hippodrome in Baltimore in 1920, and following that, at the Century Theater, on Central Park West, and at Lewisohn Stadium, both in New York. Michel Fokine, as choreographer, had enlarged traditional technique to include freer arm and leg movements that broke with the strict rules for classic positions. Fluidity and relaxation superseded conventional rules. He changed the traditional dress requirements of tutu (short ballet skirt) and male tights to more comfortable and informal attire. And he elevated the subservient male dancer to a central figure.

Ballet Russe de Monte Carlo

After many financial and artistic crises in Europe, Leonide Massine succeeded Fokine; then Nijinsky took over as master choreographer. The Ballets Russes became the Ballet Russe de Monte Carlo and gave its first American performance in 1933 at the St. James Theater in New York. Massine staged weekly productions at New York's Roxy Theater and also danced in the productions. He danced with remarkable rhythm and strength. Both the Metropolitan Opera House in New York and the Academy of Music in Philadelphia featured his *Sacre du Printemps*. The Forrest Theater in Philadelphia welcomed *Union Pacific* with music by Nicholas Nabokoff. Dancing in that production were Massine, David Lichine, and André Eglevsky. New York's Majestic Theater hosted *The Three-Cornered Hat* and *La Boutique Fantastique*, two of Massine's masterpieces.

George Balanchine and the School of American Ballet

Another Russian artist, George Balanchine, came to America

in 1933 after serving, at age twenty-one, as Diaghilev's Ballet Master and having created a Stravinsky ballet, *Le Rossignol*, for ballerina Alicia Markova. Balanchine, together with Lincoln Kirsten, established the School of American Ballet in New York in 1934. The American Ballet was the precursor of the New York City Ballet. The School of American Ballet presented Balanchine's *Mozartiana* and *Serenade* among others at Avery Memorial Theater in Hartford, Connecticut, that year.

Balanchine was innovative—his bent knee on points and a turned-in foot position were radical ideas. He interwove acrobatics into classical technique, and a different sort of technical virtuosity was evident in the combination of folk steps, stunts, and theater in *Western Symphony* and *Square Dance*. In 1935 the American Ballet, under Balanchine's direction, became the resident ballet company at the Metropolitan Opera House. Lew Christensen, Erick Hawkins, and Lillian Moore, among others, joined the company. The idea at that time was to promote ballet works by American rather than import talent from Europe. The company performed *Billy the Kid* by Aaron Copland, *Filling Station* by Elliot Carter, and *Yankee Clipper* by William Carter. In their ballets the story was prominent and was based on native American material.

Balanchine worked on Broadway in 1936 in *Ziegfeld Follies* and in Hollywood in 1937 in *Goldwyn Follies* with Vera Zorina. By the 1940s he had created a distinctive kind of dancer for his ballets: quick, supple, energetic, mobile, unemotional, and particularly American. He placed choreography above the dancer in importance, prefering movement and music to a story line. He worked with Hindemith's music in *Four Temperaments*, and with Stravinsky's music in *Agon*, *Symphony in Three Movements*, and *Violin Concerto*. *Gounod Symphony*, performed by Maria Tallchief in 1962, was one of his most impressive works. His recent death in 1983 saddened the artistic world.

The Ballet Theater

The Ballet Theater, now called the American Ballet Theater (ABT), was founded by dancers Lucia Chase and Richard Pleasant. The presentation of *Sleeping Beauty* in 1940 at the Center Theater in New York's Rockefeller Center marked its beginnings. Since that time, other ballet companies have appeared: the Joffrey, Eliot Feld, and the Dance Theater of Harlem (all in New York); the Philadelphia Ballet; the Boston Ballet; the Washington, D.C. Ballet; the Maryland Ballet.

Some artists who rose to fame with the ABT are Lupe Serrano, Agnes De Mille, Jerome Robbins, Robert Joffrey, and Maria Karnilova. The American Ballet Theater operates schools in New York, Washington, D.C., Denver, and Detroit. The schools are open to native talent. Jerome Robbins became co-director with Balanchine of the ABT at New

York's City Center in 1949. Robbins worked with a ballet-jazz style and choreographed *Fancy Free* to the music of Leonard Bernstein. This ballet contributed humor to dance. *Fancy Free* was featured at the Metropolitan Opera House in 1944. Robbins's *Interplay* also weaves classical dance with jive, and *West Side Story* another work by Robbins/Bernstein, is a fusion of dance, jazz, and drama. One of his latest is *Gershwin Concerto* premiered in 1982. It's set to the Concerto in F and contains jazz and symphonic elements.

The New York State Theater, part of the Lincoln Center complex at Sixty-fifth Street and Broadway, opened its doors to dance in 1964 and became the home of the New York City Ballet and the American Ballet Theater. Little more than a decade later, the ABT came under the artistic direction of Mikhail Baryshnikov, the dancing personality of the 1970s and 1980s. The Joffrey Ballet and the Alvin Ailey Dance Theater assumed control of the City Center, with the Joffrey planning to move to Los Angeles in 1984.

Katherine Dunham

A famous American dancer, Katherine Dunham, mixed dance with song, black history, and sexual elements. She danced in the 1930s at the Forty-eighth Street Theater and at the Martin Beck Theater, both in New York. She was the first person to organize a black troupe. Dunham's *Tropical Revue* was heated with West Indian and native American music, a blending of eroticism, humor, and lyricism.

Martha Graham

A living legend, Martha Graham, dancer and choreographer, has proven to be an innovator par excellence. Her dances express social conflicts, psychological themes, drama, and Far Eastern mysticism. Significant dance movements are kneeling, squatting, contracting, and unfolding from the floor as base. Graham gave her dance recital at the Forty-eighth Street Theater in New York in 1926, and several years later she danced at the Academy of Music in Philadelphia, where she performed Stravinsky's *Sacre du Printemps*. She is well known for her arrangement of *Deaths and Entrances*, a study in psychological austerity.

She responds to history, myths, and human experience in a traditional but free manner. Graham worked on Americanizing ballet in *Frontier: An American Perspective of the Plains*; in *Horizons*, a ballet that told of migration and new trails; in *El Penitente*, a ballet about a southwestern Indian sect; in *Letter to the World*, about the life and art of Emily Dickinson; in *Salem Shore*, about the New England coast; and in *Appalachian Spring*.

In addition to the Forty-eighth Street Theater, Graham danced at the Fifty-fourth Street Theater, 152 West Fifty-fourth Street, at City

Center, and on Broadway. Today, her works are presented mostly in Broadway theaters for limited engagements, and many of them are commissioned by Aaron Copland, Dello Joio, and William Schuman.

Agnes De Mille

Agnes De Mille was the first artist to utilize dance to illustrate character development, plot, and atmosphere, as in *Oklahoma*, the 1943 Broadway musical. De Mille further embellished cowboy steps and tap dancing in her choreography for *Rodeo*. Her style is highly personal and eclectic. Other well-known works of hers are *Tally-Ho*, to the music of Gluck, and *Fall River Legend*, to the music of Gould. De Mille has danced and choreographed for ballet for more than five decades.

Ruth St. Denis and Ted Shawn

This husband and wife dancing team brought Eastern dance to America and taught such students as Martha Graham in their Denis-Shawn classes. Their style consisted of simple, emotive, unencumbered body movements using the floor as an integral foundation for expression. They introduced mobile scenery on stage and employed multi-ethnic members in their dance groups. Speech was occasionally incorporated into dance and wearing leotards as costumes was their idea. Jacob's Pillow, in the Berkshire Mountains in Becket, Massachusetts, is the famous home of the Ted Shawn Summer Theater for International Dance.

It is no longer simple to differentiate between ballet and modern dance. The styles have overlapped, merged, and interacted. Folk steps, country dance, tap, cowboy struts, jazz steps, and even rock and roll mix with ballet. Dance frequently contains acting, contemporary themes, and sometimes speech.

Dance in Education

The summer Bennington School of the Dance in Bennington, Vermont and the Bennington Festivals were founded by Martha Hill in 1934. She extended the Bennington idea to Connecticut College in 1948 with New York University's co-sponsorship and also created the American Dance Festival, now at Duke University in Durham, North Carolina. To her credit, too, is the first dance department created at the Juilliard School in New York in 1951. Hill stressed not only professional training, but the importance of creating new works while in training and teaching. Many of the major liberal arts colleges and universities throughout the Northeast have dance departments that give performances all year round.

Smaller Dance Companies

The Elgin, a movie house on Eighth Avenue and Nineteenth

Street in New York's Chelsea district, was remodeled into New York's first theater designed for small dance groups. Renamed the Joyce Theater, it has 475 seats and serves as home to the Eliot Feld Ballet, which recently premiered *Over the Pavement*, set to music by Charles Ives.

Merce Cunningham founded his fourteen-member company in 1953. A formalist in dance, he stresses interaction of movement with time and space and no story. Sound that has no necessary relationship to the dance is sometimes added for effect. His *Winterbranch* and *Torse* were heralded as "avant-garde" when first performed.

Other small dance companies are the Paul Taylor group, the Eglevsky Ballet, the Pilobolus Dance Company, and the José Limon Dance Company.

There are many places for operatic, symphonic, and dance performances in the northeastern states, some of which are listed below. They are incomplete, though, without the prime ingredient for significance and success—you, the audience.

CONNECTICUT

Bridgeport
Summer concerts, which include symphonic music, at the Barnum Festival, 820 Main Street.

East Haddam
The Simbury Light Opera Company performs the works of Gilbert and Sullivan at the Goodspeed Opera House, at the Plaza.

Falls Village
Chamber music ensembles, such as the Manhattan String Quartet, give concerts throughout the summer atop Music Mountain, in the foothills of the Berkshire. Travel two-and-a-half miles east on CT-126, then to the top of Music Mountain Road.

Hartford
Many music events take place in Bushnell Memorial Hall on the east flank of the capitol building. Some of the groups which perform in the hall are the Hartford Symphony Orchestra (with soloists such as pianist Emanuel Ax and cellist Lynn Harrell), the Bushnell Symphony, the Connecticut Opera Association, and the Albano Ballet.
The Hartford Symphony Band gives concerts in Elizabeth Park in the summer.
The Festival of Greater Hartford takes place in Constitution Plaza, on Main Street, during the summer.

New Canaan
The Silvermine Chamber Music Series takes place in Gifford Auditorium in the Silvermine Guild Center of the Arts, during July and August.

New Haven
The New Haven Symphony Orchestra performs at Woolsey Hall, on College and Grove Streets, from October through April.
The Starlight Festival of Chamber Music takes place in the Yale Law School Courtyard, Wall near York Street, in June.
Yale University Art Gallery, in the heart of New Haven at 15 Hillside Avenue, has an excellent collection of musical instruments. There are instruments from early times to the present in the collection. There are permanent as well as changing displays at the gallery.
The Connecticut Ballet and the Hartford Ballet both perform in New Haven.
New Milford
Concerts by resident artists take place at the Charles Ives Center for American Music.
Norfolk
Yale Chamber Music Concerts take place in the Music Shed on the Stoeckel Estate at US-44 and CT-22. Some of the historic greats have performed at these concerts in the past (pianist Josef Hofmann, violinist Fritz Kreisler, and composer Sergei Rachmaninoff, who played his own works on the piano).
Norwalk
Chamber Music Summer Festival, at 1037 Silvermine Road.
Stamford
The Stamford Symphony Orchestra performs at Westhill Auditorium at Long Ridge and Roxbury Roads. A recent program featured Beethoven's Sixth and Eighth Symphonies and Mendelssohn's Violin Concerto in E Minor, with violin soloist Glenn Dicterow.
Stratford
Not only Shakespeare, but ballet, symphonic music, opera, and pops are billed at the American Shakespeare Theatre/Connecticut Center for the Performing Arts, at 1850 Elm Street.
Torrington
Concerts are given during the Torrington Arts Festival in August.

DISTRICT OF COLUMBIA
The John F. Kennedy Center for the Performing Arts, on New Hampshire Avenue and F Street NW, is the leading place for symphonic music, opera, and ballet. The center has several halls: Concert Hall, Opera House, Eisenhower Theater, Terrace Theater, and American Film Institute Theater. The National Symphony Orchestra, under the musical directorship of Mstislav Rostropovich since 1977, performs in Concert Hall with such soloists as pianist Vladimir Ashkenazy and flutist Julius Baker. The Opera House has welcomed soprano Leontyne Price, the Washington Ballet, and the Joffrey Ballet. The Terrace Theater has fea-

tured the Houston Symphony, pianist Alicia de Larrocha, and dance groups such as the Royal Danish Ballet and Grand Kabuki.

The Library of Congress, at First Street and Independence Avenue SE, offers concerts. The Audubon Quartet has appeared here and the Juilliard String Quartet has a regular season here from October through April. The instruments used for concerts are taken from regular displays in the library. In addition, the Library has exhibits and a wealth of musical data.

"Pops" concerts take place at the Carter Barron Amphitheater, in Rock Creek Park, at Sixteenth Street NW and Colorado Avenue.

The National Gallery of Art, at Constitution Avenue and Sixth Street NW, presents free concerts in the East Garden Court. Chamber music, choral works, and recitals are given by the National Gallery Orchestra and guest artists. American music is emphasized, especially the music of Hanson, Barber, Copland, and George Crumb, at their American Music Festival in April and May.

The Phillips Collection, a gallery at Twenty-first Street NW, offers free concerts and recitals in its living room.

The Smithsonian Institute, on Jefferson Drive between Ninth and Twelfth Streets, boasts many musical programs in the Museum of Natural History's Auditorium.

The Marvin Theater of George Washington University has frequent dance programs.

MAINE

Bangor
The Bangor Symphony performs in Peakes Auditorium, 885 Broadway, during its regular season, October through May.

Bar Harbor
A music festival takes place at the College of Atlantic Auditorium. Musical fare consists of traditional and light classics.

Acadia National Park offers concerts by the Acadia String Quartet.

Blue Hill
There is a chamber music school at Kneisel Hall, on the slope of the Blue Hill Mountains. Violinists Joseph Fuchs and Fritz Kreisler taught there in past years. The cellist Leslie Parnas is currently the school's music director.

Bowdoin
Henry Wadsworth Longfellow's alma mater, Bowdoin College, on Maine, Bath, and College Streets, has an active music department that organizes chamber music concerts in summer.

Brunswick
The Bowdoin College Summer Music School holds a Summer Festival in Kresge Auditorium. The Aeolian Chamber Players, the resident ensemble, plays traditional and modern music.

Castine

The Downeast Chamber Music Center, at the Maine Maritime Academy, is an extension of the Manhattan School of Music's preparatory division.

Hancock

This is the home of the Pierre Monteux Domaine School for Conductors and Orchestra Players, on sixty-eight acres of farmland along Route 1. Chamber music from classical to modern is studied and played. In the summer the Monteux Memorial Festival takes place in the 350-seat Hancock Corner Hall.

Ogonquit

This area is an art colony, with summer concerts held in the Barn Gallery, about half a mile south on Shore Road at Bourne's Lane.

Portland

The City Hall Auditorium at Portland City Hall, 389 Congress Street, houses the Portland Symphony Orchestra. The auditorium has three-thousand seats. Here too is the Kotschmar Memorial Organ, one of the largest in the world, used for concerts with its 6,500 pipes.

The Cumberland County Civic Center, One Civic Square, hosts professional artists in concerts.

Rockport

The Rockport Opera House features the Bay Chamber Concerts in the summer. In past years instructors such as Gian-Carlo Menotti, Gregor Piatigorsky, and Bidu Sayao, with the Philadelphia Curtis Institute of Music, taught summer sessions here.

Waterville

Colby College boasts a Wolcker organ in Lorimer Chapel designed by Albert Schweitzer.

The Bixler Art and Music Center, on Mayflower Hill, presents works of European and American composers.

Wiscosset

Musical Wonder House, at 18 High Street, is a private museum. In it one can see and hear antique music boxes and other restored musical mechanical instruments.

MARYLAND

Annapolis

Many fine performances are offered at the Annapolis Opera, Inc., on Constitution Avenue.

Baltimore

The Peabody Conservatory is a famous music school having such people as conductor and pianist Leon Fleischer on staff.

The Lyric Theater, 128 West Mt. Royal Avenue, is Baltimore's oldest music hall, and former home of the Baltimore Symphony. It was replaced in 1982 by a new music hall, the Maryland Concert Center, 1212 Cathedral Street. The Lyric will continue to house the Baltimore Civic Opera Company and guest performances by groups such as the Philadelphia Orchestra and the Ballet Russe de Monte Carlo. Saturday night "pop" concerts are given here too.

In the summer the Baltimore Symphony performs at Symphony Woods, at Merriweather Post Pavilion, off US-29.

Pier 6/Inner Harbor, with nautical setting, at 110 West Baltimore Street, presents a Harborlights Music Festival in the summer.

Bowie

The Performing Arts Center in Whitemarsh Park is the site for numerous musical events.

College Park

Tawes Recital Hall and Theater at the University of Maryland features the Maryland Dance Theater Group among others.

Cumberland

Constitution Park at City Hall has a summer concert series.

Frederick

Hood College hosts a series of Bach concerts during the academic year. The Weinberg Center for the Arts, 20 West Patrick Street, is Frederick's popular musical building.

Glen Echo

Glen Echo Park on MacArthur Boulevard has an open-air pavilion and large ballroom for dance concerts throughout the summer. Some groups who have appeared here are the Washington, D.C., Ballet and the Hoffman Touring Ensemble.

MASSACHUSETTS

Boston

Symphony Hall on Massachusetts and Huntington Avenues, home of the Boston Symphony Orchestra, is Boston's leading cultural institution. "Pop" concerts can be heard here in May and June.

Hatch Shell, along the Charles River, houses Esplanade Concerts in July. The concerts are free for twenty-thousand listeners.

Many other places also have music programs. Some of them are: John Hancock Hall, New England Mutual Hall, Boston University Concert Hall, Jordan Hall, the Museum of Fine Arts (465 Huntington Avenue), Gardner Museum (280 the Fenway), Bush-Reisinger Museum (on Kirkland Avenue), Hines Memorial Auditorium (at Prudential Center), and Harvard's Sanders Theater (on Quincy Street).

"Summerthing" is a gala affair that carries concerts to the entire city.

The Boston Opera Company is headquartered at 539 Washington Street in the Opera House. Past performances were *Aida*, *La Boheme*, and *Die Soldaten*, conducted by Sarah Caldwell.

65

The Boston Lyric Opera in 1982 performed Wagner's "Ring" Cycle on four successive Sundays during the summer in the twelve-hundred-seat Alumni Auditorium of Northeastern University.

The oldest U.S. choral group is the Handel and Haydn Society, still standing at 158 Newbury Street. The New England Conservatory of Music is on Huntington Avenue. One may look around here.

Falmouth

The College Light Opera Company performs at Highfield, off Depot Avenue on MA-28.

Gloucester

The Hammond Museum, 80 Hesperus Avenue, houses an interesting pipe organ that contains eight-thousand pipes. Concerts are also given here all year round.

Ipswich

Castle Hill, a large Georgian mansion overlooking Massachusetts Bay, is the home of the Castle Hill Festival, which takes place in July and August. Opera, chamber music, and dance are performed in the barn and casino. Baroque and Renaissance music are the specialties and the music of these eras is played as authentically as is possible: trumpets have no valves; stringed instruments are played on gut rather than wire; a harpsichord, lyre, and zither are used, and sometimes there is no conductor.

Becket

World-famous for Jacob's Pillow Dance Festivals, the Ted Shawn Theater welcomes visiting dancers and international companies performing ballet and modern dance. Maria Tallchief and Martha Graham danced here as did the Paul Taylor Dance Company and Les Grands Ballets Canadiens.

Lenox

This is the site of the Berkshire Music Center in the Berkshire Mountains, and Tanglewood is the main attraction on 250 beautiful acres. The Music Shed, which has five-thousand seats, is used for symphony concerts and choral works. The lawn outside the shed provides enormous space for many more listeners. You'll hear ensembles, and if you're interested, lectures and seminars are given too in inside rooms. One may observe classes and rehearsals at Chamber Music Hall. Leonard Bernstein, Erich Leinsdorf, and Seiji Ozawa are some of the many conductors who have performed at Tanglewood since Koussevitsky. Some of the guest artists who have played here have been pianist Alfred Brendl, and singer Maureen Forrester. The repertory covers a very wide range, from Vivaldi to George Crumb.

Lowell

The University of Lowell, at One University Avenue, organizes ensembles during the academic year in Durgin Hall Performing Arts Center.

New Marlborough
Red Fox Music Camp at new Marlborough Music Center is situated in a renovated barn on seventy-five acres of farmland in the southern Berkshires. Each summer, students perform chamber music and orchestral works from Baroque to contemporary repertory.

Pittsfield
South Mountain Concerts are given each summer in an historic landmark building located on South Street off US-7 and US-20. Opera and chamber music have been performed here by such artists as pianists Dame Myra Hess and Ruth Laredo, the Guarneri String Quartet, and the Empire Brass Quintet.

Rockport
The Cape Ann Symphony and the Chamber Music Society of Cape Ann both perform here.

Springfield
Renovated Symphony Hall, on the northwest side of Court Square, features concerts and dance. The thirty-mile view of the Connecticut River Valley and the three-hundred foot bell tower add to the attractions.

Worcester
Worcester has the oldest October Music Festival in the country—126 years old.

Symphonic works, choral works, and "pops" are performed at Memorial Auditorium. Recently, the Buffalo Philharmonic and Baltimore Symphony excited audiences here as Jenny Lind and Nellie Melba must have done more than a century ago.

The Wart Museum, 55 Salisbury Street, offers concerts.

NEW HAMPSHIRE

Center Harbor
The New Hampshire Summer Music Festival takes over in several locations with music by different groups and ensembles: Silver Hall, Plymouth; the Academy at Moultonboro; Gilford Middle School; and the Lakes Region area.

Jaffrey
Monadnock region is saturated with music in summer played in about fifteen churches.

Hanover
Hopkins Center for the Arts, at Dartmouth College, Main and Wheelock Streets, offers concerts in Spaulding Auditorium by resident and visiting artists.

Manchester
The New Hampshire Performing Arts Center, 80 Hanover Street, houses the New Hampshire Symphony in the Palace Theater.

Milford
The American Stage Festival, just off NH-101, takes place from June through August. Concerts and theater are plentiful here.
Peterborough
The American composer, Edward MacDowell (1861–1908), lived here. He composed music for piano ("Norse" and "Keltic") and for orchestra ("Indian Suite"). His widow founded the MacDowell colony for artists, writers, and composers on High Street.

NEW JERSEY
Hackensack
Orrie de Nooyer Auditorium offers opera by Opera Classics and guests.
Holmdel
The Garden State Arts Center, a nine-thousand-seat amphitheater in Telegraph Hill Park, features concerts of classical and "pops" music as well as the New Jersey Ballet, from June through September.
Montclair
The Whole Theater Company, 544 Bloomfield Avenue, is a resident professional company that performs modern dance and opera.
Newark
Symphony Hall, 1020 Broad Street, houses the New Jersey State Opera, the Garden State Ballet, and the New Jersey Symphony Orchestra.
Ocean City
At Music Pier, there are concerts all summer long.
Princeton
The McCarter Theater, at Princeton's University, offers ballet and symphonic music from the fall through spring.
Stanhope
Waterloo Village, which was known originally as Andover Forge (during the Revolutionary War), is noted today for the Waterloo Summer Music Festival. Under a large circus tent, a great variety of music is performed, including symphonic music and chamber music. Pablo Casals played cello and conducted here in 1970 at the age of ninety-three. Other artists who have performed here are Byron Janis, Eugene Istomin, and Phillipe Entremont all pianists. Gerard Schwarz is currently the music director.
Trenton
The New Jersey State Capitol Cultural Complex, at 205 West State Street, presents concerts frequently.

NEW YORK
Binghamton
Roberson Center for the Arts and Sciences, 30 Front Street, presents regular symphonic concerts during the year and a Summer Arts Festival in July.

Buffalo

A concert series, including open rehearsals, are provided by the Buffalo Philharmonic in Kleinhans Music Hall, 370 Pennsylvania Street.

Chautauqua

Chautauqua Amphitheater, on the western shore of Chautauqua Lake, is headquarters for the Chautauqua Symphony Orchestra. Ballet, recitals and other music events also take place here.

Norton Memorial Hall houses operatic performances, many performed in English. Notable artists who have performed here are Arthur Fiedler and the Boston Pops, soprano Marilyn Horne, violinist Ruggiero Ricci, and the Eglevsky Ballet.

Glens Falls

The Lake George Opera Festival, in the Opera Festival Auditorium, exit 19, off I-87, features artists from leading American and European opera companies singing operas in English from both traditional and modern repertory.

Katonah

The Caramoor Festival takes place on the Caramoor Estate in northern Westchester, off NY-137. The Festival is devoted to chamber music and choral works. Recently, the Caramoor Festival Orchestra under Julius Rudel performed Brahms' Hungarian Dance in G Minor. Other artists who have performed here are soprano Beverly Sills, the Tokyo String Quartet, pianist Rudolf Firkusny, and soprano Elly Ameling. The estate includes a Venetian theater and an open-air Spanish courtyard.

Mamaroneck

Concerts, recitals, and other musical events take place throughout the year at the Emelin Theater for the Performing Arts, on Library Lane. The quality is high.

New York City

New York City abounds in musical entertainment, so selectivity is essential.

Lincoln Center for the Performing Arts on Broadway between Sixty-second and Sixty-sixth Streets consists of Avery Fisher Hall, Alice Tully Hall, the Metropolitan Opera House, the New York State Theater, and originally the Vivian Beaumont Theater. A great variety of music is performed in these buildings, which host the New York Philharmonic, the Metropolitan Opera, the New York City Ballet, New York City Opera, and the Chamber Music Society of Lincoln Center. And the Juilliard School of Music is right next door.

Carnegie Hall, at Fifty-seventh Street and Seventh Avenue, is no longer the home of the New York Philharmonic, but remains a revered favorite with artists and public alike. Carnegie Recital Hall is right across the street.

Interior of Carnegie Hall, New York (Courtesy Carnegie Hall)

The following is a listing of some of the other places in New York City where one can attend concerts:

The Manhattan School of Music, at 120 Claremont Avenue.

The Manhattan School of Dance, at 78 Fifth Avenue.

Abraham Goodman Concert Hall, just around the corner from Lincoln Center at 129 West Sixty-seventh Street, offers regular symphonic presentations.

Town Hall, 123 West Forty-third Street, does not have as busy a schedule of concerts as it had in past years, but it occasionally bills a top artist.

The Ninety-second Street "Y," on Lexington Avenue, offers a great variety of music. The Bach Aria Group is one of the many ensembles which perform here.

City Center, 131 West Fifty-fifth Street, features a number of dance companies, such as the Martha Graham Dance Company, the Alvin Ailey, and the Joffrey Ballet (soon to be moved to Los Angeles). Downstairs at City Center, in an area called Space, other dance companies perform, such as Paul Sanasardo and Dance Company and the Joyce Trisler Danscompany.

The Metropolitan Museum of Art, Fifth Avenue at Eighty-second Street, in addition to offering the Waverly Consort playing Vivaldi and Scarlatti, and the Grace Rainey Rogers Auditorium hosting numerous concert series and lectures, displays a most impressive collection of four-thousand musical instruments representing all time periods from all parts of the world. There are three Stradivarius violins made by the Italian Cremona lutemaker (there is today a string quartet called Cremona). There is also, a remarkable group of keyboard instruments, some decorated with paintings and sculpture, such as the first pianoforte built in France in 1720 by Cristofori, and the Spinettina made in Venice in 1540 for the Duchess of Urbino. There are lutes, zithers, and guitars from seventeenth-century Europe, and Far Eastern and African instruments, which are played in Museum concerts (similar to the concerts in the Library of Congress).

The Whitney Museum, on Madison Avenue at Seventy-fifth Street, presents concerts featuring American music. *Atlas* and *Eclipticalis* by John Cage could be heard there a short time ago.

Symphony Space, at Broadway and Ninety-fifth Street, offers dance as well as music concerts. Two groups that have appeared here are the Fantastic Symphony Steel Orchestra, doing Handel, Chopin, and Strauss; and Dancemobile with Rod Rogers Dance Company.

Madison Square Garden, at Thirty-third Street and Seventh Avenue, occasionally holds a symphonic event for thousands of people.

New York University's Main Building in Washington Square holds a large collection of rare antique musical instruments dating from Middle Ages and Renaissance periods. The University has its own dance company, the Second Avenue Dance Company, which performs at the NYU Theater Department, on Second Avenue between Sixth and Seventh Streets.

The Joyce Theater, on Eighth Avenue and Nineteenth Street, now houses the Eliot Feld Ballet which premiered *Over the Pavement* with music by Ives.

The Dance Theater of Harlem performs at its own theater at 466 West 152nd Street.

The Schomburg Center for Research, 515 Lenox Avenue at 135th Street, contains interesting exhibits pertaining to such personalities as Alvin Ailey, Katherine Dunham, and Pearl Primus.

Somewhat unexpectedly, the Abyssinian Baptist Church, a 175-year-old building, has occasionally welcomed the New York Philharmonic, under Zubin Mehta's baton, with pianist André Watts, and soprano Kathleen Battle. A makeshift stage was built over the church's altar to accommodate the performances.

Concerts and operas are presented in parks throughout the city and in

Nassau County during the summer. Free concerts are available in Damrosch Park at Lincoln Center; the Great Lawn in Central Park (one-half mile long with room for one-hundred-fifty-thousand);Van Cortlandt Park in the Bronx; Marine Park in Brooklyn; Cunningham Park in Queens (successor site in 1965 to Lewisohn Stadium); Clove Lake Park in Staten Island; and Eisenhower Park in Nassau County. Some of the conductors who have performed in the parks are Leonard Bernstein, Pierre Boulez, Lorin Maazel, and André Kostelanetz.

The Brooklyn Academy of Music (known as BAM), at 30 Lafayette Avenue, is Brooklyn's outstanding musical building. Its resident Orchestra is the Brooklyn Philharmonic Symphony. Other notable groups that have performed here are the Pennsylvania Ballet, the Dutch National Ballet, and the Beaux Arts Trio.

Brooklyn College has welcomed the Joffrey Ballet dancing the premiere of *Madrigal*.

The Fulton Ferry landing offers chamber music concerts on a barge all summer long.

Long Island has a number of theaters and concert halls, some of which are:

Coe Hall, in Oyster Bay, is popular for concerts.

C. W. Post College, in Greenvale, presents opera and chamber music.

The John Drew Theater, in East Hampton, presents opera and chamber music. Guild Hall, 158 Main Street in East Hampton, offers dance concerts.

South Hampton College presents summer concerts.

The Parish Art Museum, 25 Jobs Lane in South Hampton, offers summer concerts.

The Adams Playhouse, in Hempstead offers ballet.

Purchase

The Performing Arts Center at SUNY Purchase, on Anderson Hill Road, presents a number of concerts featuring music (including choral works) and dance all year round.

Rochester

Eastman Theater, on Main and Gibbs Streets, is the home of the Rochester Philharmonic Orchestra. The Theater also presents recitals, and opera.

The Dome Arena, at Monroe County Fairgrounds, has symphonic and dance programs.

The famous Eastman School of Music, at 26 Gibbs Street, is open to visitors. In the school is the Howard Hanson Recital Hall. Part of the Eastman School is the Sibley Music Library, at 44 Swan Street, which covers an outstanding collection of musical literature, rare scores, and original manuscripts.

Saratoga Springs
The Saratoga Performing Arts Center, nestled in the Adirondack foot-hills (the address is South Broadway), is a huge amphitheater amidst a natural setting. There are 5,100 seats under cover and space for thou-sands more on the lawn. The New York City Ballet usually performs here in July and the Philadelphia Orchestra is here in August.

Syracuse
Civic Center of Onondaga County, at 411 Montgomery Street, presents opera, concerts, and dance programs.

The city parks have summer concerts.

Tarrytown
The Lyndhurst Summer of Music-on-Hudson Festival, at 655 South Broadway, has a tent and lawn to accommodate listeners. Tchaikovsky's *1812 Overture* is performed with real cannons on the shores of the Hudson River.

Woodstock
Woodstock Playhouse, at Junction NY-212 and 375, is a location for dance festivals.

Maverick Concerts are presented on Maverick Road, with performers such as violist Jaime Laredo, and pianist Grant Johannesen.

PENNSYLVANIA

Bethlehem
Lehigh University is famous for its Bach Festival held in Packer Memo-rial Chapel each May (See Section I. Chapter 3).

Lancaster
The Fulton Opera House, 12 North Prince Street, originally built on the foundation of an old jail, has served many purposes: a convention site, a hospital, an armory during the Civil War, and a theater for entertain-ment.

Philadelphia
The Academy of Music, on Broad and Locust Streets, is the home of the Philadelphia Orchestra. The Academy also hosts the Opera Company of Philadelphia, where Luciano Pavarotti joins the winners of a voice com-petition in an opera production. The Lyric Opera and several ballet com-panists can be seen here as well.

Mann Music Center, formerly Robin Hood Dell, is the lovely outdoor site in West Fairmont Park for summer orchestra events. It's a large outdoor amphitheater. Light classics have been on the program in the past with conductors James Levine and Mstislav Rostropovich.

The Shubert Theater, 250 South Broad Street, houses the Philadelphia Ballet. The Walnut Street Theater, 825 Walnut Street, houses the Phila-delphia Dance Company. The Trocadero, 1003 Arch Street, is an inter-esting building. Originally an opera house, it then became a burlesque house; now it's an opera house again as well as a Chinese movie theater. The Pennsylvania Opera Theater performs here.

The Curtis Institute of Music, 1726 Locust Street, was mentioned previously.

The Temple University Music Festival, at Broad Street and Montgomery Avenue, offers with it classical and popular music and ballet. The Pittsburgh Symphony also performs here in the summer.

The City of Brotherly Love marked its three-hundredth birthday in 1982 with the Philadelphia American Music Festival, a colossal musical celebration which took place at many sites, including the Academy of Music, Mann Music Center, JFK Plaza, Gallery, and Independence Mall, and offered all varieties of music. It was so successful that it may be repeated annually.

Pittsburgh

Heinz Hall for the Performing Arts, 600 Penn Avenue, houses the Pittsburgh Symphony Orchestra and also presents opera and ballet. This is *the* place.

The Pittsburgh Chamber Music Society, Fifth and Balfield, attracts groups such as the Budapest String Quartet and the Juilliard String Quartet.

Three Rivers Stadium, 600 Stadium Circle, offers music and dance programs in the summer.

RHODE ISLAND

Kingston

The University of Rhode Island at Kingston presents dance events during the year.

Newport

Concerts of nineteenth-century instrumental music, vocal works, and ballet, are given in mansions along Bellevue Avenue in July. Violinist Erich Friedman and soloists from the Royal Danish Ballet have attracted numerous people.

Trinity Church offers frequent concerts. The Newport Cultural Foundation sponsors symphonic music.

Providence

Music Mansion, 88 Meeting Street, provides free concerts.

The Rhode Island Philharmonic performs at Westminister Mall.

The Barrington College School of Music, Middle Highway, is active in music performance.

The Peloquin Chorale performs at the Cathedral of Saints Peter and Paul in downtown Providence.

Rhode Island College Orchestra and Chorus and the Civic Chorale and Orchestra perform at 600 Mt. Pleasant Avenue.

VERMONT

Bennington

Bennington School of the Dance is considered a center of modern dance. Dance Festivals at the school, begun by Martha Hill over fifty years ago, are very popular. In addition, there's a Choral Society and an orchestra at the College.

Brattleboro

Famous for its Music Center in West Brattleboro, the West Village Meeting House, on South Street, offers many events, including a Bach Festival in the fall and a choral group, the Liederkreis Ensemble.

The Brattleboro Museum, on Vernon Street, displays a permanent collection of Estey organs.

Burlington

The University of Vermont Concert Series.

The Vermont Mozart Festival, patterned after "Mostly Mozart" in New York, takes place in August with dozens of concerts given at many sites, such as the University of Vermont Show Barn, on Spear Street, an arched arena with seating capacity of twelve-hundred; Lake Champlain ferryboats, boarding at the King Street Dock in Burlington; the Cathedral Church of St. Paul, a handsome, modern building at Battery and Pearl Streets; the Fletcher Library on College Street in the Carnegie Building with a new modern wing; the Atrium, Burlington Square Mall with high ceilings and good acoustics; Shelburne House, a Tudor-style mansion, in Shelborne Farms; in the Basin Harbor Club; and Bundy Museum in Waitsfield.

Manchester

South Vermont Music Pavilion features the Vermont Symphony Orchestra's "pops" concerts in the summer.

Marlboro

Marlboro College Campus is the location of the renowned Marlboro Music Festival. Set in the lush foothills of the Green Mountains in southern Vermont, eight miles west of Brattleboro on VT-9, chamber music concerts are performed each summer. The Marlboro Music school is directed by pianist Rudolph Serkin.

Middlebury

Sheldon Museum, One Park Street, displays old pianos in addition to presenting concerts in Mead Chapel.

And so we come to the end of our journey searching for symphonic music, opera, and dance. Obviously, there are too, too many to list all in these pages, but you can get some idea of what's available where, and explore further on your own while traveling.

JAZZ AND SWING

Jazz

New York City, always a center of musical activity, fostered jazz in the 1920s in an environment tinged with vice and crime, a pattern familiar to other parts of the nation as well. Jazz musicians moved up North from the South and Midwest in search of jobs that were dwindling with the oncoming depression. Musicians were willing to work for meager wages, and jazz enjoyed a northern heyday in the mid-twenties. In the early thirties, jazz became part of swing and the big band era, which lasted until the end of World War II. The distinctive world of New York jazz welcomed jazz musicians from the deep South and the Midwest; their music would mix with the music of the northerners and cross-fertilize jazz. The mixture of big band jazz and swing resulted in more of a "soft jazz," with more educated players joining the fold.

On the black jazz scene, Harlem was to New York what Storyville and the South Side were to New Orleans and Chicago respectively. Harlem clubs were run by white entrepreneurs offering black entertainment to mostly white clientele. The area from 125th to 145th Streets, between Fifth and Eighth Avenues, was dotted with jazz sites, most of them no longer in existence. Had you looked for places to visit, you would have found: the Sugar Cane Club, Saratoga Club, Bamboo Inn, Bamville Club, Capitol Palace, Lenox Club, Nest's Club (a warehouse today), Cotton Club, Small's Paradise (later known as Big Wilt's, owned by Wilt Chamberlain), Connie's Inn (later known as Hilda's Admiral Cafe), Edmond's, Renaissance, Royal Cafe, Apollo Theater (under possible conversion to a cable TV studio), Alhambra Ballroom, and Savoy Ballroom. The Savoy, on 140th Street and Lenox Avenue, had a wide marble stairway that led to a large room for drinking and dancing. The room was decorated with circulating spotlights. An evening at any of these clubs would have been filled with laughter, noise, smoke, boisterous activity, and bootleg liquor, a reminder that control was, in large part, in the hands of gangsters. Décor ranged from a makeshift assortment of chairs to fine table linen. Most important, you would have enjoyed the best black musical talent to be found.

The Cotton Club

The center of Harlem entertainment and its most famous jazz symbol in the twenties was the Cotton Club, located between Lenox and Fifth Avenues. Called the "Aristocrat of Harlem," the nightspot was frequented predominantly by whites seeking Broadway entertainment uptown. Among the club's notable visitors were Mayor Jimmie Walker, Walter Winchell, and Ed Sullivan. The Club was posh and expensive, glowing with purple lamps, arranged with horseshoe seating of seven hundred on two levels and in booths along the walls. A burly bouncer at the front door made certain that the audience was well-mannered, and those few blacks admitted as guests were carefully screened. Chorus girls chosen were lightskinned, glamorous, and sexy. And among the jazz musicians who established their own reputations and propelled the Cotton Club to fame was Duke Ellington, who performed at the Club in the late twenties.

Edward Kennedy "Duke" Ellington, born in 1899, in Washington, D.C., had a twelve-piece band called the Washingtonians. The band played music that was composed and arranged by its leader/pianist. The band was engaged at Gibson's Standard Theater on South Street, in Philadelphia, and at the Kentucky Club, a basement cafe on Forty-ninth Street and Broadway, when they were booked into the Cotton Club. Some of the musicians in the band, in addition to Ellington on piano, were Rudy Jackson on tenor saxophone, Louis Metcalf on trumpet, James (Bubber) Miley on trumpet, Wellman Braud, on bass, Otto Hardwick, on alto sax, and Sonny Greer, on drums. The group produced an earthy, rhythmic, almost primitive African sound, so much so that they changed their name to Duke Ellington's Jungle Band. Some of their early hit tunes were "Jungle Jamboree," "Jungle Blues," and "Jungle Nights in Harlem." Characteristic of much black music was vocalization of the instrumental tone, as heard in "Harlem River Quiver."

The Duke composed profusely, continually changing and experimenting, and his arrangements became more and more sophisticated and complex. Among his masterpieces are "Ko-Ko," "Black, Brown, and Beige," "Mood Indigo," "Take the 'A' Train," and "Double Check Stomp." At the Cotton Club lavish revues with singing, dancing, and colorful costumes, accompanied his music, adding drama and the flair of the theater. *Sophisticated Ladies*, made into a Broadway musical in 1981, is representative of this era. Ellington left the Cotton Club in 1930, followed by others who rose to fame during the Club's heyday.

Cab Calloway succeeded the Duke and popularized the songs "Between the Devil and the Deep Blue Sea" and "Minnie the Moocher." During one performance Calloway forgot the words to "Minnie" and substituted the syllables "Heigh-de-ho." The syllables fit so well that he adopted them as his theme song and became known as the "Heigh-de-ho" man.

Ethel Waters appeared in *Cotton Club's Revue in Harlem* in the early thirties and turned out the hit song "Stormy Weather." Lena

Horne, Josephine Baker, tap dancer Bill Robinson, and Jimmie Lunceford's Orchestra, with Sy Oliver on trumpet, followed as major attractions. Songwriter Harold Arlen composed "I've Got the World on a String" and "New Kind of Rhythm" in the early years of the depression. With the deepening depression, violence and unrest in Harlem became widespread. "Brother Can You Spare a Dime" became popular for its symbolic meaning, and the glamorous Cotton Club opened a free kitchen for handouts. The Club closed its doors in 1936 and moved downtown for a brief time to Broadway.

The Broadway Cotton Club

The Cotton Club and its performers moved downtown to the theater district on Forty-eighth Street and Broadway, still catering primarily to white clientele. It occupied the former Palais Royal with its elaborate jungle decor, its theater boxes, and its fancy terraces.

Bill Robinson opened the festivities at the new location, singing "Bojangles" while dancing up and down the steps of the stage. The audience loved it and the routine became his trademark. Following his act, Ethel Waters sang "Happiness is Just a Thing Called Joe." One of the Club's numerous lavish revues took place in 1936 and featured Robinson, Cab Calloway and the Tramp Band, Katherine Perry, and the Cotton Club Girls who introduced the Suzie-Q, a dance that became a national craze.

Duke Ellington returned to present his famous composition, "It Don't Mean a Thing If You Ain't Got That Swing." His was the first song to use the term "swing" to mean jazz, with descriptive "do-wop" phrases. Jazz had begun to fuse with popular songs used for dancing, and a dancing beat became the mainstay of jazz swing bands. The Club played to over fifty-thousand dancing people, turning away overflow crowds regularly.

The Cotton Club closed for good in 1940, becoming the Latin Quarter in 1942 (also no longer in existence). On the site of the old Harlem Cotton Club today is a housing development. But nostalgia for the early New York jazz scene has been evident in recent Broadway shows: *Sophisticated Ladies*, *Bubbling Brown Sugar*, *Ain't Misbehavin'*, and *One Mo' Time*.

Pre-Swing

During the Cotton Club era, a lot of money was spent, and jazz expanded downtown into white territory along the West Fifty-second Street area. Some of the better-known places were: Texas Guinan's, Helen Morgan's Club, Club Richelieu, Silver Slipper, Peter's Blue Hour, The Onyx Club, Famous Door, 18 Club, and Roseland. The Onyx Club, a representative club of the prohibition era, was a second-floor speakeasy.

You had to enter through the basement of a rundown brownstone building and walk up a dark flight of rickety stairs. Roseland, on the other hand, was a public dance hall with mirrored walls, electric stars on its ceilings, and courteous hostesses taking charge of guests. A remnant of yesterday, but lacking much of the original, spontaneous charm associated with the big bands, Roseland Ballroom is still open to the public for dancing. Frequently, for a dollar a dance, one can dance with a professional host or hostess to the strains of popular music, jazz, rock, or Latin American rhythms. The exterior of Roseland is open in several places to permit outsiders to look in and decide whether or not they want to come in.

One of the top names in the pre-swing era was that of pianist/arranger, Fletcher Henderson, who was booked at Roseland for several years. As a college student, Henderson listened to popular music on player-piano rolls; and he listened to Louis Armstrong, Ma Rainey, and Bessie Smith sing the blues. He built an orchestra of highly skilled musicians, both ensemble players and soloists, among whom were Coleman Hawkins and Benny Carter on saxophone, and Joe Smith on trumpet. Bessie Smith sang with the orchestra first at Club Alabam (no longer in existence), and later at Roseland, as did Louis Armstrong. Some of the band's specialties were "King Porter Stomp," "Sugar Foot Stomp," and "Hot and Anxious." Very early arrangements were made in hot jazz style.

Henderson was an original arranger; his piano style soon incorporated boogie-woogie in the bass with numerous variations turned toward popular tunes. His arrangements were suited to jitterbugging on the dance floor. "Henderson Stomp" and "Rocky Mountain Blues" displayed these tonal varieties. "Hard-Hearted Hannah" featured an interesting clarinet trio. "Wrappin' it Up" introduced four choruses for twelve instruments, and a thirty-two-bar chorus which broke down into two sixteen-bar halves using solo brass instruments to answer each other playfully. Riffs or repetitive phrases such as "yeah," "oh," or "right" that were shouted, played, or murmured for effect at certain moments, moved against each other in antiphonal style. The swing break phrasing was made to glide gently rather than jolt abruptly. In the mid-thirties, the band's activity waned. The band left Roseland. Henderson joined Benny Goodman in 1939, for whom he arranged such tunes as "Sometimes I'm Happy" and "Blue Skies."

Another pre-swing figure was the flamboyant conductor, Paul Whiteman. New York at this time was noted as the place where bands were booked, songs were promoted, and orchestral jazz was set. A huge broadcasting industry was developing, with radio and recordings coming into prominence. And showman Paul Whiteman, known as the "King of Jazz," was instrumental in promoting many talented performers who rose to fame: Jimmy Dorsey on alto saxophone; Bunny Berrigan playing

"It's Only a Paper Moon"; Jack Teagarden with "Ain't Misbehavin' ";
and Joe Venuti, Mildred Bailey, Johnny Mercer, and Bing Crosby.

Whiteman, above all, was credited with elevating jazz by combining it with swing, and making it acceptable to the public. He brought
the concept even further along by introducing George Gershwin's
"Rhapsody in Blue," a blend of symphonic music and jazz. Aeolian Hall
(no longer in existence), the Palais Royal, and the Paramount Theater in
Times Square were places of note where the King of Jazz entertained.

The Casa Loma Orchestra, led by Glen Gray, made the historic
transition into the swing era in the mid-thirties by combining big band
jazz with slow, sentimental ballads. Gray and his orchestra succeeded in
reaching audiences emotionally from two different directions, achieving
overall a unifying and satisfying effect. Up-tempo brass mixed with glid-
ing guitar strings to create a mellow mood for dancing the fox-trot to
"Honeysuckle Rose," "It's the Talk of the Town," and "For You." Harmony, melody and rhythm were made appealing to the public in arrangements (some of which were done by Glenn Miller and Ray Conniff) sung
by Bob Crosby and featuring Bobby Hackett on trumpet.

The Casa Lomans appeared at Roseland, the Hotel New Yorker,
the Rainbow Room, the Paramount Theater, and the Glen Island Casino.
They performed in formal dress, a new touch. Glen Island Casino was a
huge rustic building on Long Island Sound at New Rochelle. The Ballroom, on the second floor, had a lovely romantic setting with moonlight
shining on the water. (It is still an active place for music and dancing
today.) The Paramount Theater, an informal, large movie palace, no
longer operative, hired numerous big-name bands, singers, and entertainers for entire stage shows. Frank Sinatra highlighted its marquee in the
forties, resulting in thousands of teen-agers standing in line to buy tickets at thirty-five cents each. Other headliners were Bing Crosby and
Mary Martin.

Gray's Band enjoyed a commercial radio series, "Camel Cara-
van," the first program to feature a swing band. Sweet sounds from the
Casa Lomans were heard until the group disbanded after World War II.

Swing

New York commercial swing had arrived with the distinctive
sounds of social dancing and theater. Such tunes as Charlie Barnet's
"Cherokee" and Bunny Berigan's "Marie" focused on increased band size
and individual musicianship, creating a stylized and personal touch. The
boogie-woogie piano style, cheerful, bouncy, with eight-to-the-bar left
hand rumbles, was imaginative as well. Proper professional dress added
a further touch of refinement to formerly crude jazz. Now, jazz gained

acceptance in academia and was studied seriously as a musical form.

By 1940, there were over two hundred dance orchestras. They performed in numerous places, among which were the Fifty-second Street Clubs (Ryan's, Famous Door, Hickory House, Kelly's Stables) These clubs were mostly bare, narrow, deep places converted from first floors of old brownstone houses. Some of the musicians who performed here were Fats Waller, Billie Holiday, and Count Basie. In the hotel ballrooms, the Pennsylvania hosted Benny Goodman, Vincent Lopez, and Glenn Miller; the New Yorker welcomed Tommy Dorsey, Charlie Spivak, and Woody Herman. The Edison, the Lincoln, the Commodore, the Lexington, and Roosevelt Hotels also featured top names in jazz and swing. Billy Rose's Music Hall was another busy place for swing.

Similar entertainment spots in the New Jersey area were: the Meadowbrook, in Cedar Grove, boasting a large dance floor and balcony, harboring strains of "Flat Foot Floogie" and "Music Goes Round and Round"; the Central Theater, Passaic; and the Adams Theater in Newark.

Connecticut had the Ritz Ballroom in Bridgeport; State Theater in Hartford; and the Roton Point Casino in South Norwalk, where swing fans, mostly in bobby socks and saddle shoes, listened rapturously as they did at the Capitol Theater in Washington, D.C. and in the Hippodrome in Baltimore.

Some of the Big Bands in the Swing Era: 1935–45

There were more than two hundred dance orchestras in existence during the swing era. Lack of space precludes mentioning more than three names representative of the swing era: Benny Goodman, Tommy Dorsey, and Glenn Miller.

Benny Goodman

The "King of Swing" clarinetist came to New York from Chicago in the early thirties after absorbing the jazz sounds of King Oliver, Louis Armstrong, Johnny Dodds, and Jimmie Noone. Goodman formed his own band and appeared on the radio show "Let's Dance" in 1934. He established a style that set standards for succeeding dance orchestras.

His most significant contribution was the swing solo for clarinet. Goodman stayed close to melodies of romantic popular songs— melodies the listener could recognize, hum, and reproduce easily. In addition, he built a powerful rhythm section for ensemble playing, with clean, crisp, well-articulated sounds. Quality was demanded and soloists were strong. Passing through his orchestra were Gene Krupa on drums; Lionel Hampton on xylophone; Fletcher Henderson on piano; Teddy Wilson on piano and Harry James on trumpet. Many of these musicians went on to form their own bands. Singers Martha Tilton and Helen Forrest sang some memorable songs ("After You've Gone," "Body and Soul," "Who," "You Turned the Tables on Me") at many of the aforementioned nightspots.

The King of Swing still appears occasionally with special one-nighters throughout the Northeast.

Tommy Dorsey

Tommy Dorsey, trombonist, was known as the "sentimental gentleman of swing," and his theme song, "I'm Getting Sentimental Over You," played against reeds and rhythm section, was his identifying sound in the thirties and forties. He was a master at creating moods, such as a warm and lilting mood in slow ballad style for dancing and listening. After working in Paul Whiteman's band in the twenties, then forming and leaving an orchestra with his brother, Jimmy, Tommy established his own orchestra and enlarged it to thirty-one players. He also added a full string section, including a harp. His objective was to build an orchestra proficient on different levels. Bud Freeman played tenor saxophone, Ziggy Elman and Peewee Erwin played trumpet, Buddy Rich played drums, and Buddy De Franco played clarinet. Singers of note were Frank Sinatra, Jo Stafford, and Dick Haymes. Dorsey's masterpieces were "Song of India," "On the Sunny Side of the Street," "You Must Have Been a Beautiful Baby," "I'll Never Smile Again," and "Boogie Woogie." Like Goodman, Dorsey played in many of the aforementioned nightspots.

Glenn Miller

Another top band that established the romantic mood of the day was that of Glenn Miller. Miller did arranging for several bands and was a trombonist in Ray Noble's band when he decided to form his own group in 1937. The Glenn Miller Band made the usual rounds plus the Raynor Ballroom in Boston.

Miller's technique of repeating riffs over and over under driving rhythm, with brass playing four beats to the bar, characterized his style on the radio program "Chesterfield Show," popular for many months. Some songs identified with the Glenn Miller Band were "Moonlight Serenade," "Serenade in Blue," "In the Mood," and "Little Brown Jug." Singers Ray Eberle, Marian Hutton, and Kay Starr, and trumpeters Ray Anthony and Billy May made names for themselves with the Miller Orchestra. Miller was a victim of World War II. He joined the Air Force to organize service bands throughout the country and died in an airplane crash over the English Channel in 1944.

Swing, for a time, was a way of life. Other bands in the swing era were those of Sammy Kaye, Les Brown, Stan Kenton, Guy Lombardo, and Artie Shaw. Big bands collapsed at the end of World War II, when the way of life changed radically.

Following the popularity of swing and dance music, the Broadway musical developed, and to this day represents one of New York's billion dollar industries.

The Broadway Musical

Broadway and the glittering "Great White Way" in New York City was established as the theater district for the entire nation, and indeed, occupies a unique position among cities of the world. Broadway sought the best talent and produced shows with lights, color, dazzle, and all the commercial effects available. A theater-goer could not help but be caught up in its fast-paced tempo and excitement.

A staggering number of theaters were built in the Times Square area during the first three decades of the twentieth century, reflecting the general prosperity in New York at that time. The district originally extended from Thirty-eighth to Fifty-ninth Streets and from Sixth to Eighth Avenues. Later the district narrowed to include the area between Forty-second and Fifty-second Streets, east and west of Times Square. A large, heterogeneous population and a strong financial community supported a concentrated, diversified center for theater.

A pioneer of Times Square at the turn of the century was Oscar Hammerstein, composer and theatrical entrepreneur. He built the Victoria Theater on the northwest corner of Forty-second Street and Seventh Avenue (now a movie theater), the Republic Theater at 207 West Forty-second Street (now a movie theater), and the Lew Fields Theater, 254 West Forty-second Street (also a movie theater). Between 1927 and 1928, one could count seventy-one theaters offering 257 productions. Ticket prices rose from $1.50 and $2.00 to $6.00.

The musical show opened with ensemble song and dance, then introduced characters and place. Songs had verse and chorus with chorus developing the main theme in the thirty-two-bar chorus or in four eight-bar sections. Lovely girls, pretty scenery, and artistic design set the tone for a happy experience.

The late twenties were peak years for the Broadway musical, with George and Ira Gershwin, Irving Berlin, Jerome Kern, and Oscar Hammerstein, among others, making musical history with such songs as "Make Believe," "Old Man River," "The Man I Love," and "Strike Up the Band." *Showboat* was a truly American musical show, depicting America's recent past from Natchez up and down the Mississippi River to Chicago and treating the subject of blacks and whites. Spirituals, ragtime, ballads, and minstrelsy captured life on the Mississippi on stage. Similarly with *Porgy and Bess.*

The noteworthy theaters held from twelve-hundred to twenty-five-hundred seats and boasted plush carpeting, crystal chandeliers, and loges and balconies. Below are listed some of these theaters that are still standing today. The productions for which they are remembered are also listed:

Forty-sixth Street Theater. 226 West Forty-sixth Street. Opened in 1924 with *Greenwich Village Follies*. *Hellzapoppin* (1938), *Finian's Rainbow* (1947), *Guys and Dolls* (1950).

Imperial Theater. 249 West Forty-fifth Street. Opened in 1923 with Mary Hay and Hal Skelly in *Mary Jane McKane*. *Rose Marie* (1924), *On Your Toes* (1936), *Annie, Get Your Gun* (1946), and *Fiddler on the Roof* (1964).

Majestic Theater. 245 West Forty-fourth Street. Opened with *Rufus LeMaire's Affairs*. *Carousel* (1945), *South Pacific* (1950), *Music Man* (1957).

St. James Theater. 246 West Forty-fourth Street. Opened in 1927 with *The Merry Malones*. *Oklahoma* (1943, ran for six years), *The King and I* (1951), and *Hello, Dolly* (1964).

And among the top musicals seen and remembered by millions are:

Oklahoma. Book and lyrics by Oscar Hammerstein, based on *Green Grow the Lilacs*, by Lynn Riggs. Music by Richard Rodgers. The title song became famous.

South Pacific. Mary Martin and Ezio Pinza. Book by Oscar Hammerstein and Josh Logan, based on *Tales of the South Pacific*, by James Michener. Music by Richard Rodgers, lyrics by Oscar Hammerstein. "Some Enchanted Evening" is one of the famous songs from this show.

Guys and Dolls. Robert Alda and Vivian Blaine. Book by Jo Swerling and Abe Burrows, based on story by Damon Runyon. Music and lyrics by Frank Loesser. "Luck Be a Lady " is a famous song from this show.

Fiddler on the Roof. Zero Mostel. Book by Joseph Stein, based on stories by Sholem Aleichem. Music by Jerry Bock, lyrics by Sheldon Harnick. "If I Were a Rich Man" is a famous song.

Broadway is very much alive today, not only for native New Yorkers, but for millions of tourists who flock to its streets yearly. Although tickets are expensive and waiting in line is lengthy, few regret the experience and most look forward to doing it again.

Although New York City is a mecca for jazz, jazz is popular throughout the Northeast. A list of jazz places follows.

CONNECTICUT

Hartford

Bushnell Hall is the main center for all musical events, and Civic Center follows closely.

The University of Hartford is particularly active in the music scene, with concerts taking place in Millard Auditorium.

Stratford

The American Shakespeare Theater, in addition to its plays, features popular music, such as the Tommy Dorsey Orchestra, in concert.

Southbury

Piccadilly Pub, on Main Street, offers jazz entertainment.

Waterbury

Park Place Cafe, 483 West Main Street.

Toad's Place, 437 Watertown Avenue, hosts jazz performers.

Wolcott

Friar Tuck's, 1585 Meridian Road, offers dancing and popular music.

Woodbury

Ray Taylor's Barnsider Restaurant, 757 Main Street, offers big band sounds after dinner.

DISTRICT OF COLUMBIA

Blues Alley, where Dizzy Gillespie and Wynton Marsalis have entertained, is a converted carriage house in an alley behind 1073 Wisconsin Avenue. It offers blues and jazz.

Mrs. Smith's, 3104 M Street NW, features a jazz pianist for dancing. It's a pleasant and relaxed place.

One Step Down, at 2517 Pennsylvania Avenue, offers a jam session on weekends.

The Ramada Renaissance Hotel is an active spot for popular music and dancing.

The Wax Museum, Fourth and E Streets NW, presents groups like Widespread Jazz.

The Harlequin Dinner Theater frequently presents entertainment such as the Glenn Miller Orchestra.

Charlie's Georgetown, 3223 K Street NW, offers a little of everything. Flickering candles, a piano bar, art on the walls, and the dance floor provide a pleasant atmosphere inside the stark, modern reddish brown brick building tucked under the Whiteburst Freeway.

The Arena Stage, Sixth and Maine Avenue SW, offers popular music and dancing.

MAINE

Bangor

During July and August, Paul Bunyan Park, on Main Street between Buck and Dutton Streets, offers band concerts with occasional renderings of yesteryear's swing.

Belfast
The Broiler Festival, in July, presents concerts of popular music with some selections in swing.

Portland
In June, the Old Port Festival takes place throughout the city, sampling jazz and other music.

Rockland
Maine's Seafood Festival, in August, offers several bands playing popular music.

Wiscasset
The Musical Wonder House, 18 High Street, holds a collection of old player pianos in that were vogue during the early twentieth century, the jazz era.

MARYLAND

Annapolis
The Maryland Inn presents popular singers.

Baltimore
Painters Mill Theater, on Painters Mill Road, offers jazz performances.
The new Meyerhoff Hall, 1212 Cathedral Street, is *the* site for all varieties of music, including performances by the Four Tops and Larry Elgart and Hooked on Swing Orchestra.
Café Park Plaza, 810 North Charles Street, presents popular singers.
There's a good deal of popular music played during the summer near Inner Harbor at Charles Center South and in the area at Charles and Lombard Streets.
Oyster Bay at Hopkins Plaza offers all-around entertainment.
The Famous Ballroom, 1717 North Charles Street, presents jazz combos.
Dunbar Performing Arts Center, Orleans and Caroline Streets, features jazz musicians, such as Dizzy Gillespie.

Olney
The Olney Inn, on Route 97, is a nightspot that offers swing music and dancing.

Rockville
Normandy Farm, on Great Falls Road, is a pleasant place to dance to popular music.

MASSACHUSETTS

Beverly
Lynch Park Bandshell offers concerts of popular music during the summer.

Boston

Boston Harbor offers jazz cruises à la Dixieland riverboat style at Long Wharf.

Lulu White's, 3 Appleton Street, presents well-known jazz performers.

Tinkers, 888 Tremont Street, experiments with a wide variety of jazz.

Papillion Gourmet Café, 1353B Beacon Street in Brookline, has mid-week jazz performances.

The Boston Globe Jazz Festival, which takes place in March, presents such attractions as Benny Goodman and Herbie Hancock. Swing is further in evidence at nightspots Last Hurrah and Dunfey's Parker House.

The Orpheum Theater on Hamilton Place is a good place to see popular music stars perform. The Berklee Performing Center, 136 Massachusetts Avenue, offers Big Band sounds.

Cambridge

Ryles, 212 Hampshire Street in Cambridge, attracts local jazz talent.

Harvard Square is a fashionable area, and during the summer, the Harvard Coop, Harvard Square T, Holyoke Mall, and Brattle Street Square keep up with the latest in jazz.

Jonathan Swift's, 30 JFK Street, presents popular music stars.

Cohasset

The South Shore Music Circus, Sohier Street, off MA-3A, features top stars in entertainment during the summer.

Dennis

Band music is available in summer concerts.

Lenox

The Berkshire Music Barn has much in the way of musical entertainment during the summer, including jazz.

Northampton

Pines Theater Festival, 300 North Main Street, offers jazz as well as other varieties of music from June through September.

The Iron Horse Bar, on Center Street, has good jazz at any time of the year.

Weymouth

Big band music can be heard during the summer at locations throughout Weymouth.

NEW HAMPSHIRE

Hampton Beach

Bands play swing on the beach during the summer.

Jefferson

The White Mountains Festival of the Arts takes place in the summer. Among its many performing artists have been Benny Goodman, Dave Brubeck, and the Preservation Hall Jazz Band.

Twin Mountain

This is another area that welcomes the White Mountains Festival of the Arts. Mt. Washington Hotel, fourteen-hundred feet above sea level in Bretton Woods, offers jazz in July.

Whitefield

Band concerts of popular music take place in July and August at White-field Commons Gazebo.

NEW JERSEY

Atlantic City

The posh hotels on the Boardwalk offer all varieties of popular music. There are dozens of hotels; some of the more well-known are:
The Claridge has featured Sarah Vaughan and Mel Torme.
The Sands has featured Shirley MacLaine.
The Superstar Theater at Resorts International, with seventeen-hundred seats, has featured Tom Jones.
Caesar's Boardwalk Regency.
The Tropicana.
The Golden Nugget.
Convention Hall.

East Rutherford

The Meadowlands. This seventy-two-thousand-seat structure has hosted hundreds of performers, including Miles Davis and Diana Ross.

Elizabeth

The Ritz, 1148 East Jersey Street, has hosted such stars as Connie Francis.

Hackensack

Orrie de Nooyer Auditorium, 200 Hackensack Avenue, has billed jazz singer Theresa Brewer and pianist George Shearing.

Lambertville

The Music Circus offers jazz under its large tent in the summer.

Ocean City

Music Pier is active all summer long with concerts of all kinds.

Parsippany

Parsippany Hilton Hotel, on Route 10, offers swing concerts and popular music.

Sayreville

Club Bene, Route 35, has welcomed the Glenn Miller Orchestra, The Spinners, and many other artists.

Somerville

The Bedell Bandshell, on Route 202S, Miltown Road, holds outdoor events, especially featuring popular music.

Stanhope

Here is one of many sites hosting New York's Summer Kool Jazz Festival.

Waterloo Village in Stanhope welcomed the Harlem Blues and Jazz Band and Dick Sudhalter recently.

Wayne

William Paterson College hosts a Jazz Room series. Tenor saxophonist Charlie Rouse and drummer Jimmy Cobb have appeared.

NEW YORK

New York City

Again, there are so many places in New York City that space precludes mentioning all but the top names.

The American Stanhope Hotel, 995 Fifth Avenue, has featured jazz flutist Herbie Mann.

Café Carlyle, Seventy-sixth Street and Madison Avenue, hosts jazz artists such as Joe Buskin.

Marty's, 1276 Third Avenue, has welcomed swing stars Vic Damone and Nancy Wilson.

Eddie Condon's, 144 West Fifty-fourth Street, is famous for Dixieland and swing.

Freddy's, 308 East Forty-ninth Street, attracted the original Jazz-at-Noon group.

Jimmy Weston's, 131 East Fifty-fourth Street, offers jazz, swing, and dancing.

Michael's Pub, 211 East Fifty-fifth Street, attracts such performers as Blossom Dearie and Shirley Horn.

Roseland is alive and well at 239 West Fifty-second Street, with jazz, swing, rock and disco. Harry James and Bob Crosby entertained there recently. If you've never been to Roseland, it's worth a visit.

Radio City Music Hall, Fiftieth Street and Sixth Avenue, frequently hosts impressive arrays of popular talent (Count Basie and Lena Horne, for example).

Duffy's Tavern, 308 West Fortieth Street, has jazz combos and big band sounds.

Broadway Joe, 315 West Forty-sixth Street.

Gregory's, 1149 First Avenue.

Jimmy Ryan's, 154 West Fifty-fourth Street.

St. Peter's Lutheran Church, Fifty-fourth Street and Lexington Avenue, an unusual site for jazz lovers, is known as the jazz church. The church holds jazz concerts on Sunday afternoons in its circular sanctuary, which has an eighty-five foot ceiling and excellent acoustics.

The New Ballroom, 253 West Twenty-eighth Street, offers yesterday's swing with such groups as the Widespread Jazz Orchestra playing "Cherokee" and "Taking a Chance on Love."

Forty West Twenty-seventh Street is the location of an unpretentious and homey loft building that holds Jazzmania sessions during the week.

Tramps, 125 East Fifteenth Street, hosted CeDell Davis.

The Lone Star Café, 61 Fifth Avenue, has hosted KoKo Taylor.

Harlem's Apollo Theater, 253 West 125th Street, the seventeen-thousand seat theater famous for jazz in the twenties and thirties, may possibly be converted into a cable TV studio, where much entertainment from the stage will be performed before live audiences.

West End, 2911 Broadway, at 114th Street, hosts performers of earlier years, such as trumpeter Jabbo Smith.

Duke Ellington's house on 115th Street and Riverside Drive is still there. Downtown and Greenwich Village have much to offer. Some of the places in these areas are: Jazz Forum, 648 Broadway; Sweet Basil, 88 Seventh Avenue South; Lush Life, 184 Thompson Street; Village Gate, 160 Bleeker Street; the Cookery, 21 University Place; Village Vanguard, 178 Seventh Avenue South; Other End, 149 Bleeker Street; Fat Tuesdays, 190 Third Avenue; the Blue Note, 131 West Third Street; Seventh Avenue South, 21 Seventh Avenue; Village West, 575 Hudson Street; and Public Theater, 425 Lafayette Street.

A major Greenwich Village Jazz Festival took place in 1982 and was such a success that there are plans to make the Festival an annual event. Artists Alberta Hunter, Hank Jones, and Reggie Workman were among those who performed at the Festival.

The Kool Jazz Festival, originally called the Newport Jazz Festival, when it was held in Rhode Island, is a major jazz event in the summer. It takes place in many locations, some of which are: Carnegie Hall, Fifty-seventh Street and Seventh Avenue; Avery Fisher and Alice Tully Halls, Lincoln Center, Sixty-fifth Street and Broadway; Roseland Ballroom; St. Peter's Church; the Guggenheim Museum, Eighty-ninth Street and Fifth Avenue; and on boatrides—the Staten Island Ferry at South Ferry; a boatride up the Hudson River, starting at Pier Forty at West Houston Street; and at the South Street Seaport, Pier Sixteen at Fulton and South Streets. Well-known stars like Benny Goodman, Lionel Hampton, Teddy Wilson, Stan Getz, Ella Fitzgerald, and Miles Davis have appeared at the Kool Jazz Festival.

No listing is complete without mention of Radio City Music Hall. Stretching down the entire length of Fiftieth Street and Sixth Avenue, and around the corner from Rockefeller Center, Radio City Music Hall is a popular showplace famous for its holiday stage shows and chorus line of Rockettes. After failing financially in the late seventies, the Music Hall has been revived and opens its doors to thousands willing to stand in line hours before the box office opens. Its elegant décor includes high ceilings, large chandeliers, plush carpeting, and a wide stage with a side pit for a solo organist who entertains before and after the main attraction.

The theater district offers numerous theaters for Broadway musicals, among which are: Shubert Theater, 225 West Forty-fourth Street; Winter Garden, Fiftieth Street and Broadway; Imperial Theater, 249 West Forty-fifth Street; Broadway Theater, 1681 Broadway; Royale Theater, 242 West Forty-fifth Street; Mark Hellinger Theater, Fifty-first Street, west of Broadway; St. James Theater, 246 West Forty-fourth Street; Forty-sixth Street Theater, 226 West Forty-sixth Street; Plymouth Theater, Forty-fifth Street, west of Broadway; and Majestic Theater, 245 West Forty-fourth Street.

PENNSYLVANIA

Ambler
The Temple University Music Festival produces an annual summer gala event with such musicians as Henry Mancini and Tony Bennett who have performed here in the past.

Devon
The Valley Forge Music Fair features top names such as Count Basie and Rosemary Clooney.

Philadelphia
Robin Hood Dell East, at Thirty-third and Dauphin Streets in Fairmount Park, has had historic concerts of popular music in the summer.

"Just Jazz" is presented at the Grog Shop, Five Penn Center.

JFK Plaza, at Sixteenth Street and JFK Boulevard, hosts jazz bands.

Rittenhouse Square at Walnut and Eighteenth Streets provides jazz events.

Khyber Pass Pub, 56 South Second Street, offers local jazz.

Rick's Cabaret, 757 South Front Street, has featured Metropole Jazz Band.

Arline, 1823 Sansom Street.

Warwick Hotel, Seventieth and Locust Streets.

Gabriel's Horn, 1420 Locust Street.

Grendel's Lair, 500 South Street.

Pittsburgh
Encore, 5505 Walnut Street in Shadyside, offers jazz.

The Heaven, 105 Sixth Street, offers some jazz.

Encore II, at 629 Liberty Avenue.

The Giraffe, 7 Parkway Green, Green Tree, has dancing.

Schenley Park, on Forbes Avenue, has a large bandstand where one can listen to popular music.

RHODE ISLAND

Newport
The Sheraton Hotel is excellent for popular entertainment and dancing. Christie's, on Thames Street, is also excellent for popular entertainment.

Blue Pelican Jazz Club, on West Broadway, has featured Razmataz in the past.

The Treadway Inn, on the Harbor, has welcomed Newport Friends of Jazz.

Harpo's Newport Jazz Club, 20 Liberty Street, is an unpretentious night-spot which is a lot of fun.

The Newport Jazz Festival, once a famous event, still takes place on a smaller scale in July, in Fort Adams State Park (the main festival moved to New York several years ago and became the Kool Jazz Festival). The Pier, at Howard Wharf, offers popular music and dancing.

North Kingston

The Lafayette Band gives concerts throughout the summer months.

Providence

The Met Café, 165 Friendship Street. The décor is not elegant, but the music is good.

Warwick

The Warwick Musical Theater, 522 Quaker Lane, has an attractive thea-ter-in-the-round, used for top entertainers in concert.

VERMONT

From Wilmington to Stowe, nightspots along Route 100 offer jazz, popular music, and dancing.

ROCK AND DISCO

The mid-1950s witnessed the emergence of rock and roll as a dynamic musical force throughout the nation. Rock has roots in white country music, black blues, and big band rhythm. It was a sensual mixture that, after taking some time to jell, exploded after the World War II years. Rock and roll swept into its fold young people who protested the traditional values of the establishment and desired a change in behavior and lifestyle. The youth listened avidly to rock and roll and spent millions on records.

Alan Freed

One of the foremost figures on the rock and roll scene in the northeast was disc jockey Alan Freed. Freed was a trombone player in Claude Thornhill's dance band and disc jockey at Cleveland's radio station WJW, where he played classical records. In 1954, he came to station WINS in New York City to play music heretofore referred to as rhythm-and-blues. He is credited with first using the term "rock 'n' roll" to describe the physical, sensual qualities of this music. Much of the music he played was characterized by a heavy beat and raw vocal sounds. Freed had a grating voice that matched the intensity of the records he spun, and he talked rapidly in slang, often preceded by little thought. The WINS Show adopted the name "Alan Freed's Rock 'n' Roll Party" and Freed became known as the "King of Rock 'n' Roll." Many disc jockeys in other parts of the country imitated his style of broadcasting. Freed organized large rock and roll concerts with artists such as Fats Domino, Chuck Berry, the Moonglows, and Jo Ann Campbell. Riots frequently accompanied the shows. But liberal New York City took them in its stride, excited about the new musical form.

Freed's popularity swelled, and he appeared in several films (*Rock Around the Clock*, in 1955; *Rock, Rock, Rock*, in 1956; and *Don't Knock the Rock*, in 1957). When *Don't Knock the Rock* opened at New York's Times Square Paramount Theater, Freed appeared on stage, wearing a loud sports jacket and gyrating and screaming "Go man, go," before an audience of fifteen-thousand teenagers, who responded in similar fashion, shouting and stomping. Owners feared the theater might collapse.

Many promotional stunts followed until 1960, when a payola scandal involving commercial bribery found Freed guilty. His career ended shortly thereafter, with drink and an early death at the age of forty-three.

Bill Haley and the Comets—Forerunners of the Rock and Roll Band

During the same year that Alan Freed came to WINS in New York, Bill Haley worked as music director at radio station WAPA in Chester, Pennsylvania. Haley, a guitarist and yodeler (complete with country twang), was interested in the new musical sounds he heard. He formed a small rock group called the Comets. He adapted big band music to his group and modified dance rhythms to an up-tempo of four beats to the bar. The northern band style of rock and roll added a touch of Dixieland jazz to the combination of country and rhythm-and-blues. Borrowed from jazz were the physical techniques of having the bass player climb on the bass or rotate it while playing, and having the saxophonist perform while lying on the floor. The musicians, in addition to executing these antics, sang in chorus.

In 1954, the Comets came to New York to record "Rock Around the Clock." This theme song of the teenage revolution was used in the film of the same name, starring Bill Haley and the Comets, Alan Freed, Chuck Berry, and Little Richard, and in *Blackboard Jungle.* For many adult viewers, the movie *Blackboard Jungle* created a link between rock and roll and juvenile delinquency.

Another hit song, "Shake, Rattle and Roll," recorded by bluesman Joe Turner, was reworked by Haley in a rock and roll arrangement that speeded up the beat, added amplification, and choked vocal syllables. Two more hits that followed were "See You Later, Alligator," and "Dim, Dim the Lights," both of which ranked high on the charts.

The popularity of Bill Haley and the Comets, considered among the forerunners of rock and roll groups, leveled out after several successful years. The group was surpassed by other rising performers, notably Elvis Presley and rockabilly artists in the South. During the early sixties; the Comets worked mostly abroad in European cities, finding receptive audiences among the youth there. They returned in 1969 to perform at a large rock and roll revival concert at Madison Square Garden in New York City. Haley died in 1981.

"American Bandstand" and Dick Clark

In 1957, while Alan Freed was rocking New York and Bill Haley and the Comets were busy recording and making films, another pioneer, Dick Clark, was shaping the face of rock and roll in Philadelphia. A lot of recording activity took place in Philadelphia, which had a strong radio and television market, including WDAS (a black station), WIBG, WPEN, WHAT, and WFIL.

Clark, an announcer originally from Utica, New York, hosted

"American Bandstand," a television program that showcased teenage recorded music. "Bandstand" was carried more than a hundred stations each day for ninety minutes after school hours. The program reached twenty-million adolescents.

WFIL television studio was located on Market and Forty-sixth Streets in a long, brick building next door to a four-thousand-seat sports complex, the Arena. The railroad ran down the center of Market Street from downtown Philadelphia and stopped at the door of WFIL. Irish and black groups of teen-agers from south Philadelphia's streets of two-story brick row houses congregated around the studio, looking for some outlet in the new rock and roll music. Two parochial high schools and one public school were within walking distance. From these sources came the audience for "Bandstand."

In sharp contrast to the raucous manner of Alan Freed, Clark was poised, debonair, and calm. His respect for the English language, his polite behavior, and his standards of dress were reassuring to those parents who feared the deterioration of values in their sons and daughters.

Generally, live artists did not appear on "Bandstand." Rather, photos of singers were projected onto screens in conjunction with the playing of their records. Occasionally, when an artist did appear in the studio, he or she did not actually sing, but would mime lyrics to the playing of his or her record. This technique is called lip-synching. This served, of course, as publicity without payment.

The local high school students were invited to drop into the studio after school and dance to records. Many did and came to regard "Bandstand" as "their" program. They bought the records, too. New dance steps were introduced on the program, including the Stroll, the Fish, and the Stomp. They were all danced to a heavy beat, in which the dancers gyrated opposite their partners but did not touch each other. The dances attained wide popularity on the show and from there traveled to the dance floors of nightclubs and hotels.

Clark even selected teenagers to rate the records he played. They rated the songs on a scale of one to ten. He then promoted the songs that were highly rated. Several artists who rose to fame as a result of teenage choices were the Monotones, singing "Little Star"; Chubby Checker, with "The Twist," a song and dance that became a world-wide craze; Dion, singing "I Wonder Why"; Fabian, with "I'm a Man"; and Frankie Avalon, performing "Venus." This last song sold one and a half million copies after publicity on the "Bandstand" show.

During the payola scandal in the sixties Clark was under suspicion and was interrogated by members of Congress. Unlike Freed, however, Clark remained largely unaffected and maintained subsequent positions as a producer and packager for television stations.

The Twist and The Peppermint Lounge

By the early 1960s the older generation began to catch up with rock and roll culture. Many parents were becoming "hip" and admitted to enjoying the body movement, emotional release, and freedom that rock and roll music inspired, especially in the dance that had turned into a sensational hit—the Twist.

"The Twist" was written by Hank Ballard and was originally recorded by the Midnighters in 1959, but the version that swept the nation was the one introduced by Chubby Checker on "American Bandstand" in Philadelphia. Professional dance studios taught the Twist, and Hollywood demonstrated it for thousands in the 1962 film, "Twist All Night," starring bandleader Louis Prima.

The Peppermint Lounge, 128 West Forty-fifth Street in New York City, was a famous nightspot for an evening's "twisting." (The Lounge is still operating today, but is much less in the limelight.) Not only did parents frequent the Peppermint Lounge, but many jet set celebrities (Greta Garbo, Adlai Stevenson, Jackie Kennedy, Lee Radziwill, and Marian Javits) flocked to its tiny dance floor to grind energetically, moving hands in the opposite direction from hips and persevering until early morning hours.

The popular band at the Peppermint Lounge in 1961 was Joey Dee and the Starlighters, which performed for over a year. Dee wrote "Peppermint Twist" as a tribute to his working locale. Other hits that attracted patrons were "Let's Twist Again," "Twistin' the Night Away," and "Slow Twistin'." This craze lasted until the late sixties when disco and psychedelic dancing came upon the popular music scene.

Rock Imports: The Beatles and The Rolling Stones

Four young men from Great Britain's working class defined American rock in the 1960s. They called themselves the Beatles. With their relatively long hair and their enormous energy, they represented a new radical teenage idol. But they also enhanced and expanded the scope of rock with their creativity and artistic uniqueness, propelling rock to a peak of emotional power and commercial success. Their fresh lyrical quality, their increased harmonic range, and their original songs and arrangements reflected positive feelings. The love of life engendered in their music was especially pleasing in contrast to the negativism of early rock music.

The four Beatles, John Lennon, Paul McCartney, George Harrison, and Ringo Starr, traveled to New York City for the first time in 1964, singing "I Want to Hold Your Hand," "All You Need is Love," and "Can't Buy Me Love." The songs were hits, accounting for more than half of all record sales at that time. Excitement and tension were evident in their accompanying guitars and drums, but the overall effect, superbly mastered, was a sophisticated excitement, rarely raucous, wild, or un-controlled.

Other new stylistic approaches could be heard in their songs. In their arrangement of "Yesterday," for example, a cello was used to convey an unprecedented touch of elegance in rock music. In "Michelle" and "Think for Yourself," they extended cultural bounds by the addition of an Indian sitar. The use of strings in rock was originated by Buddy Holly. (See Section IV, Chapter 3.)

The Beatles were the rage throughout the sixties. They broke up in 1970 to pursue individual careers. In 1980 the world was stunned by the tragic murder of John Lennon in New York City.

Another English group, the Rolling Stones, was almost as popular as the Beatles. Their style, however, was closer to the counterculture that identified with the group's wild outrage and deliberate provocation of the establishment in a high-speed, high-decibel, gruff delivery. Leader Mick Jagger sang grating songs, including "Something Happened to Me Yesterday," a song about LSD; and "I Can't Get No Satisfaction," carrying an attitude of flaunting bohemianism.

The Stones toured America in 1972 with more best-selling hits ("Exile on Main Street" and "Sticky Fingers"). The group was followed by many other imports such as Led Zeppelin and The Who.

Bob Dylan and Folk Rock

The Beatles' records had some competition on the home front in Bob Dylan, who, like the Beatles, added an original touch to rock and established a new direction.

Dylan was a folk singer who had come to New York because of Woody Guthrie. He and other folk singers communicated their feelings about social injustice through their folk music. A stylistic change came about in 1965 at the Newport Folk Festival in Rhode Island where Dylan took the heavy beat and loud instrumentation of rock and fused these elements with the personal statements of folk music. (See Section I, Chapter 4.) The nuclear threat was expounded in "A Hard Rain is Gonna Fall," war was vilified in "Masters of War," and racial prejudice was attacked in "The Lonesome Death of Hattie Carroll." There were all highly personal lyrics sung to a throbbing rock beat. Loose and loud, sometimes intensified by a drugged performer's abandon, the sound became known as folk-rock.

After this musical transition was made, the folk-rock style was adopted by such artists as Paul Simon, The Lovin' Spoonful, and the Mamas and the Papas. Dylan, in a more relaxed frame of mind, turned to writing tenderhearted, almost poetic lyrics, for example "Restless Farewell" and "My Back Pages." The music of this multi-talented man reigned in the sixties.

Dylan starred in the film, *Woodstock*, made after the Wood-stock Music Festival in 1969. Held at a farm in White Lake, in upstate New York, the Festival symbolized youth solidarity. More than three-hundred-thousand young people jammed the farm grounds for a week-end of rock music. Unfortunately, wild behavior and poor safety precautions culminated in several deaths. Shortly after the Woodstock Festival, Dylan underwent a religious conversion and emerged as a Born-again Christian, returning, it seems, to his country roots.

Disco

Disco emerged at the end of the sixties from the rock culture. This new form of music went beyond rock's statement of challenge and hostility to the frankly sexual. Unlike the Twist in earlier years, disco dancing meant dancing under psychedelic lights with sexual body movements (often heightened by drugs). It was an expression of total self-absorption that lost itself in movement.

Legend has disco beginning in gay colonies in Fire Island, New York, then moving into such private New York clubs as the Loft and the Tenth Floor in Manhattan. Unsyncopated 4/4 meter is typical of the disco sound. It can be heard in George McCrae's hit, "Rock Your Baby," and in the music of Isaac Hayes and Barry White. Frequently, percussive instrumentation overrides the voice so that the music sounds like one continuous beat-driven tune. Sybil's and Studio 54, still here today, sprang up to accommodate disco lovers.

After a group called Village People recorded "Macho Man" and "YMCA," Greenwich Village's Christopher Street became a mecca for disco. New arrangements were made of old tunes and, although there were cries of decadence, the beat went on.

The disco era culminated with the film, *Saturday Night Fever*, starring John Travolta. It was shot at the real 2001 Odyssey Club in Bay Ridge, Brooklyn. The music featured was that of the Bee Gees; it cut across all lines of class, age, and sex. The film was later televised, and is occasionally revived. Disco peaked and then tapered off in the late seventies.

The Splintering of Rock

Rock in the seventies was splintered into as many groups as there were names available: funk, punk, acid, new wave, and other over-lapping varieties. This was more or less the last gasp of rock. The Mercer Arts Center (no longer in existence), near the Bottom Line, New York's popular rock club in Greenwich Village, contained the original Kitchen, a forum famous for experimental music. Several groups were active here, including the New York Dolls, calling themselves punk or new wave. The terms punk and new wave describe groups that have a sexually ambivalent image, a snarling manner, and an almost primitive style. Velvet Underground, also a raw group, entertained in the Bowery, as did the Talking Heads, whose lead singer and songwriter, David Byrne, was concerned with social commentary as heard in the albums, "Songs About Buildings and Food" and "Fear of Music."

A popular star to emerge in the seventies was Deborah Harry, the blonde lead singer of the group, Blondie, with the hit, "Heart of Glass," at the Mudd Club. You can visit the club today. The music of Blondie and the Talking Heads is evident in some measure today.

The institution of rock and roll is part of music history. Although the revolution is over, there are still places in the Northeast where you can enjoy varieties of rock and be temporarily transported back into the colorful milieu of musical aggression, escape, fun, and vitality. Below is a partial list of such places in the Northeast.

CONNECTICUT

Hartford
The Civic Center has featured Speedwagon with Survivor. Near the Hartford Civic Center, there is a large entertainment center downtown, containing many clubs.

New Haven
Peace Train gives concerts on the Green in summer which feature genuine rock and folk-rock.

Stamford
The Palace Theater on Atlantic presents rock concerts frequently.

Waterbury
Toad's Place, 437 Watertown Avenue, has welcomed Crystal Ship.

Westport
Levitt Pavilion on Saugatuck River is a center for all kinds of music, including rock.

DISTRICT OF COLUMBIA

Bojangles, 2100 M Street NW, is a nightspot for rock and disco. During the summer, rock groups perform outside on the patio.
Charlie's Georgetown, 3223 K Street NW, features some rock.
Capital Center has hosted Linda Ronstadt and Largo.
The Bayou, 3135 K Street NW, features performers such as Asbury Dukes and Shooting Star.
9:30 Club, 930 F Street, offers rock and popular music.
The Warner Theater, 513 Thirteenth Street NW, regularly attracts artists such as Gladys Knight and the Pips.
Constitution Hall, Eighteenth and D Streets NW, has billed the O'Jays.

MAINE
Portland

The Playroom, 121 Center Street, is an attractive and fairly expensive nightspot with plenty of action.

In June the Old Portland Festival offers a little of everything including rock.

MARYLAND
Baltimore

Baltimore Civic Center, 201 West Baltimore Street, has rock concerts and popular music galore.

Inner Harbor abounds in music during the summer.

Club Venus, in the Perring Plaza Center, is fine for rock music.

Two O'Clock, 400 East Baltimore Street, also features rock music.

The area of North Charles Street near Mt. Royal Avenue is a busy nightlife strip.

Holiday Inn Circle One, 301 West Lombard Street, has a revolving rooftop, where one can dance and listen to rock concerts.

MASSACHUSETTS
Boston

The Metro, 15 Landsdowne Street, is a popular disco.

The Spit, next door to the Metro at 13 Landsdowne Street, offers punk rock and disco. You'll see some outlandish dress here.

Narcissus, 533 Commonwealth Avenue, features disco.

Celebration, also on Commonwealth Avenue, offers disco.

Back Bay Theater hosted Jackie Wilson.

The Berklee Performing Center, 136 Massachusetts Avenue, is a prime spot for musical variety.

The Hynes Auditorium, 900 Boylston Street, holds many events.

The Oxford Ale House, 36 Church Street, is informal, offering a variety of music.

Cambridge

Inman Square is the place to go for rock and disco.

Northampton

Rahar's, on Main Street, offers punk rock music.

The Iron Horse Bar, on Center Street, also offers punk rock music.

Pittsfield

Oh Be Joyful offers rock and roll music.

Jonathan's, 446 West Housatonic, offers rock and roll music.

Worcester

Centrum, 50 Foster Street, frequently has rock stars. Crosby, Stills and Nash were there recently.

NEW HAMPSHIRE

Bretton Woods
The Mt. Washington Hotel Amphitheater has many musical events, among which are rock bands in concert.

NEW JERSEY

Atlantic City
The Boardwalk hotels are your best bet for musical entertainment. Diana Ross has appeared at Resorts International, the Beach Boys at the Sands, The Spinners at Caesar's, and many stars have appeared at Convention Hall.
Little John's, Tennessee and Pacific Avenues, and Chez Paree are discos with flashing lights and mirrors.

East Rutherford
Meadowlands in the Byrne Arena has rock concerts. Recently, Crosby, Stills and Nash and Asbury Dukes entertained here.

Hackensack
Orrie de Noyer Auditorium, 200 Hackensack Avenue, presents all kinds of musical events.

Hoboken
Maxwell's, 1039 Washington Street is a rock club. Human Switchboard and the Individuals have been among their featured guests.

Passaic
The Capitol Theater, 326 Monroe Street, has featured such stars as Graham Parker and new wave rock.

Wildwood
Gloria's, Decatur and Beach Avenues, holds two-hundred listeners for rock concerts. John Prine appeared here recently.
The Playpen, Atlantic Avenue, offers rock and disco music.
The Penalty Box, Pacific and Cedars Avenue, offers rock music.

NEW YORK

New York City
Roseland, 239 West Fifty-second Street, has a large disco room, and has attracted such artists as Bruce Springsteen and the East Street Band.
The Peppermint Lounge, 128 West Forty-fifth Street, offers a variety of rock groups including Flesh Eaters, a heavy metal band, and Furious Five.
Studio 54, 254 West Fifty-fourth Street, and Sybil's, 101 West Fifty-third, are popular clubs.
Michael's Pub offers the latest in popular music.
Other discos are New York, New York, 33 West Fifty-second Street, a multi-level complex; Regine's 502 Park Avenue, a very lively place; Madison Square Garden, Thirty-third Street and Seventh Avenue, offers big rock events.

Downtown are the Bottom Line, 15 West Fourth Street, which always features quality rock and roll (the Mystics, the Harptones, and the Capris were here recently); The Ritz, 119 East Eleventh Street, the Palladium, Fourth Street between Third and Fourth Avenues; the Mudd Club, 77 White Street, for artists such as Tav Falco and Panther Burns; CBGB, which stands for country, bluegrass, and blues), now features rock. It's a long, dark Bowery bar, with guests such as The Mob and Cool it Rheba. The Lone Star Café, Thirteenth Street and Fifth Avenue, is another popular spot.

Several other large sites for rock concerts outside of Manhattan are Shea Stadium in Queens, and the Nassau Veterans Memorial Coliseum in Uniondale, Long Island. Elton John and Rick James were among their performers.

PENNSYLVANIA
Philadelphia
The Spectrum Theater, Broad Street and Pattison Avenue, and the Shubert Theater, 250 South Broad Street, feature such stars as Dionne Warwick.

Ripley Music Hall, 608 South Street, has presented The Sensory Fix.

The Tower Theater, Sixteenth Street and Ludlow Avenue, has featured Devo.

Robin Hood Dell East has an outdoor theater with rock concerts in summer.

JFK Plaza, Sixteenth Street and JFK Boulevard, holds summer concerts with rock stars.

Rittenhouse Square, Eighteenth and Walnut Streets, also holds rock concerts outdoors.

Stars, Second and Bainbridge Streets, is the place for new wave rock. The Library, 2 Bala Plaza on City Line, Bala Cynwyd, offers disco music.
Pittsburgh
The Razzberry Rhinoceros, 5534 Walnut Street in Shadyside. It attracts quality rock bands. The Marriott Inn, 101 Marriott Drive in Greentree, is a popular disco nightspot. Heaven, 105 Sixth Street, is said to be Pittsburgh's hottest nightclub. A former bank building, it boasts a large dance floor with colored lights.

RHODE ISLAND
Newport
The Shamrock Cliff Hotel, on Ridge Road, is a lovely place for rock and disco music. One Pelham East, on Thames Street also offers rock and disco music. The S.S. Newport is a floating lounge and restaurant, and a favorite for dancing. Pappy's at West Main Road Center has featured Charlie Cash among its stars. Jubilee Clock, 102 Connell Highway should

please you, as will Cliff Walk Manor, 82 Memorial Boulevard.
Woonsocket
Diamond Hill State Park, off Diamond Hill Road in Cumberland Hill,
holds rock concerts during the summer.

VERMONT

Brattleboro
Mole's Eye, Brookshouse, presents a variety of music, sometimes rock.
From Wilmington to Stowe, there are rock and disco nightspots along
Route 100.

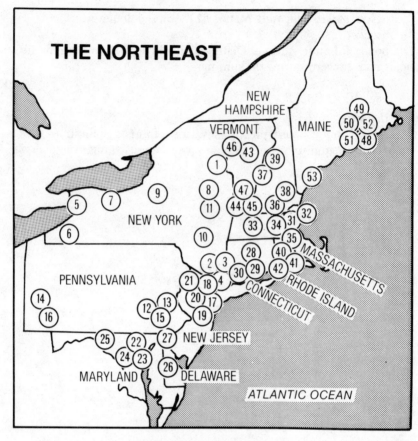

The Northeast

1. **Petersburg, NY**—Fox Hollow "Traditional Music in the Woods" with psalm singing
2. **Croton-on-Hudson, NY**—Clearwater Revival, for folk and country
3. **Katonah, NY**—Caramoor on Girdle Ridge Road, for symphonic music
4. **Purchase, NY**—Performing Arts Center at SUNY on Anderson Hill Road, for all varieties of music
5. **Buffalo, NY**—Kleinhans Music Hall, 370 Pennsylvania Street, home of Buffalo Philharmonic
6. **Chautauqua, NY**—Chautauqua Amphitheater on western shore of Chautauqua Lake, home of Chautauqua Symphony Orchestra
7. **Rochester, NY**—Eastman Theater, Main and Gibbs Street, home of Rochester Philharmonic

8. **Saratoga Springs, NY**—Saratoga Performing Arts Center on South Broadway, for symphonic music, dance, and many varieties of music
9. **Syracuse, NY**—Civic Center, 411 Montgomery Street, for varieties of music
10. **Woodstock, NY**—Woodstock Playhouse, junction NY 212 and 375, for dance festivals
11. **Rensselaer, NY**—Fort Crollo State Historic Site, a restored house at 9½ Riverside Avenue, where a British surgeon may have written words to **Yankee Doodle** in the late 18th century
12. **Kutztown, PA**—Pennsylvania Dutch Folk Festival at Fairgrounds
13. **Bethlehem, PA**—Lehigh University for the Bach Festival in May. Former home

of old Moravian Collegium Musicum in 1744

14. Pittsburgh, PA—Home of Stephen Foster (1826–1864). The University of Pittsburgh, Fifth Avenue and Bigelow Boulevard, contains his memorabilia. Heinz Hall, 600 Penn Avenue, home of Pittsburgh Symphony

15. Schwenksville, PA—Philadelphia Folk Festival at Poole Farm

16. Uniontown, PA—Fiddling and country music in Fayette County

17. Bayonne, NJ—Veterans Memorial Stadium, 267 F Street, for musical events

18. E. Rutherford, NJ—Meadowlands, off NJ-50, exit 20, for all varieties of music

19. Holmdel, NJ—Garden State Arts Center, Telegraph Hill Park

20. Newark, NJ—Symphony Hall, 1020 Broad Street, home of New Jersey Symphony

21. Stanhope, NJ—Home of Waterloo Summer Festival in Waterloo Village

22. Baltimore, MD—Meyerhoff Hall, home of Baltimore Symphony at 1212 Cathedral Street. Fort McHenry in Baltimore Harbor, where Francis Scott Key wrote words to The Star-Spangled Banner in 1814. Star-Spangled Banner House, 844 Pratt Street, exhibits memorabilia

23. Annapolis, MD—Home of Annapolis Opera, Constitution Avenue

24. College Park, MD—Tawes Recital Hall and Theater, University of Maryland, for musical events

25. Frederick, MD—Weinberg Center for the Arts, 20 W. Patrick Street

26. Harrington, DE—Grand Opera House, Wilmington Square

27. Wilmington, DE—Brandywine Arts Festival, Josephine Gardens

28. Hartford, CT—Bushnell Memorial Hall, east flank of Capitol, home of Hartford Symphony, Bushnell Symphony, and CT Opera. Other music too

29. New Haven, CT—Woolsey Hall, College and Grove streets, home of New Haven Symphony. Yale Law School Courtyard concerts, Wall near York Street. Peace Train folk music on The Green

30. New Canaan, CT—Silvermine chamber music at Silvermine Guild Center of the Arts

31. Salem, MA—Former Assembly House at 138 Federal Street (1782), built to accommodate informal concerts and chamber music

32. Rockport, MA—Cape Ann Symphony and Chamber Music Society of Cape Ann

33. Worcester, MA—Memorial Auditorium for musical events

34. Concord and Lexington, MA—Fife and Drum event on Patriot's Day, April 19th, each year, downtown

35. Stoughton, MA—First American performing vocal organization established 1800, The Stoughton Musical Society

36. Peterborough, NH—Home of American composer Edward MacDowell (1861–1908). MacDowell Colony for artists and composers on High Street.

37. Hanover, NH—Hopkins Center for the Arts at Dartmouth College, Main and Wheelock streets.

38. Manchester, NH—New Hampshire Performing Arts Center, 80 Hanover Street, home of New Hampshire Symphony

39. Franconia, NH—Bluegrass and square dancing at Muster Field, Franconia Village

40. Providence, RI—Providence Civic Center, LaSalle Square, for folk. Rhode Island Philharmonic at Westminster Mall

41. Newport, RI—Bellevue Avenue mansions, for 19th-century music concerts

42. University of Rhode Island at Kingston, for musical events

43. Barre, VT—Barre Auditorium, Seminary Hill, for folk and country

44. Bennington, VT—Bennington School of the Dance at Bennington College

45. Brattleboro, VT—Music Center in western Brattleboro

46. Burlington, VT—One site of "Mostly Mozart" Festival

47. Marlboro, VT—Marlboro Music School and Festival of symphonic music

48. Bar Harbor, ME—Mountain Desert Island, Acadia National Park, and Village Green Park on Main Street, for folk festivals and workshops

49. Old Town, ME—Penobscot Reservation, for Indian songs and dances

50. Bangor, ME—Bangor Symphony in Peakes Auditorium, 885 Broadway

51. Blue Hill, ME—Kneisel Hall Music School and concerts

52. Hancock, ME—Pierre Monteux Domaine School for Conductors and Orchestra Players on Route 1

53. Portland, ME—Portland City Hall Auditorium, 389 Congress Street, home of Portland Symphony

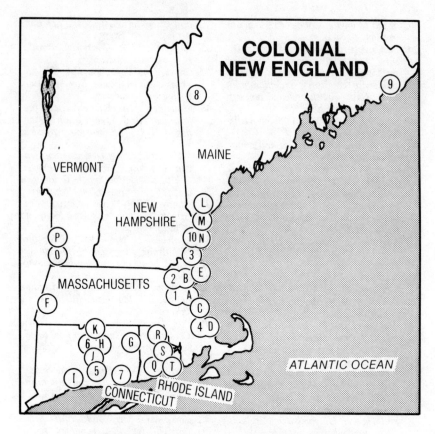

Colonial New England

1. *Boston, MA—Colonial home of Thomas Brattle, importer of first organ from England; Edward Bromfield, maker of first American organ in 1740s; Rev. Cotton Mather, advocate of "regular singing" and director of first singing school in 1720 in his schoolhouse. Home of Handel and Haydn Society, 158 Newbury Street.*

2. *Cambridge, MA—First book printed in North America in 1640 by Matthew Daye, The Bay Psalm Book, with 50 English hymn tunes.*

3. *Newburyport, MA—Colonial home of Rev. John Tufts (1689–1750), who wrote first instruction book on singing in 1712*

4. *Plymouth, MA—Home of first Pilgrim settlement in 1620 and site of reenactment of "Pilgrim's Progress" semi-annually with psalms sung*

5. *Durham, CT—Colonial home of Rev.*

Nathaniel Chauncey, 18th century advocate of "regular singing."

6. *Hartford, CT—Colonial home of composer Andrew Law. CT archives in library on Main Street holds petition from Law requesting copyright of his works*

7. *New London, CT—Place where pamphlet on "regular singing" was printed in 1728 by Rev. Chauncey.*

8. *Roxbury, ME—Originally in MA, Colonial home of Rev. Thomas Walter (1696–1725), who published a book of singing instructions in 1721*

9. *Machias, ME—Colonial home of composer James Lyon, who wrote famous psalm collection, Urania, in 1761*

10. *Portsmouth, NH—Site of St. John's Episcopal Church (1807) at 101 Chapel Street that hold Brattle's successor organ as well as some frayed Colonial prayerbooks with psalms*

*SOME SITES OF RESTORED COLONIAL
CHURCHES IN NEW ENGLAND WHERE
PSALMODY PREVAILED THAT MAY BE
VISITED TODAY*

A. *Boston, MA—Old South Meeting House
(1729)
Washington and Milk
streets
King's Chapel (1686)
Tremont and School
streets
Old North Church (1723)
193 Salem Street*

B. *Cambridge, MA—Christ Church (1761)
Garden Street at the
Common*

C. *Hingham, MA—Old Ship Church
(1681)
90 Main Street*

D. *Plymouth, MA—First Parish Church
and Church of Pil-
grimage (early 17th
century)
Leyden Street*

E. *Salem, MA—First Church of Salem
(1634)
316 Essex Street*

F. *Stockbridge, MA—Mission House
(1739)
Main and Ser-
geant streets*

G. *Brooklyn, CT—Old Trinity Church
(1771)
Off Route 6*

H. *Hartford, CT—Center Church (1638)
60 Gold Street*

I. *New Haven, CT—Trinity Church (1752)
The Green on Church
Street*

J. *Wethersfield, CT—First Church of
Christ Congrega-
tional (1685)
Main and March
streets*

K. *Windsor, CT—United Church of Christ
Congregational
75 Palisade Avenue*

L. *Kennebunk, ME—First Parish Church
(1773)
Main Street and
Portland Road*

M. *Kittery Point, ME—First Congregational Church
(1659)
Pepperrell Road*

N. *Portsmouth, NH—St. John's Church
(1732)
101 Chapel Street*

O. *Bennington, VT—Old First Church
(1762)
Monument Avenue*

P. *Arlington, VT—St. James Church (1764)*

Q. *North Kingston, RI—Smith's Castle
(1678)
Post Road*

R. *Providence, RI—First Baptist Meeting
House (1638)
75 N. Main Street*

S. *Wickford, RI—St. Paul's Church (1707)
55 Main Street*

T. *Newport, RI—Trinity Church (1698)
Church and Spring
streets*

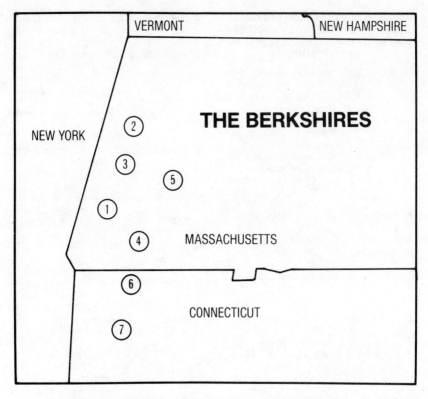

Berkshire Area: MA and CT

1. Great Barrington, MA—Great Barrington Fair, Fairgrounds on Route 7, folk,
country, and popular music. St. James
Episcopal Church has Aston Magna performing chamber music
2. Pittsfield, MA—South Mountain Concerts, South Street off US-7 and 20, symphonic and chamber music, and music
colony. Pittsfield Art Festival in summer. Jonathan's, 446 W. Housatonic, has
rock
3. Lenox, MA—Tanglewood summer concerts: symphonic and chamber music,
choral works, open rehearsals, seminars, etc. Home of Boston Symphony. Off
US-7 and 20. Home of Berkshire Music
Center and Berkshire Music Barn with
varieties of music
4. New Marlborough, MA—Red Fox Music Barn and Camp, off US-57
5. Becket, MA—Jacob's Pillow Dance Festival, off US-20, world-renowned dance
events
6. Norfolk, CT—"Yale in Norfolk" chamber music, summer music school, off US-
44
7. Falls Village, CT—Music Mountain
concerts on CT-126

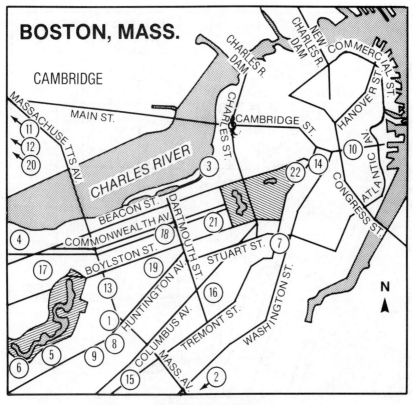

Boston, MA

1. Symphony Hall, Massachusetts and Huntington avenues, home of Boston Symphony

2. Opera House, 539 Washington Street, home of Opera Company of Boston

3. Hatch Memorial Shell, Esplanade along Charles River. Site of musical events

4. Boston University Concert Hall, Charles River Campus, Back Bay. Site of musical events

5. Museum of Fine Arts, 465 Huntington Avenue. Concerts and chamber music

6. Gardner Museum, 280 the Fenway. Concerts and chamber music

7. Boston Music Hall, former home of Boston Symphony

8. New England Conservatory of Music, 290 Huntington Avenue

9. Northeastern University, 360 Huntington Avenue, site of musical events

10. Black Rose, 160 State Street, for folk and country

11. Passim, 47 Palmer Street, for folk and country

12. Cantab Lounge, 738 Massachusetts Avenue, for Bluegrass

13. Berklee Performing Center for Big-Band sounds, 136 Massachusetts Avenue

14. Dunfey's Parker House and Last Hurrah, places for jazz and swing, on School Street

15. Tinkers at 888 Tremont Street, for a wide variety of jazz

16. Lulu White's, 3 Appleton Street, for jazz

17. Metro, 15 Lansdowne Street, for disco Spit, 13 Lansdowne Street, for punk rock and disco

18. Narcissus, 533 Commonwealth Avenue, for disco

19. Hynes Auditorium, 900 Boylston Street, for all musical varieties

20. Oxford Ale House, 36 Church Street, for popular music

21. Home of Handel and Haydn Society, 158 Newbury Street

22. Former home of Reverend Samuel Smith, composer of America, sung at Park Street Church, 1 Park Street, on July 4, 1831

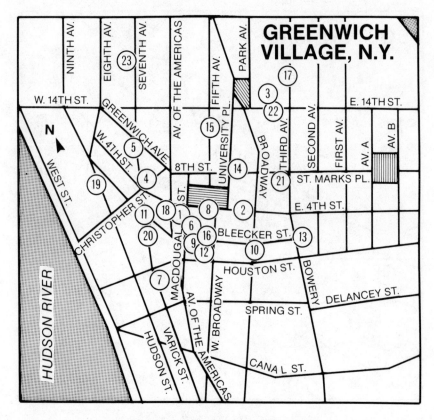

New York City, NY
(Greenwich Village)

1. Folk City, 130 W. Third Street, for folk
2. The Bottom Line, 15 W. Fourth Street, for folk, jazz, and rock
3. Tramps, 125 E. Fifteenth Street, for jazz and blues
4. City Limits, Tenth Street and Seventh Avenue, for folk and country
5. Village Vanguard, 178 Seventh Avenue, for jazz
6. Speakeasy, 107 MacDougal Street, for jazz and country
7. Ethnic Arts Folk Center, 179 Varick Street
8. NYU, Washington Square, for collection of musical instruments
9. Village Gate, Bleecker and Thompson, for folk and country
10. Jazz Forum, 648 Broadway, for jazz
11. Sweet Basil, 88 Seventh Avenue S., for jazz
12. Lush Life, 184 Thompson Street, for jazz
13. CBGB, 315 Bowery, rock and country
14. The Cookery, 21 University Place, jazz
15. Lone Star Café, 61 Fifth Avenue, for rock and country music
16. Other End, 149 Bleecker Street, for rock
17. Fat Tuesday's, 190 Third Avenue, jazz
18. The Blue Note, 131 W. Third Street, jazz
19. Village West, 575 Hudson Street, jazz
20. Seventh Avenue South, 21 Seventh Avenue, jazz
21. Cooper Union, Third Avenue and Seventh Street, folk
22. The Palladium, Fourteenth Street between Third and Fourth avenues, for folk, jazz and rock
23. Joyce Theater, Nineteenth Street and Eighth Avenue, home of Eliot Feld Ballet

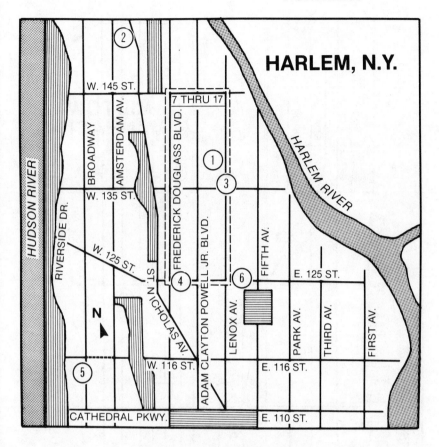

New York City, NY (Harlem)

1. *Abyssinian Baptist Church, 132 W. 138th Street, hosts symphonic events*
2. *Dance Theater of Harlem, 466 W. 152nd Street, headquarters for renowned dance group*
3. *Schomburg Center for Research, 515 Lenox Avenue, music history of black artists*
4. *Apollo Theater, 253 W. 125th Street, landmark in Harlem jazz in early 20th century*
5. *West End, 2911 Broadway, current jazz spot*
6. *Former home of Cotton Club, symbol of Harlem's early jazz, between Lenox and Fifth avenues on 125th Street*

Popular jazz clubs in the early 20th century between Lenox and Eighth avenues, from 125th to 145th streets

7. *Sugar Cane Club*
8. *Saratoga Club*
9. *Bamboo Inn*
10. *Lenox Club*
11. *Bamville Club*
12. *Small's Paradise*
13. *Savoy Ballroom*
14. *Alhambra Ballroom*
15. *Connie's Inn*
16. *Royal Café*
17. *Nest's Club*

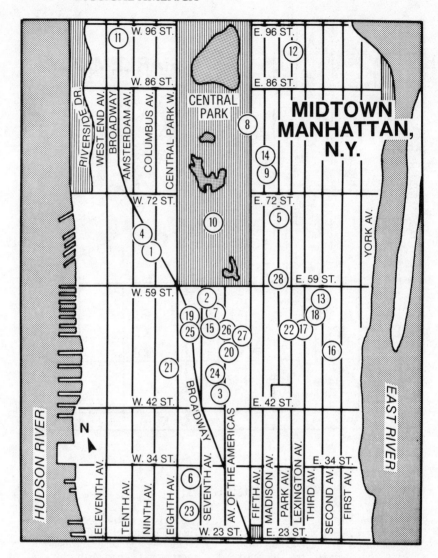

New York City, NY
(Mid-Manhattan)

1. Lincoln Center Complex between Sixty-second and Sixty-sixth streets on Broadway. Home of NY Philharmonic, NY Metropolitan Opera, NYC Ballet, American Ballet Theater, Juilliard School of Music

2. Carnegie Hall and Carnegie Recital Hall, Fifty-seventh Street and Seventh Avenue, former home of Philharmonic and site of concerts and recitals

3. Town Hall, Forty-third Street and Sixth Avenue, place for musical events

4. Abraham Goodman House, 129 W. Sixty-seventh Street, hosts symphonic and chamber music concerts and recitals

5. *Hunter College, 695 Park Avenue, for concerts and recitals*

6. *Madison Square Garden, Thirty-third Street and Seventh Avenue, hosts large popular musical events*

7. *City Center, 131 W. Fifty-fifth Street, hosts dance events*

8. *Metropolitan Museum of Art, Eighty-second Street and Fifth Avenue, for music and instrument collection, chamber music concerts*

9. *Whitney Museum, Seventy-fifth Street and Madison Avenue, for symphonic music and chamber concerts*

10. *Central Park, Fifty-ninth Street and uptown, sites of summer concerts of symphonic and popular music*

11. *Symphony Space, Ninety-fifth Street and Broadway, for symphonic and popular music*

12. *92nd Street Y, Ninety-second Street and Lexington Avenue, for symphonic, chamber, folk, and popular music*

13. *Sundown, 227 E. Fifty-sixth Street, for folk*

14. *Café Carlyle, Seventy-sixth Street and Madison Avenue, jazz and popular music*

15. *Eddie Condon's, 144 W. Fifty-fourth Street, jazz and swing*

16. *Freddy's, 308 E. Forty-ninth Street, jazz*

17. *Jimmy Weston's, 131 E. Fifty-fourth Street, jazz and swing*

18. *Michael's Pub, 211 E. Fifty-fifth Street, jazz*

19. *Roseland, 239 W. Fifty-second Street, landmark spot for jazz, rock, and disco*

20. *Radio City Music Hall, Fiftieth Street and Sixth Avenue, popular music*

21. *Broadway Joe, 315 W. Forty-sixth Street, jazz and rock*

22. *St. Peter's Church, Fifty-fourth Street and Lexington Avenue, the Jazz Church*

23. *New Ballroom, 253 W. Twenty-eighth Street, jazz and swing*

24. *Peppermint Lounge, 128 W. Forty-fifth Street, landmark for rock and disco*

25. *Studio 54, 254 W. Fifty-fourth Street, rock and disco*

26. *Sybil's, 101 W. Fifty-third Street, rock and disco*

27. *New York, NY, 33 W. Fifty-second Street, rock and disco*

28. *Regine's, 502 Park Avenue, rock and disco*

113

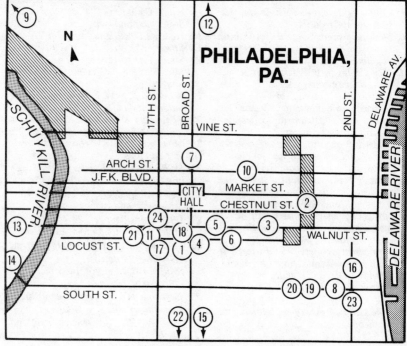

Philadelphia, PA

1. **Academy of Music,** Broad and Locust streets, home of Philadelphia Orchestra. Hosts Opera Company of Philadelphia
2. **Independence Mall,** site for American Music Festival in 1982
3. **Walnut Street Theater,** 825 Walnut Street, home of the Philadelphia Dance Company
4. **Shubert Theater,** 250 S. Broad Street, home of the Philadelphia Ballet
5. **Forrest Theater,** 1111 Walnut Street, place for musical events
6. **New Locust Theater,** 1411 Locust Street, place for musical events
7. **Pennsylvania Academy of Fine Arts,** Broad and Cherry streets, for concerts
8. **Theater of Living Arts,** 334 South Street
9. **Mann Music Center,** West Fairmount Park. Summer home of Philadelphia Orchestra, and site of numerous outdoor concerts
10. **Trocadero,** 1003 Arch Street. Opera House that hosts the Pennsylvania Opera Theater
11. **Curtis Institute,** 1726 Locust Street. Renowned music school
12. **Temple University Music Festival,** Broad Street and Montgomery Avenue, for music festivals and events
13. **University of Pennsylvania,** Thirty-fourth and Walnut streets. A variety of musical events
14. **Civic Center,** Thirty-fourth Street and Civic Center Boulevard, for folk festivals and musical events
15. **JFK Stadium,** City Hall, music festival and events
16. **Khyber Pass Pub,** 56 S. Second Street, jazz club
17. **Warwick Hotel,** Seventeenth and Locust streets, jazz and popular music
18. **Gabriel's Horn,** 1420 Locust Street, jazz and popular music
19. **Grendel's Lair,** 500 South Street, for rock
20. **Ripley's Music Hall,** 608 South Street, for rock
21. **Rittenhouse Square,** Eighteenth and Walnut streets, for rock concerts
22. **Spectrum Theater,** Broad and Pattison, for rock
23. **Stars,** Second and Bainbridge streets, rock
24. **Former home of Waller and Crawford,** publishers of broadsides at Seventeenth Street between Chestnut and Walnut

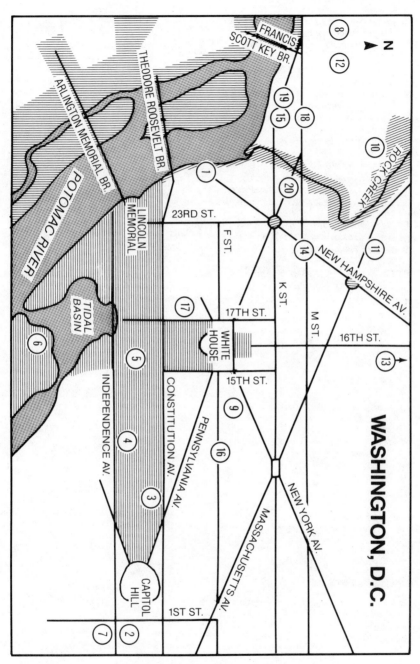

Washington, DC

1. John F. Kennedy Center for the Performing Arts, New Hampshire Avenue and F Street, home of National Symphony, and houses all kinds of music including symphonic, opera, ballet, folk, and popular

115

2. *Library of Congress, First Street and Independence Avenue SE. Concerts and chamber music, musical exhibits*
3. *National Gallery of Art, Constitution Avenue and Sixth Street NW. Concerts and chamber music*
4. *Smithsonian Institute, Jefferson Drive between Ninth and Twelfth streets. Music memorabilia and concerts of all kinds*
5. *Washington Monument Grounds. Folk concerts and popular music*
6. *Jefferson Memorial Grounds. Popular, patriotic, and varieties of concerts*
7. *Thomas Jefferson Building, First Street and Independence Avenue SE. Folk concerts*
8. *Georgetown University, Thirty-seventh and O streets NW, for concerts*
9. *Warner Theater, 513 Thirteenth Street NW. Folk concerts*
10. *Childe Harolde, 1610 Twenty-ninth Street NW, for Bluegrass*
11. *Phillips Collection, 1600 Twenty-first Street NW, for symphonic and chamber music concerts*
12. *The Cellar Door, 1201 Thirty-fourth Street, for popular music*
13. *Carter Barron Amphitheater, Sixteenth Street NW and Colorado Avenue in Rock Creek Park, for "pop" concerts.*
14. *Bojangles, 2100 M Street NW, nightspot for rock and disco*
15. *The Bayou, 3135 K Street NW, for rock*
16. *Nine-Thirty Club, 930 F Street, for rock and popular music*
17. *Constitution Hall, Eighteenth and D streets NW, varied musical events*
18. *Mrs. Smith's, 3104 M Street NW, for jazz*
19. *Charlie's Georgetown, 3223 K Street NW, all popular music*
20. *One Step Down, 2517 Pennsylvania Avenue, for jazz*

S·O·U·T·H

INTRODUCTION

Music of historical prominence in the South is generally thought of as twofold: (1) black ragtime/blues/jazz and (2) white hillbilly or country music. Today, all styles have overlapped to a certain extent and a bit of everything can frequently be heard in some of the current music.

Traditionally, New Orleans was the haven for black music after the Civil War. Blacks were heir to generational patterns of spontaneous, natural rhythm, straight-forward musical beat, and volatile emotional lives that supported gut feelings for blues and jazz. Colorful saloons, brothels, and gambling houses in the French Quarter (Vieux Carré) of Storyville were breeding grounds and forum for the development of American jazz in the late nineteenth and early twentieth centuries.

At the turn of the century, out of the mountain regions of the rural South came a genre of country music symbolic of the white inhabitants' impoverishment, isolation, and personal resignation. Mountaineers sang simple folk tunes and ballads filled with emotion. They sang in their kitchens, on back porches, at country fairs, and eventually, before large audiences in commercial places such as the historic Grand Ole Opry in Nashville, Tennessee. The simple heartfelt ballad underwent a transformation to become popular country music and a multimillion dollar industry.

FOLK AND COUNTRY MUSIC

Folk music in the Northeast, from the seventeenth century until the early twentieth century, was based largely upon the native music of three very different segments of the population: American Indians, Afro-Americans, and European immigrants.

Indians, the first Americans, were a tribal people who used song and dance in communal activities. Their music reflected their culture and mythology. Meters were simple (2/4 and 4/4 time) and the melodies consisted of simple chanting with no harmonization. The Iroquois Indian verse, shown below, is typical of American Indian music. This verse sung to the accompaniment of rattles and drums.

> *The deer is taking away the daylight*
> *After taking away the daylight*
> *   he named it darkness.*

Afro-Americans came to America from western Africa beginning in 1619. Although they and the great majority who followed lived their lives in slavery in the South, their musical influence was felt in all parts of the country. The blacks, like the Indians, were descended from a tribal people, who incorporated much singing and dancing into their daily life.

Their songs were especially rhythmic and intricately patterned, as seen in the response and refrain of the following primitive African song, "The Story of Tangalimlibo."

> *It is crying/ it is crying*
> *Siham/ba Ngenyan/go*
> *The child of the walker by moonlight*
> *Siham/ba Ngenyan/go*

Frequently, cries, hollers, hand-clapping, and the use of call and response were adapted from African songs to American songs which expressed the slaves' experiences in cotton picking, corn shucking, stevedoring, and working on the railroad. The music of the black slaves told the story of their lives and expressed their feelings of oppression, dreariness, resignation, and hope.

> call—*March on, Lawd, and you will gain the victory*
> response—*March on, Lawd, and you will gain the victory*
> call—*March on my brother and you gwine gain the day*
> response—*March on my brother and you gwine gain the day.*

The narrative song, "John Henry," first sung in the 1870s, when slavery had ended, reflected the personal experience, as would the developing American folk song.

> *John Henry hammered in the mountain . . .*
> *He worked so hard, it broke his poor heart . . .*
> *And he laid down his hammer and he died.*

The European Immigrants

Country music reflected essentially the backwoods life in the poor, white, rural South. This music, which seems so American, had immigrant origins. More than three centuries ago, hordes of settlers from England, Scotland, and Ireland began arriving in the southern part of North America. Some crossed the Appalachian Mountains in 1775. They brought with them folk songs and ballads handed down through generations.

Country music developed in the mountain regions of Virginia, North and South Carolina, Georgia, Alabama, Mississippi, Arkansas, Tennessee, Kentucky, and West Virginia. The songs that came out of this area were full of simplicity, sincerity, reality, and deep feeling. Prolonged poverty and isolation heavily influenced mountain folk music as they were etched unforgettably on the face of Appalachia.

Ballads as Folk Music

In the eighteenth and nineteenth centuries the poor mountaineers in Appalachia relieved the toil and monotony of everyday life by clinging to the old ballads that they knew from the British Isles. Singing was a major outlet and source of recreation, as men and women gratefully anticipated some relaxation with music after a hard day's chores. Ballads spoke of love, friendship, nature, and religion. They were simple and narrative, filled with human emotion.

The ballad was usually sung in a high register, producing a shrill, nasal sound. Sung to the accompaniment of a violin, called fiddle, the song repeated phrases and lines for emphasis and feeling:

120

> *Georgie Collins drove home one cold winter night,*
> *Georgie Collins drove home so fine;*
> *Georgie Collins drove home one cold winter night,*
> *Was taken sick and died.*

New local surroundings and events changed names and words in English ballads, as illustrated in "The Cuckoo."
Original English version:

> *The cuckoo is a pretty bird*
> *She warbles as she flies,*
> *She brings us glad tidings*
> *And tells us no lies.*

American version:

> *The cuckoo is a pretty bird*
> *She wobbles as she flies,*
> *And she never sings "cuckoo"*
> *Till the fourth day of July.*

First-hand emotional experience was expressed in the music of the mountain people, as they made the conventional narrative ballad into a more personal statement. The following nineteenth-century ballad expresses the direction of the evolving American folk song, reflected in these two stanzas:

> *I wish to Lord I'd never been born,*
> *Or died when I was young,*
> *I never would have seen your sparkling blue eyes*
> *Or heard your lying tongue.*
>
> *All the good times are past and gone*
> *All the good times are o'er,*
> *All the good times are past and gone*
> *Little darlin', don't you weep no more.*

Unhappiness and despair in the human condition are exemplified in "Man of Constant Sorrows," an Appalachian song of loneliness:

> *I am a man of constant sorrow,*
> *I have seen trouble all my days;*
> *I bade farewell to old Kentucky,*
> *The place where I was born and raised.*
> *For six long years I've been in trouble,*
> *My pleasure here on earth is done;*
> *For in this world I have to ramble,*
> *I have no friends to help me now.*

By the middle of the nineteenth century, the American home-grown folk song, interlaced with poverty, loneliness, unrequited love, and resignation, was the music of the white rural southerner. Generations of folks learned these songs from mama, in the kitchen, and from papa, at night. "Pretty Polly," "Powder River," "Come All You Fair and Tender Maidens" are just a few examples.

Hillbilly Music as a Forerunner of Country Music

In contrast to settlers in more densely populated regions, Appalachians were cut off from outside influences. Clashes developed between neighboring clans, often followed by feuding and fighting. Because of their insular mountain dwellings, they came to be known as "Hillbillies" in the early twentieth century. That name also identified their folk music. "Hillbilly" evokes an image of a poor white, uneducated, conservative, religious worker in the fields; whiskey-drinking, proud, with a fierce temper, who carries a gun for sport and safety. In an uncomplimentary fashion, Southern hillbillies commonly were called "Arkies," "crackers," "rednecks," "hicks," and "trash."

Hillbilly music denotes the beginning of what we call "country music" today. Lyrics then, as now, were realistic and emotional, communicating the values of the people who lived here: family, kinship, good-will, religion. Some favorites were "Cumberland Gap," "The Little Old Log Cabin in the Lane," and "Old Zip Coon" ("Turkey in the Straw"). All were simple, unsophisticated tunes, in some cases hymnlike, with straight-forward melodies, basic harmonies of only three or four chords, and simple meters, like 2/4 and 4/4 time.

The voice, distinctive in hillbilly music, was deliberately nasal, twangy, and whiny, scratching out pure corn with a rural inflection that came straight from the gut as in "Pretty Polly."

> *Polly, pretty Polly, come go along with me,*
> *Before we get married some pleasures to see.*

People picked up tunes easily and learned music by ear. There was music notation but it took the form of "shape notes" (notation in which the shape of the note, rather than its position on the written staff, determined its pitch). But regardless of whether they could read music, or even read at all, people in the hills sang or made music.

Hillbilly Concerts and Fiddling

As traditional folk music, hillbilly music never purported to make money. People played and sang on front porches, while looking out at the chickens; they congregated at special social events for musical entertainment. There were barnraisings, quilting parties, log-rolling, molasses-making days, and fiddlers' conventions all over Appalachia, family affairs that celebrated a heritage. Music was made in open spaces, often to a background of children crying. Some of the instruments were homemade: a banjo with a wooden neck attached to a hollow gourd, a fife made of a whittled reed; a possum skin stretched over a log for a drum; other instruments were dulcimers, autoharps, and fiddles.

Lifestyle in the backwoods was reflected in the backstep dance with arms akimbo, head thrown back, both heels moving in staccato rhythm, and foot stomping. Pa fiddled, ma sang, and youngsters clapped hands till they collapsed.

Well-attended "medicine shows" in the late nineteenth and early twentieth centuries provided continuous exposure for mountain music; the "doctor" sold products of corn salve, tonic water, soap, and candy, as marvelous cures for disease, while fiddlers contributed to the ambience.

Fiddling, an element in hillbilly music which carried a peculiar southern flavor, was popular in many regions of the nation. Tunes fiddled were also picked, sung, and danced to; they were reminiscent of the early English, Irish, and Scottish tunes brought to the New World and passed on through generations. Very little music was written down; the melody was simple with no embellishments (not even grace notes), no amplification, and no drum accompaniment.

Representative of an old-time fiddler's convention is one in the small town of Galax, Virginia, sixty miles southwest of Roanoke, near the North Carolina border. The center of activity is in Felts Park, where musicians and dancers rehearse in the parking lot before going on stage to compete for prizes.

Felts Park has a covered grandstand, with seating for five-thousand and for thousands more outside on blankets. In 1978 there were over one-thousand contestants and over twenty-five-hundred visitors.

Rhythm, timing, authenticity, and expression will win prizes for contestants who have had no formal training and are over fifty, but who are able to preserve the quality of old-time music. Local color adds to the fun of the music where old-timers exchange stories, friendships are renewed, and reunions are established.

There is a lot of spontaneous music-making at fiddler's conventions. A fiddler will begin to play an ancient fiddle tune, such as "The Eighth of January," which tells of Andrew Jackson's victory at the battle of New Orleans. He will be joined by a guitarist accompanying the melody. A bass player will add his beat. If a banjo player wanders by, he will listen for the key and join in. Soon, he will take the melody lead. Crowds gather and it goes on and on.

Radio

With the advent of radio in the 1920s, large new audiences opened up for hillbilly music. Station WSB in Atlanta, Georgia, was the first radio station to play hillbilly music in 1922. "It Ain't Gonna Rain No Mo' " and "Arkansas Traveler" were among the many songs broadcast. More than ninety radio stations sprang up all over the South and broke through rural isolation. Recorded mountain music became a craze. Sales of radios totaled in the millions of dollars, although early performers were rarely paid for their music-making. The radio has played a vital role in expanding the popularity of mountain and country music and still does. Some of the many radio stations which broadcast mountain music were: WSM in Nashville, Tennessee, with Grand Ole Opry; WWVA Jamboree Sessions in Wheeling, West Virginia, playing the music of Grandpa Jones, Doc Williams, Cousin Emmy and her Kinfolks, and the Osborne Brothers; WRVA in Richmond, Virginia, featuring Red Battle, Mac Wiseman, and Quincy Snodgrass; WNOX in Knoxville, Tennessee; KTHS in Little Rock, Arkansas, where Hank Williams was its first star; and KWTO in Springfield, Missouri.

Music for Money

The "cracker" who attained popularity and initiated the trend toward recording music was fiddlin' John Carson of Atlanta in 1923. He fiddled "Old Hen Cackled" for Okeh Records and the record sold five-hundred copies in two weeks, an astounding number for that day. Carson has been remembered as "a crude, common man who drank rough whiskey and fiddled all night." His career marked the beginning of hillbilly music's commercial era. Other early recording groups were the "North Carolina Tar Heels," the "Piedmont Log Rollers," the "Hoss-Hair Pullers," complete with nasal twang, fiddles, and banjos playing "Down on the Farm," "The World is Not My Home," and "Can the Circle Be Unbroken." Performers increasingly wrote the music they performed.

Then, inevitably, commercialism continued to develop in the late 1920s and offered recompense to the mountaineers for singing and playing music that had become as natural to them as breathing. Ralph Peer, a talent scout who had formerly been with Okeh Records and was at that time with Victor, came to Bristol on the Tennessee/Virginia border in 1927 to see what he could discover in "them thar hills." He advertised in the local newspaper for musicians and among those responding were a young man, Jimmie Rodgers, and a family of three, the Carter family (A. P. Carter, his wife, Sara, and sister-in-law, Maybelle Carter). All four were destined for stardom. Rodgers, born in Meridian, Mississippi in 1897, was living in the mountains of Asheville, North Carolina, when he traveled to Bristol to audition for Peer. He sang "Peach Pickin' Time in Georgia."

The original Carter Family, from Maces Spring, Virginia, had A. P. singing bass, Sara singing lead and playing autoharp, and Maybelle singing tenor and playing guitar. Maybelle, who became the queen of country music, was the mother of Helen, Anita, and June (who married Johnny Cash). Classic hit songs of the Carters were "Wildwood Flower," "Keep on the Sunny Side," "Little Darlin' Pal of Mine," and "Little Moses."

Early in their careers the Carter Family performed mostly at barn dances, in schoolhouses, church socials, and community centers throughout North and South Carolina, Virginia, West Virginia, Kentucky, and Alabama. Their stages were most often made of wooden planks and lit by kerosene lamps to counter the effects of the ubiquitous mountain fog.

In the early forties mother Maybelle and daughters performed on radio stations WRNL and WRVA in Richmond, Virginia; on WNOX in Knoxville, Tennessee; and on KWTO in Springfield, Missouri. They later joined the Grand Ole Opry.

Son-in-law Johnny Cash recorded for Columbia records and toured extensively throughout Tennessee, Arkansas, and Louisiana.

A. P. Carter's original country store has been converted into a memorial music center and museum in a wooden shed with a stage and a thousand seats. Old-time country music shows take place on Saturday nights. In August there is usually a two-day Carter Festival with all the country trimmings.

Origins of The Grand Ole Opry in the Twenties

Shortly before Peer discovered Jimmie Rodgers and the Carter Family, several other events took place in Nashville, Tennessee, which would greatly change and expand the world of mountain music. The events involved a radio station in Nashville, WSM. Station WSM was owned by the National Life and Accident Insurance Company, whose slogan, **We S**hield **M**illions, gave the station its call letters.

In 1925, Uncle Jimmy Thompson, an eighty-year-old fiddler from the Tennessee mountains, came down to WSM to play some tunes for the WSM "Barn Dance," a program directed by George D. Hay (known as the "Solemn Old Judge"). Thompson fiddled for hours, and was such a big success with the listening audience that Hay featured Uncle Jimmy playing his fiddle for the next few weekly shows. Soon other musicians came to perform on the program. In 1927 the WSM "Barn Dance" became known as the "Grand Ole Opry," named by Hay. The show featured many performers including Jimmie Rodgers, Maybelle Carter, Roy Acuff doing "Great Speckled Bird," and Ernest Tubb, who appeared at Carnegie Hall in New York in the 1970s.

The "Tennessee Barn Dance" was also being broadcast from Knoxville's Station WNOX at this time, and many future country stars who came to Nashville began their careers at WNOX.

Because of its overwhelming popularity, the Nashville Grand Ole Opry needed larger quarters. The show moved first to the War Memorial Auditorium and then, in 1941, to the Ryman Auditorium. Originally the Union Gospel Tabernacle on the corner of Broadway and Opry Place, the Ryman was the home of Grand Ole Opry until 1974, at which time even this theater was no longer able to accommodate the thousands of people who waited outside its doors.

Uncle Dave Macon did "Bully of the Town," Grandpa Jones beat out "Here, Rattler, Here" on his banjo, Porter Wagoner sang "If Jesus Came to Your House," Hank Williams, an example of the hungry, tortured hillbilly singer, sang "Lovesick Blues," Jimmie Dickens wailed "Sleeping at the Foot of the Bed," Jim Reeves bemoaned "Four Walls," the Stoney Mountain Cloggers square danced to "Arkansas Traveler," Red Foley interpreted "Precious Memories," and Minnie Pearl was introduced and became a grand lady of country music. Charlie Pride made it here too, virtually the only black singer in this area of music.

Shortly after the Ryman opened its doors, the Rose-Acuff Music Publishing Company was founded, followed by the influx of large recording companies seizing the opportunity to make it big. They recorded talented fiddlers, singers, banjo players, dancers, and comedians. Publishing houses, music stores, and talent agencies sprang up in and around Nashville to be near the Ryman. Many of these firms are located along several blocks of Sixteenth Avenue South on Music Row and are still in business today. One of the most historic buildings along Music Row is Studio B, which once housed the entire Nashville operation. Chet Atkins and Hank Snow recorded big hits here. Recording artists still use the studio, but it's now open to the public. On a tour, you can examine its multi-track recording equipment.

Ryman Auditorium, former home of the Grand Ole Opry from 1943 to 1974. (Courtesy Tennessee Tourist Development, Nashville)

The "Nashville Sound"

Nashville turned quickly into "Hillbilly Haven," the home of hillbilly music (it was not called country music until well after World War II) and the "Nashville Sound" was born. The term is attributed to Chet Atkins in the early 1960s. Atkins, a guitarist from Luttrell, Tennessee, just north of Nashville, learned to play fiddle and guitar from his father, a classical musician and singer, and from his grandfather, who played and built fiddles.

The Nashville Sound refers to a more slick and sophisticated style of playing country music that developed in the sixties. It has been described as loose, relaxed, easygoing, jazzy, and subtle. The vocal sound

127

was less twangy and there was the addition of the background chorus (often made up of trained singers). The instrumentation, too, was more sophisticated. The country bands now used bass, drums, piano, guitars (including electric guitars), and only sometimes a fiddle. Floyd Cramer, Boots Randolph, and Jerry Reed were especially notable for commercially capitalizing on these techniques.

Country went from Opry, to the road, to clubs, to studio recordings that sold in the millions. Glen Campbell came from Arkansas to Nashville to record "Wichita Lineman," "By the Time I Get to Phoenix," and "Gentle on My Mind." Bob Dylan was cutting the Nashville Sound with drums and electric guitar in "Nashville Skyline" and the bands of Woody Herman and Ray Anthony came to Nashville to play the Ryman, decked out with full electronic technology. Professional song writers, rather than singers themselves, wrote "Help Me Make It through the Night," and "Behind Closed Doors." Rock and roll was stiff competition for country at this time, and the Nashville Sound with its innovations helped sustain country through its lean years.

The Grand Ole Opry and The Country Music Hall of Fame Today

The home of the Grand Ole Opry since 1974, is in Opryland, 2800 Opryland Drive. This fifteen-million-dollar building is part of the 110-acre, twenty-eight-million-dollar amusement park complex. It is located just off Briley Parkway, four miles from downtown Nashville. Its heavy wooden slot doors with large metal straps and bolts are an imposing sight, as are its twenty-one-foot wood-beamed ceilings and forty-four-hundred cushioned church pew-type seats. Dolly Parton opened early festivities with "Sacred Memories" and Hank Snow sang "I Don't Hurt Anymore."

In addition to presenting two shows every Saturday night, a Saturday matinee in summer, and a show on Friday night from February till November, the Grand Ole Opry is the largest broadcast studio in the world, heard throughout the United States and Canada. Today, in the early eighties, the styles of music at the Opry include rock, pop, blues, and jazz as well as country. Two performances of the Opry have been given at the White House and have been televised. Tours are generally available at all times, but you must purchase tickets to a performance well in advance to avoid disappointment. Order them long before you expect to arrive in Nashville.

Interior of the Grand Ole Opry House from which live performances are broadcast over WSM radio. (Courtesy Tennessee Tourist Development, Nashville)

The Country Music Hall of Fame and Museum, in downtown Nashville on Music Row, was created to hold memorabilia of stars and to elect them to membership. There are seventeen-thousand square feet of floor space in the Hall of Fame and Museum. That space houses two movie theaters showing rare film and television clips, many exhibits of early home-made mountain musical instruments, such as the fretless banjo, made from hog skin and white oak wood, original manuscripts of hit songs written on old grocery lists, Minnie Pearl's straw hat with flowers and the price tag, Kenny Rogers' outfit for the TV movie, *The Gambler*, and Chet Atkins' first guitar. Here too is Elvis Presley's gold Cadillac with its gold-plated telephone, gold-plated record-player, and gold television set sitting under the car ceiling, which is lined with gold records.

In another of the Museum's rooms, there is a colorful wall chart outlining the roots of country music from English ballads, and other regional influences of blues, jazz, and pop music. The Artists' Gallery is a large room holding recordings and large color photos of country stars. Recordings of Jimmie Rodgers, Kitty Wells, Waylon Jennings, Merle Haggard, and Donna Fargo are but a few. A simulated recording session is even offered to visitors to show you how it's done. There are numerous tours and many opportunities available for viewing the history and development of country music.

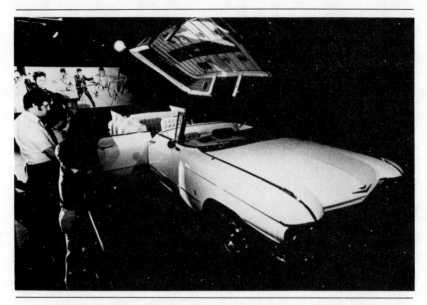

Elvis Presley's 1960 Cadillac now on view at the Country Music Hall of Fame. A 24-karat gold-plated television set, gold refreshment bar with gold trays, and an engraved gold phone are some of its special features. (Courtesy Tennessee Tourist Development, Nashville)

Bluegrass

A segment of country music that retained the flavor of the traditional Appalachian heritage and resisted newer electronic techniques was bluegrass. In bluegrass music the emphasis was on pure entertainment rather than baring the soul with raw emotion. Individual virtuosity and showmanship were its style, as exemplified with Bill Monroe on the mandolin and the Blue Grass Boys beginning in 1938. William "Bill" Monroe from Rosine, Kentucky, described bluegrass as "a combination of church music, jazz, and mountain fiddling. There is much stomping of the feet and wild exhortation in bluegrass. When you've heard it, you'll know it." A more formal definition of bluegrass might be: polyphonic vocal and instrumental music played on unamplified instruments brought from the British Isles to Appalachia—five string banjo, guitar, fiddle, mandolin, and bass fiddle. It operates in much the same way as chamber music does in that it places the emphasis on skillful ensemble work. Bluegrass also has an element in common with jazz, a quick response of improvisation (to the hot licks of fiddle and banjo).

Another bluegrass devoté is Grandpa Jones who performs on the banjo with the "drop thumb" method, whereby the thumb drops from the first and second strings down to the fifth string. Even today he claws and flails his banjo, jumps into the air, stomps on the floor, yelps and yodels, and tells cornpone jokes. He usually opens with "Mountain Dew" and closes with "Are You from Dixie?" Earl Scruggs demonstrated that the banjo could lead in addition to playing background music with his "three-finger roll" of picking on a five-string banjo. Lester Flatt usually sang the lead. After leaving the Blue Grass Boys, Flatt and Scruggs formed their own group, The Foggy Mountain Boys, which included Mac Wiseman on the guitar. Of the favorite bluegrass songs, "Blue Moon of Kentucky" and "Salty Dog" have always been popular. Any number of towns in the eastern Tennessee mountains has a group playing bluegrass at almost any time. One can go to a backyard barbecue in Chattanooga, for example, and hear musicians from three states who will stay and play for several days.

There are many delightful bluegrass festivals today all over the South. One, in particular, is held in Elizabethton, Tennessee, in late June. Another, Slagle's Bluegrass Festival, features music in a pasture, complete with animals, creating the feeling of yesteryear. It's usually a three-day celebration for the entire family.

Country Music Changes

Country music in Appalachia underwent changes that represented social and political issues after the mid-twentieth-century wars. Shifts in population, great mixings of people, civil rights, restlessness, changing sexual mores and values, all affected the "pure" and simple style of country music. Westward migration, the black people's blues, jazz, rock and pop mixed with and changed country music. Singers no longer came from isolated areas, but moved down from the hills and participated in big business. They could even read music, written mostly in numbered chord progressions. A new breed came forth as exemplified by Roger Miller's "King of the Road," "Sixteen Tons" by Ernie Ford, "I'm Just a Coal Miner's Daughter" by Loretta Lynn, Bobby Bare's "Detroit City," and Ted Daffan's "Born to Lose."

Johnny Cash, from Arkansas, fused music styles (country, folk, and pop) and sang of his term spent in "Folsom Prison." "Little Green Apples" and "Honey" of Bobby Goldsboro carried us into the seventies along with Bobbie Gentry's "Ode to Billy Joe" and Jeanne C. Riley's "Harper Valley PTA," a gut story about small town hanky panky that sold over five-million copies.

As a result of these changes, country music is no longer strictly country, but a hybrid of several styles. One can hear the differences by listening to modern performers side by side with the old-timers who are still giving their all at the Grand Ole Opry as well as throughout the nation for audiences that number in the millions. Some of today's country singers are Willie Nelson, Dolly Parton, John Denver, Lynn Anderson, Tammy Wynette, Ricky Scaggs, and Barbara Mandrell. These performers demonstrate that country music today is big-time business, a far cry from its beginnings when it was simply a personal pastime that one engaged in for emotional release.

Folk, Country, and Bluegrass Today

Country music is alive and well. One can see musical landmarks and hear splendid performances of folk, country, and bluegrass music throughout the South. The following is a partial listing.

ALABAMA

Athens

In the Cumberland Foothills, the first week in October brings the ever popular Tennessee Valley Old-Time Fiddler's Convention to Athens State College on Beaty and Pryor Streets. The gym holds four-thousand seats from which fiddling and banjo-picking jam sessions can be heard and enjoyed. Earlier, in April, Athens boasts a musical explosion throughout the city with traditional mountain music predominating.

Birmingham

Exciting events occur at the Birmingham/Jefferson Civic Center, located between Ninth and Eleventh Avenues North and Nineteenth and Twenty-first Streets. The Complex extends the length of four square blocks. Among the varied musical programs in the April Birmingham Festival of the Arts is folk music of a different country each year. Belgium, France, Spain, and Germany have already enjoyed their day. Some enjoyable night spots that feature country music are the Cone Break at 2936 Fourth Avenue, the Bachelor's Showboat, and the Cobblestone on Morris Avenue.

Homewood

Several miles east of Birmingham in nearby Homewood is the Wrangler's Club, 113 South Jackson, a country music haven. Close by, the Lowenbrau Haus features bluegrass music.

Fort Payne

In July finds there is the Mentone Festival with traditional mountain music in City Park on Lookout Mountain, on Route 117 E.

Montgomery

South of Fort Payne is Montgomery where Hank Williams Sr. "picked" his guitar and made it big with "Lovesick Blues." He died en route to a performance on New Year's Day in 1953; his memorial is at Oakwood Annex Cemetery, 1305 Upper Wetumpka Road. A great singer, musician, and songwriter, Williams delivered an earthy style of country music. He played with numerous local bands, and was completely self-taught.

ARKANSAS

Arkadelphia

A traditional old-time Fiddler's Contest takes place in September.

Eureka Springs

This tiny Victorian town, nestled in the beautiful Ozark region, hosts a Mid-American Banjo Rally in September for banjo pickers from many states. In early November there is the Ozark Folk Festival, where serious amateur musicians play American folk tunes. There is jigging and clogging to fiddles and banjos, and even harmonicas. For the sheer fun of it, join in. This is the oldest resort city in the Ozarks and people there are always glad to welcome visitors.

Fordyce

Redbug Football Field is where country stars perform. Recently, Johnny Cash and June Carter Cash entertained local citizens and music-loving travelers here.

Harrison

Harrison is the home of the northwestern Arkansas Bluegrass Festival. If you're in these parts in August, a merrier event is hard to find. Go from there to North Arkansas Community College. The Pioneer Pavilion presents country music concerts frequently.

Little Rock

Little Rock, in central Arkansas, is proud of its jumping nightspot, Kountry Klub, at 5512 Patterson Avenue, which attracts such stars as Johnny Paycheck and "Festus" of "Gunsmoke."

Mountain View

Mountain View is southeast of Eureka Springs on US 62 and Highway 14, a paradise for folk and country music at the Ozark Folk Center. Snuggled in the Ozark foothills with blue mountains rising in all directions, clear streams, limestone bluffs dropping into deep valleys, and wildlife and forest lands abounding, it provides a spectacular setting for listening to music.

FLORIDA

Although rock and disco are predominantly popular in the Florida hotels and nightspots, there are some selective places that play folk and country music.

Clearwater

Woody Riley's Warehouse at North Garden Avenue and Drew offers country sessions occasionally. Not an elegant place—old jeans and tee shirts are common attire—but the music is good quality. Don Dee's and Joyland Country Nightclub, slightly more elegant places downtown, provide an evening's entertainment.

Dade City

The Pasco County Fair represents the musical activity in February over at the Fairgrounds, one mile west on FL-52. Among other styles, country and bluegrass hold their own. Following this event in the spring is the Heart of Florida Folk Festival to remind you that country is still highly appealing in spite of stylistic competition.

Fort Lauderdale

The best place to find country, unlike its name, is Beethoven's, in the Pier 66 Hotel and Marina, 2301 SE Seventeenth Street Causeway. Beethoven's is truly an engaging beach spot, clean and attractive, with several decorative glass enclosures.

Key West

Frequented by Ernest Hemingway in past decades is Captain Tony's Saloon, and Sloppy Joe's on Duval and Greene Streets. Papa Hemingway heard country and bluegrass played here, as you can today. Some of it in style tends to be lowdown.

Kissimmee

Known as the gateway to Walt Disney World, it offers an authentic Bluegrass Festival in March. If you're traveling from up North, the ideal weather will increase your musical enjoyment.

Miami and Miami Beach

Discos mostly are prevalent in the Gold Coast hotels, but you'll catch some country at Howard Johnson's Golden Glades, 16500 NW Second Avenue in north Miami and at Omni International, Biscayne Bay and Sixteenth Street. At Bayfront Park, from NE Fifth to SE Second, between Biscayne Bay and Biscayne Boulevard, an International Folk Festival surfaces in late May with ethnic costumes accompanying folk music of many countries. Miami Beach, America's international playground, houses many splashy nightclubs in hotels: the Deauville, 6701 Collins Avenue; the Sans Souci, 3101 Collins Avenue, and the Sheraton Bal Harbour, 9701 Collins. These are dressy places, and even though the country music is informal, the audience is not.

Orlando

A block long entertainment complex at Church Street Station, 129 Church, displays themes of earlier days, translated into folk and bluegrass especially at Apple Annie's Courtyard. The Courtyard is charming, built around a colorful Victorian garden in a country setting.

Pensacola

Saville Square, between Government and Main Streets, is best known for its boisterous nightclub, Rosie O'Grady. If you're feeling tired, save it for another night.

Sarasota

A fairyland sight beholds the visitor at the 68-acre estate of John Ringling of circus fame, 3 miles north on US-41. A most appealing event awaits you in March: a medieval fair, bedecked with madrigal singers and dancers, who recreate original folk songs from the British Isles.

St. Petersburg

Not too unlikely a place is Clancy's Irish Pub, downtown, for rowdy country and bluegrass. And the Bayfront Center prepares for the St. Petersburg International Folk Festival in fall. Several miles west of St. Petersburg, the Mid-Florida Fiddler's and Bluegrass Jamboree frolics in the spring.

Tallahassee

As we move on, Tallahassee is situated in the rolling hills and vast oak forests of the Florida Panhandle. The Zellwood Sweet Corn Festival, as its name suggests, is busy with bluegrass in the spring. More bluegrass is available, rather tastefully too, at the Ramada Inn West, 2121 West Tennessee Street.

Tampa

Along the riverfront at 600 Ashley Drive is Curtis Hixon Convention Hall, host to a variety of musical events including country. A swinging nightclub in the area is the Hall of Fame Inn, 2222 North Westshore Boulevard. July is steamy, and you can cool off at the Tampa Bay Bluegrass Festival, twelve miles southeast of the city in Riverview. Any remaining energy can be spent at Old Orleans, 2055 North Dale Mabry, on its large dance floor to the strains of country.

West Palm Beach

In January and February, the Fairgrounds at 9067 Southern Boulevard goes all out in a jamboree of country and bluegrass.

White Springs

A Fiddler's and Bluegrass Festival and Florida Folk Festival are presented at the 250-acre Stephen Foster Center, showing off fancy guitar picking, fiddling, and dulcimers. It's clearly a grass roots attempt to preserve the prolific past.

GEORGIA

Atlanta

A pleasant place for leisure is the Café Erewhon, 60 Fifth Street NW. This softly-lit club offers folk music regularly with an extra touch of gentility. On weekends, try the Admiral Benbow Inn in two locations:

1419 Virginia Avenue, and 1470 Spring Street NW. Both are recommended for country and bluegrass. In downtown Atlanta, some hour will find you at the Peachtree Center and Omni Complex, catching a glimpse of literally dozens of clubs and lounges. Country's here! Folk is around also in the Underground Atlanta Complex on Central Avenue and Martin Luther King Drive. The cobblestone streets are original and the storefronts date back to 1890. In mid-May, Atlanta presents an Arts Festival in Piedmont Park, featuring a potpourri of blues, jazz, and country. Don't forget that Station WSB in Atlanta was the first to play mountain music back in 1922.

Cumming

Cumming has picturesque Lanierland County Music Park, about two miles from the city, off GA-306, hosting music every other weekend.

Helen

Helen offers an authentic clogging event in May, identical to the clogging on the Grand Ole Opry stage.

Hiawasseee

For a touch of old-flavor folk, drop in at the Georgia Mountain Fair at the Towns Recreation Park during August. You can refresh with southern "ahce tea" as you watch and hear replicas of Appalachian mountain life with hominy-and soap-making, quilting parties, and likely hear strains of "Old Zip Coon" complete with hillbilly twang. In May and October, there are Bluegrass Festivals at the Mountain Fair Music Hall.

Three special happenings occur in spring in:

Crawfordville; Stephens State Park produces the Folklore Festival. Gainsville presents the Georgia Mountains Jubilee. Howard has the Great Crackerland Country Fair, epitomizing the hillbilly era.

Macon

Macon goes country in April and late September with Georgia Music Week, a gala celebration.

Marietta

Bobby Bare has been among the performers at the Buckboard Country Music Showcase, 2080 Cobb Parkway.

Newnan

Newnan is just below Atlanta; it is the site of the Powers Plantation, ten miles west on GA-34. What is more authentic than country music on a southern plantation? And here it is in September—the Powers Crossroads Country Fair and Art Festival. You might need to look at your digital watch to see what year it is, the flavor is so reminiscent of a bygone era.

Perry

Perry is in the center of the state with a Farm-City Festival and emphasis on square dancing in October. For year-round country, visit the Holiday Inn on US 341 at I-75.

Savannah

Savannah is the traveler's delight. Famous for its "Night in Savannah," international folk dances whirl in Johnson Square in April. Earlier, in February, Georgia Week is filled with country music, followed by the world-famous Scottish Games in May at Old Fort Jackson, 1½ miles east on President Street. The pipe drumming and square dancing are ancestral throwbacks. Two local hotels are excellent country spots: the relaxed De Soto Hilton at Liberty and Bull Streets, and the hospitable Master Hosts Inn, Abercorn Expressway and I-95.

KENTUCKY

Barbourville

Traveling into historic Daniel Boone country in the valley of the Cumberland River, you'll encounter a Daniel Boone Festival of old-time fiddling, square dancing, and for effect, a rifle shoot between simulated neighboring states. This in October.

Berea

Appalachian mountain music and dancing define the merry Mountain Folk Festival in April.

Renfro Valley

Renfro Valley is 4 miles to the north of Berea; here barn dances have gone on since 1939. Two large imposing barns stand: one for country and bluegrass; the other for new country combining electronics and rock and roll. Mac Wiseman is around in July and in August, there's also a gospel sing. The McLain Family Band from Berea are top performers who host a celebration in August at their Big Hill Farm residence outside Berea. They also travel widely. Berea College on US-25 is the home of the Indian Fort Theater, open in May and October for folk musicals.

Elizabethtown

Elizabethtown, northwest of Corbin, offers an old-time Fiddler's Contest and Convention each May.

Harlan

Harlan, deep in Appalachian coal country, is noted for the Poke Sallet Celebration in June, and Kingdom Come Swappin' Meeting at Southeast Community College in October.

Henderson

Henderson produces a Big River Arts Festival and County Fair in October and July respectively.

Hodgenville

Hodgenville is the site of Robert Hodgen's Mill, and of the historic Lincoln Jamboree, two miles south on US-31E. Folk and country music surround the area all year at the place where Abe Lincoln came to grind corn from his home several miles away.

Lexington

In June and July, a lively Bluegrass State Fair at Masterson Station Park takes place two miles northwest on US-421. For bluegrass fans, this is the place. Also, the Rupp Arena in the Lexington Center is the setting for regular bluegrass concerts. John Hartford, Doc and Merle Watson, and the Dillards are among those who perform here. A fancier place is the Breeding Nightclub, 1505 New Circle Road. Watch for J. D. Crowe's Band, The New South.

Louisville

The Executive West, Freedom Way at the Fairgrounds, a half mile west of I-65, has great bluegrass, as does the Lords of London at the Marriott Inn, 505 Marriott Drive in Clarksville. The Kentucky Derby in spring at Churchill Downs, 700 Central Avenue, is usually accompanied heavily by country, bluegrass, and square dancing. The famous Bluegrass Music Festival of the U.S. is held at Riverfront Plaza in June and September, and has had on its slate almost every country artist in the business.

Madisonville

This picturesque area of hills and rivers presents a Gospel Music Fest in early September. It's a serious and interesting event.

Morehead

An enjoyable occasion is in June, when the Appalachian Celebration features early folk.

Pikesville

At the eastern tip of Kentucky, where the legendary Hatfields and Mc-Coys feuded, visit the appropriate Hillbilly Days Spring Festival, heavy on authentic mountain music and stomping.

Pippa Passes

Pippa Passes holds another Appalachian Festival in September with ballads and folk music that go back as far as Chaucer's England.

Prestonburg

Here is the Kentucky Highlands Folk Festival at Jenny Wiley State Resort Park in fall, about 3½ miles east on US-23.

Other events hither and yon in the state are: a Big Singing Day in Benton in May focusing on ancient songs; an American Folksong Festival at Grayson, about forty miles from Ashland in June; a high-spirited Summer Festival in Paducah, in the home of the Duke of Paducah, country singer Whitey Ford; and Carson Park, 301 Clifton Drive is lively in June, boasting the Kiwanis West Kentucky-McCracken County Fair, featuring gospel singing. Top it off with the ever-popular Kentucky State Fair in August, which is held simultaneously in many places in the bluegrass state.

LOUISIANA

New Orleans

In this relaxed atmosphere, find Jed's at 8301 Oak for both traditional country and newer electronic country. Also, Jimmy's, 8200 Willow, can be recommended. The major center for entertainment is of course the French Quarter or Vieux Carré, mostly lower Bourbon Street. Jazz prevails here, but occasionally a strain of country escapes to identify Louisiana as a southern community. You'll have to watch for listings, though.

Shreveport

Tune in Station KWKH for broadcasts of the Louisiana Hayride, as it used to be, with hillbilly tunes, and for more recent electronic country.

MISSISSIPPI

Bluegrass is a favorite in Mississippi and among some of the well-known events are these:

Jackson

Top names appear at the Mississippi State Fair in October.

Vicksburg

Hear a charming concert of folk and bluegrass on the Court House Lawn in April, attended by many local officials.

Kosciusko

Kosciusko features the Natchez Trace Festival in April.

Meridian

Meridian is the home of Jimmie Rodgers, and they don't forget it. Highland Park houses the Jimmie Rodgers Museum with memorabilia of the "father of country music" including his guitars and sheet music. A Memorial Festival in his honor pervades the entire city in May.

Natchez

A significant event in October is the Great River Roads Fair with dulcimer playing. A memorable experience is the Mississippi Medicine Show performed at the Natchez Little Theater Playhouse, Linton Avenue and Maple Street. Mountain life ambience is recreated by "doctors," quilters, and fiddlers.

Oxford

The museum at the University of Mississippi carries recordings of stars born in Mississippi—Jimmie Rodgers, Charlie Pride, and Leontyne Price.

Philadelphia

August finds country artists at the Neshoba County Fair.

MISSOURI

Branson

Up high in the Ozarks, Branson is a place for representative mountain music. Traveling west on US-76 any time from April till October, you can attend the Baldknobbers Hillbilly Jamboree, the Plummer Family County Music Show, Bob-O-Link's Country Hoe Down, and Presley's Mountain Music Jubilee. Branson is a stomping town.

Kansas City

The Worlds of Fun amusement park, 13 miles northeast of the city, has a 153-acre theme park with folk music from around the world, May through September. Then in September and October, a Renaissance Festival takes place on the grounds of the Agriculture Hall of Fame. Folk music is the theme.

Lebanon

Bennett Spring State Park, 12 miles west on MO-64, hosts Hillbilly Days in June,

Osage Beach

A real treat in Osage Beach is the Ozark Opry, patterned after Grand Ole Opry, featuring singers, dancers, and comedians from April through November. In addition, catch the Ozark Jamboree on Highway 42 during the same months.

Springfield and St. Charles

These cities sport their own country fairs in August, the latter with a rifle shoot.

St. Louis

The riverfront has many establishments on Laclede's Landing on Fourth and Market Streets, and they're esthetically appealing with cast-iron balconies and delicate grille work all along the wharf. At the foot of Washington Avenue, riverboats Tom Sawyer, Huck Finn, and Sam Clemens are docked, waiting for the evening hours to cruise on the Mississippi with lots of music for dancing including country. Put this high on your priority list.

Table Rock Lake Area

Folk music pervades the entire park and crosses over to the Arkansas border.

NORTH CAROLINA

Apex

Apex in April is noted for an Old North State Clogging Competition.

Asheville

Asheville, up in the Blue Ridge Mountains, has lively musical events going on. Civic Center on Haywood Street is the site of the Mountain Dance and Folk Festival in August, reminding one that ballads, dulcimers, clogging, 5-string banjos and gut-string fiddles were the way it used to be. Civic Center also hosts the colorful Gathering of the Scottish Clans with bagpipes and pipe bands. The Great Smokies Hilton Hotel at One Hilton Drive has fine country music for natives and travelers alike. Rather a nice touch in March is the Mountain Youth Jamboree, in which youth groups perform ballads, folk dances, and instrumental music. They did indeed learn these tunes from previous generations in the South. Going all-out is Shindig-on-the-Green at the City-Country Plaza, College and Spruce Streets, performing country and bluegrass and clogging during the summer months. A day of rest will be welcome after this.

Barnardsville

Slightly north of Asheville is Barnardsville, boasting a big Ivy Ramp Festival at the Big Ivy Community Center, the heart of local entertainment in May.

Brasstown

The John Campbell Folk School on Route 1 trains young people in traditional folk and presents a Fall Festival in October.

Brevard

Try to catch up with the Festival of the Arts in July.

Burlington

Burlington hosts the Summer Arts Festival all summer long at Snow Camp, off NC-87.

Charlotte

The Ramada Inn Coliseum at 3501 Independence Boulevard, Charlotte, offers good entertainment as does the one in Durham on I-85 at the Guest Road Exit. Also in Durham, July brings festival for the Eno. It's clogging at Eno River City Park. Fiddler's conventions, bluegrass, and folk festivals are on-going summer highlights in Cullowhee at Western Carolina University; Eden at Cedar Hill Bluegrass Park; Franklin (Macon County); in Jefferson at Ashe County Park; in Mount Airy at Veteran's Memorial Park; in Mooresville at the Roland Morgan Auditorium. This last event is the oldest fiddler's convention in North Carolina and takes place in March.

Laurinburg

Laurinburg in September comes alive at Market Park with Sandhills Clogging Competition.

Linville's

Linville's attraction is held at Grandfather Mountain and brings together highland games and ballads of one hundred Scottish Clans in "Singing on the Mountain."

Murfreesboro

Murfreesboro holds the Heritage Festival in April, with fine folk and country representative offerings.

Raleigh

Dress up and go to the Velvet Cloak Inn, 505 Hillsborough Street. If you're around in May, you'll enjoy the Springfest at the Civic Center, folk singing and dancing.

Nag's Head

Laid-back and fun is the Sound Side Folk and Ale House, Milepost 6½ on Avalon Drive.

Ocracoke

Passing through Ocracoke, if you have time, the Pirates Gallery near the shore has ambience as well as country music.

Union Grove

The Van Hoy Amphitheater is open to the public for an old-time Fiddler's Convention in April, complete with banjo, dulcimer, and clogging. However, in May, the Old-Time Fiddler's and Bluegrass Festival, held at Fiddler's Grove Campsite in the woods by a lake, can be attended by invitation only; the invitation extended by Mr. Van Hoy of Union Grove. This latter concert includes gospel singing and psaltery as well as Appalachian music.

Wilmington

October ushers in a colorful Riverfront Celebration, preceded in May by the Coastal Carolina Folklife Festival at the Popular Grove Plantation on Route 1.

Winston-Salem

The Rodeway Inn at 5025 Market Street is an old reliable spot for year-round country, as is the Holiday Inn North at Thirtieth Street and Cherry Marshall Expressway. July ushers in the Bluegrass Show at the Dixie Classic Fairgrounds.

SOUTH CAROLINA

Charleston

R & R's on St. Phillips and Wentworth Streets is a small, unpretentious club that plays bluegrass in a friendly atmosphere. The Blue Marlin on Cumberland Street is housed in a converted warehouse with nautical motifs. A canoe is suspended from the ceiling and the band plays country in a rather loud and rowdy fashion. The Best Western, 5020 Rivers Avenue, plays country and is a fairly dressy nightspot, as is the Sheraton Charleston, 170 Lockwood Drive.

Myrtle Beach

The Grand Strand consists of fifty miles of beach starting five miles south of the North Carolina border and has two places offering quality country: the Breakers, 2006 North Ocean Boulevard, and the Sand Dunes, 201 Seventy-fourth Avenue North.

Again, hither and yon are fiddler's conventions in the state: Ehrhardt in August; Kingstree on Main Street in September; Salley with the "Chitlin Strut" in November; Spartanburg at the Arts Center, 385 South Spring Street; Mountain Rest Community Club in Mountain Rest; Winnsboro at Hoods Park in August, and a Spring Hoedown at Oconee State Park in Walhalla.

Once attending any of these events, it's impossible to forget the entertainment value in addition to enriching your knowledge of music history.

TENNESSEE

Practically every corner of Tennessee shows some activity in country and bluegrass.

Bristol

You remember Bristol on the Tennessee-Virginia border is where it all started commercially, when Ralph Peer came here to see what talent he could discover in "them thar hills." He found Jimmie Rodgers and the Carter Family, and Bristol celebrates heartily at Steele Creek Music Park with Country Music Days in May. Festivities include a parade on State Street, a gospel sing, and a slide presentation of the history of country music at the Appalachian Music Museum. October brings a Southeastern Band Festival with non-electric, original Appalachian music. The Holiday Inn on I-81 carries through this music theme in its entertainment.

Chattanooga

A refreshing trip in the fall might take you to Chattanooga in the Eastern Tennessee Mountains and Grand Canyon of the Tennessee River. What more delightful time can you have than to listen to its Fall Festival?

Clarksville

This city is famous for the State of Tennessee Old-Time Fiddler's Convention in April at Dunn Center, Austin Peay State University, 601 College Street. Mandolins, banjos, guitars, and even harmonicas make music joyfully.

Cosby

Catch the Dulcimer Convention here in June, and the continuous workshops and impromptu performances of dulcimers and traditional mountain instruments.

Crossville

Crossville hosts a Cumberland County Fair and Fiddler's Contest in September.

Elizabethton

Many nationally known bands play at the Bluegrass Festival in Slagle's Pasture, two and a half miles north on TN-19 in June. Stars entertain in a meadow surrounding the Doe River Covered Bridge during Country Music Week.

Gatlinburg

Gatlinburg produces a Folk Festival of the Smokies in June and September.

Jonesboro

Jonesboro presents an Old-Time Country Radio Reunion. This is a country music jamboree in the style of live country radio of the 1920s and 1930s, when broadcasts were conducted at barn dances, high schools and fiddling contests. Broadcasts included gospel, clogging, and square dancing. Some old-time artists who participated in Jonesboro were Cord and Ruby McConnell, and Walter and Howard Hensley. May is when this happens, and in August, Jonesboro goes all out with a sensational Appalachian Fair on the Fairgrounds, fifteen miles northeast on Boones Creek Road and TN-137. You'll see quilting, molasses-making, soap-making, and hear mountain music ad infinitum.

Knoxville

Every April Knoxville has a Dogwood Arts Festival at Market Square Mall, playing bluegrass to symphonic music. And there was of course the 1982 World's Fair in Knoxville. A six-month international exposition featuring entertainment from around the world brought Knoxville back to fame in country music with its Folklife Festival in the Tennessee Amphitheater on the Fairgrounds. Even the working moonshine whiskey still added to the ambience.

Memphis

Don't forget Memphis. Its new Civic Center is the location for many musical events, The Memphis Music Heritage Festival in September, the Mid-South Fair at the Fairgrounds, also in September, and the Music Festival in August are the main country events. Lucy Opry held at Forest Drive Civic Club on Fite Road is a "pass the hat" kind of event. You'll hear bluegrass and country performed spontaneously and be inspired to drop a coin in the hat. Nightspots are the brawling Golden Nuggett, 2491 Elvis Presley Boulevard; the quieter Hernando's Hide-Away, 3210 Old Hernando Road, and the more elegant Eddie Bond's Ranch Supper Club, 87 West Mitchell Road. The latter plays country music in a ballroom.

Nashville

Nashville is Music City, U.S.A. Although it's not possible to list every place for country, it's equally impossible to miss hearing it on any trip through Nashville. If you begin at Music Row at the corner of Sixteenth Avenue South and Division Street, you'll encounter literally hundreds of music publishing companies, dozens of recording studios, including the famous Studio B, numerous talent agencies—the Jo Coulter Studio grooms talent for television, and Hubert Long International is probably the number one talent agency. Find scores of music stores selling instruments, records, and sheet music. The Country Music Hall of Fame is along Music Row and so is the Wax Museum, where you'll gaze unbelievingly at the likenesses of 51 great country artists, such as Uncle Dave Macon and Uncle Jimmy Thompson. All are attired in authentic costumes with their own instruments. This trip is mind-boggling, as you might expect. The old Ryman Auditorium, now museum, stands at 116 Fifth Avenue North, home of the Grand Ole Opry from 1943 to 1974. North of the city is Johnny Cash's and June Carter's house on Old Hickory Lake, and south of the city is the Governor's Mansion flanked on one side by singer Minnie Pearl's house, and on the other by singer Webb Pierce's. About six miles out of town to the east on Briley Parkway is Opryland, U.S.A.

at 2800 Opryland Drive. This vast entertainment park hosts all kinds of music today, although it began with just country. There's a regular program of "I Hear America Singing" and "Country Music, U.S.A.," plus performances on the weekend. Grand Ole Opry House of course is where it all comes together and reserved seats must be ordered well in advance. Events are in motion continuously.

In June, a special occasion is the Country Music Fan Fare and Old-Time Fiddling Championship. In October, don't miss the National Quartet Convention and the Deejay Convention, when country disc jockeys and performers compete for "people of the year" titles. Back in downtown Nashville, off Union Street between Third and Fourth avenues, is Printer's Alley and half a dozen nightclubs with top name artists. The area has of late developed a somewhat unsavory reputation, though. Tootsie's Orchid Cafe at 422 Broadway is extremely popular; stars come here to relax after shows. Rock City plays new country at 107 Second Avenue North, off Broadway. The Bluegrass Inn, 1914 Broadway, is said to have the best bluegrass in town. Other nightspots are Maxwell House, 2025 MetroCenter Boulevard, and Music City Rodeway Inn, One Briley Parkway near the Grand Ole Opry House. Nashville is always busy and bustling, so be prepared for crowds and noise. Finish traveling through the city in September and hear Tennessee Grassroots Days—a celebration combining the music, folklife, and old-time flavor of Tennessee

The Smithville Jamboree, one of the many old-time fiddlers' jam-borees popular in Tennessee. (Courtesy Tennessee Tourist Development, Nashville)

working people. Everything from blues to bluegrass is played and sung and it's a lot less hectic than the Opry.

Oak Ridge
The Appalachian Music Festival at the Children's Museum, 461 West Outer Drive, during April and May, is fun.

Savannah
Here's where the noted Tennessee River Bluegrass Festival can be heard in June and July. Look for top names.

Smithville
Old-Time Fiddler's Jamboree for musicians, singers, and dancers here. Listen to continuous, spontaneous jam sessions under the tree close to the De Kalb County Courthouse. All over Smithville, similar events are happening: "Fire on the Mountain," "Foggy Mountain Breakdown," and "Hot Corn, Cold Corn" ring out from the entire city.

Tullahoma
Visit Tullahoma for a Fiddler's and Peddler's Day in June, and pleasantly absorb the flavor of mountain music.

Sewanee
In June and July, attend a concert at the Sewanee Summer Music Center. It's delightful.

VIRGINIA

Abington
Abington, in the Virginia Highlands, offers a Spring Sampler of country music in May. If you're still here in August, the renowned Virginia Highlands Festival is a worthy activity.

Alexandria
In July, see and hear Virginia Scottish Games with bagpipes and drums. 901 North Fairfax Street is the address of the Ramada Inn-Old Town, a place for quality country at night.

Galax
Remember Felts Park in August for traditional mountain music with autoharp, dulcimer, and clogging, and an old-time Fiddler's Convention. Newer country can be heard at the Midtown Hotel, 303 North Main Street.

Bluegrass and Fiddler's Conventions abound in Virginia, and you'll catch up with one in Dublin, Marion, Martinsville, Middletown, Narrows, Saltville, and Stuart in the summer months.

Norfolk
The address for the Sheraton Inn is Military Circle, where many like to listen to country.

Roanoke
Visit Festival in the Park in June for folk music. The Roanoke Hotel has

the Regency Room at 19 North Jefferson Street for country with the Nashville Sound.

Vienna
Wolf Trap Farm Park for the Performing Arts, 1624 Trap Road, is famous for its varieties of musical performance. There are 3500 seats under the amphitheater roof and much room on the lawn. A fire in 1982 destroyed Wolf Trap amphitheater, and it is in the process of being rebuilt. Catch the National Folk Festival in August.

WEST VIRGINIA

Athens
Concord College presents the John Henry Folk Festival in July along with other events year round.

Charleston
The Cultural Center at the Capitol Complex holds most of the city's musical fare, significant among which is the Vandalia Gathering—a festival of West Virginia's traditional arts including fiddle and banjo contests in May. In September, you'll be in time for the Sternwheel Regatta with much music. Wanting more, visit the Holiday Inn-Downtown, 600 Kanawha Boulevard East for dancing.

Clarksburg
Salem College, 12 miles west in Salem, produces a Salem College Heritage Arts Festival on Campus in April.

Franklin
A wonderful Treasure Mountain Festival is here in September including square dancing and mountain music. "Country Roads," the song that John Denver popularized, comes to life here.

Huntington
Huntington is the home of Marshall University at Fourth Avenue and Sixteenth Street, that organizes a busy program and holds a Square and Round Dance in June.

Moundsville puts on a splendid Folk Music Festival in Grand Vue Park in July, as does Ripley at Cedar Lakes.

Steubenville
There are happy times in Steubenville, with a Country River Jamboree taking place on board the Gateway Clipper Fleet at Monongahela Wharf under Fort Steuben Bridge. Sailing will add to your pleasure as you listen to such artists as Bill Ross, Crazy Roy and Turkey Neck Band.

Wheeling
This city is a landmark in country music. Famous for Jamboree U.S.A. at its Capitol Music Hall, 1015 Main Street, live radio shows have been presented by Station WWVA since 1933. Recently, Ricky Skaggs and Jacky Ward entertained with "I'm Cryin' My Heart Out Over You." Darnell Miller and Bobby Mackey play here frequently. Equally famous

is Jamboree in the Hills at Brush Run Park, 15 miles west off I-70. Anytime at all, you'll hear top names. Oglebay Park is used regularly for folk dancing and festivals.

West Williamson

West Williamson offers a King Coal Festival sporting square dancing and traditional mountain music.

Visiting any one or more of the places mentioned in the previous pages will linger pleasantly in memory and add to your knowledge of folk and country music.

RAGTIME, BLUES, AND JAZZ

The music of jazz is a synthesis of different elements from three continents: from Africa came rhythm and beat; from Europe, harmony and form; from America, brass instruments and extension of the blues. The South put it all together more than one hundred years ago, and created a tradition enjoyed by millions since that time.

Storyville

Jazz developed in New Orleans, Louisiana, just before the turn of the twentieth century, in the famed red-light area of Storyville, bounded by North Basin, Robertson, St. Louis, and Iberville Streets. Storyville

Some "girls" dancing to the jazz beat in Hilma Burt's "house" in Storyville, 1903. (Courtesy the Louisiana State Museum)

was exceedingly hospitable to blacks, and contained a large population of blacks who had flocked there at the end of the Civil War. The emotional climate of Storyville was conducive to the growth and development of jazz, with its improvisational thrusts, high tension beat, guttural, throaty sounds and honky-tonk styles, which found natural outlets in saloons, gambling halls, nightclubs, and brothels. The downtown area below Canal Street, including Storyville and the French Quarter (Vieux Carré), gave rise to the traditional form of jazz associated originally with Armand Piron and John Robichaux, who played in Club Forrest, the St. Charles Hotel, and the Lyric Theater (places of a bygone era).

Early in the 1900s, "Professor" Jelly Roll Morton, the New Orleans Storyville jazz and ragtime pianist, entertained in private homes, gambling halls, and brothels. One of the most flamboyant establishments was Hilma Burt's, at 209 North Basin Street. Morton incorporated the rolling rhythms of marching bands into his improvisations; he orchestrated jazz and ragtime; and he arranged his own piano compositions in a style known as "hot" jazz, a sound meant to convey tortured, heavy feeling. He also epitomized ragtime in a lighter vein in "I'm Alabama Bound." He played frequently in Mahogany Hall, 355 Basin Street, a well-known bordello, no longer in existence. Mahogany Hall had beautiful sitting rooms with expensive decor and beautiful women.

New Orleans was the only city in America in which prostitution was licensed. Then, in 1917, the Federal Government closed it down. This marked the end of Storyville as a red-light district, and jazz and its disciples began to move northward.

The Origins of Jazz, Blues and Ragtime

Jazz, an integral part of blues and ragtime, was derived from the emotional life of the black people in the United States, as expressed in their spirituals, gospels, work songs, and dances (which were all interrelated). This form of jazz first appeared as a musical style in the early minstrel and cakewalk shows, and in the music played by brass and military bands.

Gospel

The gospel hymn, originally a secular folk tune of British or Scottish origin, sung to a religious text (a religious offshoot of American folk hymnody) absorbed a great deal of black influence in the late nine-teenth century. Under this influence the hymn changed: the rhythm and melody were emphasized and the words were simplified. For example, the words

> *The one eternal God*
> *Ere right that now appears*
> *The first, the last, beyond all thoughts*
> *His timeless years . . .*

were modified in the black idiom to become:

> *God is a God*
> *God don't never change*
> *God is a God*
> *And always will be God.*

Black gospel was imbued with deep feeling, expressing the "spirit" or "soul" of black life, history, and aspirations. The songs were sung in poor, rickety store-front churches and at camp "revival" meet-ings throughout the South. Body movement accompanied the songs. Often, songs served as a psychological force, religiously motivating crowds and uniting them in common purpose.

A few of the popular refrains, having characteristic repetition of words and lines, are:

> (1) *Let us gather at the river*
> *Let us gather at the river*
> (2) *In the sweet by and by*
> *In the sweet by and by*
> (3) *Oh, when the saints,*
> *Oh, when the saints,*
> *Oh, when the saints go marchin' in . . .*

Soloists, groups, and choirs participate in the singing of gospel songs. The male quartet is the foundation for later rhythm-and-blues and jazz. Some of the characteristics of the music were the tension between beats, the aroused expectations and climaxes. Listen to the heavy bass and falsetto, even female basses and male sopranos exuding long moans.

Black churches often provided training in gospel singing. Fancy choir robes were, and still are worn by the church choirs. Pianos and organs accompany the singers. The audience is often caught up in the emotional frenzy created by the singing with hand-clapping, swaying, and crescendoing ecstasy. "Ain't No Grave Can Hold My Body Down" and "There's a Man over the River" express some of this feeling.

A noteworthy church offering gospel singing, one that can be visited today, is the Lively Stone Church of God Apostolic at 4015 St. Louis Avenue in St. Louis, Missouri. A former one was Highway and Hedges Fire Baptized in Atlanta, Georgia, no longer open. Fiske University in Nashville has a gospel choir. Other churches, such as Black Holiness or Sanctified churches, Pentecostal, churches of God in Christ, and churches of God Apostolic, have services that include significant gospel singing.

The Spiritual

The gospel hymn gave rise to the spiritual, an antebellum religious song sung in church and at camp meetings. Some of the characteristics of spirituals are freer rhythms, the addition of notes that are foreign to the key (like the flatted third), and changes from major to minor without regular modulations. Some of the popular spirituals before the Civil War were "I Got Religion and I Can't Sit Down" and "If I Had My Way I'd Tear the Building Down," with the refrain:

> If I had my way oh Lawdy, Lawdy,
> If I had my way oh Lawdy, Lawdy,
> If I had my way oh Lawdy, Lawdy,
> I'd tear the building down.

Some spirituals used a call-and-response chant, as found in "Great Camp Meeting" and "Shout for Joy." A slow, sustained melody as in "Nobody Knows the Trouble I've Seen" was another variety of spiritual. A third style of spiritual was consisted of a highly syncopated melody, as in "Little David Play on Your Harp." In churches and at meetings the leader would set the pitch and tempo of the spiritual, singing the verses first before the audience joined in. Meetings in the woods, often lasting several days, frequently supplemented singing with an African dance called ring shout. Ring shout consisted of large circles of people shuffling their feet to and fro, a precurser of ragtime.

Some churches today have spirituals designated as "Brother Brown's Song" or "Sister Anne's Song." In black southern churches you're bound to hear "Roll, Jordan, Roll," "Swing Low, Sweet Chariot," and "Nobody Knows the Trouble I've Seen" at some time.

The Work Song

The work song, close in feeling to the spiritual, was born on

the Southern plantation. Sung by black slaves while laboring and disseminated by them up and down the Mississippi River, work songs
helped make the time pass bearably. The call-and-response pattern predominated, with a leader or top hand calling out something like "Hail
Lawd" to which the field crew responded, "Hail Lawd." Some popular
work song lines were:

> *call—I'm glad to see the evenin' sun go down*
> *response—I'm glad to see the evenin' sun go down*
> *call—So I can go back home and lay down*
> *response—So I can go back home and lay down*

One of the techniques used in the work song was the flatting
of the third and seventh notes of the scale, which produce a melancholy
sound. This technique was used in the blues, and the flatted notes became known as blue notes. Like the gospel and the spiritual, the work
song reflected the hardships of black slave life.

In the late 1880s, blacks and Creoles gathered on Sundays in
Congo Square, now Beauregard Square, in front of the municipal Auditorium on Rampart Street, to sing and play their music. In Congo Square
drums were beaten with fingers, fists, and feet; gourd triangles and banjos played while African voodoo dances broke out with much thigh-
beating, breast-patting, swinging, and writhing. Sunday was the holiday
for slaves; they could gamble, get drunk, watch cock fights, and make
music. You can visit historic Beauregard Square today.

Minstrelsy was a type of black-American entertainment that
also served as a precursor of jazz. Between 1895 and 1900, traveling
minstrels sang songs like "Jump Jim Crow" and danced the cakewalk on
the streets, collecting money from anyone who cared to listen. In this
way, the general public was introduced to black song and dance. Some of
the favorite theatrical performing groups were the Christy Minstrels, the
Georgia Minstrels, and the Young Colored Minstrels. A popular verse
was this one, done to a cakewalk:

> *Hoe de corn, hoe de corn, Moses*
> *Hoe de corn, Moses, hoe de corn;*
> *Come away from dat winder,*
> *My lub and my dub,*
> *Come away from dat winder*
> *Don't you hear me: Oh my.*
> *Come some udder night,*
> *For dere's goin' to be a fight.*
> *Dere be razors flyin' in de air.*

The Military Band

Another link in the evolutionary chain of jazz was the military band, which was European in origin. Popular in New Orleans, and designed after the Napoleonic French fashion of the early 1800s, it exists mostly in memory. These bands adopted European instruments (trombone, cornet, and clarinet) and played at parades, concerts, riverboat excursions, and funerals. Many blacks joined secret burial societies that entitled them to have funerals accompanied by the music of a brass band. A slow blues or lament was played on the way to the burial, and on the way back, the band would strike up a lively tune. The bands were Eureka, Olympia, and Young Tuxedo, marching down Bourbon Street, Third Street, and playing in the cemeteries of Mt. Olivet, Carrollton, and Lafayette. This tradition declined in the sixties and has all but disappeared today.

Stephen Foster

Stephen Foster (1826–1864), although born in Lawrenceville, Pennsylvania, and living most of his life north of the Mason-Dixon Line, is included in this discussion of the South because his music expressed the indigenous spirit of the southern part of the United States in both the black and white styles. His songs reflected working days on the Mississippi River, the coming of the steamboat and the railroad, minstrelsy, and historic plantation life in the Old South. No chapter on blues and jazz is complete without mentioning his name.

As a boy, Foster spent a good deal of time at the levees along the Ohio River. He thus developed an understanding of the poor, black deck hands playing banjos, singing, and dancing on the riverboats, and of the well-to-do, educated Louisiana planters and their fine ladies in splendid garb. He gained a feeling for both, and as he absorbed the black and white bustling, picturesque traffic of the river scene, he began to write songs such as "Oh Susanna" and "Old Uncle Ned."

While still a young man, Foster visited his cousin, Judge John Rowan in Bardstown, Kentucky, one mile east on US-150. (It is now a state park.) Here was a spacious, antebellum house on a hill, with winding walks and a gently curving driveway lined with tall tulip and maple trees. The scent of myrtle undoubtedly filled the warm air. Behind the house were barns housing cows and horses, drenched with the sweet smell of hay. Slave quarters were next to the barns and the budding composer observed their life first hand.

After the dinner chores were completed, blacks strummed on their banjos, sang softly, and occasionally incorporated a dance step or two into the music. As Foster listened, and looked out at the moonlight, and heard the night birds chirping, he was inspired by the peaceful, gentle plantation scene and wrote "My Old Kentucky Home."

Some years later Foster married Jane McDowell, who sang in a church choir. She was known to friends as "Jeanie" and was the inspiration for "Jeanie with the Light Brown Hair." The old black servant at the McDowell house, Joe, an old man with a shock of white hair, heavily-lined, tired eyes, bent over, and limping with rheumatism was "Old Black Joe," but Joe had succumbed to the "gentle voices" before the song was finished.

The composer wrote many other songs which are classics in American music. Two of them are "Old Folks at Home" and "Camptown Races." He came upon hard times after the Civil War started and died in Bellevue Hospital in New York in 1864, leaving a small purse containing thirty-eight cents and a slip of paper with the words "dear friends and gentle hearts." The purse and its contents and other Foster memorabilia can be seen at the Foster Hall collection at the University of Pittsburgh (see Section I.4, listing under Pittsburgh). Other memorabilia can be seen at the Stephen Foster Center in White Springs, Florida on the bank of the Suwannee River.

Ragging and Ragtime

Around the turn of the twentieth century, the cakewalk gave way to "ragging," a largely shuffling style of dance, with exhortations of glee coming from the dancer, and hand-clapping, feet-stomping, and banjo accompaniment from on-lookers.

The essence of ragtime piano lies in maintaining both a syncopated and an unsyncopated beat at the same time; while the left hand plays a steady beat, the right "rags" or syncopates. Although anyone who could read music could play it in its simplest form, the more difficult rag pieces were reserved for the truly good pianists who had a jazz-oriented sense of rhythm, who were able to improvise a variety of rhythmic suspensions, unusual accents, and between-the-beat effects. Ragtime, cheerful and swingy in mood, was limited to the piano. It became the national craze at the end of the depression of the 1890s, most likely due to its intrinsically cheerful nature.

St. Louis is considered to be the birthplace of ragtime. St. Louis, located on the Mississippi River, was a stop on the railroad where hundreds of traveling musicians arrived, played, stayed, and then left. They found an easy and fast life with much night life, drugs, and prostitution.

Indeed, every city with a population of over five-thousand had its red-light district.

In the Rosebud Café in the center of the Chestnut Valley red-light district, Tom Turpin, a pioneer in ragtime, was busy writing rags and handling underworld activities as well. Tom weighed a modest three-hundred pounds and had his piano hoisted up on several large blocks in order to play standing up, a position more comfortable than playing over his corpulence. His "Harlem Rag" became famous around 1900. Turpin worked with Louis Chauvin, another rag composer, and together they played at parties, in riverfront saloons, in honky-tonks, and on excursion boats that cruised up and down the Mississippi River. Fate Marable and Red McKenzie were others who joined them.

Scott Joplin, born in Sedalia, Missouri, of parents who were newly-freed slaves, played his popular "Maple Leaf Rag" at the Maple Leaf Club on Lamine and Main Streets in 1899 and shortly thereafter moved to St. Louis where ragtime skyrocketed onto the musical scene for over a decade. Joplin met Turpin at the Rosebud Café where he wrote "Rosebud March." Joplin went on to work at the Silver Dollar Saloon for Turpin's father, "Honest John" Turpin. Moving back and forth between Sedalia and St. Louis, Joplin played at the Woods Opera House in Sedalia, staging "Ragtime Dance." He wrote "Elite Syncopations" and "Peacherine Rag" before moving to New York in 1907, when he died of syphilis.

St. Louis Ragtime Festival

Since 1965, every summer on the Goldenrod Showboat there is a gathering of ragtime piano players. It has become an annual event lasting one week and has featured almost every major ragtime performer in the country. There is continuous entertainment taking place in at least five locations on and around the boat, including all-night sessions on the levee. Hosting the gala event is a group known as the St. Louis Ragtimers, dedicated to preserving the ambience of yesteryear. The film *Ragtime* (produced in the 1980s) was an attempt to recreate the era between 1890 and 1920.

The Blues' Origin and Early Development

The blues, at the center of the jazz tradition, has remained in great favor up to the present day. Its bittersweet mood reveals the attitude, "I'm laughing on the outside, crying on the inside," and is expressed in deceptively simple language, which belies an underlying skepticism about life. What makes this particular form of jazz distinct is its tonality, made up of blue (flatted) notes, slow tempo, and melancholy air. The blues are sorrow songs that bemoan one's fate. Written in a combination of major and minor modes playing against each other, the music of the blues expresses tension, emotional restlessness, and the conflicting moods mentioned above.

The blues are believed to have been born along the Mississippi Delta as thousands of anonymous blacks traveled north and sang of their woes as cotton pickers, dockhands, and slaves. Blues songs gradually evolved when a listener heard a phrase, embellished it, and repeated it to others or wrote it down.

Such was the case with the esteemed W. C. Handy, born in Florence, Alabama in 1873. Handy himself traveled up and down the Mississippi in the early 1900s and found inspiration from the music he heard in the cotton fields, on the waterfronts, and at back doors of the delta country. Of this experience he said: "I find music all around—in the ripple of a brook, and in the sigh of wind in the trees. I call it the 'blues.'" He wrote down these sounds, orchestrated them, introduced a lowered or flatted seventh note in harmony, and had them published. Handy traveled extensively with the Knights of Pythias Band, based in Clarksdale, Mississippi, to small towns to play for dances and social events. He not only arranged and improvised, but composed the classics, "St. Louis Blues," "Memphis Blues," and "Beale Street Blues." His style has been described as music with an itch. Although many talented, unknown black musicians before Handy were occasionally playing similar music, it was he who popularized the blues and earned for himself the title, "Father of the Blues," in Memphis, with "Memphis Blues."

Huddie Ledbetter (Leadbelly) from Shreveport, Louisiana, was another early star of the blues, who recorded for the Library of Congress in Washington, D.C. Leadbelly was a heavy strummer on a twelve-stringed guitar. He sang songs of oppressed blacks in a powerfully persuasive voice. The notorious red-light district, Fannin Street, in Shreveport, was his local stomping grounds. Gambling houses, street fights, hard drinking, and "high yaller" women were part of Fannin Street. Leadbelly had served a prison sentence for murder in another city, and was polite, almost servile to whites, pouring his pent-up emotions into song.

Once having heard his "Rock Island Line" and "This Hammer," people found it impossible to forget his mesmerizing appeal. Leadbelly veered toward folk music, joining Woody Guthrie and Pete Seeger in the Almanac Singers in the Northeast.

Blues from 1920s On

The first phonograph recording by a blues singer was not made until 1920 by Mamie Smith. "That Thing Called Love" and "You Can't Keep a Good Man Down" were followed by the hit, "Crazy Blues." She was a star performer at the Booker T. Washington Theater in St. Louis.

Perhaps the greatest and most loved blues singers of all times were Gertrude (Ma) Rainey and Bessie Smith. Rainey, a poor girl from Columbus, Georgia, belted out songs in an early, warm, moaning style, suggesting a rural, down-home appeal. "Black Cat Hoot Owl Blues" and "Chain Gang Blues" of 1928 were her trademarks. She sang in Memphis's Beale Street clubs and toured the South before going to Chicago to work with Louis Armstrong, Coleman Hawkins, and Fletcher Henderson.

Bessie Smith's demeanor was somewhat more sophisticated, although she too was a poor girl—from Chattanooga, Tennessee. With a fierce temper and amazing physical strength she immortalized "Poor Man's Blues," in which she implored the rich man to open his heart and mind.

> Mister rich man, rich man, open your heart and mind,
> If it wasn't for the poor man, mister rich man, what would you do?

In the 1930s, clubs, halls, and poolrooms on Decatur Street in Atlanta, Georgia were the places where black musicians played and sang the blues. Willie McTell, a blind boy, entertained with his twelve-stringed guitar; Peg Leg Howell and his gang were heard by many in "New Prison Blues" and "Low Down Rounder Blues."

Other well-known places where one could hear the blues were the Lyric Theater in New Orleans, and the Dream Theater in Columbus Georgia. Memphis's Beale Street, inundated with gambling halls and honky-tonks, was a blues mecca. You could have visited the Midway, Hole-in-the-Wall, Red Light, Blue Light, Pee Wee's Saloon (you can visit Pee Wee's today), the Palace Theater, and the Pastime Theater. W. C. Handy was given his title, "Father of the Blues," on Beale Street. Jed Davenport's was a popular club; the Memphis Jug Band and Gus Cannon's Jug Stompers played there.

The blues could be heard in other parts of the South, too. Count Basie was making it big all along the River City area nightclubs in Kansas City, Missouri. Morgan Street was the favorite hangout in St. Louis, especially Deep Morgan's, a sleazy sort of club, but typical of the day.

Jazz and the Jazz Band

What exactly is this music called jazz? The best answer to that question is a nonverbal one. Only after you feel it do you experience the answer—it is a unique combination of melody, harmony, and rhythm that makes you want to tap your foot, sway your body, and wiggle your toes. Rhythm is the distinction between jazz and other forms of music, for it is its heart; syncopation stresses the weaker beats and persuades the listener's pulse to beat attentively. Improvisation, an integral part of jazz, uses printed music merely as a guideline, while the performer creates his own melodic and rhythmic subtleties.

The jazz band, back at its inception around 1900, consisted of crude instruments such as cigar box fiddles, old kettles, cowbells, pebble-filled gourds, bull fiddles, half barrels, and harmonicas, not to mention sundry whistles and horns. It evolved gradually into a band of banjo, drums, tuba, trombone, and trumpet. Finally, by the 1920s, the piano and bass replaced the tuba and banjo, and wood wind instruments were added. The drum, piano, and banjo make up the rhythm section, and the horns can be thought of as the melodic voices; trumpet or cornet playing the tenor part, trombone playing the bass part, and clarinet playing the soprano part. Alto horns, saxophone, clappers, and guitar were also included when desired.

Dixieland and Dixieland Names

New Orleans jazz, known as traditional jazz or Dixieland, is the style from which all jazz varieties stem. In Dixieland, musicians improvise around a recognizable melody against a strong beat. Sometimes they all play together, occasionally, someone makes his own statement with a short instrumental solo, but the music remains faithful to the same theme throughout. African influence is heard in the whooping falsetto yell, which is incorporated into jazz instrumentation. This occurs when the musician uses the instrument as an extension of his own voice.

A memorable early artist was Charles "Buddy" Bolden, who put together the first real jazz band at the now-vanished Come Clean Hall, at around 1900 in New Orleans. His band played at dances, funerals, socials, and parades. The Razzy Dazzy Spasm Band, later called simply the Jazz Band, played "hot" jazz, pouring forth the same searing quality that Jelly Roll Morton introduced. The number one group, however, was the Original Dixieland Jazz Band, which made the first jazz recording in 1917, with "Original Dixieland Onestep" on one side of the record, and "The Livery Stable Blues" on the other. The record sold one million copies, an incredible sale for that day. The notable Dominick James "Nick" LaRocca played cornet in this band. Leon "Bix" Beiderbecke listened to and was influenced by these records, and went on to surpass LaRocca in fame with such groups as the "Wolverines."

One of the world's great trumpeters and a big name in jazz, Louis "Satchmo" Armstrong, got his start in a marching band in New Orleans before World War I. Armstrong helped popularize the "scat" style of singing (a substitution of syllables such as "da-da-de-dad" for words). He was highly successful, too, in his practice of gradually "crying up" to a note on the trumpet, rather than striking it immediately. His long, carefully drawn-out high notes added further to his appeal.

Names to come out of New Orleans during its heyday in the early twentieth century were: Bix Beiderbecke; Dominick "Nick" La-Rocca; King Oliver and his Jazz Band, playing such tunes as "High Society Rag" and "Chattanooga Stomp" at Pete Lala's at Customhouse and Marais Streets; Sidney Bechet, saxophonist; Kid Ory, and Louis Prima, who operated the Five-Hundred Club on Bourbon and St. Louis Streets some time later; the New Orleans Rhythm Kings, and the Creole Jazz Band. New Orleans had created a style of Dixieland with a unique flavor, and its advocates, for the most part, could not read a note of music.

Dixieland spread northward, and was not revived in New Orleans until well after World War II. The establishment of Preservation Hall on St. Peter Street as a musical landmark immortalized jazz and houses performances today. The Preservation Hall Jazz Band and Sweet Emma Barrett and her Band are two outstanding groups that play historical jazz. And they are featured at Preservation Hall.

Preservation Hall

The store-like entrance from the street level, at 726 St. Peter Street, discloses a poorly-lit aisle leading to the back of the one-room hall where the musicians perform.

The hall is dingy, dusty, musty, and drab, with lighting fixtures from yesteryear. Seating is provided on paint-chipped, narrow wooden benches or on faded stuffed pillows, some of which are split from use with the stuffing popping out. You can sit on the floor, too. There is no air-conditioning and you bring your own drinks.

Equipment for the performers consists of old rickety, worn-out music stands and an upright piano. The board covering the keys on the piano is missing; the flat surfaces of the piano serve as a repository for used coffee cups and empty Coke cans.

In this seedy atmosphere glorious Dixieland music is played to an audience offering bits of "yeah," and "right on" during the performance, with thunderous applause and shouting following the session. During breaks, you can talk with the performers.

Jazz Expands

In the 1920s and 1930s, Kansas City, Missouri became one of the three leading jazz cities, along with New Orleans, and Chicago. As New Orleans did, Kansas City supported speakeasies and gambling halls. Count Basie reigned at the nightclubs along the River City area, producing his rhythmic "Kansas City Sound" on the piano. Basie actually prepared the blues for big band form. Charlie "Yardbird" Parker, who later made it big in New York, played in Kansas City and introduced a "cool" style of jazz, described best as having an aura of haunting lyricism and mild, soft-toned nuances, which added considerably to listening pleasure. "Cool" made jazz more respectable by reducing the honky-tonk effect.

Radio stations in the thirties began to offer blues and jazz programs as daily entertainment. Station KFFA in Helena, Arkansas, produced the famous "King Biscuit Time" program; and there was KGGI in Little Rock; KNOE in Monroe, Louisiana; and WAZF in Yazoo City, Mississippi.

Jazz and Blues Mix with Rock and Roll

The many technological advances that took place after World War II ushered in an era of electronics which pointed music in the direction of rock and roll. Jazz and blues mixed with rock the way everything mixed with rock, and resulted in stylistic changes. Purists were disturbed and barely recognized jazz-blues singer Joe Turner in Kansas City, when he turned toward rock in "Shake, Rattle and Roll." Roy Brown combined blues, jazz, and rock in "Trouble at Midnight," and paved the way for future blues singers to do the same. Heightened individual showmanship and body movement were desirable elements then, as B.B. King from Memphis became "King of the Blues," with his electric guitar and long swooping notes, belting out "Worry, Worry." Bobby (then Blue) Bland captured audiences in "Stormy Monday" with smooth, cultivated phrasing, and Ray Charles adopted a style of country or rhythm and blues in numerous recordings, which is still popular today.

Since the 1950s it has been very difficult to categorize music precisely; country, rhythm and blues, jazz, and rock have all influenced each other.

The new breed of jazz-blues singer in the fifties and sixties found expression in John Lee Hooker from Clarksdale, Mississippi. He played electric guitar, stomped his feet, and embellished notes widely. His style? Country-rhythm-blues-rock style. From original Delta country, he introduced "Hobo Blues" and "Sally Mae," both high on the top ten records list. Also from the Delta was the late Muddy Waters, blues singer, who formed his own band, featuring Little Walter on amplified harmonica and Jimmy Rogers on guitar. Waters himself played slide guitar, wearing the appropriate slide on the little finger of his left hand.

The Alabama-based rhythm and blues band, Wet Willie, rocketed singer and saxophonist, Jimmy Hall, into fame in the seventies. Songs like "Sleepin' on the Beach Tonight" and "Cadillac Tracks" helped him along the way.

CeDell Davis, a Mississippi guitarist, unlike many musicians who brought the blues North, stayed in the South to carry on the tradition. He has performed in the 1980s at the Jack Rabbit Club in Pine Bluff, Arkansas. He's interesting because he sings songs written by Joe Turner, Muddy Waters, and B.B. King, and styles them according to original Dixieland.

Progressive or New Wave Jazz

This is a polyphonic variety of jazz with little orchestration since three or four instruments improvise simultaneously on a melody. There's more to listen to at the same moment in this style, and the music is controlled. Some well-known virtuosi are listed below:

Ornette Coleman—an innovative saxophonist, who came to New Orleans in 1949 and played all over the city. His band Prime Time has recently recorded "Of Human Feelings."

Joe Newman—trumpeter, famous for his solo in Count Basie's recording of "April in Paris."

Ellis Marsalis—jazz pianist.

Willie Tee—pianist-singer.

Jim Singleton—bassist.

These musicians starred frequently in New Orleans at the Old Absinthe House and at Tyler's.

Soul Music

Soul music has its roots not only in the blues but in the earlier music of the black spirituals and gospels. It picks up the repetition of words and music and crescendoed effects of feeling, sometimes with a call-and-response pattern. It seems to have come full circle.

Little Johnny Taylor, a successful soul-blues singer, began as a gospel singer. Wilson Pickett, Dionne Warwick, and Aretha Franklin also sang gospel in church in their early years. Perhaps the most renowned gospel singer of all times was Mahalia Jackson, remembered for "Precious Lord." The Staple Singers, a Mississippi gospel group, added some folk to its gospel and turned toward soul in "Respect Yourself" and "Be What You Are." James Brown achieved fame as a Soul Brother in "Say It Loud, I'm Black and I'm Proud." The essence of Soul lyrics calls for unity and commitment to each other among all blacks, as distinguished from straight blues of individual lament.

Many blues singers, such as Bobby Bland and B.B. King, combined blues and Soul and called it Soul. Styles are no longer clearly defined; they're blends and mixtures, with borrowed elements.

And the beat goes on! Jazz and blues are alive and well today. The following pages list jazz spots throughout the South.

ALABAMA
Fairfield
Miles College, at 5500 Avenue G, is a black college with a gospel choir that performs soul music during the year.
Florence
On W. C. Handy's birthday, November 16th, there is an annual celebration held in his home (and museum) at 620 West College Street. This restored birthplace holds mementos and memorabilia, including the trumpet and piano with which he composed "St. Louis Blues"; there are also testimonials to him by Louis Armstrong and George Gershwin. Tours are available.
Mobile
In March, a Mardi Gras with brass bands and jazz galore celebrates Shrove Tuesday.

ARKANSAS
Jonesboro
The Forum presents the New American Ragtime Ensemble in April.
Little Rock
Little Rock Convention Center Music Hall welcomes all artists. Herbie Mann, jazz flutist, played here recently.
Pine Bluff
The Jack Rabbit Club has hosted many fine jazz musicians, including Dixieland artist CeDell Davis.
Springdale
The Albert Brumley Gospel Festival, featuring Soul-blues, takes place in August.

FLORIDA

Clearwater

Woody Riley's Warehouse, at North Garden Avenue and Drew, plays Dixieland jazz in an informal atmosphere (as the name suggests).

The Traveler's Motel Lounge, at 4767 NW Thirty-sixth Street, can be counted on for jazz and jam sessions.

The Bilmar Hotel, in Treasure Island, close to the Clearwater area, features jazz.

Miami and Miami Beach

Many of the big hotels and motels are rock and disco oriented, but one can, nevertheless, find jazz.

The Sheraton Bal Harbour, at 9701 Collins Avenue, is comparable in quality to Las Vegas or San Juan.

The Flamenco Supper Club, at 991 NE Seventy-ninth Street, features jazz Flamenco and a Latin beat.

The Metamorphosis Lounge, in Miami Airport Inn, 1546 NW LeJune Road, offers jazz.

The Village Inn, 3131 Commodore Plaza in Coconut Grove, a nearby suburb of Miami, offers jazz.

Palm Beach

The Paddlewheel Queen, a riverboat, plays Dixieland while embarking from Ft. Lauderdale, reminiscent of yesteryear's exciting musical excursions.

The Time Out Lounge offers music and dancing. The interior features lovely hanging plants.

The Vintage Star Room features superstars in elaborate Las Vegas style shows. The Dave Brubeck Quartet and Patti Page have performed here.

Panacea

The Blue Crab Festival presents gospel singing with Soul in August.

Tampa

The Tampa Theater occasionally plays host to the Newport Jazz Festival.

White Springs

On the northern bank of the Suwannee River is the 250-acre Stephen Foster Center, Amphitheater, and Museum. Surrounded by large oak trees, the museum has a plethora of early musical instruments and Foster memorabilia. There are musical events year-round. Particularly noteworthy is the big music festival in September, at which "Jeanie with the Light Brown Hair," "Old Folks at Home," and "Camptown Races" are performed.

GEORGIA

Albany

The Albany Jazz Festival, in Thronateeska Plaza downtown, in April.

Atlanta

Atlanta has hosted many big names in jazz and is a city of nightspots featuring all kinds of jazz, from Dixieland to cool to progressive. Some outstanding places are:

The Keyboard Lounge, 3861 Roswell in Buckhead, an informal spot where natives, visitors, and visiting jazz artists gather to play, listen, talk shop, and just relax to music. The jazz sessions go on all evening.

Peachtree Center Plaza, Peachtree and Cain Streets, and the Hyatt Regency, Peachtree and Baker Streets, are two spectacular hotels, with interior glass elevators, floating lounges, and revolving bars. The entertainment is also spectacular. Trumpeter Joe Newman and pianist-singer Willie Tee have starred here.

The Omni Complex, at Marietta Street and Techwood Drive, has many clubs, some of which have hosted the Manhattan Yellow Pages.

The Marriott schedules jazz artists regularly.

The oldest part of the city is Underground Atlanta, and Dante's Down the Hatch, 84 Old Pryor Street, boasts good cool jazz. The Paul Mitchell Trio, noted for its elegant, low-key sound, has performed here. The building is antebellum and part of original Atlanta. The dining room is a replica of an eighteenth-century sailing frigate with three-hundred-year-old hand-carved Polish and English figureheads. The well in the entrance was the water source for Atlanta's first volunteer fire department.

Pascal's La Carrousel Lounge near the Atlanta University Campus Center has been called the best black entertainment motel in America. The nation's top jazz people have been frequenting this place for years and loyal Atlantans patronize it regularly. You'll probably need reservations.

The Atlanta Stadium, on Capitol Avenue, hosts the Jazz Festival in June.

Savannah

April is the time for the "Night in Old Savannah," with music by the renowned New Orleans Preservation Hall Jazz Band.

Night-Flight Café, an old cotton warehouse at 113 East River Street, has different groups performing, including Soul-blues groups.

KENTUCKY

Bardstown

Bardstown's reputation is built on the fact that Stephen Foster visited the town. Foster was born in the North near Pittsburgh, Pennsylvania in 1826. Although many of his songs tell of black southern life, he visited the South only once. In 1852 he visited his cousin, Judge Rowan, at his home, one mile east on US-150. Judge Rowan's home is now a 235-acre "Old Kentucky Home State Park," and programs of Foster's melodies are presented from June through September in the attractive Talbot Amphitheater. (See also Section I. Chapter 4, listing under Pittsburgh.)

LOUISIANA
New Orleans

The French Quarter (Vieux Carré) bounded by the Mississippi River, and Canal and Rampart Streets, is where to go if you love jazz. There are scores of nightclubs in this area. Iron-lace railings overhang wisteria gardens and sidewalks. Preservation Hall, 726 St. Peter Street, offers only traditional Dixieland. The Preservation Hall Jazz Band plays here when not touring. Sweet Emma's band is also based here.

A great deal of activity goes on at night, especially on Bourbon Street, where the activity continues almost endlessly. By the way, the street was named for the Royal Family and not the drink.

The Old Absinthe House, 240 Bourbon Street, is a hopping club that contains all the antique fixtures of the Old Absinthe House, formerly located just down the street. Interesting items are a long marble-topped bar and an old water dripper used to drip water into Absinthe. There are hundreds of calling cards plastered over the walls, a carry-over of an old custom begun by patrons. Ornette Coleman and progressive jazz musicians have been featured here.

The Paddock Lounge, 309 Bourbon Street, has a Dixieland band and features entertainers such as Wallace Davenport.

Famous Door, 339 Bourbon Street, hosts Santo Pecora, the Dukes of Dixieland, and Sharkey.

Your Father's Mustache, 426 Bourbon Street, is noisy, with a brass band that plays in the gay nineties style.

Al Hirt's, 501 Bourbon Street, offers sweet sounds.

Old Court Tavern, 624 Bourbon, is a small, pleasant club that has entertainment such as a pianist, a popular jazz trio, or a blues singer.

Crazy Shirley's, 640 Bourbon Street.

Maison Bourbon, 641 Bourbon, offers jazz both afternoons and evenings. Clive Wilson's Original Jazz Band, among others, plays here.

Dixieland Hall, opened in 1962, is a small concert hall that attracts traditional artists.

Tipina's, 501 Napoleon Avenue, offers jazz and blues.

Clubb (sic) 77, 810 North Claiborne, is a black nightclub which offers modern and far-out jazz.

Mason's Americana, 2309 South Claiborne Avenue, is a black motel-nightclub which offers blues.

The Hyatt Hotel features jazz artists such as Ornette Coleman.

The Esplanade Room, in the Royal Orleans Hotel, 621 St. Louis Street, is a relatively low-toned spot for music lovers. Ragtime pianist Armand Hug was billed here recently.

Maple Leaf Bar, 8316 Oak, features the Louisiana Repertory Jazz Ensemble. The group is a seven-piece traditional jazz band established by the Tulane University Jazz Archive.

Fat City, bounded by Veterans' Boulevard, North Causeway, West Esplanade, and Division Streets, has no less than 70 nightspots, restaurants and shops.

Pete Fountain's Inn at the Hilton Hotel on Poydras Street presents jazz with a touch of modern influence.

Tyler's, at 5345 Magazine Street, features new wave style jazz.

The President is an old-time sidewalk steamboat that cruises up and down the Mississippi River. The boat leaves from Canal Street and the River and features such groups as the Crawford-Fergusen Night Owls.

The Jazz Archive at the Tulane University Library, on the corner of Freret Street and Newcombe Boulevard, holds fascinating memorabilia: thousands of reels of taped interviews with jazz people, huge record collections, sheet music, band arrangements, programs and posters. A must for jazz lovers.

The big event of the year is the famous New Orleans Jazz and Heritage Festival. Each spring, from the end of April to early May, stars of jazz, ragtime, and blues gather together at this unstructured celebration to play music.

The festival is divided into daytime and evening events, and held in various sites throughout the city: The Fairgrounds, Municipal Auditorium, the Marriott Hotel, the Royal Sonesta Hotel Ballroom, the steamboat President, and the Theater of Performing Arts.

MISSISSIPPI
Biloxi
The Mardi Gras reigns supreme on Shrove Tuesday.
The Biloxi Beach Motor Inn, at 115 Beach Boulevard, offers jazz.
Gulfport
The Best Western, 2922 West Beach Boulevard, offers jazz.
Jackson
The Ramada Inn Coliseum, at 400 Greymont Avenue, offers jazz.

MISSOURI
Kansas City
The Museum of History and Science, 3218 Gladstone Boulevard, has historical exhibits of jazz.
The Strawberry Patch, 8725 State Line Road, offers jazz.
Milton's Tap Room, 3241 Main Street, offers jazz. Count Basie and Charlie Parker played here in their heyday.
Sedalia
Scott Joplin played his "Maple Leaf Rag" in 1899 at the Maple Leaf Club at Lamine and Main Streets. The listeners went wild as ragtime was born. There is a monument to Joplin in front of the club.

St. Louis

The Annual National Ragtime Festival, in the Goldenrod Showboat, 400 North Wharf Street, in mid-June. This is the big event in St. Louis. In the early 1960s, the St. Louis Ragtimers bought this boat, which had been lying dormant in St. Louis levee since 1937. From 1965 on, the Goldenrod has been the permanent Festival site, and the time for a yearly pilgrimage for ragtime lovers all over the world. It has featured such international talented ragtimers and jazz performers as the Bix Beiderbecke Memorial Jazz Band, the Storyville Dandies from Japan, Turk Murphy Band from San Francisco, the Saint Louis Ragtimers, Eubie Blake, Mike Montgomery, and Tex Wyndham, among others.

There is room for fourteen-hundred people at the Festival, since various boat decks, dining rooms, and lounges are used, as well as nearby barges. Festivities go on nonstop until the early morning hours with after-hour levee sessions. The Goldenrod also provides regular weekly entertainment.

NORTH CAROLINA

High Point

High Point Theater and Exhibition Center, 220 East Commerce Street, presents one-thousand years of jazz in March.

Raleigh

The Velvet Cloak Inn, 1505 Hillsborough Street, offers all kinds of quality popular music, including jazz.

The Hilton, near the velvet cloak, at 1707 Hillsborough, also presents all kinds of popular music, including jazz.

Wilmington

All kinds and varieties of music take place at 5025 Market Street.

Winston-Salem

The Dixie Classic Fair, at the Fairgrounds, in the fall, offers original Dixieland jazz. An enjoyable group is the Traveling Jazz Band connected with the North Carolina School of the Arts.

SOUTH CAROLINA

Charleston

One of the nation's renowned events is the Spoleto Festival, which takes place in May and June. Professional and amateur musicians look forward to this varied musical celebration. Music abounds—all kinds and lots of it. The event is a direct replication of the Spoleto Festival in Italy, founded over twenty years ago by Gian-Carlo Menotti, composer of "The Medium" and "The Telephone." Sally's Place, at 43 John Street, plays jazz all week.

The Best Western Rivers, 5020 Rivers Avenue, offers jazz.

Hilton Head
Sea Pines Plantation, at Hilton Head Island, a charming site with much old-world ambience, features top musicians.
Mount Pleasant
You'll find jazz in April on the grounds of Boone Hall Plantation. The sessions are full of ante-bellum atmosphere.

TENNESSEE
Henning
Toby's Pub, at the junction of US-51 and 87, provides music on weekends. The name Toby is the one Kunta Kinte in "Roots" chose for himself

A jam session around the statue of W.C. Handy in Handy Park in Memphis, Tennessee. (Courtesy Tennessee Tourist Development, Nashville)

when he came to America, and this Pub is named for that "Roots" character. The African influence is felt here in the jazz that is played. There's Soul too.

Memphis

This city pays special homage to W. C. Handy. There is a statue of the "Father of the Blues" in Handy Park, on the corner of Third and Beale Streets. Today, Memphis is in the middle of major reconstruction; the Beale Street Development Corporation is slowly restoring entertainment and bringing new life back to this former blues city.

Handy Park offers free summer concerts, beckoning old-time blues artists.

Blues Alley has nightspots which offer music, but one must be careful about wandering there at night.

Blues Alley Restaurant and Bistro, 60 South Front Street, one block east of the Mississippi, is a one-hundred-year-old cotton warehouse converted into a showplace. It has featured outstanding Memphis blues singers (in ways reminiscent of former Beale Street clubs) such as Ma Rainey and Bessie Smith.

Pee Wee's Saloon, on Beale Street, is an extremely popular entertainment place.

The Birth of the Blues, 1748 Madison, is also popular.

Bud's Hot Biscuits offers jazz.

Many top artists have appeared in all these Memphis sites, including Bessie Smith, Furry Lewis, Memphis Slim, B.B. King, and Bobby Bland.

Number One Beale Street, a fairly new establishment, offers a good deal of Soul blues.

Festivals in Memphis are gala.

The Annual National Blues Music Awards is held every November sixteenth (Handy's birthday) to honor outstanding people who have made significant contributions to the blues.

The International Festival, held all May long, is a tribute to the blues at the Beale Street Music Festival. There are four separate stages for all performing groups and artists.

Memphis Cotton Carnival, in Lakeland Park, is another May jazz and blues celebration.

Dixieland and Blues, at the Metropolitan Opera, in May, is an event that brings together blues artists from the entire country.

The Mid-South Fair can be seen at the Fairgrounds in September. Traditional jazz is featured here.

Nashville

Fisk University has a famous gospel choir.

VIRGINIA
Charlottesville
The West Virginian (in Virginia), 1521 University Avenue, offers a good-sized dance floor.
The Odyssey Night Club, Route 250 East, also has a large dance floor. Blues is featured here.
The Mine Shaft, 1106 West Main Street, offers blues.
Hampton
The Hampton Jazz Festival, at the Hampton Roads Coliseum, 413 West Mercury Boulevard, in June. It's the jazz event of the year, and there's no shortage of talent.
Vienna
Music lovers were saddened when, in April of 1982, a fire ravaged the Wolf Trap Farm Park for the Performing Arts, on Trap Road near Fairfax, on US 7. This was the second such fire since it opened in 1971. The Filene Center at Wolf Trap that seated thirty-five-hundred under the roof was destroyed, and makeshift arrangements under a large tent were provided until the area was due to be restored. Many organizations, including the United States Government, contributed money towards the twenty-million-dollar reconstruction. Wolf Trap, in the hills of the Blue Ridge Mountains, is world-famous for its varied, high-caliber musical programs. Ella Fitzgerald and Count Basie are among many who have performed here.

WEST VIRGINIA
Beckley
The John Henry Blues and Gospel Festival, in September, with authentic music ranging from religious to modern in flavor.
Charleston
The Cultural Center Theater, in the Capitol Complex, hosts the West Virginia Jazz Festival each year from late March to early April.
Wheeling
Oglebay Park, on WV-88, is a well-used site for varied musical activities, especially Oglebay Festival in October which features jazz.
White Sulphur Springs
The Valley Barn, off Route 92N, is actually a 1938 barn. Redecorated several times, it offers dancing to the music of jazz in a semi-formal atmosphere.

    The South is proud of its heritage of jazz and blues and it keeps it alive through these many presentations in nightspots and halls and at festivals. Historical museums help preserve mementos of jazz days gone by. The French Quarter at night, downtown Atlanta, or the St. Louis Ragtime Festival all provide opportunities to experience the magic of jazz.

ROCK

The time was post-World War II, 1954; the place, southern United States; the situation, dissatisfaction and restlessness among the young, who challenged values of the establishment. Youth, emerging as a social group, sought to change lifestyles and define themselves in their casual dress, promiscuous sex, drugs, and radical-sounding music. The different kinds of music already in existence (white pop and country, and black blues and jazz) interacted and fused, to which youth further added a pounding piano, a bleating saxophone, amplified electric guitars, and ever-beating drums. Crude lyrics delivered by raw voices cut through these funky sounds to convey the hard realities of the day. The teenage revolution had arrived, represented by rock and roll.

Rockabilly: The Beginnings of Southern Rock in the Fifties

A group of singers from Memphis (a blues mecca in the early twentieth century) promoted a sound infused with a regional mixture of country music plus rhythm-and-blues. It became known as country rock or rockabilly. In contrast to the early northern sound of Bill Haley and the Comets, who accentuated the blues/jazz element in rock, rockabilly emphasized country, although the dance beat in both styles came from rhythm-and-blues. Rockabilly singers displayed a personal manner and touch of warmth in their delivery. There was no singing in chorus by the musicians, as in Haley's band; the singing was done by one performer, who looked to the lead guitarist for strong accompaniment.

The first million-dollar rockabilly recording was made by Carl Perkins in 1956. Perkins wrote, sang, and strummed "Blue Suede Shoes," and his plea for personal identity appealed strongly to teenagers. Perkins was born in Jackson, Tennessee, in 1932, and his first guitar was made from a small cigar box, wire, and a broomstick. At age five he got a real guitar and learned to play as he spent time with black cotton pickers, who sang rhythm-and-blues. He worked at local spots beginning at age sixteen, and shortly thereafter wrote and recorded such songs as "Boppin' the Blues" and "Your True Love." Perkins's career, however, did not survive the competition posed by another rising young singer from Memphis at this time—a boy named Elvis Presley.

Elvis Presley

Elvis Presley, with his long hair, sideburns, flashy jewelry, and slinky outfits, was a revolutionary force and the most important rock star to emerge in the fifties. As a singing idol, whose every gyrating body movement reflected sensual feeling, his popularity surpassed that of any other artist and lasted until the Beatles' music appeared in the 1960s.

Born in Tupelo, Mississippi, in 1935, Elvis regularly attended church and revival meetings, and sang gospel hymns. The family moved to Memphis, where Elvis got his first guitar as a teenager. He imitated country ballads, spirituals, popular tunes, and blues he heard on the radio. He liked blues the best, which prompted him, a white singer, to emulate the black sound.

Elvis developed an intense emotional quality in a vocal style that shifted abruptly from high to low notes, choked on words, gulped, groaned, and exhorted. A breathless haze purported to sweep up listeners in warmth, tension, and release.

Audiences clamored for more and were rewarded with "Heartbreak Hotel," "That's All Right Mama," "Good Rockin' Tonight," and "Love Me Tender" (also a film). Between 1956 and 1958, several million-selling singles ("Hound Dog," "Jailhouse Rock," and "Treat Me Nice") helped to buy Elvis a shiny gold Cadillac which one can see today in Nashville's Country Hall of Fame and Museum, together with other Presley memorabilia.

The U.S. Army drafted the singer in 1958, and upon his discharge several years later, his image had changed somewhat to that of a pop singer. He was more clean cut and quieter, singing subdued songs, injecting a new religious element, as in "Cryin' in the Chapel," and a homey touch, as in "Kentucky Rain." His life was fraught with personal problems in the sixties that lasted until his death in 1975. He died at his Graceland Estate in Memphis, apparently from an overdose of drugs.

Graceland

At 3764 Elvis Presley Boulevard on Highway 51S in Memphis, going in the direction of Mississippi, stands the thirteen-acre Graceland Estate of the late singer. Hidden by a five-foot stone wall, is a curved driveway leading to a white-columned mansion on a grassy slope set back from the highway, and a wrought iron gate with musical notes looming large in metal.

Graceland, Elvis Presley's home in Memphis. (Courtesy Tennessee Touri., Development, Nashville)

Gardens and greenery abound. A swimming pool, stables, and offices are tucked away in back of the house. Graceland is not open to the public except by arrangement with private Graceland tours. Presley bought the house in 1959 and died in the second-floor bathroom in 1975. The bathroom was also a lounge with a large club chair, sunlamps, and reading lights. The main floor has high pile red carpeting in the front hallway. Meditation Garden is off to the side of the house and holds several familial burial plots. Presley, however, is buried in a six-crypt family room in Forest Hill Cemetery Mausoleum in Memphis.

Jerry Lee Lewis

Born in Ferraday, Louisiana, in 1935, Jerry Lee Lewis, like Elvis Presley, had a strong church background and listened to black blues singers. B. B. King, Ray Charles, and Bobby "Blue" Bland were his early models. After performing at the Blue Cat Club in Natchez, Mississippi, and at the Wagon Wheel Club, Lewis came to Memphis to record "A Whole Lotta Shakin' Goin' On," which he accompanied by wild stage antics, sighs, moans, panting, and a series of knocks, kicks, and thumps on the piano as he played. Once he was said to have sprinkled lighter fluid on the piano top, lit a match to it, and jumped off the stage. His was a style to remember.

"Breathless" and "Great Balls of Fire" were two hits that followed in the late fifties. His ratings declined at this time because of an unpopular marriage to a fourteen-year-old cousin. Even though this act was in keeping with the radical lifestyle of rock, colleagues frowned upon it. Lewis turned to recording country/Western music and soon had another hit, "Another Place, Another Time." Country radio stations today play his music regularly. Among the many Memphis rockabilly singers, such as Roy Orbison, Ronnie Hawkins, and Gene Vincent, Jerry Lee Lewis has been ranked second to Elvis.

New Orleans Rock

New Orleans was a city steeped in blues and jazz tradition, as was Memphis, and rock and roll emerged here in several styles. One characteristic style was that of a relaxed, shuffling, boogie-woogie piano, exemplified in the playing of Fats Domino.

Antoine "Fats" Domino was born into a musical family in New Orleans, in 1928. His father played violin and arranged for his son-in-law to teach Fats to play the piano. At the age of fourteen Fats quit school to find work in local clubs. One of these was the Hideaway (still here today), where music agents who heard him were impressed with his rolling piano, his high-pitched nasal voice, and his simple, unaffected manner, which contrasted sharply with the often hysterical performances of other rock artists. A recording session was arranged and "The Fat Man," Fats's first hit, became a million-seller in a short time. Saxophone, trumpet, guitar, bass, and drums accompanied him. Other hits followed: "Ain't it a Shame," "I'm in Love Again," and "Blueberry Hill." Far from being a sex symbol, Fats's delivery was clean, offering simple charm. His style influenced later New Orleans performers such as Shirley and Lee, Frankie Ford, and Huey "Piano" Smith.

Another version of New Orleans rock came forth in the music of Guitar Slim (Eddie Jones), born in Greenwood, Mississippi, in 1916. Slim played lead electric guitar with a tone so spellbinding that he claimed to have drawn people in from the streets to listen to his sound. Slim sang raw blues mixed with gospel, frequently accompanied by horns, reminiscent of a church choir. Many of the tunes he sang were arranged by Ray Charles, including "The Things I Used to Do," a top-selling recording. As with other artists, Slim died a young man (at age thirty-two, in 1959) of drink and poor health. His electric style was borrowed by later performers such as Jimi Hendrix.

A third New Orleans style, similar to that of Memphis's Jerry

Lee Lewis, was a wild and flamboyant one, seen and heard in perfor-mances of Richard Penniman, better known as Little Richard. Born in Macon, Georgia, in 1932, Little Richard sang in a church choir and learned to play piano in church. As a teenager, he seemed unusually wild and energetic, singing and playing at the Tick Tock Club, in Macon, at age fourteen. He won a talent show in Atlanta at age sixteen, which led to recording contracts. He turned out several powerhouse songs that were full of chaotic piano playing and howling vocalization: "Rip It Up," "Keep a-Knocking," and "Long Tall Sally." On stage, his clothes were garish, his hair, slinky, and his jewelry, ornate. Hard-rocking saxo-phones, amplified guitars, and pulsating drums kept pace with Little Richard as he executed his gyrations.

As though coming full circle, Little Richard left rock and roll in 1958 to become a minister in a Seventh Day Adventist Church. This lasted for several years until he returned to recording, but this time he sang traditional gospel tunes in a more subdued manner.

Ray Charles: The High Priest of Soul

All varieties of music began to appear, and the late fifties and sixties witnessed a particular mixture of gospel, blues, jazz, and pop, with a heavy beat, introduced by Ray Charles. Charles set the southern scene for a style which was to become known as Soul.

Ray Charles was born in Albany, Georgia, in 1930. He became blind as a young boy as a result of glaucoma. The family moved to Greenville, Florida, where he attended St. Augustine's School for the Blind and Deaf. Here, he learned to read and write music in braille and play piano, organ, trumpet, and clarinet. Church going provided an op-portunity for singing as well.

At the age of fifteen he quit school to look for work singing and playing piano. At first, he performed in the smooth, popular manner of a Nat "King" Cole and then in a blues-jazz style. His travels took him to New Orleans and Atlanta, where he combined a little of all the different kinds of music he knew to create a unique, eclectic sound—Soul. "Drown in My Tears" and "Hit the Road Jack" are some examples.

He added a kind of gospel choir, the Raelettes, consisting of three women utilizing the call–and–response technique (familiar in early black music) in the song "What'd I Say." A bass guitar accompanied Charles's fever-pitched voice that swooped exuberantly in wild abandon. His body swayed at the piano as he played, trance-like, full of gospel revival fervor. Audiences nicknamed him the "Reverend." "Georgia on

My Mind" and "I Can't Stop Lovin' You" were two more of his hits in the sixties, followed by "Don't Change on Me" and "Feel so Bad," in the seventies.

Ray Charles, who grew up poor, black, blind in the rural South, still performs and records today. Having suffered bouts of drug addiction, he has recovered and maintains his most descriptive title of "High Priest of Soul." His style has been adopted by many southern performers, notably: James Brown; Otis Redding, as in "These Arms of Mine"; Wilson Pickett, as in "If You Need Me"; and Mary Wells, as in "Two Lovers."

There are places in the South that have not let rock and its varieties pass from the musical scene. A list of such sites follows.

ALABAMA
Birmingham
The Birmingham/Jefferson Civic Center Concert Hall, 2114 First Avenue, is the place for large rock concerts. Recently, Lou Rawls and Roberta Flack entertained thousands here.

Foy Ballroom, Auburn, and Hulsey Center at the University of Alabama occasionally offer rock.

The Sheraton Mt. Brook Inn, 2800 US-280, the Holiday Inn, 5000 Tenth Avenue North, the Cane Break, 420 Twentieth Street South are reliable spots for rock.
Mobile
Chez Paree, in St. Francis Motel, off US-90.

FLORIDA
Boynton Beach
The Vintage Star Room, 715 South Federal Highway.
Clearwater
Woody Riley's Warehouse, North Garden Avenue at Drew, has occasional rock performances and some disco.
Fort Lauderdale
Mr. Pips, on Federal Highway, is noted for its disco, with several thousand lights flashing from mirrored ceilings.

The Candy Store Disco, Route A1A, between Los Olas and Sunrise Boulvard.

Carmen's Disco, near the Candy Store Disco.

The Four O'Clock Club, 2520 Miami Road, usually has three bands playing rock and disco.
Hallandale
The Limelight Disco, 1001 North Federal Highway, presents rock groups.
Key West
Sloppy Joe's and Captain Tony's Saloon at Duval and Green Streets offer rock groups.

Miami/Miami Beach

Your Place or Mine, 7995 West Flagler Street, offers disco.

Almost all the hotels along Collins Avenue, including the Fountainbleau Hilton and the Deauville, feature rock entertainment.

Hemingway, 219 North Twenty-first Avenue in Hollywood.

Oscar's, 901 SW Eighth Street in Calle Ocho.

The Miami Marine Stadium, a place for large groups, has welcomed Ray Charles.

Horatio's, in the Coconut Grove Hotel, overlooking Sailboat Bay.

Orlando

Phineas Phogg's Ballroom Works has a disco in Lili Marlene's Aviator's Pub. In addition to the balloon museum, there are three dance floors.

Palm Beach

The Palm Beach Ocean Hotel, 2830 South Ocean Boulevard, offers quality entertainment in rockabilly.

Sarasota

Ruby Tuesday's, 465 John Ringling Boulevard.

Tampa/St. Petersburg

Big Daddy's, 5701 Park Boulevard North, presents rock groups.

Forty Second Street Station, 4202 Bush Boulevard East, presents rock groups.

The Gallery Lounge, Blind Pass Road, presents rock groups.

Dr. Rubiconti's has a nineteenth-century setting and a sunken dance floor.

GEORGIA

Atlanta

Omni, downtown, presents groups such as All Turtles.

The Agora Ballroom, 665 Peachtree Street NE, is the most popular rock club in Atlanta, featuring such stars as Men at Work.

The Great Southeastern Music Hall is another favorite for large concerts.

The 688 Club, 688 Spring Street, offers rock bands such as the Swimming Pool Qs.

The Fox Theater, 660 Peachtree Street NE, offers name entertainment. Linda Ronstadt has performed here.

The Moonshadow Saloon, 1880 Johnson Road.

Rumors, North Decatur and Clairmont. Carl Perkins has been a guest artist here.

Savannah

Night-Flight Café, 113 East River Street, is an old cotton warehouse used for musical events including rock.

Malone's, Barnard Street ramp off River Street, has a large disco floor.

KENTUCKY
Ashland
The Paramount Arts Center, 1300 Winchester Avenue, presents performers such as Mac Frampton.
Lexington
The Center for the Arts, 430 West Vine Street, offers a variety of music.
Louisville
The Palace, 625 Fourth Avenue, is a newly restored theater with three-thousand seats. Crystal Gayle and Rick Springfield have been billed here. The Mill Run Theater and Louisville Gardens, have presented performers such as Nazareth and Billy Squire.
Masterson's, 1830 South Third Street, offers rock combos.

LOUISIANA
New Orleans
The Hideaway, 2601 Orleans, has featured Fats Domino.
The Godfather Disco, 3012 North Arnoult Road, has accompanying lights.
Fletcher's Nightery, 3208 North Arnoult Road, has video effects and a computerized dance floor. It's referred to as the "disco pacesetter of the South."

MISSISSIPPI
Tupelo
The birthplace of Elvis Presley, 306 Elvis Presley Drive. The small white frame house where Presley lived for the first thirteen years of his life can be visited.

MISSOURI
St. Louis
The Fox Theater, 527 North Grand Boulevard, features top names. Dionne Warwick sang here in recent months. The Checkerdome, 5700 Oakland, has featured Jefferson Starship and Shooting Star.

NORTH CAROLINA
Greensboro
The Greensboro Coliseum, 1921 West Lee Street, presents large rock concerts.
Carolina Theater, 310 South Green Street, hosts such stars as Herbie Mann and Betty Carter.
Nags Head
Atlantis, on the beach, is an informal spot. Dress in jeans and listen to rock combos.

Ocracoke
The Pirates Gallery occasionally features rock entertainment.
Winston-Salem
Convention Center, 301 West Fifth Street, is busy with all kinds of musical events, including rock.
The Forum, at Parkway Plaza Center, offers rock.

SOUTH CAROLINA
Charleston
The Dock Street Theater, 135 Church Street, will feature a rock star every now and then.
The Gaillard Municipal Auditorium, 77 Calhoun Street, also features a rock star occasionally.

TENNESSEE
Memphis
Graceland Mansion, Elvis Presley's home at the time of his death, is located at 3764 Elvis Presley Boulevard. It is open to the public by tour arrangement
Sun Recording Studio, 706 Union Avenue, is the site where Presley made his first recordings, followed by Jerry Lee Lewis and Roy Orbison, among others. The studio has been restored, and a variety of 1950s rock guitars, as well as other memorabilia, can be seen in the spring and summer.
Number One Beale Street features many varieties of rock.
The Memphis Music Heritage Festival, in September.
The Memphis in May month, in May.
Nashville
Check Section II.2 (Folk, Country and Bluegrass) under Nashville. All the places that formerly hosted country music host country-rock and rockabilly today. In addition, there are the following places:
Rock City, 107 Second Avenue North.
Spinners, 2600 Nolensville Road, offers disco.
Tennessee Performing Arts Center's Jackson Hall, where Jerry Lee Lewis, Carl Perkins, and Kris Kristofferson have entertained.

VIRGINIA
Alexandria
The Birchmere, 3901 Mt. Vernon Avenue, is a favorite spot for groups like Foggy Bottom.
Charlottesville
The West Virginian, 1521 University Avenue, has a good dance floor for blues, jazz, and rock.
The Mine Shaft, 1106 West Main Street, also has a good dance floor for blues, jazz, and rock.
The Odyssey Night Club, Route 250E, offers blues, jazz and rock.

Richmond

The Richmond Coliseum, 601 East Lee Street, always has something going on.

WEST VIRGINIA

Charleston

The Cultural Center, Capitol Complex, recently welcomed Nat Reese in concert.

Charleston Civic Center, 200 Civic Center Drive, is active all year round.

Huntington

Huntington's Civic Center holds musical events of all kinds.

OPERA, SYMPHONIC MUSIC, AND DANCE

Opera

New Orleans Opera in the Eighteenth and Nineteenth Centuries

New Orleans, the first city to provide a regular season of French opera, did so for a century and a half. New Orleans was considered the music center of the South. Its opera history began in 1791, when Santo Domingo refugees, Monsieur Louis Tabary and his troupe of actors, acquired a tiny building on Rue St. Pierre. The building, located at 732 St. Pierre Street, soon became known as Le Spectacle de la Rue St. Pierre. What began as a bare, damp, wooden, oil-lit structure was to house the first successful theatrical troupe performance. The threatre was so rudimentary that Tabary, himself, would come out on stage to announce the change of scenes, as there were no programs. Although grand opera was not yet performed, a short opera was presented along with the drama. The public reacted enthusiastically to this new form of entertainment, and soon the St. Pierre Theatre became a popular meeting place for the townspeople. The street is now St. Peter Street.

When the small building became inadequate for the throngs of people who frequented it, Tabary built another, more elaborate opera house in 1808—Le Theatre St. Philippe on St. Philippe Street, between Royal and Bourbon Streets. "Elaborate" meant a parquet, two tiers of boxes, and seats for seven-hundred people. The New Orleans of the late 1700s to the early 1800s was a gay, lively city, full of fancy dress balls and gala social affairs, due largely to the influence of the Creoles, who set the tone for social life. Because of their French heritage, light French opera, or opéra-comique, predominated. Some French opéra-comique composers whose works were performed at the St. Philippe Theatre were: Étienne Méhul (1763–1817), Francois Adrien Boieldieu (1775–1834), Daniel Francois Auber (1782–1871), and Ferdinand Hérold (1791–1833).

As opera and the St. Philippe theater became a major focus of social life, another new theater was needed to accommodate the ever-increasing numbers of opera-goers. The Theatre d'Orleans, built in 1813 at 721 Orleans Street, just off Royal Street, served as the successor to the St. Philippe Theatre. In 1816, it burned to the ground, but it was rebuilt by John Davis, also a Santo Domingo refugee, and reopened in 1818. Soon d'Orleans became one of the most fashionable places to be seen in in America. This theater had a spacious parquet, two tiers of boxes, several galleries, and "loges grilles" (latticed boxes) for people in need of privacy, namely mourners and pregnant women. Davis also added the New Orleans Ballroom wing, famous for "bals du Cordon Bleu" (quadroon balls) for Creole men. In 1828 the Theatre d'Orleans featured *The Vestal*, a grand opera in three acts. Beginning in the 1820s, Davis would bring a group of singers and musicians from France to perform here yearly, and during the mid-nineteenth century, it became common practice for impresarios to recruit European artists. Audiences were always large at the Theater d'Orleans, with Anglo-Saxon, Creole, and even slaves, accommodated in a special gallery for such purpose. Davis operated the Theatre d'Orleans for eighteen years, and his troupes staged hundreds of performances.

In 1835, the more lavish St. Charles Theatre was built at 432 St. Charles Street by the English actor, James Caldwell. Caldwell, who had studied the great opera houses of Europe, designed the St. Charles Theatre, which was comparable in magnificence. It seated about four-thousand, had a domed interior and a huge gas chandelier. Fire destroyed the St. Charles Theatre in 1842, but the following year it was rebuilt by Noah Ludlow and Sol Smith. The new St. Charles Theatre was as large as but less ornate than the first.

As opera flourished in New Orleans, it became an important element of correct social life. When theater managers recruited their artists from Europe, shops and schools would close as crowds lined the docks to watch prima donnas coming off the boats and driving through the streets in open carriages. The mid-nineteenth century was the golden age of opera in New Orleans.

Grand opera continued to captivate the people of New Orleans, and one Charles Boudousquie furthered the cause even more. In 1859, Boudousquie built the French Opera House, "The Lyric Temple of the South." This temple, located in the Vieux Carré, five blocks from Canal Street on the uptown corner of Bourbon and Toulouse Streets, was a four-story, brick building that seated about two-thousand comfortably, and housed twenty-five-hundred during gala occasions. Supposedly the best-designed opera house in the United States because every seat afforded a full view of the stage, it became the new music and social center of the city. It was also the scene of many carnival balls, receptions, and parties.

Rossini's *Guillaume Tell*, marked the beginning of a highly successful season at the French Opera House for Boudousquie. Boudousquie engaged an Italian-American soprano, Adelina Patti, who had made her opera debut in New York City at eighteen years old as Lucia in Donizetti's *Lucia di Lammermoor*. Hailed by critics, "Little Miss Patti" was an enormous hit in her role of Gilda in *Rigoletto* in 1860 at the French Opera House, and stayed on in New Orleans to perform for three months, becoming one of the most famous opera stars in history. The French Opera Company performed at this theater and became one of the South's finest contributions to musical culture.

In New Orleans, Sunday night was considered French opéra-comique night, and those who performed on Sunday night were *not* the weekly performers. At first, much of the Anglo-Saxon population considered the opéra-comique too risqué and inappropriate for young ladies, and only occasionally did a married or elderly woman venture to the opera on Sunday. However, the excitement of the opera soon succeeded in captivating the city and dispelling these strait-laced notions.

Rules and Duels

Since opera was an important part of social life in nineteenth-century New Orleans, opera lovers took themselves quite seriously. Each opera house had a strict set of rules which, if not obeyed, would result in heavy fines or even imprisonment. Proper attire (white gloves for women and full dress coats for men) was required at all times except on Sunday nights. The carrying of canes or swords by men was forbidden, as was noisy applauding, hissing, or throwing things onto the stage (at the risk of a $25 fine).

Regarding swords, it was not unusual to see rival impresarios fighting a duel. As in Paris, dueling was very much in vogue, concerning such issues as the relative merits of the prima donnas. It was wise to become an expert swordsman, especially if one was a manager.

People made a night of the opera. Arriving at six, those who did not leave at midnight to attend mass, watched expectantly as a great swinging floor was brought down over the parquet, so that they might dance until dawn. Gentlemen were requested, of course, to leave all weapons in the dressing room before they went into the ballroom, to prevent any dueling.

"The Swedish Nightingale"

Nineteenth-century New Orleans was graced by P.T. Barnum's protégée, soprano Jenny Lind, who not only captured audiences in new Orleans with her enormous vocal range (she could hit high G), but in every city in the United States in the early 1850s. When Lind arrived in New Orleans, the crowds that lined the levee to catch a glimpse of her must have intimidated this shy, retiring lady, for she apparently could not bring herself to walk down the gangplank in front of them. P. T.

Barnum hit upon a clever ruse, and unbeknownst to the throngs of admirers, veiled his sister and walked the plank with her to the waiting carriage. The crowds, thinking this was Lind, went home satisfied, and a little later, the real Lind inconspicuously boarded her coach and rode to her quarters.

Lind's first concert resulted in a sellout at the St. Charles Theatre, as did all her subsequent performances. Some of the tickets for her concerts were sold at auction, and the highest price was $240. Her fame quickly spread to rural areas, and even river planters put aside their bales of cotton to come and hear the "Swedish Nightingale." On her tour she sang such classics as arias from Bellini's *Norma, I Puritant,* and *La Sonnambula,* as well as arias by Mozart, Weber, and Meyerbeer. Some English and Scottish songs were included in her repertory, such as "The Last Rose of Summer." She also sang the American song, "Home, Sweet Home."

After the Civil War

The Civil War largely phased out the musical life of New Orleans, and musical societies and groups disbanded. However, just when it seemed that opera was gone, along came the brothers Alhaiza. In 1866, after the war, Marceline and Charles Alhaiza embarked on a journey to France to recruit a troupe for revival of New Orleans French Opera. But Marceline died in Europe, and on the way back to New Orleans, the ship carrying Charles and his newly-acquired troupe of fifty-seven French artists sunk in a violent storm off Tibee Island, Georgia. A third brother, Paul, assembled a troupe at the French Opera House in New Orleans, and for a few years, between 1880 and 1887, opera thrived. Opera revival in New Orleans at this time was due too to some of the city's most capable musicians, among whom were:

Giuseppe Ferrata. A pupil of Liszt, Ferrata taught at the Sophie Newcomb College of New Orleans for many years, and wrote many compositions.

Gregorio Curto. This Spaniard was responsible for training a generation of singers. He also wrote church music and taught music.

Mme. Jane Feodor and Ernest Gargano. Both were well-known vocal teachers and singers.

Although opera was revived in the late nineteenth century, people began to turn away from it as a form of entertainment, preferring, instead, jazz. The Opera House was used less and less and it slowly deteriorated. Seasons went by without a single opera performance. Then, in 1915, a fierce storm devasted the already decrepit building.

There were still those for whom opera had a special place, however, and the philanthropist, William Radcliffe Irby, bought the French Opera House and presented it to Tulane University, providing funds for its restoration. At the end of the first World War, the French Opera House opened again, trying desperately to rekindle the grace and elegance of the mid-nineteenth century. But, in 1919, after a performance of *Les Hugue-nots,* the ill-fated building was again destroyed, this time by fire. This marked the physical end of the theaters and of the opera heyday in New Orleans.

Symphonic Music

Mentioned in other chapters was the heavy influx of German immigrants to America in the early and mid-nineteenth century. They brought with them to the South their cultural heritage of Austro-German music, an outstanding example of which could have been heard in St. Louis, Missouri, where the groundwork was laid for what is today the St. Louis Symphony Orchestra.

Early Music in St. Louis and Forerunners of the St. Louis Symphony Orchestra

Historically, St. Louis got its first taste of serious music in its infancy. In 1818, interest in classical music was apparent after A. C. van Hirtum offered piano-forte classes, and Mme. Marie Victoire Adelaide Le Masurier de Perdreauville, former lady-in-waiting to Marie Antoinette, opened up an academy for young ladies with instruction in voice and instrumental music. Classical music soon became a standard course in schools for women. Following that, some of the noteworthy German-Americans who were responsible for the interest in classical music in St. Louis were Johann Weber, William Robyn, and Charles Balmer.

Johann Weber came to St. Louis in 1834 and brought with him some full orchestral compositions of Bach, Beethoven, Gluck, Handel, Haydn, and Mozart. Weber established the St. Louis Sacred Music Society. William Robyn came and taught music at St. Louis University, organized and trained the St. Louis Brass Band, and served later as a conductor of the St. Louis Musical Society, Polyhymnia.

Charles Balmer, a prolific composer, arrived in St. Louis as accompanist to Madame Carodoni-Allan, a celebrated singer. In 1848, with C. Henry Weber, he opened a music store and publishing house.

Gradually, with this impetus, choral and instrumental groups began to develop under different auspices (church, theater, and school). There grew such widespread interest in classical music that the J. C. Dinnies Company of St. Louis sold Italian, German, and French instruments (violins, clarinets, trombones, bassoons, guitars, trumpets, flutes, and piano-fortes). Some St. Louis citizens began to form music ensembles. The early traditional orchestra was the Polyhymnia, which presented concerts between 1845 and 1852. This orchestra was about the size of an eighteenth-century Haydn orchestra, consisting of thirty-five musicians.

Between 1848 and 1854, another group, the Germania Orchestra, made up of twenty-five musicians, carried forward the musical spirit. The orchestra toured, playing in many major cities. In 1853 the people of St. Louis heard Beethoven's Second Symphony in its entirety for the first time. The following year, the orchestra gave a series of five concerts, and there followed a desire to establish a permanent orchestra. Thus, the St. Louis Philharmonic Society was founded, and in 1860, the eminent German-American operatic composer and conductor, Fredrich Eduard de Sobolewski (1808–1871) was engaged as its conductor.

Sobolewski had been a pupil of Carl-Maria von Weber in Dresden from 1821 to 1824. He had also been a co-worker of Robert Schumann on his musical journal, *Neue Zeitschrift für music,* in which Schumann introduced such then unknowns as Chopin and the young Brahms. In Germany, Sobolewski had produced and conducted opera, and when he entered the United States in 1859, he assumed a post in Milwaukee where he staged his opera, *Mohega.* Under Sobolewski, the St. Louis Philharmonic Society grew and flourished, combining choral and symphonic works, and offering monthly concerts. Later, in 1869, the Theodore Thomas Orchestra of New York appeared in St. Louis on a national tour, which further inspired musical interest in the city.

In 1880, the St. Louis Choral Society was organized by Joseph Otten, organist and conductor. The society offered choral works of the highest calibre, including Handel's *Messiah,* Beethoven's "Mass in C," and Gounod's *Redemption.* Otten presented several concerts in the spring of 1881, and at times, collaborated with the visiting Theodore Thomas Orchestra in local festival productions.

Due to financing by Robert S. Brookings, the president of the Choral Society, the Society grew and broadened its program to include orchestral numbers as well as choral works. Then, in 1890, the St. Louis Philharmonic Society and the St. Louis Choral Society merged, becoming the St. Louis Choral-Symphony Society, today's St. Louis Symphony Orchestra.

Some Early Conductors of the St. Louis Symphony Orchestra

Alfred Ernst
This young German pianist first assumed leadership of the St. Louis Symphony in 1894. Although an excellent musician, some criticized him for spontaneous improvisation which was thought to overshadow the strict interpretation of the score. Under his baton, however, the orchestra grew in significance. From 1900 to 1901, the fifty-five musi-

cians and the two-hundred members of the chorus presented three oratorios and three symphony concerts. Then, between 1905 and 1906, Ernst introduced a series of Sunday afternoon "Pops" concerts. At the end of 1907, Ernst returned to his native Germany to supervise a production of his own operatic works.

Max Zach

The St. Louis Symphony Orchestra needed a new conductor in 1907, and Max Zach, a violinist from the Boston Symphony Orchestra, took up the baton. Zach had been brought to the United States in 1896 by Wilhelm Gericke, conductor of the Boston Symphony Orchestra from 1884 to 1889, and then again from 1898 to 1906. Zach had conducted the Boston Pops from 1887 to 1897 and had been a member of the Adamoski String Quartet. Unlike Ernst, Zach was highly disciplined and a strict interpreter of musical scores. Under his leadership, the number of concerts increased, regular concert seasons were established, the orchestra expanded, tours were begun, and repertory was expanded to include French and Russian works (Saint-Saens, Berlioz, Franck, Tchaikovsky and Rachmaninoff) as well as standard Austro-German fare. Zach also presented works by some American composers. He continued the Sunday afternoon Pops concerts begun by Ernst.

Interior of Powell Symphony Hall, St. Louis, Missouri (Courtesy St. Louis Symphony Orchestra)

Rudolph Ganz

In midseason of 1921 Zach died, and Rudolph Ganz replaced him. Ganz was a gifted pianist, but had had little orchestral experience. His main contribution was made in the area of children's concerts, which were so successful that other regional orchestras sought to follow this pattern. Ganz resigned in 1927 to rejoin the staff of the Chicago Music College, where he had worked in previous years. After World War I, under Ganz, the American repertory gave way to more standard Austro-German music.

Vladimir Golschmann

During several years after Ganz left, the St. Louis Orchestra was taken over by a series of guest conductors. Public interest waned until Damrosch, of New York, and Koussevitzky, of Boston, recommended a Frenchman of Russian parentage, Vladimir Golschmann, to succeed Ganz. Golschmann took over in 1931, having come to the attention of the music world with his "Concerts Golschmann" in Paris in 1919. These concerts had introduced young, avant-garde French composers and were so successful that in 1924 Golschmann was invited to New York for his first United States appearance.

As conductor of the St. Louis Symphony Orchestra, from 1931 to 1957, Golschmann helped to establish the Orchestra as a major ensemble through excellent technique and broad repertory. With his romantic temperament and dramatic nature, he championed new, unfamiliar music of French composers along with the familiar works of Beethoven and Brahms. In 1941 he conducted the orchestra in *La Sultane* by Francois Couperin, orchestrated by the twentieth-century French composer, Darius Milhaud. Golschmann performed Sunday Pops concerts only infrequently during the remainder of his term.

In 1957, he put down the baton to go to Tulsa, and then to the Denver Symphony Orchestra through the 1969–70 season.

The St. Louis Symphony Orchestra originally performed in Odeon Hall, destroyed by fire, and then in Kiel Municipal Auditorium. Kiel was larger than Odeon, with a seating capacity of about thirty-five hundred. Today, the orchestra performs in Powell Hall in downtown St. Louis and has an active music schedule. The current conductor is Leonard Slatkin.

Dance

Charleston, South Carolina, was one of the leading cultural centers of the American colonies in the eighteenth century. Dancing began when Englishman Henry Holt, the first professional dancer to appear in America, came to Charleston in 1734, and opened a dancing school. Holt went on to arrange America's first ballet (then called pantomime), *The Adventures of Harlequin and Scaramouch with the Bourgo'master trick'd*, in 1735. This performance took place in the Courtroom of the Exchange Building overlooking the harbor, since there were not yet any theaters in Charleston. Holt helped erect the Dock St. Theatre, one of America's earliest playhouses, which was reconstructed two-hundred years later in 1936, and is in use today. Then, in 1765, one Thomas Pike offered the first course in the art of dancing.

Other dancing masters appeared in Charleston, but not until 1794 was full scale ballet performed, with the arrival of Santo Domingo refugees as well as refugees from the French Revolution. Of the numerous artists, two who especially contributed to the development of ballet, giving Charleston its first resident company and season of performances, were the choreographers, Alexandre Placide and Jean Baptiste Francisqui.

Alexandre Placide, an actor, rope-dancer, acrobat, mime, and entrepreneur, had studied at the Paris Opera Ballet School. Francisqui, a classical dancer and choreographer, had also danced in France.

In 1794, The French Theatre opened on Church Street, with a program which included Jean Jacques Rousseau's musical interlude, *Pygmalion*, and a ballet pantomine, *The Three Philosophers, or the Dutch Coffee House*, which starred Francisqui as dancer, and Placide on the tightrope. Placide's wife, Suzanne, made her début the next evening as Rosetta in *The Bird Catchers*, which Placide had introduced two years earlier in New York. *Robinson Crusoe*, with Francisqui as Friday, was also presented.

Soon, the French dancers moved to the more spacious Charleston Theatre. This theater had a good orchestra, machinery for special effects, and skilled artists for building scenery.

The 1794–95 season featured dancing along with opera and drama at the Charleston Theatre. About thirty ballets in all were produced. In 1799, Jean Marie Legé and his wife became leading dancers in the Charleston Ballet. Old ballets were revived, and new ones produced. One of the most elaborate pantomimes was *The Birth Day of General George Washington, or the Triumph of Virtue*. Ballet was prominent in Charleston until 1812 when Placide died. Subsequent season failed to achieve the same splendor of the late-eighteenth century, and ballet faded from the scene.

North Carolina Dance Theater

A major Southern dance company today is the North Carolina Dance Theatre, in Winston-Salem, created in 1970 by Robert Lindgren. This company was begun as a student group. Lindgren, who had had a lengthy dancing career, performed with the Ballet Russe de Monte Carlo in 1942, with the American Ballet Theatre of New York, and the New York City Ballet, and was co-director of a ballet school in Phoenix, Arizona. In 1965, he became Dean of the School of Dance at the North Carolina School of the Arts.

Salvatore Aiello, originally with the Royal Winnepeg Ballet, came to Winston-Salem in 1980. He, like Lindgren, has had considerable background in dancing, having been a principal dancer with the Eglevsky Ballet and made many guest appearances in such companies as the Ballet de San Juan, the Frankfurt Ballet, and the Alvin Ailey Dance Theatre.

The North Carolina Dance Theatre tours the United States extensively for most of their season. Sixteen dancers perform both classical and contemporary works by many choreographers, from Petipa to Driver. Some examples are: *Pas de Dix*, by Glazounov; *Allegro Brillante*, by Tchaikovsky; *Concerto Barocco*, by Bach; *Valse Fantasie*, by Glinka; *Dichterliebe*, by Schumann; *Women*, by Slick; and *Resettings*, by Purcell.

A Major Southern Festival Today

A particularly lovely southern festival, featuring many forms of music, takes place in historic Charleston, South Carolina in May and June. It is the Spoleto Festival.

In 1958, Italian composer, Gian-Carlo Menotti founded the Spoleto Festival in Italy, just north of Rome. When Menotti came to America, he looked for a place that could be an American counterpart in symphonic music, opera, and dance, and in 1977, he selected Charleston, South Carolina, because of its charming colonial architecture, its musical heritage, and its beautifully preserved eighteenth-century homes, gardens, plantations, and churches.

The Festival is held all over the city in theaters, auditoriums, courtyards, parks, and plantations, including the Dock Street Theater, the Garden Theater, the Gaillard Municipal Auditorium, and the College of Charleston. International visiting artists perform diverse works of high caliber. Some who have appeared have been cellist Yo-Yo Ma and the Eliot Feld Ballet. The quiet charm and hospitality of Charleston imbue the event with old-world, pre-Civil War southern gentility and ambience, and heighten the musical experience.

Opportunites are abundant in the South for performances of symphonic music, opera, and dance. The following pages list such places.

ALABAMA

Auburn

Auburn has a symphony orchestra that plays in Union Ballroom and in Foy Ballroom.

Birmingham

The Birmingham/Jefferson Civic Center, between Ninth and Eleventh Avenues North and Nineteenth and Twenty-first Streets, is a large building (it extends four square blocks) which is used for many events. It's home to the Birmingham Symphony and the Civic Opera, and host to many musical and dance groups. The concert hall has three-thousand seats and the theater, almost one-thousand.

The Greater Birmingham Arts Alliance, 2114 First Avenue. Samford University Concert Hall, Eight-hundred Lake Shore Drive.

The University of Alabama Theater.

Fort Payne

The old Opera House, built in 1889, located at 510 Gault Avenue North, is the oldest Alabama theater in use today. It was restored in 1970 as a Cultural Arts Center.

Greenville

The Ritz Theater welcomes chamber music groups.

Huntsville

Big Spring Park offers semi-classical music in a "Pops-in-the-Park" program, performed by the Huntsville Symphony, in May.

The concert hall in Von Braun Civic Center, 700 Monroe Street SW.

Mobile

There's a Mobile Symphony here and a Civic Music Association.

Montgomery

Tullibody Music Hall at Alabama State University, South Jackson and I-85, has regular musical fare.

The Montgomery Museum of Fine Arts, 440 South McDonough Street, offers a concert series.

Tuscaloosa

The University of Alabama, University Boulevard, between Thomas Street and Ninth Avenue, presents a concert almost every day.

The Bama Theater, 600 Greensboro Avenue, offers chamber music.

Wetumpka

Jasmine Hill, off US-231, presents dance groups from the spring through the fall.

ARKANSAS

Eureka Springs

The Music Chapel in Miles Musical Museum, on Highway 62, is a special attraction. Organs and many stringed instruments are on display there.

Inspiration Point Fine Arts Colony, on Route 2 presents a Festival of Music, with instrumental works, opera, and dance, in the summer.

Fayetteville
The Fine Arts Center at the University of Arkansas, Garland Avenue, is very active musically.

Hot Springs
Convention Auditorium holds varied musical programs.

Little Rock
Convention Center Music Hall, Markham and Broadway, welcomes the Arkansas Symphony Orchestra, the Arkansas Opera Theater and the Ballet Arkansas.

The Fine Arts Building at the University of Arkansas, Little Rock, welcomes guest artists.

Arkansas Repertory Theater, 712 East Eleventh Street, presents chamber music during the year.

FLORIDA

Coral Gables
Gusman Concert Hall, at the University of Miami, Miller Drive, presents recitals and concerts including chamber music.

Fort Lauderdale
The War Memorial Auditorium, 800 NE Eighth Street, presents symphony concerts.

Hollywood
Young Circle Bandshell, in Young Circle Park, hosts concerts given by the Greater Hollywood Philharmonic Orchestra. A Seven Lively Arts Festival is given here in March.

Miami/Miami Beach
Dade County Auditorium, 2901 West Flagler Street, is always busy with opera, chamber music, symphony orchestras, and dance. Some of the groups that have performed here are the Florida Philharmonic Orchestra, the Alberni String Quartet, and the Miami Ballet Company.

Gusman Cultural Center, 174 East Flagler Street, has a similar schedule to the Dade County Auditorium.

The Theater of the Performing Arts, 1700 Washington Avenue, presents the Miami Beach Symphony.

The Miami Beach Convention Center features a Festival of the Arts and many programs.

The Marine Stadium, off Rickenbacker Causeway, offers many programs. Bayfront Park, between Biscayne Bay and Biscayne Boulevard, from NE Fifth Street to SE Second Street, has Civic Auditorium and Chapin Plaza.

Orlando
The Bob Carr Performing Arts Center, 401 West Livingston, is the musical hub of Orlando. It welcomes the Florida Symphony Orchestra, and numerous music, dance, and opera groups.

Palm Beach

West Palm Beach Auditorium, Palm Beach Lakes Boulevard, has presented the Florida Gulf Coast Symphony, the Oakland Ballet, and soloists such as Itzhak Perlman and Aldo Ciccolini.

Four Arts Plaza, at One Four Arts Plaza, is another cultural center.

Pensacola

The Great Gulf Coast Festival, with all varieties of music, takes place in November.

Sarasota

Van Wezel Performing Arts Hall, 777 North Tamiani Trail, presents concerts, opera, and ballet. The inside of the hall is painted deep purple for majestic effect.

The Asolo Theater, 5401 Bayshore Road, has eighteenth-century interiors, which were imported piece by piece from an Italian castle in Asolo, Italy. Concerts and operas are given here with opera in English by the Asolo Opera Company.

The campus of the University of Southern Florida presents a New College Music Festival in June. Artists such as flutist Julius Baker, trumpeter Robert Nagel, and violinist Joseph Silverstein have appeared.

Music of Yesterday, 5500 North Tamiani Trail, has musical antiques on display.

Tallahassee

Florida State University has a Fine Arts Festival with varied musical fare in February.

Tampa/St. Petersburg

McKay Auditorium, at the University of Tampa, Kennedy Boulevard, and Bayfront Auditorium, St. Petersburg, present performances by the Florida Gulf Coast Symphony.

Winter Park

Rollins College, Park and Holt Avenues, has a Bach Festival in February. The room where the programs take place is decorated with stained glass windows, wood carvings, and works of art.

GEORGIA

Atlanta

Symphony Hall, in the Atlanta Memorial Arts Center, 1280 Peachtree Street NE, presents the Atlanta Symphony Orchestra as well as numerous other musical companies.

The Atlanta Civic Center, Piedmont and Forest Avenues, presents the Metropolitan Opera as well as other groups.

Piedmont Park, Tenth Street and Piedmont Avenue, hosts outdoor musical programs, such as Arts Festival of Atlanta in May.

The Fox Theater, 660 Peachtree Street NE, hosts the Atlanta Ballet and popular musical programs. A former movie palace, the Fox has elegant 1930 interiors, impressive Moorish architecture, and stars and clouds painted on its ceilings.

Columbus

The old Springer Opera House, 103 Tenth Street, is a restored Victorian theater, open for musical performances.

Macon

The Coliseum, 200 Coliseum Drive, presents many concerts.

The Grand Opera House, 651 Mulberry Street, was originally an Academy of Music in 1884. It has been restored for community cultural events. Such notables as Van Cliburn have appeared here.

Savannah

Telfair Academy of Arts and Sciences, 121 Barnard Street, is the oldest art museum in the Southeast and presents concerts throughout the year.

KENTUCKY

Frankfort

Capitol Plaza, at Civic Center, is active in musical events.

Horse Cave

Horse Cave Theater, 107 Main Street, is in the renovated Thomas Opera House, built in 1911, and features musical programs.

Lexington

The old Opera House, built in 1886, at 401 West Short Street, has been restored and reconstructed to house ballet and musical events.

The University of Kentucky Center for the Arts is very active in classical music.

Louisville

A new Kentucky Arts Center opened in 1983, which comprises two auditoriums with a total of three-thousand seats. Formerly, the Louisville Orchestra and Kentucky Opera performed at Macauley Theater, 315 West Broadway.

Memorial Auditorium, 970 South Fourth Street, hosts the Louisville Ballet.

Oxmoor Center, 7900 Shelbyville Road, hosts "pop" concerts during the Kentucky Derby Festival.

The Palace Theater, 625 Fourth Avenue, hosts all musical events.

The University of Louisville School of Music presents programs regularly.

Prestonburg

Jenny Wiley State Park is a site of many musical events held in the Summer Music Theater.

Shelbyville

The theater building, 800 West Main Street, offers a variety of music, including recitals.

LOUISIANA

Baton Rouge

Since 1944, the Louisiana State Festival of Contemporary Music has been a highlight in April. Twentieth-century music is offered by composers Carlos Chavez, Otto Luening, and Elie Siegmeister.

New Orleans

The renovated Orpheum Theater, at University Place near the French Quarter, hosts the New Orleans Philharmonic Symphony. The theater's interior has restored Beaux-Arts décor, and just under two-thousand seats. The facade has polychrome terra cotta, complete with cherubs and maidens.

Municipal Auditorium, former home of the Philharmonic, hosts many musical groups including dance and opera.

Shreveport

Convention Center, 600 Clyde Fant Parkway, is where the Shreveport Symphony, Civic Opera, and other musical groups are featured.

Hargrove Memorial Band Shell at Centenary College, 2911 Centenary Boulvard, holds summer concerts.

MISSISSIPPI

Biloxi

The Cultural Center, Le Meuse Street, hosts all the performing arts.

The Saenger Theater is a new theater under reconstruction to become a center for the performing arts.

Jackson

The Arts Festival, featuring concerts and ballets, in April.

Mississippi Arts Center, 201 East Pascagoula Street, is home to Opera South (the only black opera company in the United States), the Mississippi Opera, Jackson Symphony Orchestra, and Jackson Ballet.

Pascagoula

A Festival of Arts takes place in April.

MISSOURI

St. Louis

Powell Symphony Hall, 718 North Grand Boulevard, hosts the St. Louis Orchestra, one of the oldest orchestras in the country. Acoustics here are excellent.

Washington University hosts Little Symphony chamber concerts during the summer.

A large amphitheater in the fourteen-thousand-acre Forest Park, Lindell Boulevard, between Skinker and Kingshighway Boulevard, offers light opera performed by the Municipal Opera Company. Dance is here also, with the stars Margot Fonteyn and Gene Kelly having appeared in past years.

Loretta Hilton Center of Webster Groves, just outside St. Louis, hosts the Opera Theater of St. Louis.
Kansas City
The Lyric Opera performs opera in English at 1029 Central.
The Municipal Auditorium, 301 West Thirteenth Street, presents symphonic music by the Kansas City Philharmonic.
The University of Missouri, 5100 Rockhill Road, offers a great deal of music.
Joplin
The Dorothy Hoover Museum, South Chifferdecker Park, on US-66, has interesting musical instruments on display.

NORTH CAROLINA
Brevard
Situated in the Smoky Mountains, Brevard is referred to as the summer cultural center of the South because of the Brevard Music Center. Symphony, choral, chamber, dance, and operatic works are presented at the Summer Festival of Music, with such distinguished guest artists as Marilyn Horne and Jerome Hines.
Burnsville
"Music in the Mountains," a chamber music series, takes place in the summer.
Charlotte
Owens Auditorium, 110 East Seventh Street, hosts the Charlotte Opera, the Charlotte Symphony Orchestra, Dance Charlotte, and many other musical companies.
Durham
Duke University, 6695 College Station, has a very active music calendar in chamber music, choral works, and dance. The America Dance Festival has its home here.
Greensboro
Guilford College hosts the Eastern Music Festival in the summer.
The Carolina Theater, 310 South Green Street, welcomes the Greensboro Symphony Orchestra, dance groups, opera companies, and a variety of music.
Raleigh
Memorial Auditorium presents the North Carolina Symphony.
Stewart Theater, at North Carolina State University, hosts all kinds of musical events. The José Limon Dance Company performed here recently.
April ushers in Artsplosure, a city-wide celebration of performing arts.
Civic Center is another site for music programs.
Winston-Salem
Reynolds Auditorium, 610 Coliseum Drive, holds many musical events,

including the Winston-Salem Symphony.

The Coliseum, on Cherry Marshall, holds all kinds of musical events.

Convention Center, 301 West Fifth Street, holds all kinds of musical events

Wake Forest University presents an Artists Series.

North Carolina School of the Arts has opera, dance and musical productions. Some native groups in Winston-Salem are the North Carolina Dance Theater, the Piedmont Chamber Orchestra, and the Moravian Music Foundation (mentioned in Section I., Chapter 3).

SOUTH CAROLINA

Abbeville

The old Opera House stands next to City Hall on the square and retains some aristocratic, if faded, elegance in its gilded box seats.

Charleston

Gaillard Auditorium, 77 Calhoun, presents the Charleston Symphony and visiting orchestras.

Simons Center, at the College of Charleston, 66 George Street, offers a great deal of music.

The Spoleto Festival is *all* in May, when symphony, chamber music, opera and ballet reign. Charleston, with its eighteenth- and nineteenth-century homes, gardens, and plantations, lends itself beautifully to this event, which lasts until June. The Dock Street Theater, the original home of the Charleston Ballet, hosts chamber music at 135 Church Street, in a reconstructed theater.

Columbia

The Columbia Museum of Art and Science, 1112 Bull Street, presents concerts.

Spartanburg

Converse College, on East Main Street, presents concerts, dance programs, and music festivals, especially a contemporary and a baroque music festival.

TENNESSEE

Chattanooga

Tivoli Theater, 709 Broad Street, hosts concerts, opera, and dance. The Chattanooga Symphony and Chattanooga Opera perform here.

Knoxville

The Knoxville Symphony Orchestra has a regular season here.

Memphis

Brooks Art Gallery, off Poplar Avenue in Overton Park, presents chamber music concerts. The Memphis Symphony Orchestra, the Opera, and Civic Ballet perform in the Civic Auditorium.

Nashville
Vanderbilt University features chamber music programs and recitals.
War Memorial Auditorium hosts the Nashville Symphony.
Sewanee
Sewanee Summer Music Center, on the campus of University of the
South, amidst woodland forests of the Cumberland Plateau, presents
concerts all summer long.
Townsend
The Tuckaleechee Cove Arts and Music Festival takes place in September.

VIRGINIA
Norfolk
Center Theater, Ninth and Granby Streets, presents concerts by the
Norfolk Symphony Orchestra.
Orkney Springs
The Shenandoah Valley Music Festival, in Orkney Springs Hotel Pavilion, offers classical music and "pops" in July. Open on all sides, with
seven-hundred seats and the lawn, the Pavilion is a lovely setting for
music. Musicians come from all over the country and more than ninety
orchestras are represented.
Richmond
The Mosque, 6 North Laurel Street, hosts the Richmond Symphony.
Staunton
Gypsy Hill Park, on Churchville and Thornrose Avenues, holds summer
concerts.
Vienna
Wolf Trap Farm Park, 1624 Trap Road, in the foothills of the Blue Ridge
Mountains, is currently being reconstructed after a fire in 1982, and will
continue to host symphonic and chamber music, opera, dance, and other
musical varieties. Shirley Verrett and Carlos Montoya have appeared
here. The programs take place during the summer.
Williamsburg
Governor's Palace, an elegant mansion of Colonial America, with ten
acres of gardens, has chamber music concerts from the spring through
the fall.

WEST VIRGINIA
Charleston
State Cultural Center, next to the State Capitol, on Washington Street
East, is the site for all kinds of musical fare, including the Charleston
Symphony Orchestra.
The University of Charleston Auditorium holds many musical events.
Civic Center, at 200 Civic Center Drive, holds many musical events.

Charles Town
Old Opera House, 204 North George.
Elkins
Harper McNeely Auditorium offers music programs.
Huntington
Smith Music Hall has welcomed the Huntington Chamber Orchestra.
Huntington Galleries, 2033 McCoy Road, Park Hills, holds concerts.
Civic Center holds concerts.
Marshall University, Third Avenue and Hal Greer Boulevard, has regular concert series.
Wheeling
Capitol Music Hall, 1015 Main Street, presents a variety of programs, including the Wheeling Symphony Orchestra.
Oglebay Park, on WVA-88, welcomes all musical fare, with such programs as the Audubon String Quartet. The park is a beautifully landscaped area of 1460 acres, pleasant for listening to "Music Under the Stars."

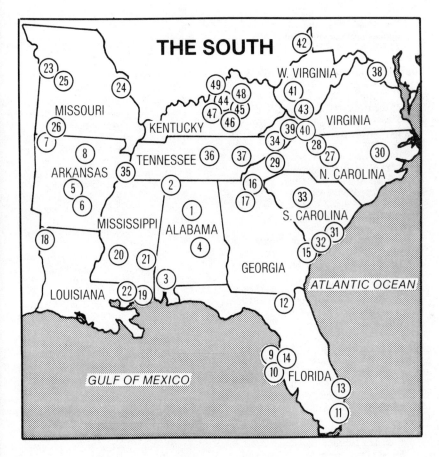

The South

1. Fairfield, AL—Miles College, 5500 Avenue G., gospel choir
2. Florence, AL—Birthplace of W.C. Handy (1873–1958), "Father of the Blues," 620 W. College Street
3. Mobile, AL—Mardi Gras on Shrove Tuesday, downtown
4. Montgomery, AL—Home of Hank Williams, Sr. (1923–1953), country music star
5. Little Rock, AR—Little Rock Convention Center Music Hall, Markham and Broadway
6. Pine Bluff, AR—Jack Rabbit Club nightspot for jazz and blues
7. Eureka Springs, AR—Site of Ozark Folk Festival
8. Mountain View, AR—Site of Ozark Folk Center, a folk music institution

9. Clearwater, FL—Woody Riley's Warehouse, North Garden Avenue and Drew Street. Place for jazz and country music
   Clearwater, FL—Traveler's Motel Lounge, 4767 NW Thirty-sixth Street. Jazz spot.
10. Treasure Island, FL—Bilmar Hotel, Gulf Boulevard, for jazz
11. Coconut Grove, FL—Village Inn, 3131 Commodore Plaza. Jazz
12. White Springs, FL—Stephen Foster Center on north bank of Suwannee River
13. Palm Beach, FL—Time Out Lounge, 3342 Shawnee Avenue. Spot for jazz and blues
14. Tampa, FL—Tampa Theater, North Franklin Street. Jazz place

15. Savannah, GA—International folk dances downtown. Night Flight Café, 113 E. River Street for jazz, blues, and soul

16. Hiawassee, GA—Mountain Fair Music Hall, Fairgrounds

17. Cumming, GA—Lanierland County Music Park, off GA-306

18. Shreveport, LA—Birthplace of Huddie Ledbetter (Leadbelly) (1888–1949), early blues singer, later folk singer. Radio Station KWKH for broadcasts of Louisiana Hayride

19. Biloxi, MS—Mardi Gras on Shrove Tuesday, downtown

20. Jackson, MS—Ramada Inn Coliseum, 400 Greymont Avenue. All varieties of popular music

21. Meridian, MS—Home of Jimmie Rodgers (1897–1933), country music star. Highland Park has the Jimmie Rodgers Museum

22. Natchez, MS—Natchez Little Theater Playhouse, Linton Avenue and Maple Street has Mississippi Medicine Shows with country music

23. Kansas City, MO—Riverfront area is where Count Basie and Charlie "Yardbird" Parker played piano and trumpet in the late 1920s–early 1930s, heyday of jazz in Kansas City. Agricultural Hall of Fame holds Renaissance Music Festivals

24. St. Louis, MO—Goldenrod Showboat, 400 N. Wharf Street for Dixieland jazz. Laclede's Landing, Fourth and Market Street on riverfront for folk and country music. Powell Symphony Hall, 718 North Grand Boulevard, home of St. Louis Symphony Orchestra

25. Sedalia, MO—Birthplace of Scott Joplin, ragtime composer (1868–1917), and "Maple Leaf Rag" played at the Maple Leaf Club, Lamine and Main Streets at the turn of the 20th century

26. Branson, MO—In Ozark Mountains, site of country music on US-76

27. High Point, NC—High Point Theater and Exhibition Center, 220 E. Commerce Street, for jazz

28. Winston-Salem, NC—Fairgrounds for Dixieland jazz. Moravian Music Foundation, 20 Cascade Avenue, for history of Moravian music

29. Asheville, NC—Civic Center, Haywood Street. Musical events including folk and mountain music and dance

30. Union Grove, NC—Van Hoy Amphitheater for Bluegrass, fiddling, gospel singing and psaltery

31. Charleston, SC—Famous Spoleto Festival with many varieties of music

32. Hilton Head, SC—Sea Pines Plantation for old-world jazz

33. Columbia, SC—Jamil Temple, Jamil Road, for gospel singing

34. Bristol, TN—Steele Creek Music Park celebrates the discovery of country music stars here

35. Memphis, TN—Beale Street for historic jazz places and current renovation. Golden Nugget, 2491 Elvis Presley Boulevard. Graceland home of Elvis Presley (1935–1975). Hernando's Hide-Away for jazz. Civic Center for varieties of music.

36. Smithville, TN—Site of Old-Time Fiddlers' Jamborees

37. Knoxville, TN—World's Fair in 1982 with country and Bluegrass in Tennessee Amphitheater on Fairgrounds

38. Vienna, VA—Wolf Trap Farm for the Performing Arts, Trap Road. All varieties of music

39. Abingdon, VA—Country music in Virginia Highlands

40. Galax, VA—Felts Park for Old-Time Fiddlers' Conventions

41. Charleston, W. VA—Cultural Center in Capitol Complex for all varieties of music

42. Wheeling, W. VA—Brush Run Park, off I-70, and Oglebay Park, W. VA-88 for country and jazz. Radio Station WWVA for country, and Capitol Music Hall, 1015 Main Street, for varieties of music

43. Athens, W. VA—Concord College has the John Henry Folk Festival

44. Bardstown, KY—Talbot Amphitheater in "My Old Kentucky Home" State Park for programs of Stephen Foster's music

45. Berea, KY—Mountain Folk Festivals regularly in Berea. Berea College has Indian Fort Theater for folk musicals

46. Renfro Valley, KY—Home of McLain Family Band at Big Hill Farm, and barn dances since 1939

47. Hodgenville, KY—Hodgen's Mill and Lincoln Jamboree on US-31E

48. Lexington, KY—Bluegrass State Fair at Masterson Station Park on US-421, Rupp Arena at the Lexington Center, 430 W. Vine Street, for Bluegrass and country, and Breeding Night Club, 1505 New Circle Road, for country

49. Louisville, KY—Riverfront Plaza holds big music festivals

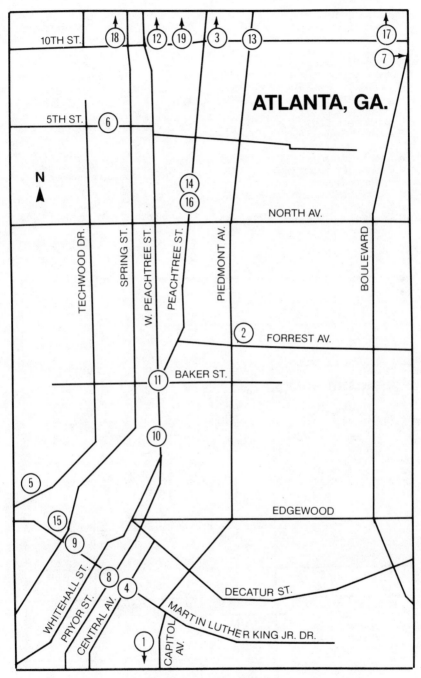

Atlanta, GA

1. Atlanta Stadium, Capitol Avenue. Site of jazz festivals and musical events

2. Civic Center, 395 Piedmont Avenue. Place for a variety of musical events

3. *Memorial Arts Center, 1280 Peachtree Street NE, for musical events and home of Atlanta Symphony in Symphony Hall*
4. *Underground Atlanta, Central Avenue and Martin Luther King Drive. Numerous places for jazz, rock, and country*
5. *Omni Complex, 120 Techwood Drive NW. Places for jazz and all popular music*
6. *Café Erewhon, 60 Fifth Street NW. Folk*
7. *Admiral Benbow Inn, 1419 Virginia Avenue, for country and Bluegrass*
8. *Dante's Down the Hatch, 84 Pryor Street in Underground Atlanta, especially good for jazz*
9. *Pascal's Carrousel Lounge, 830 Martin Luther King Drive, for jazz*
10. *Peachtree Center Plaza, Peachtree and Cain streets, for jazz and all popular music*
11. *Hyatt Regency Hotel, Peachtree and Baker streets, for jazz*
12. *Radio Station WSB, 1601 W. Peachtree Street NE. First radio station to play mountain music in 1922*
13. *Piedmont Park, Tenth Street and Piedmont Avenue, outdoor musical programs and Arts Festival of Atlanta*
14. *Agora Ballroom, 655 Peachtree Street NE, for rock*
15. *Six Eighty-Eight Club, 688 Spring Street, Big-Band sounds*
16. *Fox Theater, 660 Peachtree Street NE, for Atlanta Ballet and popular music*
17. *Moonshadow Saloon, 1880 Johnson Road, for rock*
18. *Another Admiral Benbow Inn, 1470 Spring Street NW, for country and Bluegrass*
19. *Keyboard Lounge, 3861 Roswell, for jazz*

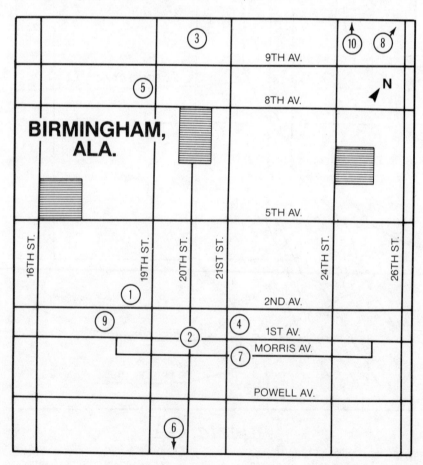

Birmingham, AL

1. Alabama Theater on Second Avenue for musical events
2. Birmingham Green for concerts
3. Birmingham/Jefferson Civic Center, Ninth and Eleventh avenues North between Ninteenth and Twenty-first streets, for varied musical programs
4. Greater Birmingham Arts Alliance, 2114 First Avenue, for symphonic music
5. Municipal Auditorium, 1930 Eighth

Avenue North, for musical events
6. The Cane Break, 420 Twentieth Street South, for country and rock
7. The Cobblestone on Morris Avenue for country
8. Holiday Inn, 5000 Nineteenth Avenue North, for rock and popular music
9. Ritz Theater, First Avenue, for musical events
10. Sheraton Mt. Brook Inn, 2800 US-280, for rock and popular music

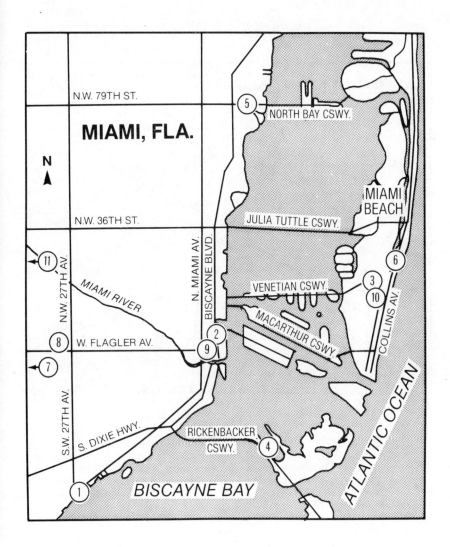

Miami/Miami Beach, FL

1. Dinner Key Auditorium, 3400 Pan American Drive, for popular music, rock, and disco
2. Miami Bayfront Auditorium, 499 Biscayne Boulevard, for folk
3. Miami Beach Auditorium and Convention Center, 1001 Convention Drive, for a variety of musical events
4. Marine Stadium, 3601 Rickenbacker Causeway, for a variety of musical events
5. Flamenco Supper Club, 991 NE Seventy-ninth Street, for jazz and all popular music
6. Collins Avenue Hotel and Nightclub Strip, for rock, disco, jazz, country-

Western: The Deauville, 6701 Collins; Sans Souci, 3101 Collins; Sheraton Bal Harbor, 9701 Collins
7. Your Place or Mine, 7995 W. Flagler Street, rock and disco
8. Dade County Auditorium, 2901 W. Flagler, opera, chamber music, dance, symphonic music
9. Gusman Cultural Center, 174 E. Flagler, symphonic music
10. Theater of Performing Arts, 1700 Washington Avenue, home of Miami Beach Symphony
11. Metamorphosis Lounge, 1546 NW Le Jeune Road, jazz and popular music

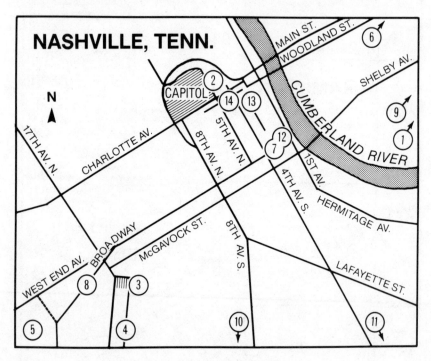

Nashville, TN

1. Opryland, USA, 2800 Opryland Drive, off Briley Parkway, six miles northeast of the center of Nashville. Home of Grand Ole Opry since 1974
2. Ryman Auditorium, 116 Fifth Avenue North. Former home of Grand Ole Opry

from 1941 until 1974. Now a museum
3. Country Music Association, 4 Music Square East. Building that houses the Country Music Hall of Fame and Museum
4. Music Row, eight blocks long, two miles

from downtown Nashville around Sixteenth and Seventeenth avenues South near Vanderbilt University. Home of numerous recording companies, music publishers, music suppliers, music agencies, etc., including Tree Recordings, Broadcast Music, Inc., RCA, Decca, and Columbia Records

5. Vanderbilt University, for chamber music and recitals

6. Radio Station WSM, 2644 McGavock Pike. Station that promoted country music in the 1920s and gave rise to Grand Ole Opry in Studio B

7. Tootsie's Lounge, 422 Broadway. Famous as an extension of Grand Ole Opry with performers taking their leisure here

8. Bluegrass Inn, 1914 Broadway, for Bluegrass and country

9. Music City Rodeway Inn, 1 Briley Parkway, for Bluegrass and country

10. Curtis Wood Lane, homes of country music stars Minnie Pearl and Webb Pierce, on either side of Governor's Mansion

11. Spinners, 2600 Nolensville Pike, a disco place

12. Rock City, 107 Second Avenue North, for rock, disco, and country

13. Printer's Alley, off Union between Third and Fourth avenues, has numerous places for popular music

14. Tennessee Performing Arts Center, 505 Deadrick, for rock and country

New Orleans, LA

1. Preservation Hall, 726 St. Peter Street. Famous jazz landmark

2–9. Bourbon Street spots for jazz: Old Absinthe House, 240 Bourbon; Paddock Lounge, 309 Bourbon; Famous Door, 339 Bourbon; Your Father's Mustache, 426 Bourbon; Al Hirt's, 501 Bourbon; Old Court Tavern, 624 Bourbon; Crazy Shirley's, 640 Bourbon; Maison Bourbon, 641 Bourbon

10. Skylite Lounge in Monteleone Hotel, 200 Royal Street. Jazz and popular music

11. Royal Orleans Hotel, 621 St. Louis Street. Jazz spot

12. Beauregard Square, formerly Congo Square, Rampart Street. Black slaves gathered on Sunday to sing and play African music that led to the development of jazz

13. 500 Club, Saint Louis and Bourbon streets, owned by Louis Prima

14. Former site of Hilma Burt's brothel at 209 Basin Street where Jelly Roll Morton played ragtime in early 1900s

15. Former site of Mahogany Hall at 355 Basin Street where Jelly Roll Morton played ragtime in early 1900s

16. Tulane University Jazz Archive, Freret Street and Newcombe Boulevard. Large collection of jazz memorabilia and history

17. Fat City, Veterans' Boulevard and West Esplanade. Site of dozens of nightspots for jazz and blues

18. Pete Fountain's Inn at the Hilton, 2 Poydras Street. Jazz and popular music

19. Bourbon Street Pub, 801 Bourbon Street. Popular for jazz and blues

20. Steamboat President that cruises up the Mississippi River for dancing to jazz and blues

21. Clubb 77, 819 Claiborne Avenue. Famous black nightspot for jazz and blues

22. Mason's Americana, 2309 S. Claiborne Avenue. Black nightspot for jazz and blues

23. Tyler's, 5345 Magazine Street. Night spot for new wave jazz

24. Fairgrounds. Site of jazz and blues festivals

25. Tipina's, 501 Napoleon Avenue. Another spot for jazz and blues

26. Maple Leaf Bar, 8316 Oak St. Ragtime and Jazz

27. Jed's, 8301 Oak St. Country and country rock

28. Jimmy's, 8200 Willow. Country music

29. Orpheum Theater, University Place, home of New Orleans Philharmonic

30. Municipal Auditorium, St. Claude Street, former home of New Orleans Philharmonic

31. New Orleans Theater for the Performing Arts and Louis Armstrong Park, St. Philip and N. Villere streets

32. Former site of first Opera House (1791), 732 St. Peter Street (then St. Pierre).

33. Civic Center, site of varied musical events

34. The Hideaway, 2601 Orleans Avenue, for rock

35. Former site of Le Theatre St. Philippe, St. Philip Street between Royal and Bourbon streets. Opera House in 1808

36. Former site of Theatre d'Orleans, 721 Orleans Avenue. Opera House in 1813

37. Former site of St. Charles Theater, 432 St. Charles Avenue, 1835 Opera House

38. Former site of French Opera House (1859), Bourbon and Toulouse streets.

39. Vieux Carré for jazz spots between Mississippi River, Canal Street, Rampart Street and Esplanade Avenue

M·I·D‑
W·E·S·T

INTRODUCTION

The Midwest added its particular nuances to jazz, country, and rock and roll music. Just as New Orleans symbolized the jazz element in the South, Chicago did the same in the Midwest. Chicago jazz kept pace with local bootlegging, crime, and underworld figures, and offered a musical counterpart in color, abandon, and fast-paced activity. The South Side's "Section," running along State Street, and The Loop, in the northern end, were historic places in the development of Chicago blues and jazz. The jazz combo gave rise to the sound of big-band swing, moving jazz out of inelegant saloons into more dignified halls and hotels, where a modified beat attracted multitudes who listened, danced to, and approved the new musical styles.

Country music underwent changes, too, as it journeyed from its isolated, backwoods, Southern mountain milieu to more open surroundings in the flat plains, picking up Western influences. The twang turned into a drawl, nasal quality became more pronounced articulation, the guitar was amplified, and dress was geared to mesh with the music.

Rock and roll found fertile ground in Detroit's Motown, where dozens of Black artists were groomed to assume a quality image and subsequently rose to fame. Back in Chicago, rock mixed heavily with country-Western and produced a genre of country-rock, prevalent today throughout the nation.

BLUES AND JAZZ, ROCK, AND COUNTRY– WESTERN

Blues and Jazz

After the jazz heyday peaked in New Orleans in the early 1900s, jazz traveled up the river to Chicago, a railway center offering jobs and attracting money. The Illinois Central Railroad, coming from Louisiana, Tennessee, and Mississippi, and stopping at Twelfth Street Station, brought men and women in ragged clothes, carrying battered luggage, and looking for work in the music field.

Much like New Orleans' Storyville, Chicago's saloons flourished, red-light districts and gambling houses abounded, and growing vice, crime, slums, and political corruption encouraged the jazz expression. Amidst the railroad yards at Dearborn Street Station, one could count eight brothels between #179 and #193 Plymouth Court. Thieves, pimps, prostitutes, gunmen, and politicians were the movers of the day. This network of organized crime supplied a lusty musical club scene of blues and jazz.

Even before Storyville shut down, many New Orleans jazz musicians, mostly black, had migrated to Chicago and joined up with midwestern musicians, black and white. A continued influx and intermingling of musicians made Chicago the nation's jazz center in the early 1920s, and further developed the "Chicago" style of jazz: driving, explosive, and searing, with an emphasis on individual performance.

Early Blues Musicians Arrive in Chicago

By 1912, Jelly Roll Morton, the famed "professor" of New Orleans ragtime piano, and Tony Jackson, a ragtime pianist, had come to Chicago and were playing regularly in the bars of the South Side's black "Section," along State Street near Thirty-fifth Street. Extending half a mile down State Street, the Section was filled with numerous saloons, cafés, cabarets, and vaudeville places, among which were the Dreamland Café, Elite Number One and Number Two, Pony Morris's, the Everleigh Club, Dago and Russells, and the Blatz Beer Garden (later known as Pekin Cabaret Theater).

Other early blues musicians began migrating to Chicago at this time, including Memphis Slim, Blind Blake, Blind Lemmon, Lonnie Johnson, Georgia White, Cora Green, and Alberta Hunter. The Grand Theater, Fountain Inn, Monogram Theater, and Eighth Street Theater were popular places for these artists. Chicago was a routine stop for acts in the Theater Owners' Booking Association (TOBA) circuit and the Orpheum circuit, both of which produced shows for black audiences.

In 1915, the Arsonia Café, at Madison and Paulina Streets, hosted a New Orleans jazz combo featuring trumpeter Emmanuel Perez, clarinetist Lorenzo Tio, trombonist Eddie Atkins, pianist Frank Haynie, and drummer Louis Cotterell, famous names in jazz history, and fore-runners of the jazz band.

The Loop

As the Section represented the black entertainment mecca on the South Side, Chicago's white entertainment area was contained largely on the northern side in an area known as the Loop: Tom Brown and his six-piece Dixieland Band played at Lamb's Café; and Stein's Band from Dixie, featuring drummer Johnny Stein, cornetist Nick LaRocca, trombonist Eddie Edwards, clarinetist Alcide Nunez, and pianist Henry Rojas, performed at Schiller's Café, at De Labbie's, and at Casino Gardens. Stein's Band from Dixie changed its name to The Original Dixieland Jazz Band and soon left for New York to make recordings.

Jazz places were ubiquitous in the Loop: Blackhawk, where Louis Prima,, Mildred Bailey and Bob Crosby would perform; The College Inn at the Hotel Sherman, which hosted swing bands growing out of jazz combos; the Brass Rail, Ambassador East, and the New Downbeat, which offered a sprinkling of jazz.

The Old Levee and the Black Belt

Immediately south of the Loop, amid grimy railroad yards, bounded by Polk Street on the north, Twelfth Street on the south, Clark Street on the west, and State Street on the east, sprawled an area known as the Old Levee. Like New Orleans, it was a red-light district housing brothels, saloons, and gambling halls. Freiberg's Dance Hall, the Silver Dollar, and Black May's were typical honky-tonk establishments that supported early jazz. The Levee was shut down in 1911, due to government crackdowns on vice and crime. Some, but not all, of the places reopened several years later, most notably among which were the Cadillac Café, Polack Ben's on Twenty-second Street, and Freddie Buxbaum's Saloon on Twenty-second and State Street—all colorful spots that were part of Chicago's regenerating vice scene.

The Black Belt, northwest of the Levee, was an area where whites and blacks co-mingled in "black and tan" cabarets. By 1920 heavy migration considerably increased the black population. Music was heard in nightspots located on Thirty-fifth Street, running six blocks between State Street and South Parkway, encompassing Wabash, Michigan, Indiana, Prairie, and Calumet Avenues. This was Chicago's heyday in jazz.

Other Places for Early Jazz

The Three Deuces, at 222 North State Street, the Southmoor Hotel on Stoney Island Avenue, and Guyon's Paradise, at 128 North Crawford, were historic places where guitarists Eddie Condon and Johnny St. Cyr began their careers, strumming out jazz in the midst of underworld hangouts. Cornetist Bix Beiderbecke worked at similar clubs—the Rendezvous Café, at One North Clark Street, and Vanity Fair, a cabaret at Broadway and Grace.

Jazz Develops

1918 brought the first "hot" jazz group exemplifying "Chicago style" to the Section. Chicago style was direct, intense, almost searing with a driving rhythmic beat. Cornetist Tig Chambers, trumpeter Sugar Johnny Smith, clarinetist Lawrence Duhé, trombonist Roy Palmer, bassist Ed Garland, and guitarist Louis Keppard, calling themselves Keppard's Creoles, performed at Dreamland Café, at Thirty-fifth and State Street, and at the De Luxe Café, a poolroom/dance hall across State Street.

The same year saw Bill Johnson's Creoles play at the Royal Gardens on North Harlem Street. (You can see it today.) It was Johnson who sent for King Oliver with his strong horn from New Orleans, and Oliver who subsequently sent for Louis Armstrong. Lincoln Gardens, no longer in existence, was the memorable site of music, music, music with these two colossi at the top of Chicago jazz.

There was more music at the Friar's Inn on Wabash and Van Buren (now an autopark). The Friar's Inn hosted the influential New Orleans Rhythm Kings, known originally as the Friars' Society Orchestra. They, and other jazz people, accepted invitations from former New Orleans musicians to play on lakeboat excursions cruising to the Michigan shore. Some who accepted were trumpeter Jim McPartland, pianist Murph Podalsky, and clarinetist Benny Goodman. At this time, reeds and saxophone added as much to Chicago jazz as the big brassy sound of the trumpet.

During the post-World War I years, Chicago jazz grew quickly, along with bootlegging and crime, and roared with the twenties. New inventions, the radio and phonograph, as well as stage shows and night clubs helped disseminate jazz. Music publishing gained impetus as did the teaching and studying of popular music. Dancing enjoyed popularity in such places as Cascades Ballroom on Sheridan and Wilson, and Toddle

Inn Roadhouse at Fox Lane.

Dancers liked a medium tempo with a bounce for the two-step and the Bunny Hug. Blues lacked a suitable tempo for these steps and hot jazz lacked mellow, dreamy mood sounds. So the jazz/blues repertory was modified to embrace a thirty-two-bar popular song rhythm pattern for dancing, a jazz that would swing, setting the stage for the sound of big bands and swing.

The Beginning of Big Bands in Chicago

The big bands took jazz/blues out of the tawdry barroom atmosphere and elevated it to the middle-class dance floor. Dancers would "swing" to syncopated rhythms ranging from soft and sweet to hot and brassy. King Oliver's Band and Louis Armstrong's Hot Five, (which became Hot Seven and then Hot Five again) in the twenties, pioneered the way for developing big bands:

Charles Elgar

Elgar's band consisted of cornet, trombone, clarinet, saxophone, violins, bass, and drums. The band occasionally produced a loud and rough sound, and at other times a softer string sound. The songs, "Nightmare," and "Brotherly Love" were two pieces played frequently at Dreamland, Arsonia Café, Savoy Ballroom, and the Sunset Café, which was the biggest Black and Tan Club in Chicago.

Erskine Tate

His band opened at the Vendome Theater and played regularly for almost a decade, with guest musicians including Louis Armstrong. About twelve pieces comprised the band. Audiences cheered wildly for songs such as "Chinaman Blues," "Static Strut and Stompoff," and "Let's Go."

Charles "Doc" Cooke

A composer/arranger, Cooke boasted among his musicians cornetist Freddy Keppard and clarinetist Jimmie Noone. They performed at Dreamland, White City Ballroom, and Club Ambassador. Noone also led his own small band at the Nest Club.

Clarence Jones

Jones played piano in the New Orleans ragtime style of Jelly Roll Morton. He was billed with his band at the Owl Theater and Moulin Rouge Café. "Wabash Blues" was a favorite number of the group.

Earl "Fatha" Hines

Hines was an important name at the Grand Terrace in 1928

and into the thirties. Joining him were clarinetists Sidney Bechet and Johnny Dodds, who were much in demand. They entertained at the Apex Club and El Grotto Supper Club as well.

Benny Goodman

Later to claim the title "King of Swing," native Chicagoan (born on Maxwell Street) and clarinetist Goodman started playing at the Congress Hotel (now the Americana Congress), at 520 South Michigan Avenue; Midway Gardens (which has a large dance floor), at 727 East Sixtieth Street; Columbia Ballroom; and Steven's Hotel, with a dance floor that accommodated four-thousand (the hotel is now the Conrad Hilton), at 720 South Michigan Avenue. Drummer Gene Krupa joined Goodman's band for a while until he left to form his own.

The depression of 1929 arrived, and when people focused on music, they called for soothing sentimentality. Songs of the day were "Sugar," "I'm Nobody's Sweetheart Now," "Baby, Won't You Please Come Home," and "Wrap Your Troubles in Dreams." The financial uncertainty of the times prompted an exodus of jazz musicians to New York, where recording was just beginning to take shape as a major industry.

Jazz was revived briefly in the early 1930s to be heard at the Sherman Hotel, the Aragon Ballroom, My Cellar, and Silhouette Club. Post-World War II prosperity hosted traveling jazz groups at the Pump Room, Preview, and Offbeat, and in the fifties at the Eleven-Eleven Club, Basin Street, and Red Arrow. But the Big-Band era, popular for so long, had essentially come to an end, and, as in other parts of the country, rock and roll came in with a bang.

The Chicago Sound

Rock and roll was developing in the blues mecca of Chicago in many of the former blues/jazz places. Notwithstanding the constant crossover, rock was splintered into three general varieties: Soul, blues, and country-Western.

Soul in Rock

Two men, Curtis Mayfield and Carl Davis, are commonly credited with pioneering Soul in Chicago.

As a young man, Curtis Mayfield had spent a good deal of time singing tenor in Chicago churches and traveling the Midwest with different gospel choirs. Mayfield and four other young men decided to form a group, which they called The Impressions. In 1958 Mayfield began to compose such pensive, Soul-type songs as "For Your Precious Love," drawing on gospel, pop, and blues. The song was recorded and, not only was it instantly successful with Chicago audiences, but it was recognized as the pivotal point for the growth of rock and roll in the Chicago area.

In 1960 Mayfield and The Impressions added a new embellishment to Soul, a Latin American rhythm expressed in flamenco guitars and castanets, and heard in the narrative song "Gypsy Woman." "Gypsy Woman" became a national hit just before the group split, and Mayfield subsequently teamed up with Carl Davis of Columbia's Okeh records. Under Davis's influence, Soul underwent a metamorphosis as Mayfield changed instrumentation by substituting heavy brass and percussion for strings. The result was that horns blared, drums dominated, and sharp vocals pierced the atmosphere in songs such as "The Monkey Time," a tune that came to identify one type of Chicago sound.

Meanwhile, the Impressions regrouped in 1963 and turned to Mayfield and Davis for direction. Former and current styles were combined in "It's All Right," utilizing lively gospel, heavy brass, and a Latin beat. To preserve Soul's status, the Impressions also started singing social message songs, as heard in "People Get Ready" and "We're a Winner."

In addition to working with Davis, Mayfield composed songs for other singers (among whom was Gene Chandler, who demonstrated a twangy falsetto that swooped up and down), returning to gospel in "Just Be True" and "Duke of Earl." The old Regal Theater in Chicago hosted many of his performances which were attended by enthusiastic teenagers.

Davis and Mayfield parted and Davis went on to discover Tyrone Davis in the late sixties, who conveyed a new Chicago sound. This new sound was bluesier and brassier and had a hard-driving delivery, similar in part to another variety of Chicago sound—the blues.

Blues in Rock

The blues aspect in Chicago rock is an indigenous link to the blues/jazz tradition that flourished in this region (noted earlier in the chapter). The outstanding artist who popularized this element in rock and roll was one Ellas McDaniels, also known as Bo Diddley.

Diddley was born in McComb, Mississippi in 1928 and moved with his family to Chicago as a young boy. He learned to play the violin before he learned guitar and spent a good deal of time listening to blues singers on the radio, as did many aspiring performers. Louis Jordan, Jimmie Reed and John Lee Hooker were especially appealing to Diddley.

The 708 Club on Chicago's South Side (no longer in existence) was an early nightspot where Diddley sang and played guitar to "Uncle John," a rock song later recorded as "Bo Diddley." The singer was raw, raspy, and noisy, performing in barroom fashion: bumping and grinding his body, while singing in the traditional syncopated rhythm of the all-pervasive, primitive African beat. Rhythm was indeed his trademark, embellished by fanciful guitar work on his square guitar, and highlighted by loud, attention-getting clothing. In "Say Man," the heavy beat accompanied humorous lyrics. "Don't Doubt Yourself Babe" epitomizes pulsating blues in Chicago rock. Diddley's style influenced the Beatles, the Rolling Stones, and other rock groups of the sixties.

Country Rock

Chuck Berry was a major Midwestern music figure. He stressed country-Western rock and bore some professional resemblance to the South's Elvis Presley. As Presley crossed racial lines (a white man appealing to blacks), so Berry cut across lines as a black man who appealed to whites. And, like Presley, Berry was a guitar player interested in teenage lifestyles.

Berry was born in Wentsville, near St. Louis, Missouri in 1926. After spending several years in reform school, he became a hairdresser in St. Louis. In 1955, Berry traveled to Chicago's South Side where he met bluesmen Muddy Waters, Howlin' Wolf, and others, who had come west from the deep South. Berry showed the song he had written, "Ida Red," to Waters, who promptly arranged for a recording session. The title was changed to "Maybelline" in 1955, and it became a hit. Its lyrics concerned a young man driving a Ford, chasing his girlfriend, who was driving a Cadillac. This was but one of Berry's classics. It was immediate and relevant, and it captured prime interests of teenagers.

Some of his other equally successful songs for youth were "No Money Down," dealing again with cars; "Roll Over Beethoven" and "Rock and Roll Music," highlighting the values of the new music; and "Almost Grown" and "School Days," addressing the problem of growing up (advocating fun, good times, and vitality in living).

Berry added fast country guitar runs to the blues and incorporated the rhythm and blues beat electronically. Alternating chords sustained the beat with much repetition. His tenor voice delivered lyrics that were simple, sometimes silly and innocently vulgar, as in "My Ding-a-Ling," a million-seller in 1972. Long and lanky, occasionally stooped, he performed a duck walk on stage to the accompaniment of his piercing electric guitar, drums, and piano.

Berry's songs reflected his own life as well as teenage lives. He twice served prison terms and composed "Have Mercy Judge," and "Tulane," a song about drugs. "Johnny B. Goode" tells the story of a young rock and roll guitarist on his way to fame. Berry starred in two films, *Let the Good Times Roll* and *American Hot Wax*.

217

Midwest Rock

Motown, Detroit

The Midwest welcomed rock and roll in the fifties, as did every region in the country. One of the most significant events in the Midwest was the development of Detroit's equivalent of Soul—the "Detroit Sound," fused with gospel, blues, pop, and a heavy beat. This style was brought to fruition by Motown, a giant recording/packaging company that cultivated its artists inside a white, two-story, frame building at 2648 West Grand Street in Detroit. One can visit the building today although Motown's headquarters moved to Los Angeles in 1971.

Detroit, or Motown (for motortown), was one of the scenes of black unrest in the fifties and sixties. The black population was the fourth largest in the country and dissatisfaction about lack of civil rights reached high proportions; there were frequent riots between blacks and the police, resulting in damage to life and property. In downtown Detroit, places like the Chit Chat Lounge, Fishmans Hardware, and Picnic Fast Foods were sites of raids and fires, producing angry crowds out of control, rampaging and looting.

The Midwest sought an outlet for its tensions and welcomed rock and roll, as did most of the nation. There was as yet no important recording company in the region until the gospel-tinged sound of black music made for one of the most significant events in the Midwest—the development of Detroit's equivalent of soul: the "Detroit Sound," fusing gospel, blues, and pop with a heavy beat. It was in Motown that the black musical image was refined and reshaped and this style brought to fruition.

The success of Motown's records was largely due to the efforts of Berry Gordy, a songwriter in the black tradition. Call-and-response pattern was familiar to him and Gordy utilized it with a female chorus in such early songs as "Come to Me," recorded by Marv Johnson. Simple lyrics and basic rock chord progressions were interestingly and elaborately orchestrated, using saxophone, bass, guitar, piano, and even tambourine and flute.

Many singers descended on Gordy's studio on West Grand Street. Jackie Wilson recorded "Lonely Tear Drops," and Smokey Robinson and the Miracles sang "Way Over There," and "The Tracks of My Tears," in a well-controlled falsetto. Gordy expanded the operation, hiring songwriters and staff, and he supervised aggressively by carefully styling and marketing his artists. He instructed singers in finishing school graces for both live and recorded performances: how to walk, talk, sit properly, and demonstrate good manners. He taught them to convey a clean, attractive public image, with a pleasing delivery and inoffensive

218

lyrics. His authoritative control of Motown's commercial package was responsible for the success of many stars in rock and roll. Some of these were the following:

The Temptations

This quintet at first represented Motown's romantic side. The combination of rich baritone and pure falsetto voices maintained an easy-going, low key manner, wedding traditional gospel/blues with the rhythm of strings in "My Girl," and "You're My Everything." The Temptations entered the disco/psychedelic era in the late sixties, recording "Cloud Nine" and "Ball of Confusion" in a style noticeably bombastic and heavy.

Four Tops

The Four Tops symbolized Motown's frenetic side, demonstrating a sharp, bellowing vocal style. It can be heard in such numbers as "Reach Out" and "I'll Be There," accompanied by unrelenting drums, rhythmic tambourines, and titillating horns.

Diana Ross and the Supremes

Perhaps Motown's most successful product was evident in the sweet, sexy, relaxed tones of Diana Ross and the Supremes who Gordy polished and patterned according to formula. The female group, singing mostly about lost or unrequited love, recorded "Where Did Our Love Go" and "Stop in the Name of Love" against a background of strings. Ross left the Supremes in 1969 to pursue a successful solo career. She enjoyed a smash hit, "Ain't No Mountain High Enough," the following year.

Gladys Knight and the Pips

Members of this group sang in gospel choirs in southern churches before coming to Motown. Gladys Knight progressed to a hard driving vocal delivery in "I Heard It Through the Grapevine."

Stevie Wonder

Stevie Wonder was a 13-year-old blind singer who achieved popularity with a raw style recording of "Fingertips." His tenor voice was frequently breathless, and his lyrics over the years have ranged from the sentimental to social and political statements. Wonder was experimental and played many instruments including the harmonica, Moog synthesizer, and electric organ. "Higher Ground" and "You Haven't Done Nothin" are further examples of his Motown recordings.

Motown's heyday declined in the early seventies, when its

headquarters moved from Detroit to Los Angeles. Although Motown's style is no longer distinctive and many of its artists have left to go out on their own, the Motown sound will be remembered as a major part of rock and roll history.

Cowboy Music and Square Dancing

Before discussing country–Western music, let's mention briefly traditional cowboy music and square dancing, both of which were central to music and leisure around the turn of the twentieth century.

Traditional Cowboy Music

Fact and fancy blended in traditional cowboy music as the history and settling of the West was recounted. The homesteaders of Kansas, Nebraska, and Iowa sang songs of the farmer, the railroad, the land they worked, and the lives they led:

> *Ho, brothers, come brothers . . .*
> *We'll sing upon the Kansas plains . . .*
>
> *Come all you folks of enterprise . . .*
> *I'll point you out the best . . .*
> *I mean the state of Kansas, the Lily of the West.*

And the musical symbol of western America is perhaps "Home on the Range," written in 1873. The original music is by Daniel E. Kelly and the words are by Dr. Higley Brewster of Kansas. There are many verses; one that is perhaps not too well-known is:

> *The bluffs and white rocks*
> *And the antelope flocks*
> *That graze on the mountain so green . . .*

Traditional cowboy music would soon be overtaken by country–Western music.

Square Dancing

In square dancing, circles or opposite lines were formed. Figures and sequences were simple and learned. The same ones were used over and over by the caller. An old favorite has always been "Buffalo

Gals." Its many verses were heard regularly throughout the early twentieth-century cowboy era.

A circle is formed while each participant walks around singing:

Buffalo Gals, won't you come out tonight—
And dance by the light of the moon—

Then the group breaks into couples, catches hands and swings with the couple on the right. The four swing around, boy swings opposite girl, then his partner. They swing again, then move on to the next couple on the right. This is repeated until each couple has been completely around the circle.

Square dancing was practiced a great deal from the Midwest through the entire West, but not heavily on the West Coast.

Country Meets Western

Country music, originally from Nashville, moved westward with Midwest migration, beginning in the 1930s, and underwent changes, influenced by a new environment and life style.

Although life was arduous and required patience and emotional outlets for survival in both regions, life in the Midwest differed from that in the South: the Midwest had dry plains, dust storms, and tall prairie grass instead of hills and benign climate; in the Midwest there was communal barroom drinking rather than moonshining on the back porch or in the basement; frontiersmen and cowboys sang around campfires instead of in church. These new elements interacted with country music and what came forth was called country-Western. Places like Abilene, Dodge City, Des Moines, and Lincoln were filled with men who worked the land and sang songs of heroes and villains, based upon a history of real outlaws such as Jesse James and Billy the Kid.

Technology, too, changed the face of country music. Railroad workers, truck drivers, steelworkers, and miners became musical heroes, as well as the cowboy, accepting challenge, seeking new adventure, and fighting danger with courage and resources. Songs such as "The Singing Brakeman," "A Different Train, a Different Time," "Idaho Red," "Widow Maker," and "Cigarettes, Whiskey, and Wild, Wild Women" were representative of the regional changes. The songs, unhappy in large part, told of actual situations with emotional impact.

Discussion of the cowboy and country-Western is treated in Section IV. Chapter 3, because of the more intense connection of the Far

West (Texas, Oklahoma, etc.) to cowboy life. Let's mention, however, the legendary cowgirl, who competed musically in a man's world and patterned behavior after such historic models as Belle Starr, Annie Oakley, and Calamity Jane.

Such a cowgirl rising to fame in the thirties was Patsy Montana, a member of the Prairie Ramblers. She starred in Chicago's famous "National Barn Dance," broadcast over radio station WLS for several hours on Saturday night (like the Grand Ole Opry in Nashville), and later from the Eighth Street Theater. Except for a skirt, Montana dressed like a man, with high leather boots, shirtwaist, cowboy hat and scarf, wide belt. She had a fiddle and guitar as well as a distinctive yodel. She elevated women in country-Western music in "I Want to Be a Cowboy's Sweetheart," which sold over a million copies in 1936. "Howlin' at the Moon" was another hit.

Early Country-Western Songs and Songwriters

Radio Station WDAF in Kansas City, Kansas, recognized singer/songwriter Carson Robison from Chetopa, Kansas in the thirties. A fiddler's son, Robison wrote more than three-hundred songs and was known as "Kansas Jayhawk." His "Way Out West in Kansas" was an early success and soon afterwards he formed his own band, Carson Robison and His Pioneers, playing such hits as "Little Green Valley," "Carry Me Back to the Lone Prairie," and "My Blue Ridge Mountain Home."

A team of songwriters, Nat Vincent and Fred Howard, were known as the Happy Chappies and worked in radio in Des Moines in the thirties. Such tunes as "When the Bloom is on the Sage" and "Strawberry Roan" gave country-Western local flavor.

Singer/songwriter Ray Price and his band, Cherokee Cowboys, were known throughout the Midwest, especially for "Don't Let the Stars Get in Your Eyes" and "Heartaches by the Number." During World War II and the early forties, Harry "Hap" Peebles from Kansas ran stage shows promoting country-Western in the Midwest. "Pistol Packin' Mama" and "Sioux City Sue" were among the favorites.

Country-Western in Cincinnati

Cincinnati was a stop on the railroad from Nashville and part of a large industrial complex encompassing sections of Kentucky. In 1937, one John Lair, who produced Chicago's WLS "National Barn Dance" came to radio station WLW in Cincinnati and began the "Renfro Valley Barn Dance" series. With him were the stars Red Foley, Slim Miller, Girls of the Golden West, and the Coon Creek Girls (the first all-girl country-Western string band on radio). The Barn Dance took place in Cincinnati's Music Hall and later moved to Renfro Valley, Kentucky, where you can see it today. The program was replaced in Cincinnati by

"Boone County Jamboree," which became "Midwestern Hayride" in 1945, a true national barn dance. A popular artist on WLW was Bradley Kincaid performing "Hound Dog Guitars."

This same year saw the establishment of the King record company by Syd Nathan. Nathan operated in an abandoned icehouse just outside Cincinnati proper. He attracted such artists as the Delmore Brothers, Hank Penny, Cowboy Copas, Hawkshaw Hawkins, and Wayne Rayney, who had been entertaining in Emery Auditorium, downtown (still here today). Bull Moose Jackson and His Bearcats singing "Why Don't You Haul Off and Love Me," also recorded at King. Another Cincinnati station, WCKY, programmed country-Western music daily for more than fifteen years, and the Metropolitan Theater (no longer in existence) was a site for up-and-coming artists, notably the Skillet-Lickers with Kiley Puckett, singer and guitarist.

Other places heavy with strains of country-Western were the Terrace Hilton, 15 West Sixth Street, the Western, 45202 Fountain Square, and Vernon Manor, 400 Oak Street.

Musical styles have crossed and interacted and forms are no longer pure. But throughout the Midwest there are places still alive with the sounds of jazz, blues, rock and roll, and country-Western.

ILLINOIS
Aurora
The Paramount Arts Center, 11 East Galena Boulevard, features jazz and other popular music.
Bensenville
Nashville North, 101 East Irving Park Road, offers authentic country-Western music.
Chicago
Rosemont Horizon, 6920 North Mannheim Road, Rosemont, for such artists as Billy Joel.

Whiskey River, 3109 West Irving Place, has entertainers such as Last Chance Band.

Fitzgerald's, 6615 Roosevelt Road in Berwyn, is noted for country-Western.

Countryside, 6200 Old Jollet Road is also noted for country-Western.

Mill Run Theater, Golf Hill Center in Niles, has featured Tom Chapin and Gordon Lightfoot.

Daley Center, Randolph and Dearborn Streets, has continuous musical events.

Somebody Else's Troubles, 2470 North Lincoln Avenue, offers a variety of music. Clearwater Saloon, 3447 North Lincoln; McGiddie's, 2423 North Lincoln, and Mr. Kiley's, 1125 West Belmont Avenue are lively places.

Navy Pier, on the lakefront, hosts Autumn Fair in October.

Andy's, 11 East Hubbard Street, features Jazz at Noon, with such performers as the Rhythmakers.

Orphans, 2462 North Lincoln Avenue, has presented the John Baney Jazz Jam and other rock groups.

On Broadway Chicago, 5246 Broadway, has welcomed Downchild Blues Band and others.

Benchley's on Broadway, 6232 Broadway, is a popular nightspot.

Sundance Social Pub, 6253 North Broadway, has disco.

Park West, 322 West Armitage, bills stars such as the Mamas and the Papas, and Chick Corea.

The Sabre Room, 8900 West Ninety-fifth Street, in Hickory Hills, has swing and rock and roll groups, such as Bill Haley's Comets, the Coasters, the Drifters, Wayne King, and Al Morgan.

The Bulls, 1916 North Lincoln Park West, is a hotspot for jazz and rock.

Crickets, 100 East Chestnut Street, has hosted Le Jazz Hot.

Hideaway Lodge, off Highway 25, St. Charles, offers rock music and groups such as the Speakeasy Jazz Band.

Highland Park boasts the famous Ravinia Jazz Festival, outdoors in June. There is plenty of jazz here.

Inmet Circle, 750 South Halsted Street, offers jazz and rock bands.

The International Amphitheater, 4220 South Halsted Street, offers jazz and rock bands.

B.L.U.E.S. 2519 North Halsted, has hosted the Sunnyland Slim Blues Band.

Kingston Mines, 2548 North Halsted Street, has offerings such as Eddy Clearwater's rock music, blues, and Big Bad Leroy Brown.

Manhattan Tavern, 1045 North Rush Street, has jazz and rock stars.

Jazz Medium, 901 North Rush, has mostly blues and jazz, as its name implies.

The Backroom Club, 1007 North Rush, offers blues and jazz.

Joe Segal's Jazz Showcase, in the Blackstone Hotel, 636 South Michigan Avenue, presents blues and jazz artists.

The Brassary, 625 North Michigan, has disco.

Civic Center, Washington and Dearborn Streets, is active with such presentations as Chicago Jazz Allstars.

Razzles, 600 North Lake Shore Drive, has presented Jim Beebe's Chicago Jazz Band and others.

Rick's Café American, in the Holiday Inn, 644 North Lake Shore Drive, is one of Chicago's most popular spots. Charlie "Yardbird" Parker's partner, Red Rodney, played hot trumpet here, and Ira Sullivan played cool style trumpet, tenor and alto saxophone.

Bar RR Ranch Western Cocktail Lounge, 56 West Randolph Avenue, is a country island in the middle of the city. It offers rock.

Koko Taylor, blues singer at ChicagoFest (Courtesy Variety Artists International, Minneapolis, photo by Steve Kagan)

The Chicago Stadium, 1800 West Madison, presents large events.

Quiet Knight, 953 West Belmont, offers blues and rock.

Dingbats, 247 East Ontario, offers disco.

George's, 230 West Kinzie Street, offers jazz. Ramsey Lewis has appeared here.

Old Town is an area up and down Clark Street with many nightspots.

Red Arrow, 6358 West Higgins Avenue, offers jazz and rock.

Navy Pier hosts the famous ChicagoFest in August. Set against the city's spectacular skyline, it's the nation's largest summer music festival. Music of every kind can be enjoyed here.

Wise Fools Pub, 2770 North Lincoln Avenue, recently welcomed blues singer Koko Taylor. Grant Park presents "A Taste of Chicago," in the summer, with all varieties of music.

Danville

Danville Civic Center, 100 West Main Street, holds concerts of all kinds.

Decatur

Holiday Inn hosts the Central Illinois Jazz Festival in February, with top artists. Rock music can be heard, too.

Civic Center, at Civic Center Plaza, offers popular music of blues, jazz and rock.

225

Edwardsville
The campus of Southern Illinois University has hosted the Mississippi River Festival every summer since 1969. All kinds of popular music are presented under a large tent.

Evanston
Northwestern University's Pick-Staiger Concert Hall, on Sheridan Road, presents jazz festivals throughout the year.

Makanda
Bluegrass Music Weekend takes place in April, with pickers, pluckers, and country-Western devotees making merry.

Peoria
Exposition Gardens, 1601 North Moor Road, is a favorite place for country-Western concerts with name performers.

Glen Oak Park, presents Steamboat Days in June, with Dixieland bands.

Rock and roll violinist, Papa John Creach, who often plays in clubs in Peoria. (Courtesy Variety Artists International, Minneapolis)

Petersburg
Lincoln's New Salem State Park presents a folk musical festival.
Illinois Country Opry is presented in the summer on IL-97.
Rockford
Metro Center, 300 Elm Street, offers varied musical fare.
Sinnissippi Park, 1401 North Second Street, is the site for "Music in the Park" programs in the summer.
Springfield
Lincolnfest is a large, jubilant Western event. Prairie Capital Convention Center, One Convention Center Plaza, hosts country-Western concerts. The Illinois State Fair takes place in August.

INDIANA

Battle Ground
The Annual Gathering of Traditional Indiana Fiddlers takes place here in July.
Bean Blossom
Bill Monroe's hundred-acre park hosts the Bean Blossom Bluegrass Festival. It is a highlight in the spring. Earl Scruggs, Lester Flatt, and Mac Wiseman have performed here.
Bloomington
The Hoosier Hills Festival is a popular event in June.
Chesterton
Dunland Folk Festival, with the emphasis on country-Western, music is noteworthy.
Columbus and Evansville
Jazz festivals with top name artists take place in April and May respectively, in Columbus and Evansville.
Fort Wayne
Summer musical performances are given in a setting marked by the juncture of the rivers of Fort Wayne.
Huntington
Huntington County Heritage Days, in June, offer square dancing and country-Western music.
Indianapolis
T.G.I. Friday's, 3502 East Eighty-sixth Street, The Garage, 831 Broad Ripple Avenue, and Max and Emma's, 8930 Wesleyan Road, offer country-Western music and dancing. Bluegrass Festival, with square dancing, and Eagle Creek Folk Music Festival take place in July.
Lafayette
There is a Fiddlers' Gathering, on Tippecanoe Battlefield, off IN-43, in June and July. A music festival takes place in January and February.
Madison
Since 1902, September has welcomed Madison's "Chautauqua of the

Arts," with jazz and blues stars among others.
Muncie
September brings Dixieland and blues to the streets of Muncie. It's a gala occasion.
Terre Haute
Fairbanks Park is the site of the Wabash Valley Bluegrass Jamboree. There's merry stomping and square dancing galore.
Winter Carnival country-Western concerts take place in February.
Terre Haute is the home of Paul Dresser, composer of Indiana's state song, "On the Banks of the Wabash." It has been restored at First and Farrington Streets, and there are tours given in the spring and summer. Dresser was author Theodore Dreiser's brother.

IOWA
Ames
The Hilton Coliseum presents jazz events.
Atlantic
A "Radio Reunion" Country Music Festival takes place in June, with traditional and country-Western music.
Britt
The National Hobo Convention, in August, offers a different rock and roll experience. Many wanderers arrive beforehand and camp out on railroad tracks. Psychedelic lights swirl for effect and rock rings out at the Convention.
Burlington
Burlington Steamboat Days and the Dixieland Jazz Festival are the main events downtown, three blocks long, on the riverfront in June. An outdoor stage overlooks a colorful garden.
Cedar Falls
Sturgis Falls Festival, in June, brings Dixieland jazz.
Band concerts offering country-Western take place all summer.
Cedar Rapids
The Paramount Theater for the Performing Arts, Paramount Building, presents jazz concerts.
Clarinda
This was Glenn Miller's hometown and it honors him with a music festival each May. Big band swing is, of course, the theme.
Council Bluffs
Old-Time Country Music Fair, in September, has scheduled and spontaneous performances of fiddle, banjo, and guitar playing.
Davenport
This is the hometown of cornetist Bix Beiderbecke. A festival with his name pays tribute to him each July in a spectacular event held on the banks of the Mississippi River at Le Claire Park. Such stars as Gene

Krupa, Hoagy Carmichael, Sons of Bix, and Salty Dogs Band have performed here. There is a museum showing Bix's memorabilia. A scholarship fund for jazz musicians has been established in Davenport.

Des Moines
The Kiwanis Jazz Festival, in West Des Moines, is the big music happening in July.

Civic Center, 221 Walnut Street, hosts jazz and rock concerts in a large amphitheater that surrounds a reflecting pool.

State Capitol Grounds at East Ninth Street and Grand, occasionally plays host to rock groups.

The Fairgrounds, East Thirtieth Street and University Avenue, hosts the Iowa State Fair, one of the largest fairs in the nation. It is held in August. This fair was the original inspiration for the book and movie, *State Fair*.

Dubuque
The Dubuque Festival, in May, features jazz on riverboats, reminiscent of Dixieland.

Iowa City
Hancher Auditorium, at the University of Iowa, has lively musical fare year round.

Mt. Pleasant
The Old Threshers' Annual Bluegrass Music Festival, in June, has continuous fiddling and country-Western music sessions.

The Museum of Repertoire America contains memorabilia of early folk music.

KANSAS
Atchison
The Atchison County Fair takes place in August.

Dodge City
Long Branch Saloon, on Front Street, offers honky-tonk, country-Western and cowboy music.

Fort Scott
The Bourbon County Fair offers jazz at the Fairgrounds.
Old Fort Days, in May, offer square dancing and country-Western music.

Hays
Fort Hays State Rodeo can be seen in April, with plenty of country-Western music.

Lawrence
Murphy Hall, in Kansas University Theater, presents a variety of musical events throughout the year.

Leavenworth
Buffalo Bill Cody Days Fair in August offers authentic country-Western music.

Wellington
Memorial Auditorium, 202 North Washington, is a site for varied programs, including country-Western music.
Wichita
Century II, 225 West Douglas Street, houses all varieties of music, including country-Western.

The Kansas Coliseum, Eighty-fifth Street and I-135, presents country-Western music. Wichita Jazz Festival takes over the streets in summer.
Winfield
The Fairgrounds hosts the Bluegrass Festival and Flat-Picking Championship Contest in September, with plenty of music.

MICHIGAN
Alma
Alma College, on West Superior Street, hosts the Highland Festival in May, with piping, drumming, banjo-playing, and square dancing. It provides a bit of genuine country flavor.
Battle Creek
Binder Winter Park offers a Bluegrass Festival in June, and rock concerts in the summer.
Dearborn
Greenfield Village presents Big Bluegrass Festivals in the summer.
The County Fair of Yesteryear takes place in May.
The Hyatt Regency Hotel, at Fairlane Town Center, offers blues, jazz and rock.
Detroit
Popular music in all forms is available in many places, among which are the following: Baber's Keyboard Lounge, on Livernois at Eight-Mile Road; Top of the Pontch, at the posh Pontchartrain Hotel, 2 Washington Boulevard; the Renaissance Center of Detroit Plaza Hotel, with outdoor performances; Hart Plaza; and the Music Hall. Many of the above have hosted the Detroit Jazz Festival each August with such stars as Chick Corea and Herbie Hancock.

Cobo Hall is a large convention center which presents rock concerts. In front of it, red trolley cars go along Washington Boulevard to Grand Circus Park. The early twentieth-century cars have brass fixtures and costumed drivers.

Bob-Lo Island, in the middle of Detroit River, has boats that depart from the island to the dock at Woodward Avenue for park jazz, big band, and rock concerts.
Flint
Flint Cultural Center, 1241 East Kearsley, offers all kinds of music.
Everett Cummings Center presents an Old-Time Fiddler's Weekend in May.

Grand Haven
The Waterfront Stadium downtown hosts special events.
Holland
Civic Center, at Eighth and Pine, holds jazz, country-Western, and rock events.
The Holland Municipal Stadium, at Sixteenth and Fairbanks, holds jazz, country-Western, and rock events.
Interlochen
Interlochen National Music Camp, situated on twelve-hundred acres of woods and lakes, fifteen miles west of Traverse City, presents jazz in Corson Auditorium, Kresge Auditorium, and The Bowl. Dave Brubeck, Teddy Wilson, and Lionel Hampton have taught and performed here.
Iron Mountain
Festival of the Arts, with square dancing and country-Western concerts, take place in the summer.
Kalamazoo
Kalamazoo Center, 100 West Michigan Avenue, presents rock concerts.
Lansing
Civic Center at 505 West Allegan, holds jazz and rock events.
West Branch
Heritage Days, in the summer, hosts country-Western music and square dancing.

MINNESOTA

Albert Lea
Freeborn County Fair is a large country fair held on the Fairgrounds in August.
Bloomington
The Thunderbird, 2201 East Seventy-eighth Street, and the Rodeway Inn, 1321 East Seventy-eighth Street, are lively spots for jazz, big bands, and rock.
Carlton Backstage, 8350 Twenty-fourth Avenue South, has hosted top entertainers.
Crystal
The Crystal Lounge, 4900 West Broadway, offers country-Western entertainment.
Fairmount
An annual Bluegrass Celebration takes place in July in a lakeside farm setting.
Minneapolis-St. Paul
Hall Brothers Emporium of Jazz, 400 D Street, Mendota, features New Orleans jazz.
Extempore Coffeehouse, 325 Cedar Avenue, hosts blues, jazz, and rock performers.

The Guthrie Theater, 725 Vineland Place, has billed The Jazz Band.

The Orpheum Theater, 910 Hennepin Avenue, has hosted jazz stars.

Walker Arts Center, on Vineland, has presented the Decoding Society.

Other jazz and rock sites are: Artist's Quarter, 14 East Twenty-sixth Street, where Eddie Berger and the Jazz Allstars have appeared; Pauline's, on County Road Eighteen and Highway Twelve; William's Pub, 2911 Hennepin Avenue South, where Gene Adams's Jazz Quartet has performed, as well as the Chuck Armstrong Jazz Quartet;

Orchestra Hall, 1111 Nicollet Mall, sometimes holds jazz festivals.

Chicago Upstairs, 23 North Sixth Street, offers top entertainment here

The Minneapolis Institute of Arts, 2400 Third Avenue South, offers all varieties of music in concerts.

The University of Minnesota programs blues and jazz in its auditorium and mall.

Horatio Hornblower's, 435 Wabasha Street.

Mears Park, downtown.

St. Paul's Civic Center, 143 West Fourth Street.

Radisson Plaza, 411 Minnesota Street, has blues/jazz/rock events.

Mississippi River paddleboats operate with jazz and blues played on board.

The Hippogriff, 450 South City Road.

Sadie's Parlour, in the Sheraton-Ritz Hotel, 315 Nicollet, overlooks downtown Minneapolis.

Duff's, 21 South Eighth Street, is a popular place.

The revolving Carousel Lounge, at the top of the Radisson Hotel, St. Paul is also a popular place.

Homestead Pickin' Parlor, 6625 Penn Avenue South.

Ryan's Corner, 201 East Fourth Street, St. Paul.

Rochester

Baldwin Memorial Pavilion, a fiberglass shell with 2,200 seats, and room for five-thousand on the lawn, has hosted the Meadowbrook Music Festival since 1964. All kinds of music have been presented at this Festival.

Roseville

Le Bistro, in Rosedale Center, offers country-Western performances.

Stillwater

Lowell Park, at the waterfront, has jazz performances in the summer. The Brown Bag Music Festival, featuring country-Western music, also takes place here.

Fatt City, 305 South Water Street, has featured Croix Country.

NEBRASKA

Blair

A Bluegrass Weekend takes place in September, with fiddling contests and country-Western music.

Crawford
A Crawford Fiddle Contest takes place in July.
Grand Island
Harvest of Harmony takes place in October, with country-Western bands and entertainers.
Lincoln
The Nebraska State Fair takes place at the Fairgrounds, Seventeenth and Clinton Streets, in September.
Norfolk
The Country Music Show in April, and the Country-Western Show in May are local favorites.
North Platte
Nebraska Days Celebration, in June, commemorates the world's first rodeo in 1882 with plenty of country-Western fare.
Cody Park, on US-83, pays homage to a former resident, Buffalo Bill, with many country-Western programs throughout the year.
Omaha
A Summer Arts Festival in June is filled with country-Western music.
The Old Market Area has Howard Street Tavern, 1112 Howard Street; Mr. Toad's, 1002 Howard Street; and M's Pub, 422 South Eleventh Street, for solid country-Western music.

OHIO

Akron
The Akron Civic Theatre, 182 South Main Street, presents top entertainment.
The Harvest Festival, in October, at Hale Farm and Western Reserve Village, 2686 Oak Hill Road, has plenty of midwestern flavor.
Shady Side Park holds a Bluegrass Festival in June.
Ashtabula
Ashtabula County Fair takes place in August, with plenty of music.
Cambridge
The Ohio Hills Folk Festival, on OH-265, Quaker City, has a dulcimer, banjo and fiddler's contest, square dancing, and country-Western music.
Cincinnati
Fountain Square, at Fifth, Vine, and Walnut, built around the madonna-like fountain statue, offers free concerts of all varieties of music. The Queen City Brass Quintet, for example has performed here.
The Cincinnati Art Museum has a fine collection of many musical instruments.
Shipley's, 2822 Vine Street, presents jazz bands.
Alexander's, at University Plaza in Corbeyville, Clifton, has a dance floor (usually crowded) for swing and disco.
The Lighthouse, 2505 Vine Street, has disco.

233

Arnold's, at 210 East Eighth Street, and Sleep Out Louie's, 230 West Second Street, offer all kinds of music.

Cincinnati, of course, is the Queen City and Riverboats Delta and Mississippi Queen provide music and nightlife in Mt. Adams.

The Public Landing, at the foot of Broadway, has many floating riverboat restaurants, and the Southwestern Classic Jazz Society has performed "Paddlewheels and All That Jazz." The Riverfront Stadium, #100, presents the Ohio Valley Kool Jazz Fest in July, with blues, Soul, and jazz.

The Riverfront Coliseum welcomed The Who in recent years.

Convention Center, Fifth and Elm, holds an Appalachian Festival in May, the largest gathering of its kind with country music.

The Sidedoor Lounge, 615 Walnut Street, offers good country-Western music.

The Netherland Hilton Hotel, Carew Tower, and Top of the Crown at Stouffer's, 141 West Sixth Street, are country-Western favorites.

The Emery Auditorium, Central Parkway and Walnut, offers musical fare.

Circleville

The Ted Lewis Museum is located at 133 West Main Street. Lewis was known in bygone years as the "Jazz King," sporting an old battered top hat, clarinet, and cane. He popularized songs such as "When My Baby Smiles at Me," "Sunny Side of the Street," and "Me and My Shadow" in a soft, shadowy voice. His memorabilia can be seen here.

Cleveland

Convention Center, 1220 East Sixth Street, holds many rock events.

Peabody's Café, 2140 South Taylor Road, has attractive décor to complement rich musical variety.

D'Poo's on the River, 1146 Old River Road in the Flats, presents local jazz and rock bands.

Fagan's, 966 Old River Road, presents concerts outdoors as the sun sets.

Cleveland Crate & Truckin' Co., 1501 Merwin Avenue, a former truck terminal, is now a spot for popular music.

Theatrical Grill, 711 Vincent Road, features country-Western music.

Public Square parks, Huron Mall, Hanna Fountains, and Chester Commons, all present musical fare, including country-Western, in the summer.

Columbus

Southern Theater, Main and High Streets, offers gospel mixed in with blues and jazz.

Ohio Theatre, 39 East State Street, just south of the State Capitol, features such attractions as Gus Giordano's Jazz Dance Chicago.

Ohio State University had the Central Ohio Jazz Festival on its grounds in past years.

The Riverfront Amphitheater, on the west bank of the Scioto River, between Brook Street and Town Street Bridges, presents entertainment on a floating stage.

Cuyahoga Falls

The Blossom Music Center, 1145 West Steels Corner Road, offers a lot of music, including some pop and jazz. Over four-thousand seats are under the roof and there's room for thirteen-thousand on the lawn. Duke Ellington and Ray Charles have entertained here in past years.

Dayton

The U.S. Air Force Museum has a regular "Tribute to Glenn Miller" concert in the summer.

Geneva

Grape Jamboree, in September, with square dancing and country-Western music.

Marietta

Band-O-Rama, in September, plays songs from yesterday's swing.
Bluegrass Reunions, on Route 15, are held in May, August, and October.

Portsmouth

Boneyfiddle Fair takes place in May.
River Days Festival takes place in August.

Rio Grande

Bob Evans Farm Festival, in October, on an 1100-acre farm on US-35, offers bluegrass music. It is a popular event.

Toledo

Country Palace, 725 Jefferson Avenue, offers country-Western music.
The Masonic Auditorium presents rock music.

Quaker City

The Ohio Hills Folk Festival takes place in the summer, with music for dulcimer, fiddle, and banjo.

Youngstown

Federal Plaza East has concerts featuring the big band sound.

WISCONSIN

Baraboo

There's a Wisconsin Opry, off WI-12, performing from May through September.

Boulder Junction

The Musky Jamboree takes place in August.

Egg Harbor

The Performing Arts Academy, Birch Creek Farm, three miles east on County Road E, offers jazz concerts in the summer.

Elkhorn

The 7000-seat Alpine Valley Music Theater, off WI-15, presents top entertainers in the summer.

Fond du Lac

The Wisconsin Folk Festival rings out in June, with country-Western music and square dancing.

Milwaukee

The Crown Room, at Pfister Hotel, 424 East Wisconsin Avenue, offers a view of the city and Lake Michigan, while you listen and dance to music. Bombay Bicycle Club, at Marc Plaza, 509 West Wisconsin Avenue, provides jazz and rock.

La Bohème, 319 East Mason, offers jazz with classics.

Dr. Feelgood's, 2178 North Riverboat Road, near Humboldt Street Bridge.

"Summerfest" is the big event during June and July, at the lakefront, and is billed as the "World's Greatest Music Festival." Seven music stages are active daily with name entertainment.

The Performing Arts Center, 929 North Water Street, presents Alewives Jazz Festival in June and July on the Center's riverfront stage.

The Milwaukee Jazz Gallery, 932 East Center Street, features some of the finest entertainment in jazz.

The Palms, 2616 West State Street, and the Metropolitan Theater, 2844 North Oakland Avenue, offer rock and roll.

The Wisconsin State Fair at State Fair Park attracts name entertainers in August.

Convention Center, between North Fourth and Sixth Streets, hosts Holiday Folk Fair in November, with plenty of singing and square dancing.

Wausau

"Summerthing" is held downtown in July.

SYMPHONIC MUSIC, OPERA, DANCE

The Chicago Symphony Orchestra is perhaps the Midwest's most active orchestra, and the Cincinnati Symphony Orchestra has long had a tradition of symphonic music.

The Chicago Symphony Orchestra

The Chicago Symphony Orchestra began with Theodore Thomas, who left the New York Philharmonic Orchestra (See Section I. Chapter 5) at the request of civic leaders to come to Chicago and develop an orchestra. Chicago businessmen, including Marshall Field, secured contributions for this purpose, and in 1890 the Chicago Orchestra Association (later the Orchestral Association) was formed. Thomas became its conductor in 1891, bringing many New York musicians with him. The Orchestra performed in the old Exposition Building (the Art Institute is there now).

From 1891 until 1905 the repertory was predominantly Austro/German, with occasional Russian and French music. The Orchestra struggled at first in spite of community support, and Thomas began touring with the Orchestra to help bolster finances. To attract larger audiences, he lightened the repertory and used the Orchestra for opera. In his stern, paternalistic but understanding way, Thomas made the Chicago Symphony Orchestra an intrinsic part of Chicago's cultural life and established the role of music director in America. Other large orchestras followed Thomas's model.

In 1899, the Orchestra moved into the Auditorium, where it performed for six years until its permanent home, Orchestra Hall, was built in 1905. The Auditorium had held thirty-five-hundred seats, but Thomas was dissatisfied with its imperfect acoustics and design. It had been built primarily for opera, with a wide stage and deep pit. Nine-thousand individuals contributed to establish a new Orchestra Hall, a nine-story building in Chicago's Loop, overlooking Lake Michigan and Grant Park. The stage was oval, with a shell-shaped stage ceiling rounded into the ceiling itself. Four seating levels, including box tiers, were an impressive sight. The dedicatory concert programmed Wagner's *Tannhauser Overture*, Strauss's *Death and Transfiguration*, Beethoven's Symphony No. Five, and the "Hallelujah Chorus" from Handel's *Mes siah*. Thomas died only several weeks after Orchestra Hall was dedicated. One can visit the Hall today.

Interestingly, there were no guest conductors during Thomas's tenure. His assistant was Frederick Stock, a violist, who succeeded Thomas, carrying on the German tradition, but playing Russian, French, and modern works as well for a term of thirty-seven years, until 1942. Stock composed and arranged works and premiered Prokofieff's *The Love for Three Oranges* and Piano Concerto No. Three in 1921.

The Stock years also saw the founding of the Civic Orchestra of Chicago in 1919, the first training orchestra affiliated with a major symphony orchestra. This started a musical tradition which served as the baisis for the orchestra's high quality. Stock also organized youth and "pop" concerts, and soon major endowment funds began to pour in.

After Stock died in 1942, three men led the Chicago Symphony Orchestra: Desiré Depauw, Artur Rodzinski, and Rafael Kubelik, who was its conductor until 1953. The next ten years belonged to Fritz Reiner, who produced many innovations, including the formation of the Chicago Symphony Chorus. In 1969, Sir Georg Solti assumed directorship, which he holds today.

An interesting fact is that the Chicago Symphony Orchestra has collection of instruments. In the collection there are two Stradivarius violins dating from 1715, and a rare instrument called a Schellenbaum. The Schellenbaum, given to Theodore Thomas by the composer Camille Saint-Saëns, is a tree-like instrument shaken by the player to produce a sound of musical bells. Other exceptional instruments in the collection are a set of Wagner tubas and a set of four silver trumpets. There is also a new Moeller pipe organ with more than four-thousand pipes.

The Cincinnati Symphony Orchestra

Cincinnati has had a tradition of symphonic music and opera because it hosted numerous German emigrants beginning in the mid-nineteenth century. In the early 1850s, the Germania Musical Society was active and held choral concerts. The city welcomed Theodore Thomas, who frequently toured with orchestras from 1870 on, performing throughout the city and in surrounding areas. On one visit in 1873, Thomas presented a May Festival, which would become tradition. Three Strauss waltzes, a polka, Beethoven's Ninth Symphony, and Schumann's Second Symphony were presented to an enthusiastic audience. The second May Festival in 1875 offered Beethoven's Seventh Symphony, as well as music by Wagner, Mendelssohn, and Schubert. Thomas conducted his last Festival in 1904 (one year before he died) with Beethoven's Ninth Symphony and *Missa Solemnis*.

In 1884, due to Thomas' influence, the Music Hall was built, a large auditorium seating thirty-six-hundred. The following year saw the creation of a local symphony orchestra (which was to be the Cincinnati Symphony Orchestra) organized by Cincinnati musicians. Its first conductor was Frank Van der Stucken, who had studied music in Leipzig, and in Weimar with Liszt. Van der Stucken introduced American music to the public (MacDowell, Foote, and Chadwick).

Van der Stucken was succeeded by Stokowski in 1909, before Stokowski went on to Philadelphia. After Stokowski came Kleinwald, Ysaye, and then Reiner in 1922. Reiner built the Cincinnati Orchestra into a major organization. Until Reiner's reign the programming was predominantly Austro/German. Reiner introduced Italian and Hungarian music (Respighi, Casella, Kodaly, and Bartok). Bartok's First Piano Concerto was presented in 1928, with the composer himself as pianist on his first visit to the United States.

The Cincinnati Symphony Orchestra serves many cities with regional concert programs, including those in Kentucky and Indiana. Music Hall displays bronze statues of Theodore Thomas and Van der Stucken in its lobby, and the May Festival is very much alive, presenting both traditional and contemporary works. Works of Bach and Leonard Bernstein were on the same program in recent years.

Chicago Opera

Chicago's opera history is colorful but uneven. It began with J. B. Rice's Chicago Theater, on Dearborn and Randolf Streets, a playhouse displaying carpets and box tiers on its elegantly furnished second floor. Indeed, it resembled a private sitting room.

In 1850, an opera group of four arrived from Milwaukee to perform Bellini's *La Sonnambula*, accompanied by a theater band and local chorus. This was actually the first of Chicago's operas, and it played to the élite of the city. Later that year a fire ravaged the theater and a fund-raising benefit was held at City Hall. A new brick theater was built on the same site, with three tiers of boxes and a saloon downstairs. There was seating available for fourteen-hundred.

Opera continued in the new building with an Italian opera troupe singing Bellini's *Norma* and Donizetti's *Lucia di Lammermoor*. Opera still appealed to the well-to-do. Rice retired from the opera scene to later become Chicago's major. His efforts in opera were carried on by James McVicker, who, in 1857, built an elaborate two-thousand-seat theater on Madison Street. Parquet boxes, two galleries, and expensive stage settings made McVicker's building even grander for opera production. The Durand English Opera Troupe presented Verdi's *Il Trovatore* and Donizetti's *The Daughter of the Regiment* here.

The Civil War halted opera performances. But afterwards, in 1865, Uranus Crosby built an elegant opera house on Washington Street, between State and Dearborn. The building was a combination opera house, art gallery and office, designed in formal Italian facade with high arches and much sculpture. Crosby's opera house added a dress circle and a family circle; the house seated twenty-five-hundred. Frescoes and portraits of composers hung on walls, and the crimson and gold décor was elegant. Opening night featured Verdi's *Il Trovatore* with the Italian Opera Company from New York. Generals Grant and Sherman were in the audience.

In 1871 the great Chicago Fire destroyed the city. When the city was rebuilt, comic opera from Paris, with Offenbach's *La Belle Hélène,* and minstrel shows and brass bands, rather than grand opera, reflected the preferences of the day. The light operas of Gilbert and Sullivan were popular along with Lilly Langtry. Not until the mid-1880's did attention turn once again to grand opera. Adelina Patti and Christine Nilsson sang German opera at the Columbia Theater, the Haverly, and the McVicker Theater. With the burning of Crosby's, however, there was no real opera house.

Finally, in 1887, plans were formulated for the construction of a new ten-story, granite opera house, to be called the Auditorium, on Michigan Avenue near the lakefront. The design was heavily Romanesque. The interior boasted marble, ivory, gold, and onyx, and seated 4,250. Opening night in 1889 presented Gounod's *Romeo and Juliet* with Adelina Patti. The experience was comparable in splendor to an evening at the Metropolitan Opera House in New York and the French Opera House in New Orleans. Following this were visits made by Walter Damrosch, conducting Wagner's *Tristan and Isolde,* and a new tenor, Enrico Caruso, singing Donizetti's *Lucia di Lammermoor* and Ponchielli's *La Gioconda.*

The Chicago Grand Opera Company was formed in 1910, performing Verdi's *Aida* in the Auditorium. Soprano Mary Garden sang in *Pelleas et Melisande* by Debussy, and *Salome* by Richard Strauss, the latter's sensuality rocking the audience's sensibilities. Nellie Melba visited for Puccini's *La Bohème* and Geraldine Farrar for Puccini's *Madama Butterfly.* Opera was ascending once again and thirty operas were produced in the 1913 season.

War again and the Opera Company disbanded, to be reorganized in 1922 as the Chicago Civic Opera. Italian opera was emphasized; even *Boris Godunov* was performed in Italian. Newcomer Gladys Swarthout sang Bizet's *Carmen,* Puccini's *Tosca,* and Humperdinck's *Hansel and Gretel.* Occasionally an opera was given in English, such as *A Witch of Salem* by Cadman, and *A Light from St. Agnes* by W. Franke Harling.

And again, a new opera house was desired. The last performance in the Auditorium was given in 1929. The opera was *Romeo and Juliet*, which was also the opera given at the first performance in the new Chicago Opera House, located on Wacker Drive.

The new Civic Opera House was forty-five stories high, literally a skyscraper. It opened several days after the stock market crash in 1929. Its marble columns, vaulted gold ceilings, and rose and gold interior contrasted sharply with the dark economic picture all around. Summer opera was presented at Lavinia Park, twenty-five miles from the Loop in a large wooden pavilion open on three sides.

But the Civic Opera Company collapsed in 1932 and the Opera House became idle. Late in 1933, the Chicago Grand Opera Company was formed and opened a new season in 1934 with Puccini's *Turandot*, sung by Rosa Raisa; Richard Strauss' *Salome*, sung by Maria Jeritza; and Wagner's *Tristan und Isolde*, with Tristan sung by Lauritz Melchior. More new names in the thirties were Kirsten Flagstad, Helen Traubel, Grace Moore, and Jussi Bjoerling. The Chicago Symphony, with guest conductors Artur Rodzinski and Fritz Reiner, accompanied the productions.

World War II at first depressed opera activity, then stimulated interest. A new resident company, the Lyric Theater of Chicago, came into existence in the early fifties. Mozart's *Don Giovanni* and Bellini's *Norma* were staged, with such opera stars as Eleanor Steber, Bidu Sayao, Maria Callas, Tito Gobbi, and Renata Tebaldi. The Company performs on Wacker Drive today and its name has been changed to Lyric Opera of Chicago. Opera is alive once again and has been revitalized for a new generation.

Dance

Several groups have made significant contributions to dance in the Midwest. Besides the Chicago Ballet with Maria Tallchief, they are the Cincinnati Ballet and the Cleveland Ballet.

The Cincinnati Ballet
Founded in 1958 as the Cincinnati Civic Ballet, it became the Cincinnati Ballet Company in 1962, performing regularly in the 3,600-seat Music Hall. Twenty-four dancers present a varied repertory in classical, romantic, and modern styles. Some recent premières by Frederic Franklin and Daniel Levans have been offered. The Company is affiliated with the Cincinnati Conservatory of Music, where it still performs in Corbett Auditorium. It is the only professional ballet company of its size

241

in the Ohio/Kentucky/Indiana area. The group tours extensively with such dancers as Lori Massie, Katherine Turner, and Kevin Ward.

The Cleveland Ballet

In 1972 a ballet school in a small dance studio in the basement of the Masonic Auditorium on Euclid Avenue was sold to a former pupil, Ian Horvath, who began a new enterprise, the Cleveland Dance Center. Horvath, at that time, was a principal dancer with the American Ballet Theater in New York and he and co-dancer Dennis Nahat formed the first professional dance company in Cleveland. The company soon moved to the Stouffer Building in Playhouse Square, and dancers were recruited from all over the nation. Lectures, demonstrations, and previews were held at Cleveland State University and at Cuyahoga Community College in an effort to attract audiences.

The Cleveland Ballet made its début in 1976 at the Hanna Theater, at 2067 East Fourteenth Street in Playhouse Square, and has grown impressively since then. Choreography is mostly by Nahat, with some ballets by Horvath, Balanchine, and Massine. In 1981, a new ballet by Nahat, "Celebrations," in four parts to the music of Beethoven's Seventh Symphony, was a resounding success. Eclecticism runs high with classical and rock styles on the same program as American ballet.

The following pages list places offering symphonic music, opera, and dance today.

ILLINOIS

Aurora

The Paramount Arts Center, 11 East Galena Boulevard, presents dance and symphonic music.

Chicago

Orchestra Hall, 220 South Michigan Avenue, is the home of the Chicago Symphony Orchestra.

The Auditorium Theater, 70 East Congress Parkway, with its high ceilings and overhanging balcony, features the Chicago City Ballet and many of the world's great dance companies.

The Chicago Cultural Center, Michigan Avenue, between Washington and Randolf Streets, holds many concerts under its glass domes.

The Civic Opera House, 20 North Wacker Drive, has thirty-six-hundred seats and a fourteen-story-high stage. It is home to the Lyric Opera Company of Chicago.

The Petrillo Band Shell in Grant Park, at Columbus Drive and Jackson Boulevard, hosts the Lyric Opera Company of Chicago during the summer. Past performers here have been soprano Lily Pons, baritone Sherrill Milnes, and conductor Julius Rudel.

The Ravinia Music Festival in Highland Park offers varied musical programs in a beautiful park setting. Artists who have performed here are Leontyne Price, Edo de Waart, and the Joffrey Ballet.

Arie Crown Theater, at McCormick Place, features many musical events.

Mandel Hall, Fifty-seventh and University Streets, welcomes chamber groups.

Vick Hall, 1100 East Hyde Park Boulevard, is another site for chamber groups.

World Playhouse, 410 South Michigan Avenue, has hosted the Beaux Arts Trio.

The Athenaeum Theater, 2936 North Southport, presents opera.

Decatur
Kirkland Fine Arts Center at Millikin University, 1184 West Main Street, features opera, dance, and classical music.

Evanston
Noyes Cultural Arts Center, 927 Noyes Street, offers all kinds of music.

Joliet
The Bandshell at Bicentennial Park Theater, Jefferson and Bluff Streets, presents concerts.

The Rialto Theater, 15 East Van Buren, is a Registered National Historic landmark featuring musical events.

Rock Island
Genesius Guild in Lincoln Park, Fortieth Street and Eleventh Avenue, offers open-air opera in the summer.

Centennial Hall hosts the Tri-City Symphony.

Springfield
Summer here is highlighted by the Springfield Muni Opera, 815 East Lake Drive.

Washington Park, Fayette Avenue and Chatham Road, offers more summer music.

Urbana
Krannert Center for the Performing Arts, at the University of Illinois, 500 Goodwin Avenue, is active musically, offering chamber music, choral works, and dance.

Woodstock
Woodstock Opera House, 121 Van Buren Street, welcomes Spring Music Series concerts.

INDIANA

Bloomington
Indiana University has a plethora of musical activities taking place in the Musical Arts Center on Jordan Avenue. The University has a fine school of music.

Evansville
Spring is the time for the Ohio River Arts Festival, and opera.

The Evansville Philharmonic Orchestra, performs from the fall through spring.

Indianapolis

Indianapolis, as well as Evansville, Fort Wayne, Kokomo, Muncie, Richmond, South Bend, and Terre Haute, all boast symphony orchestras.

Clowes Memorial Hall, 4600 Sunset Avenue, seating twenty-two hundred, is where the Indianapolis Symphony Orchestra performs. Especially enjoyable is the Romantic Music Festival in May.

Butler University, West Forty-sixth Street and Sunset Avenue, has welcomed guest artists Jorge Bolet and Aaron Rosand. The University also has a School of Music.

Indiana and Purdue University (merged in 1969), 1100 West Michigan Street, has an extremely active musical department with many events year-round.

Booth Tarkington Civic Theater, 1200 West Thirty-eighth Street, offers a variety of music programs.

The Indianapolis Ballet performs at 1831 North Meridian Street.

Indiana Convention Center, 100 South Capitol, offers many music programs. The Fort Wayne Ballet, among other groups, performs here.

Michigan City

A Michigan City Summer Festival comes with many varieties of music in July.

Muncie

Emens Auditorium at Ball State University, Riverside and University Avenues, features classical music.

New Harmony

Murphy Auditorium for Performing Arts, Tavern Street and Thrall Theater Complex, has concerts and musical fare.

Pendleton

The Paramount Theater (Anderson), 1124 Meridian, hosts the Pendleton Festival Summerfest in the summer, presenting symphonic music and opera. Such stars as soprano Roberta Peters have performed here.

South Bend

Century Center, 120 South St. Joseph Street, has a Performing Arts Center active in the performance of chamber music and choral works.

IOWA

Charles City

Bend Park, on Court Street, hosts Art-A-Fest in August, offering music and dance.

Davenport

Masonic Auditorium, hosts the Tri-City Symphony.

Des Moines

Iowa State University (Ames), Drake University, and Simpson College host chamber groups, operatic stars and the Des Moines Symphony.

Simpson College hosts the Metro Summer Festival of Opera in June and July. It attracts many listeners.

"Music Under the Stars" on the Capitol Grounds also attracts many listeners.

Civic Center, at 221 Walnut Street, offers ballet.

Dubuque
The University of Dubuque, 2050 University Avenue, presents concerts.

Iowa City
Hancher Auditorium, at the University of Iowa, has welcomed chamber groups and opera stars, including soprano Leontyne Price.

Mason City
The Summer Arts Festival takes place in August.

Mount Vernon
The Cornell College Music Festival, in May, offers a great variety of music. The St. Louis Symphony, the Indianapolis Symphony, pianist Eugene Istomin, and mezzo-soprano Marilyn Horne have been among many guest artists performing on campus.

King Chapel houses a Moeller pipe organ.

Sioux City
Grandview Park, Twenty-fourth Street and Grandview Boulevard, features Sioux City's symphony orchestra and other musical events.

KANSAS

Iola
Bowls Fine Arts Center, 205 East Madison, presents the Iola Area Symphony Orchestra.

Lawrence
The Lawrence Arts Center, Ninth and Vermont Streets, offers concerts and dance programs.

Lindsborg
Bethany College, East Swensson and First Street, hosts the Messiah Festival, consisting of several oratorios of Bach and Handel, the St. Matthew Passion, and other choral works.

Burnett Center is another site for the performance of choral works and chamber music.

Manhattan
City Park hosts Arts-in-the-Park concerts in the summer.

Wellington
Memorial Auditorium, 202 North Washington, offers classical music.

Wichita
Civic Center's Century II, 225 West Douglas, hosts the Wichita Symphony. Not only are major Classics Series presented, but chamber music, "pops" and the River Festival Concert, too.

Friends University, 2100 University Avenue, hosts the "Singing Quakers," who are noted for their choral presentations.

MICHIGAN

Ann Arbor

Hill Auditorium, at the University of Michigan, features regular musical programs with such stars as violinist Yehudi Menuhin, soprano Joan Sutherland, tenor Dietrich Fischer-Dieskau, and the Philadelphia Orchestra, which has performed at its May Festival.

Power Center for the Performing Arts offers dance as well.

Calumet

The old Calumet Theater, 340 Sixth Street, was built with boomtown wealth, and restored in 1976. Enrico Caruso and John Philip Sousa performed here.

Coldwater

Tibbits Opera House, on South Hanchett Street, presents winter concerts.

Detroit

Ford Auditorium, 20 Auditorium Drive, hosts the Detroit Symphony Orchestra.

Oakland University, Rochester is the Orchestra's summer home.

The Performing Arts Center at the University of Detroit, 4001 West Mc Nichols Road, holds concerts all year.

Masonic Temple, 500 Temple, offers a Metropolitan Opera series.

Orchestra Hall, 3711 Woodward, presents concerts.

The Detroit Institute of Arts, Woodward and Farnsworth Avenues, features "Brunch with Bach," informal chamber music concerts in the Crystal Gallery.

Flint

Cultural Center at Flint College, 1401 East Court Street, offers music in the summer.

Grand Haven

An Arts Festival takes place in the summer.

Dewey Hill has the world's largest electronically controlled musical fountain.

Grand Rapids

De Vos Hall, Grand Center, offers opera.

Interlochen

The famous National Music Camp is here. All varieties of music are taught and performed amidst a twelve-hundred-acre pine forest, on MI-137.

Jackson, Kalamazoo, Lansing, and Saginaw have symphony orchestras.

Midland

Midland Center for the Arts, 1801 West St. Andrews, presents music concerts, dance programs, and chamber music programs.

Muskegon

Seaway Festival takes place in the summer, with all forms of musical fare.

Whitehall

The White Lake Music Shell, Dowling Street, offers summer concerts.

MINNESOTA

Minneapolis/St. Paul

Orchestra Hall, 1111 Nicollet Mall, hosts the Minnesota Orchestra. There are fine acoustics inside and spacious walkways, and lovely fountains, trees, and flowers outside.

The Walker Art Center, 725 Vineland Place, hosts concerts and ballet.

The Minneapolis Institute of Arts, 2400 Third Avenue South, hosts concerts and ballet.

Stage Coach Museum, off MN-101, is a former opera house which now offers varied musical fare.

The University of Minnesota, in Minneapolis, hosts the Metropolitan Opera every spring.

Minneapolis and St. Paul have their own opera company—the Minnesota Opera Company, 75 W. Fifth Street in St. Paul. St. Paul also has a Chamber Orchestra and a Civic Opera

Keyboard Instrument Museum, 75 West Fifth Street, St. Paul, has an interesting display of nineteenth-century instruments.

Concentus Musicus, at 905 Fourth Avenue South, is a Renaissance-costumed ensemble playing medieval music with krummhorns, sackbutts, and shawms.

Summer performances of classical and contemporary music are given by the Minneapolis Chamber Symphony.

Hennepin Center for the Arts, 528 Hennepin Avenue, presents choral works by the Minnesota Chorale.

St. Paul Arts and Science Center, 30 East Tenth Street, a large center for the performing arts, has an auditorium for musical programs.

Rochester

Mayo Civic Auditorium Theater, 30 South East Second Avenue, presents the Rochester Symphony Orchestra.

NEBRASKA

Omaha

The Orpheum Theater, 409 South Sixteenth Street, and the Joslyn Art Museum, 2200 Dodge Street, both present evening and afternoon performances of the Omaha Symphony. Dylana Jenson, violinist, and Lorin Hollander, pianist, have recently appeared here. Opera and ballet companies, and visiting orchestras and chamber groups also perform at these two theaters.

The lobby of the Orpheum Theater, home of the Omaha Symphony, during intermission. (Courtesy Omaha Symphony)

OHIO

Berea
Baldwin-Wallace College, 275 Eastland Road, has hosted the Baldwin-Wallace Bach Festival since 1930.

Canton
Cultural Center for the Arts, 1001 Market Avenue North, has a recital hall which is used for symphony, opera, and dance programs.

Cincinnati
The Cincinnati Art Museum, Eden Park, displays a large collection of musical instruments.

Sanders Theater, at the University of Cincinnati Conservatory of Music, offers classical and experimental music.

The eight-hundred-seat Corbett Auditorium, presents the Civic Ballet.

The Music Hall, 1241 Elm Street, hosts the Cincinnati Symphony Orchestra, Cincinnati's Ballet Company and Summer Opera. The Music Hall has been renovated with crystal chandeliers and French décor, and with over thirty-five-hundred seats it is second in size to New York's Metropolitan Opera House. Soprano Eileen Farrell, tenor Richard Tucker, bass Ezio Pinza, and mezzo-soprano Rise Stevens have appeared here.

There's a gala May Festival each year that began more than a century ago. The Cincinnati Chamber Orchestra plays at outdoors Eden Park in Seasongood Pavilion. Various dance groups perform at Shillito's, Seventh and Race Streets. Memorial Hall holds musical events at 1225 Elm Street. Springfest welcomes Queen City Brass to Fountain Square, Fifth Street between Vine and Walnut Streets.

Cleveland

Severance Hall, Euclid Avenue and East Boulevard, is home to the Cleveland Orchestra.

Blossom Music Center, Cuyahoga Falls, near Akron, is the Orchestras summer home.

Convention Center, Lakeside at East Sixth Street, hosts the Metropolitan Opera in the spring.

The Hanna Theater, 2067 East Fourteenth Street, presents the Cleveland Ballet.

The Music Hall, East Sixth Street and St. Clair Avenue, presents dance companies.

The Cleveland Institute of Music, 11021 East Boulevard, is open to visitors.

Columbus

Capitol Grounds is the site for the Summer Festival of the Arts in June.

The Ohio Theater, 39 East State Street, hosts the Columbus Symphony Orchestra as well as dance companies and opera. The Eliot Feld Ballet and cellist Lynn Harrell have performed here.

Cuyahoga Falls

Blossom Music Center, 1145 West Steels Corner Road, is a busy place. In addition to being the summer home to the Cleveland Orchestra, it has hosted the San Francisco Ballet. In addition, *Madame Butterfly* has been presented here and cellist Yo-Yo Ma has performed here.

Oberlin

Oberlin College, at junction OH-10 and 58, has had an active Conservatory of Music since the mid-twentieth century.

Sandusky

The Sandusky Bay Festival offers concerts in May.

Springfield
A Summer Arts Festival takes place at many sites throughout town. The Civic Opera performs in the winter, spring, and fall.
Toledo
The Masonic Auditorium, 4645 Heatherdowns, hosts the Toledo Symphony and the Toledo Ballet. Soloists who have performed with the Symphony are pianists Horacio Gutierrez and André Watts.
The Toledo Museum of Art, 2445 Monroe, also hosts the Toledo Symphony.
Crosby Gardens, 5403 Elmer Drive, hosts a Festival of the Arts in the spring and fall.
Youngstown
The Youngstown Symphony Center, 260 Federal Plaza West, presents ballet and concerts by the Youngstown Symphony Orchestra.
Stambaugh Auditorium, Fifth and Park Avenues, offers concerts.

WISCONSIN
Appleton
The Conservatory of Music at Lawrence University, College Avenue and Union Street, is open to visitors.
Fish Creek
Gibraltar High School Auditorium in Door County hosts the Peninsula Music Festival, with such soloists as Sidney Harth and Jan De Gaetani. Ravel, Stravinsky, Weber, and Beethoven are sample fare.
La Crosse
The Fine Arts Center at Viterbo College, 815 South Ninth Street, holds musical events all year.
Milwaukee
Uihlein Hall, in the Performing Arts Center, 929 Water Street, overlooking the Milwaukee River in Père Marquette Park, hosts the Milwaukee Symphony Orchestra, the Milwaukee Ballet, the Florentine Opera, and Bel Canto Chorus. Uihlein Hall, holds over two-thousand seats.
Washington Park and Humboldt Park, host "Music under the Stars" in the summer. Soloists such as mezzo-soprano Rosalind Elias and tenor John Gary have appeared. Comic opera, particularly Gilbert and Sullivan is performed at 813 North Jefferson Street.
Pabst Theater, 144 East Wells, has a large stage for dance groups.
Sheboygan
Kohler Arts Center, 608 New York Avenue, presents concerts.

THE MIDWEST

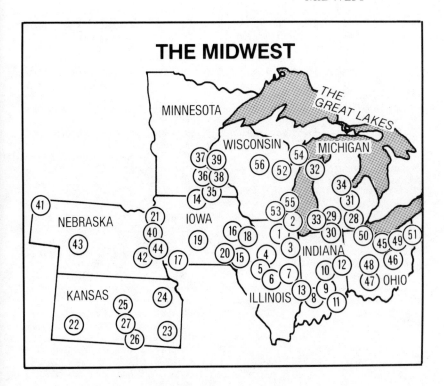

The Midwest

1. Aurora, IL—Paramount Arts Center, 11 E. Galena Boulevard, for all popular and symphonic music
2. Bensenville, IL—Nashville North, 101 E. Irving Park Road, has country-Western
3. Joliet, IL—Concerts at Bicentennial Park Theater in the Bandshell, Jefferson and Bluff streets
4. Peoria, IL—Exposition Gardens, 1601 N. Moor Road, has country-Western concerts
5. Petersburg, IL—Illinois Country Opry in summer on IL-97
6. Springfield, IL—Springfield Muni Opera, 815 E. Lake Drive, in summer
7. Urbana, IL—Krannert Center for the Performing Arts at the University of Illinois, 500 Goodwin Avenue, presents chamber music, choral works, and dance
8. Bloomington, IN—Indiana University has continuous musical events on Jordan Avenue
9. Bean Blossom, IN—Bill Monroe's 100-

acre park is site of Bean Blossom Bluegrass Festival in spring
10. Indianapolis, IN—Clowes Memorial Hall, 4600 Sunset Avenue, is home of Indianapolis Symphony. Indiana University has an active music department, 100 W. Michigan Street. Indiana Convention Center, 100 S. Capitol, has many musical presentations. Eagle Creek Folk Music Festival takes place in July
11. Madison, IN—"Chautauqua of the Arts" heralds all kinds of music
12. Muncie, IN—Ball State University, Riverside and University avenues, features classical music in Emens Auditorium
13. Terre Haute, IN—Bluegrass, country-Western at Fairbanks Park
14. Britt, IA—Railroad tracks hold rock and roll concerts at National Hobo Convention in August
15. Burlington, IA—A Dixieland Jazz Festival takes place in June on the riverfront

251

16. Cedar Rapids, IA—Paramount Theater, Paramount Building, for jazz concerts

17. Clarinda, IA—Hometown of Glenn Miller and a music festival in his honor in May

18. Davenport, IA—Hometown of and a music festival for cornetist Bix Beiderbecke in Le Claire Park

19. Des Moines, IA—Iowa State Fair on Fairgrounds, E. 30th Street and University Avenue, in August. Civic Center, 221 Walnut Street, hosts jazz, rock, ballet, and other events

20. Mt. Pleasant, IA—Bluegrass Music Festival in June

21. Sioux City, IA—Grandview Park, Twenty-fourth Street and Grandview Boulevard, for musical fare

22. Dodge City, KN—Long Branch Saloon on Front Street offers honky-tonk and country-Western

23. Iola, KN—Bowlus Fine Arts Center, 205 E. Madison, houses the Iola Area Symphony

24. Lawrence, KN—Lawrence Arts Center, Ninth and Vermont streets, for concerts and dance

25. Lindsborg, KN—Bethany College, E. Swensson and First Street, presents Messiah Festival in spring

26. Wellington, KN—Memorial Auditorium, 202 N. Washington, for all kinds of music

27. Wichita, KN—Century II, 225 W. Douglas Street, for all varieties of music. Home of Wichita Symphony

28. Ann Arbor, MI—Hill Auditorium in University of Michigan offers regular musical programs

29. Battle Creek, MI—Binder Winter Park for Bluegrass and rock concerts

30. Coldwater, MI—Tibbits Opera House on S. Hanchett Street holds winter concerts

31. Flint, MI—Cultural Center, 1341 E. Kearsley, offers all musical varieties

32. Interlochen, MI—Site of National Music Camp where all kinds of music are taught and performed

33. Kalamazoo, MI—Kalamazoo Center at 100 W. Michigan Avenue presents rock concerts

34. Midland, MI—Midland Center for the Arts, 1801 W. St. Andrews, features chamber music and dance

35. Albert Lea, MN—Fairgrounds for a gala country fair in August

36. Bloomington, MN—E. Seventy-eighth Street for jazz and rock spots, The Thunderbird and Rodeway Inn

37. Crystal, MN—Crystal Lounge, 4900 W. Broadway, for country-Western

38. Rochester, MN—Baldwin Memorial Pavilion for classical and popular music. Mayo Civic Auditorium Theater, 30 SE Second Avenue, for the Rochester Symphony

39. Stillwater, MN—Fatt City, 305 S. Water Street, for rock groups

40. Blair, NB—Bluegrass and country-Western in fall

41. Crawford, NB—Fiddle Contests in summer

42. Lincoln, NB—The Nebraska State Fair is held on the Fairgrounds, Seventeenth and Clinton streets in fall

43. North Platte, NB—Cody Park on US-83 is site for world's first rodeo in 1882. Heavy on country-Western

44. Omaha, NB—Old Market Area on Howard Street, for Howard Street Tavern and Mr. Toad's. M's Pub, 422 S. Eleventh Street, for country-Western. The Orpheum Theater, 409 S. Sixteenth Street, is home to the Omaha Symphony. The Joslyn Art Museum, 200 Dodge Street holds frequent concerts, opera, and dance performances

45. Akron, OH—The Akron Civic Theater, 182 S. Main Street provides varied musical fare. Bluegrass concerts in Shady Side Park

46. Canton, OH—Cultural Center for the Arts, 1001 Market Avenue N., holds symphonic, opera, and dance performances

47. Circleville, OH—133 W. Main Street is site of Ted Lewis Museum

48. Columbus, OH—Columbus Symphony, opera, and dance groups perform at the Ohio Theater, 39 E. State Street. The Riverfront Amphitheater on the west bank of the Scioto River provides musical fare on a floating stage

49. Cuyahoga Falls, OH—Blossom Music Center, 1145 W. Steels Corner Road, is active in all kinds of music including housing the Cleveland Orchestra in summer

50. Toledo, OH—The Toledo Symphony performs at Masonic Auditorium, 4645 Heatherdowns and Toledo Museum of Art, 2445 Monroe

51. Youngstown, OH—Youngstown Symphony Center, 260 Federal Plaza West, for concerts and ballet. Federal Plaza East has Big-Band sound concerts

52. *Appleton, WI—The Conservatory of Music, Lawrence University, is located on College Avenue and Union Street.*

53. *Elkhorn, WI—Alpine Valley Music Theater, off WI-15, hosts musical fare in summer*

54. *Egg Harbor, WI—The Performing Arts Academy, Birch Creek Farm, 3 miles east on County Road E, has summer jazz concerts*

55. *Milwaukee, WI—Uihlein Hall in the Performing Arts Center, 929 Water Street, hosts the Milwaukee Symphony, the Milwaukee Ballet, the Florentine Opera, and Bel Canto Chorus.*

Pabst Theater, 144 E. Wells, offers dance groups. Comic opera is performed at 813 N. Jefferson Street. The Milwaukee Jazz Gallery is located at 932 E. Center Street. Dr. Feelgood's, 2178 N. Riverboat Road, plays popular music. "Summerfest" is held at the lakefront. The Pfister Hotel, 424 E. Wisconsin Avenue, has all popular music. La Bohème, 319 E. Mason, offers classics and jazz. The Palms, 2616 W. State Street, and the Metropolitan Theater, 2844 N. Oakland Avenue, for rock

56. *Wausau, WI—"Summerthing" is a gala festival in July*

Chicago, IL

1. **Auditorium Theater**, 70 E. Congress Parkway. Former home of Chicago Symphony. Host to Chicago City Ballet and many dance companies
2. **Civic Opera House**, 20 N. Wacker Drive, home of Lyric Opera of Chicago
3. **Orchestra Hall**, 220 S. Michigan Avenue, home of Chicago Symphony
4. **Chicago Cultural Center**, Michigan Avenue between Washington and Randolf streets, for concerts
5. **Grant Park**, Columbus Drive and Jackson, site of summer concerts in Petrillo Bandshell
6. **World Playhouse**, 410 S. Michigan Avenue, hosts chamber music groups
7. **Athenaem Theater**, 2936 N. Southport, for opera
8. **Daley Center**, Randolph and Dearborn streets, has continuous musical events
9. **Somebody Else's Troubles**, 2470 N. Lincoln, for popular music
10. **Clearwater Saloon**, 3447 N. Lincoln, for popular music
11. **McGiddie's**, 2423 N. Lincoln, for popular music
12. **Orphans**, 2462 N. Lincoln, for rock
13. **Andy's**, 11 E. Hubbard Street, for jazz
14. **On Broadway Chicago**, 5246 Broadway, for blues and jazz
15. **Benchley's on Broadway**, 6232 Broadway, a popular nightspot
16. **Sundance Social Pub**, 6253 Broadway, a popular nightspot
17. **The Bulls**, 1916 N. Lincoln Park West, for jazz and rock
18. **Crickets**, 100 E. Chestnut, hot jazz
19. **Inmet Circle**, 750 S. Halsted Street, blues, jazz, rock
20. **International Amphitheater**, 4220 S. Halsted Street, jazz, rock
21. **Kingston Mines**, 2548 N. Halsted, blues, jazz, rock
22. **Manhattan Tavern**, 1045 N. Rush Street, for jazz and rock
23. **Backroom Club**, 1007 N. Rush Street, for blues and jazz
24. **State Street**, historic black area for development of jazz
25. **Jazz Showcase**, 636 S. Michigan Avenue, for jazz
26. **The Brassay**, 625 N. Michigan Avenue, for rock and disco
27. **Civic Center**, Washington and Dearborn streets, for all kinds of musical events
28. **Razzles**, 600 N. Lake Shore Drive, jazz
29. **Rick's Café American**, Holiday Inn, 644 N. Lake Shore Drive, a popular nightspot
30. **Bar RR Ranch Western Cocktail Lounge**, 56 W. Randolf Street, for rock
31. **Chicago Stadium**, 1800 W. Madison, rock concerts
32. **Dingbats**, 247 E. Ontario, jazz and rock
33. **George's**, 230 W. Kinzie Street, for jazz
34. **Old Town**, up and down Clark Street, with dozens of nightspots
35. **Wise Fools Pub**, 2770 N. Lincoln, for blues and jazz
36. **Navy Pier**, ChicagoFest in August, world renowned festival
37. **Highland Park** features Ravinia Music Festival

Cincinnati, OH

1. Convention Center, Fifth and Elm streets, holds an Appalachian Festival in May and numerous other musical events
2. Emery Auditorium, Central Parkway and Walnut, for varied musical fare
3. Music Hall, 1243 Elm Street, home of Cincinnati Symphony, Cincinnati Ballet, and Summer Opera
4. Riverfront Coliseum on Front Street, for rock concerts
5. Riverfront Stadium, Front Street, for blues and jazz
6. Memorial Hall, 1225 Elm Street, for musical events
7. Cincinnati Art Museum, Eden Park, has musical fare
8. Seasongood Pavilion in Eden Park, summer concerts by Cincinnati Chamber Orchestra
9. Shillito's, Seventh and Race streets, hosts dance groups
10. Fountain Square, Fifth Street between Walnut and Vine, all varieties of music
11. Shipley's, 2822 Vine Street, jazz
12. The Lighthouse, 2505 Vine Street, disco
13. Arnold's, 210 E. Eighth Street, jazz and rock
14. Sleep Out Louie's, 230 W. Second Street, jazz and disco
15. Public Landing, foot of Broadway, many floating riverboat spots offering jazz and popular music
16. Sidedoor Lounge, 615 Walnut Street, country-Western
17. Top of the Crown at Stouffer's, 141 W. Sixth Street, country-Western

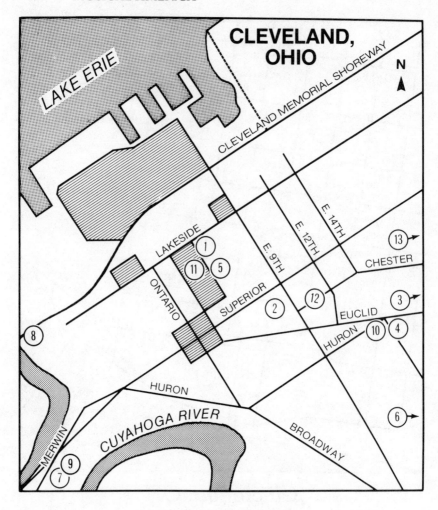

Cleveland, OH

1. *Convention Center, 1220 E. Sixth Street, rock concerts and musical events*
2. *Theatrical Grill, 711 Vincent Road, for country-Western*
3. *Severance Hall, 11001 Euclid Avenue, home of Cleveland Orchestra*
4. *Hanna Theater, 2067 E. Fourteenth Street, home of Cleveland Ballet*
5. *Music Hall, E. Sixth Street and St. Clair Avenue, hosts dance companies*
6. *Peabody's Café, 2140 S. Taylor Road, all popular music*
7. *D'Poos on the River, 1146 Old River Road, for popular music*
8. *Fagan's, 966 Old River Road, for popular music*
9. *Cleveland Crate and Truckin' Co., 1501 Merwin, popular music*
10. *Huron Mall, Huron Avenue, popular music in parks*
11. *Hanna Fountains, popular music in parks*
12. *Chester Commons, Chester Avenue, popular music in parks*
13. *Cleveland Institute of Music, 11021 East Boulevard*

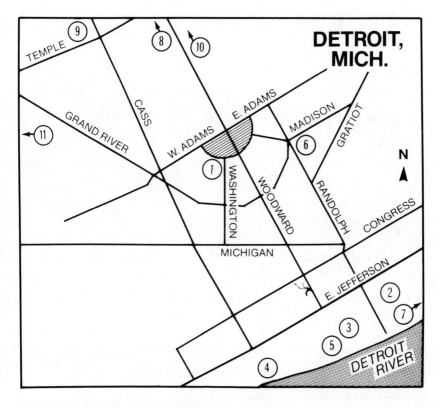

Detroit, MI

1. Top of the Pontch, Pontchartrain Hotel, 2 Washington Boulevard, for all popular music
2. Renaissance Center, Detroit Plaza Hotel, Atwater Street, for all popular music
3. Ford Auditorium, 20 Auditorium Drive, home of Detroit Symphony
4. Cobo Hall, center for rock concerts, Civic Center Drive
5. Hart Plaza, off Woodward, for popular music
6. Music Hall, Randolf Street, for popular music
7. Bob-Lo Island in middle of Detroit River has boats from Island to dock at Woodward for jazz, swing, and rock concerts
8. Orchestra Hall, 3711 Woodward, for concerts
9. Masonic Temple, 500 Temple, for opera
10. Detroit Institute of Arts, Woodward and Farnsworth, for chamber music
11. University of Detroit, 4001 W. Mc-Nichols Road, concerts and many musical events

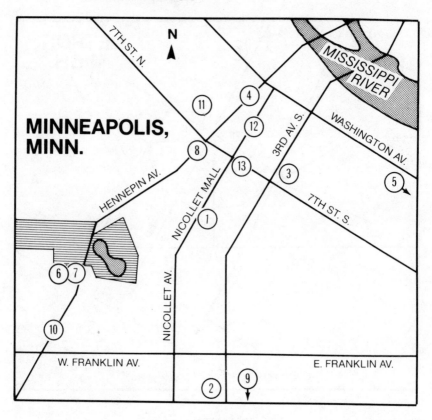

MINNEAPOLIS, MINN.

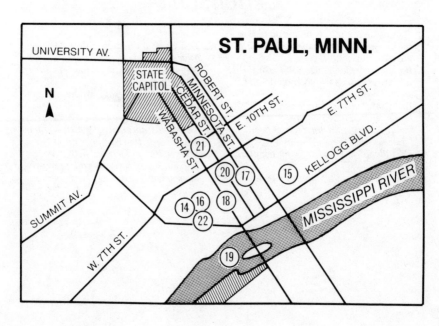

ST. PAUL, MINN.

Minneapolis/St. Paul, MN

1. Orchestra Hall, 1111 Nicollet Mall, home of Minnesota Orchestra
2. Minneapolis Institute of Arts, 2400 Third Avenue S., for concerts and ballet
3. Concentus Musicus, 905 Fourth Avenue S., ensemble playing of medieval music
4. Hennepin Center for the Arts, 528 Hennepin Avenue, site for concerts and choral works
5. University of Minnesota, off Washington Avenue, hosts musical events
6. Walker Arts Center, 725 Vineland Place, concerts, ballet, jazz
7. Guthrie Theater, Vineland Place, for musical events
8. Orpheum Theater, 910 Hennepin Avenue, for jazz
9. Artist's Quarter, 14 E. Twenty-sixth Street, for jazz
10. William's Pub, 2911 Hennepin Avenue S., for jazz
11. Chicago Upstairs, 23 N. Sixth Street, jazz
12. Sadie's Parlour, Sheraton-Ritz Hotel, 315 Nicollet, for popular music
13. Duff's, 21 S. Eighth Street, popular place for popular music
14. Civic Center, 143 W. Fourth Street
15. Ryan's Corner, 211 E. Fourth Street, jazz and rock
16. Keyboard Instrument Museum, 75 W. Fifth Street, 19th-century instruments on display
17. Radisson Plaza, 411 Minnesota Street, blues, jazz, rock
18. Horatio Hornblower's, 435 Wabasha Street, for popular music
19. Paddleboats cruise the Mississippi River offering jazz and blues
20. Extempore Coffeehouse, 325 Cedar, blues, jazz, and rock
21. St. Paul Arts and Science Center, 30 E. Tenth Street, for musical programs
22. The Minnesota Opera Company will soon be performing at their new theater at 75 W. Fifth Street in St. Paul

W·E·S·T

INTRODUCTION

The spread of jazz, swing, and country–Western music continued, following heavy migration patterns to the western part of the country. Large dance halls opened up as major sites of musical recreation, and the West, with its distinctive cowboys, horses, wide-open spaces, freedom, friendly and unfriendly nature, put its stamp on music.

San Antonio, Dallas, Oklahoma City, Omaha, and Denver were cities where, collectively, almost one hundred bands were formed. Ballrooms brought the "Battle of the Bands" to their doors as thousands of listeners danced into the early morning hours.

Symphonic music, opera, and dance moved along slowly and, although less prominent than other regions of the country, groups such as the Utah Symphony, the Albuquerque Symphony, and Ballet West were heavily identified with their respective communities.

When the rock revolution reached the West, it fused with country–Western, producing a regional combination evidenced in the "Tex-Mex" sound—a unique musical genre distinctive in its soft quality and white sound in contrast to the black, bluesy sound of other regions. It was advanced briefly but notably by Buddy Holly, who met an untimely death while pursuing a musical career.

SYMPHONIC MUSIC, OPERA, DANCE

Two orchestras, the Utah Symphony and the Albuquerque Symphony Orchestra, are well-known in the West, closely associated with their locales.

The Utah Symphony

The Utah Symphony, in the heart of Salt Lake City's Mormon country, is an orchestra heavily identified with its community. A special Mormon ethical quality based upon a philosophy of community service helps establish the orchestra as an integral part of life.

The Utah Symphony was founded in 1940 as a WPA group, and in 1947, conductor Maurice Abravenal, originally from Turkey, then Switzerland, came to Salt Lake City to assume directorship of the new orchestra. Money for funding was scarce in the city and state, and some of the musicians worked for minimal salaries or no salaries. Abravenal, himself, worked at very low salary and, in addition to his musical duties, he devoted time to raising funds from citizens by appealing to the common value of sacrificing today for rewards in the future. He was successful, and the orchestra grew, performing in Salt Lake City Tabernacle, built in 1863 of wood and stone and housing over five-thousand people in church pews.

Abravenal had studied for a time in the twenties with Kurt Weill in Berlin. He developed eclectic musical taste. Works by Ernest Bloch, Stravinsky, and Honegger were added to traditional Austro/German repertory. The Symphony's activities were expanded to include working closely with Ballet West and the University of Utah's Music Department, hiring more outside players, establishing a resident opera company, and instituting youth concerts and tours. Abravenal is widely noted for his benign, sympathetic attitude toward the musicians, and indeed toward people in general, in contrast to some major historic disciplinary conductor-figures in other regional symphony orchestras.

In 1957 the Symphony began recording and joined the ranks of other prominent orchestras. Handel, Mahler, and Tchaikovsky suites for Ballet West, and choral works with the University Choir are among its best-known recordings. The Symphony is still subsidized by its players

263

and community members, very little by the Mormon Church and wealthy benefactors. Home base has moved to the Concert Hall in Salt Palace, where acoustics are better.

The Albuquerque Symphony Orchestra

Another growing modern orchestra is the Albuquerque Symphony Orchestra, set in a totally different Western milieu. Albuquerque, the largest city in New Mexico, is a blend of American Indian, Spanish, Mexican, and Anglos (white Americans), living amidst not infrequent racial tension and violence.

Orchestral activities were begun by Anglos at the University of New Mexico in 1932 under the leadership of Grace Thompson Edminster, head of the Music Department. Known as the Albuquerque Civic Symphony, forerunner of the present Albuquerque Symphony Orchestra, the group performed its first concert at the University in that post-depression year. After Edminster left the University, she was succeeded by William Kunkel and then by Kurt Frederick in 1945, both of whom worked to develop a significant orchestra and musical activities.

Frederick was Viennese and had studied violin and viola before coming to the Civic Orchestra as violist and conductor of the student group. He programmed works by Hindemith, Milhaud, and Schoenberg, and in 1948 presented the premiere of Schoenberg's *A Survivor from Warsaw*. The audience was mostly apathetic, not only to "new" music, but to works of Beethoven as well.

The orchestra experienced growing pains and had a difficult time in reaching the public at large. Frederick was replaced by Hans Lange, then by Maurice Bonney. Time and improvements helped move the Symphony along: repertory was increased and the caliber of the playing was augmented by outsiders as well as students; Popejoy Hall, in the Fine Arts building of the University of New Mexico, was completed in 1968 with a large stage and fine acoustics.

In 1970, Japanese-born Yashimi Takeda, former conductor of the Tokyo Symphony Orchestra, apprentice to George Szell in the Cleveland Orchestra, and later conductor of the Honolulu Symphony, took up the baton of the Albuquerque Symphony Orchestra. Repertory began as Austro/German, and then expanded to include such colorful pieces as Ravel's *Rhapsodie Espagnol*, Mussorgsky's *Pictures at an Exhibition*, and Respighi's *Pines of Rome*. Takeda expanded the scope, introducing educational programs to youth. He worked diligently to win status for serious music in the community. Unfortunately, although the New Mexico area is rich in natural, physical resources, there is no extensive financial support for cultural activities. Nevertheless, the Albuquerque Symphony has grown and shows signs of continuing to do so.

The Santa Fe Opera

A city high up in the mountains of New Mexico is noted as a significant musical landmark—Santa Fe, for the Santa Fe Opera.

In 1954, one John Crosby established a summer outdoor opera company in a well-equipped theater. Singers were apprentices who came to Santa Fe for training, and orchestras were drawn from different professional groups throughout the country. Both American and European singers participated in such traditional and modern repertory as Puccini's *Madama Butterfly*, Rossini's *The Barber of Seville*, Strauss' *Arabella*, Stravinsky's *Rake's Progress* (at which Stravinsky himself attended rehearsals), and a modern American work, *The Tower*, by Marvin David Levy. All the operas are sung in English.

The physical climate of Santa Fe lends itself to scenic outdoor productions, as in the production of *Madama Butterfly*, when the rear doors of the stage open onto the shining lights of the town of Santa Fe below, emulating the Japanese city of Nagasaki.

The opera house is perched on a mesa between the Jemez and Sangre de Cristo mountains, six miles outside Santa Fe, and is made of redwood and stucco. The colorful Indian motif augments the beauty of the music. The stage is shaped like a gramaphone horn, divided in the middle. It was originally separated from the auditorium by a large pool reflecting light and stars.

In 1967, just prior to a performance of Hindemith's *Cardillac*, a fire ravaged the Opera House. The Theater was rebuilt the following year.

A memorable event took place in August, 1982 with the production of *Die Fledermaus* by Johann Strauss. The costumes were dazzling in the swirling action of the ballroom waltz scene. Sets were elaborate and airy with arching girders and walls and walls of windowpanes.

The theater continues today as a lovely site for opera, playing to more than forty-thousand a season.

Other Outdoor Festivals

Red Rocks Park

The most famous of a chain of Denver mountain parks is the Park of the Red Rocks, about thirteen miles west of downtown Denver. An open-air theater situated on an incline commands a spectacular view of red rocks tinged with green, gray, and white streaks forming the stage. The acoustics are nearly perfect on cool summer evenings bathed with fresh mountain air, as ten-thousand listeners flock to hear world-renowned talent perform high above sea level. The constant play of light and shadow add to the visual charm and pure, clear sound.

Aspen

Here is a beautiful outdoor community nestled in a valley of Roaring Fork River in the Rocky Mountain range. It is the top most part of the Continental Divide, with rugged landscape and pine-clad bluffs. Towering eight-thousand feet above sea level, it is surrounded by seven peaks, all over fourteen-thousand feet tall.

Composer Darius Milhaud has been active in summer music festivals here since 1949, and in establishing the Aspen Music School. Special tribute was paid to him on his seventieth birthday, in 1962, when he conducted the American première of his work, a harp concerto, *Chants Populaires Hebraiques,* with vocalist Jennie Tourel. The main concerts are held in the large white circular tent seating sixteen-hundred.

Dance

Ballet West

A rising dance company and the most notable in the region is Ballet West of Salt Lake City, Utah. It performs at the renovated two-thousand-seat Capitol Theater, with thirty-nine dancers giving about 120 performances each year. During the summer, the company travels to Aspen/Snowmass, Colorado, where it takes up residence for two months.

William Christensen (brother of Lew Christensen, director of the San Francisco Ballet) founded the group in 1963, calling it the Utah Civic Ballet. It became Ballet West in 1968, when the Federation of Rocky Mountain States designated it the official ballet company of the Federation. Christensen also established the group as the first university-affiliated ballet school with the University of Utah. Such works as *La Fille Mal Gardée, Cinderella,* and *Swan Lake* were memorably choreographed by Christensen. After he retired, dancer and choreographer Bruce Marks arranged *Don Quixote, Sanctus,* and *Inscape.* In addition, varied pieces are in the repertory, among which are works by Balanchine and Michael Smuin.

The pages that follow guide you in visiting places that offer symphonic music, opera, and dance.

ARIZONA
Flagstaff

The campus of Northern Arizona University, on I-17, hosts the Flagstaff

Festival of the Arts. Symphonic music, chamber music, dance, and theater are the programs.

Phoenix

Kerr Cultural Center, 6110 North Scottsdale Road, presents symphonic and choral music. Such artists as the Bach Aria Group perform here.

Arizona State University, Tempe, is a major site for concerts, dance, and theater in the Frank Lloyd Wright-designed Gammage Auditorium. The acoustics are close to perfect here. The University also has a museum of musical instruments.

The Phoenix Art Museum, 1625 North Central Avenue, hosts chamber music events.

Civic Plaza Symphony Hall, North First Avenue and Van Buren, is where the Phoenix Symphony Orchestra holds its regular season. The Arizona Opera also performs in Civic Plaza.

The Sun City Dome, 19403 R. H. Johnson Boulevard, offers much music, including performances by the Arizona Opera.

The Phoenix Chamber Music Society performs in Scottsdale, as does the Scottsdale Symphony.

Tucson

Community Center Music Hall, 260 South Church Street, hosts the Tucson Symphony Orchestra. Symphonic music and "pops" are offered. An Artists Series is presented by the University of Arizona.

The Southern Arizona Light Opera Company and the Tucson Metropolitan Ballet also perform in Tucson.

COLORADO

Aspen

The Aspen Music Festival, from late June through August, brings such well-known artists as Mischa Dichter, Lilian Kallir, and Walter Trampler to play with the Aspen Chamber Symphony and Aspen Festival Orchestra. There's a music school here, too, with almost a thousand students. Concerts are given in a large tent and there is additional lawn seating with a splendid view of the board valley of Roaring Fork River in the Rocky Mountain Range (an altitude of 7,900 feet). In 1962, Darius Milhaud celebrated his seventieth birthday in Aspen with singer Jenny Tourel. Aspen High School Performing Center, on Castle Creek Road, hosts Utah's Ballet West during the summer.

Boulder

A Colorado Music Festival comes to Boulder in the summer.

Colorado Chautauqua in Chautauqua Park, 900 Baseline Road, provides symphonic concerts. The Civic Opera and Boulder Symphony perform here in the spring.

Central City

Central City is known for its operas held in the Old Central City Opera

House on Eureka Street. The 1878 Opera House is Victorian in décor, with crystal chandeliers, hickory chairs, and murals hung on solid granite walls. Casts from all over the country perform two major operas in the summer.

Colorado Springs
The Fine Arts Center, 30 West Dale Street, offers classical music from time to time.

Denver
Denver Center for the Performing Arts has four theaters for music and dance. The Denver Symphony Orchestra plays in Boettcher Hall, one of the four theaters, at Fourteenth and Curtis Streets. The music performed includes "pops" and classical. In the summer, the Symphony plays "Concerts in the Parks." Boettcher Hall has seating for twenty-five-hundred on several levels built around the orchestra, and is said to be acoustically perfect. Central City Opera performs here too.

The Arvada Center for the Arts, 6901 Wadsworth Boulevard, presents chamber groups, ballet, and opera. Recently, Les Ballets Trocadero de Monte Carlo were featured.

Red Rocks Park and Amphitheater on I-70 presents all varieties of music and a Music Festival in the summer. Especially beautiful is an Easter Sunrise Service in a natural setting of huge red rocks.

Bonfils Theater, East Colfax and Elizabeth Streets, hosts The Colorado Concert Ballet.

The Houston Fine Arts Center, on Quebec Street and Montview Boulevard, offers chamber music and choral works.

Evergreen
Center for the Arts, 27640 Colorado Highway 74, hosts Summerfest Evergreen in June. The Colorado Philharmonic can be heard at this Festival.

Fort Collins
Lincoln Community Center, 417 Magnolia, has a concert hall and the Theatre for the Performing Arts, both of which are active.

Leadville
The restored Tabor Opera House, 308 Harrison Avenue, was built by silver king Horace Tabor, whose tragic second marriage to Elizabeth Doe was the subject of the American opera, *The Ballad of Baby Doe*, by Douglas Moore. (This opera provided New York Opera star Beverly Sills with one of her first roles.) The Opera House is now a museum.

Pueblo
Memorial Hall, Union and Grand Avenues, is home to the Pueblo Symphony. A Mozart Festival takes place here in January.

Steamboat Springs
The Perry Mansfield School of Stephens College is a dance and drama school that has interesting productions during the year.

Vail
The Vail Institute, 395 East Lionshead Circle offers many musical events.

IDAHO
Boise
Music Week rings out in May with city-wide music programs in abundance.
Boise has a Philharmonic Orchestra.
Boise State College has a community orchestra.
Northwest Nazarene College, 623 Holly Street, has a madrigal choir.
Pocatello
Idaho State University, 741 South Seventh Avenue, presents concerts throughout the year.
Julia Davis Park, Boise Park, and Ross Park offer summer concerts.

MONTANA
Billings and Helena
Both Billings and Helena have symphony orchestras.
Helena offers band concerts in the summer.
Bozeman
The Loft Theater, which presents summer drama, occasionally offers musical events too.
Great Falls
Concerts are given in the spring and summer throughout Great Falls.

NEVADA
Carson City
Brewery Arts Center, 449 West King Street, has welcomed the Saxophone Quartet Plus Two.
Las Vegas
The University of Nevada, 4505 South Maryland Parkway, presents a Masters Series, usually in the fall, with such artists as Zubin Mehta and André Previn. Chamber music, dance programs, and choral works are also presented. The Aladdin Theater for the Performing Arts, Las Vegas Boulevard South, is a concert facility.
Artemus Ham Concert Hall, at the University, is also a concert facility. It seats two-thousand.
The Charleston Heights Arts Center, 300 South Torrey Pines Drive, offers chamber music.
Whipple Cultural Center, 821 Las Vegas Boulevard North, has welcomed the Civic Symphony.
The Library, 1401 East Flamingo Road, has hosted the Nevada String Quartet.

Reno

Pioneer Theater, 100 South Virginia, hosts the Reno Philharmonic.
The Masonic Theater hosts the Reno Chamber Orchestra.
The University of Nevada, Reno, has hosted the Annapolis Brass Quintet.

NEW MEXICO

Albuquerque

Popejoy Hall for the Performing Arts at the University of New Mexico, on Central Avenue, is the home of the Albuquerque Symphony Orchestra. Light opera, ballet and chamber music events are featured in Popejoy as well. There is an annual Music Festival in June.

Santa Fe

The number one attraction is the Santa Fe Opera, which performs in the summer. Both traditional and modern operas are performed, all in English. Many famous artists sing here. The outdoor theater is located off US-84.

The Santa Fe Chamber Music Festival, with the Orchestra of Santa Fe, performs symphonic music, giving concerts in the following places:

St. Francis Cathedral, 275 East Alameda.

St. Francis Auditorium at the Museum of Fine Arts, 113 Lincoln.

St. John's College in the Great Hall, Camino de Cruz Blanca.

Santuario de Guadalupe Church. In the church altar bells are rung to

Orchestra of Santa Fe on the stage of the St. Francis Auditorium, Santa Fe. (Courtesy Orchestra of Santa Fe, photo by Marilyn Foss)

signal the end of the concert, instead of turning up lights. Alfred Brendel and the Vermeer Quartet have been among the guest artists appearing with the Festival. Works of Vivaldi, Telemann, and C.P.E. Bach have been featured.

Taos
The Taos School of Music holds a Summer Chamber Music Session from mid-June through July, and offers concerts in the Taos Community Auditorium on North Pueblo Road. David Diamond has been the composer-in-residence for some years.
The Taos Festival of Music takes place in October and
The New Mexico Music Festival takes place in the summer.

NORTH DAKOTA
Bottineau
The International Music Camp, close to the Canadian border offers music, dance, and drama, with concerts and guest artists in the summer. More than two-thousand students and teachers from all continents take part in music activities.
Fargo
Imagination Arts Festival takes place in September.
Medora
The Gold Seal Amphitheater, an open-air site overlooking Medora countryside, offers music.

OKLAHOMA
Ardmore
Charles B. Goddard Center, First Avenue and D Street SW, welcomes symphonic music and ballet.
Bartlesville
The Bartlesville Symphony and Choral Society.
Oklahoma City
Civic Center Music Hall, 201 North Dewey, is home to the Oklahoma City Symphony Orchestra. Performing here also are the Oklahoma City Opera and Oklahoma City Ballet. Interestingly, several of the world's leading ballerinas are Oklahomans, including Maria and Marjorie Tallchief, Rosella Hightower, and Yvonne Chouteau.
Lyric Theater, 2501 North Blackwelder Avenue, presents musical evenings.
Stillwater and Norman
Both campuses of Oklahoma State University are active in symphonic events.
Tulsa
Theater Tulsa, 1511 South Delaware Avenue, features musical evenings. The Performing Arts Center, Second and Cincinnati, hosts the Tulsa Philharmonic, The Tulsa Opera, and the Tulsa Ballet.

271

Weatherford
Southwest Festival of the Arts, in April, provides numerous concerts.

SOUTH DAKOTA
Aberdeen
Northern State College, on South Jay Street, has an active music department. The Dakota String Quartet is in residence.
Lead
The restored Homestake Opera House, 309 West Main Street is a 1914 gold and ivory studded theater with Tiffany light fixtures and a Wurlitzer pipe organ.
Vermillion
The Shrine to Music Museum, on the campus of the University of South Dakota, Clark and Yale Streets, houses more than twenty-five-hundred antique musical instruments from all over the world—bugles of copper with silver trim, echo-horns, trombones in the shape of dragons, zithers built like crocodiles, and hand-painted Persian drums.

TEXAS
Austin
Zilker Park Hillside Theater, 2000 Barton Springs Road, offers concerts under the stars from the spring through the summer.
Palmer Auditorium, Fifty-first and West Riverside, hosts the Austin Symphony Orchestra.
The Fine Arts Complex in the University of Texas also hosts the Austin Symphony Orchestra.
Dallas
The Music Hall in Fair Park, off I-30, hosts the Dallas Symphony Orchestra, the Dallas Ballet, and the Dallas Civic Opera. A new hall was built in 1983.
Starfest Concerts take place year-round throughout the city in Dallas parks.
The Majestic Theater, 1925 Elm Street, hosts dance groups.
El Paso
El Paso has a Symphony Orchestra, as do thirty other Texas cities.
Civic Center, One Civic Center Plaza, presents music programs.
The University of Texas at El Paso frequently presents ballet programs.
Fort Worth
Casa Manana at Amon Carter Square, 3101 West Lancaster, has a large area theater used for concerts and varied musical fare.
Tarrant Hall Convention Center, 1111 Houston, offers symphonic music.
Galveston
An old Grand Opera House, now restored in Granbury in the Strand, is a

272

cultural arts center.

Galveston Island State Park, an eighteen-thousand-seat amphitheater with a 150-foot wide, very deep stage, offers music programs.

Houston

Jones Hall, 615 Louisiana Boulevard, hosts the Houston Symphony Orchestra, Houston Grand Opera (which produces opera in English), and the Houston Ballet.

Miller Outdoor Theater, in Hermann Park, hosts the same performing organizations in the summer.

Theater Under the Stars, the Cabaret Theater in the Shamrock Hilton Hotel, 6900 Main Street, and the Music Hall, 810 Bagby Street, host dance companies.

San Antonio

The Theater for the Performing Arts, HemisFair Plaza, South Alamo, hosts the San Antonio Symphony Orchestra's winter season.

Grand Opera Festival takes place in the spring, with famous opera stars.

The Arneson River Theater, 503 Villeta Street, hosts Summer Festival. The stage is on one side of a river, the audience on the other. One climbs the steps through the theater and walks through the arch.

UTAH

Provo

Brigham Young University, University Hill, organizes symphonic programs.

Salt Lake City

The Bicentennial Concert Hall of the Salt Palace, West Temple and South Temple Streets, hosts the Utah Symphony.

The Tabernacle, on Temple Square, is the home of the world-famous Mormon Tabernacle Choir. Here is the great organ with over ten-thousand pipes, up to thirty-two feet in length. Marvelous acoustics make recitals and works such as Handel's *Messiah* (performed at Christmas) particularly enjoyable. Temple Square is ten acres long with a high granite wall enclosure and three towers holding an angel statue on the top.

The University of Utah, University Street and 300 South, hosts Ballet West, the Utah Symphony, and other groups which perform classical music.

Capitol Theater, 50 West 200 South, presents dance groups.

WYOMING

Casper

Casper Events Center, One Events Drive, is the site where the Casper Symphony and Casper Comic Opera perform.

Cheyenne

Cheyenne Civic Center, 510 West Twentieth Street, offers symphony and ballet.

Sheridan

The Wyo Theater, 36 East Alger Street, offers music events.

Jackson

Jackson Hole Opera House, 220 South Glenwood, is an old opera house. Teton Village, on the lower slope of Grand Teton Mountains, hosts the renowned Grand Teton Music Festival in the summer. Situated a mile high in the Rocky Mountains, there is often snow on some peaks in the summer. Trees, brooks, and big game provide spectacular views. Such artists as Phyllis Curtin and John Stewart have sung here.

Laramie

The Concert Hall in the Fine Arts Center of the University of Wyoming hosts many musical events throughout the year. It houses a Walcker pipe organ, one of the largest in the U.S.

JAZZ, WESTERN SWING, COUNTRY-WESTERN, AND ROCK

From mid-1920s until the end of World War II, the shifting population to the West created a demand for the blossoming jazz dance bands. San Antonio, Dallas, Oklahoma City, Omaha, and Denver were among those cities where almost a hundred bands were formed. Jazz spread westward from such earlier places as New Orleans, St. Louis, and Chicago. Ballrooms sprang up and the commercially profitable "Battle of the Bands" developed: a local band called "territory band" played opposite a visiting band at home, while several thousand people listened to the jam sessions and danced into the early morning hours. Three of these territory bands were in the foreground of the musical scene.

Alphonso Trent

Alphonso Trent's band was Texas's most influential group. Trent was a pianist and arranger, born in Fort Worth, Arkansas, in 1905. In 1915, he began working in Dallas with an eight-piece combo. They played in the ballroom of the Adolphus Hotel (one can visit it today), and were the first black band to broadcast regularly on Radio Station WFAA. In the group was trombonist Lawrence "Snub" Mosley, purported to be an outstanding jazz soloist. The entire brass and rhythm sections consisted of distinctively strong players.

In most Western bands, blues were part of the repertory, many blues singers (Tex Alexander, Jimmy Rushing, and Blind Lemmon Jefferson) having come originally from Texas and Oklahoma. Trent, in arranging, experimented with standard repertory, however, and went beyond the blues pattern. He arranged "chase choruses," which utilized a reed and a brass instrument soloing alternately, each for four bars. Trent further thought to use a vocal jazz trio, rather than only one vocalist.

In 1926, the band left the Adolphus Hotel after more than a year's engagement to tour the West. Listeners in places like the Ritz Ballroom in Oklahoma City were especially receptive to such songs of theirs as "After You've Gone" and "I've Found a New Baby."

From 1928 to 1930 Trent added trumpeters Peanuts Holland

and Lee Hilliard, and trombonist Gus Wilson (Teddy Wilson's brother), and they became known for their recording of "Clementine," which demonstrated expressive riffs, the repeated musical phrase that became the identifying sound of big-band swing.

Walter Page

Another Western figure in the early twenties was Walter Page, a bassist and arranger, who traveled on the road with the Billy King Show and took over the band in Oklahoma City, reorganizing it as Page's Blue Devils. The group consisted of Buster Smith on alto saxophone, Eddie Durham on trombone, Oran "Hot Lips" Page on trumpet, pianist Bill (Count) Basie, and vocalist Jimmy Rushing. Considered to be an excellent jazz orchestra, the Blue Devils battled the bands of Vincent Lopez and Lawrence Welk in such places as Louvre Ballroom in Tulsa, Oklahoma, and Lamond Ballroom in Longview, Texas. Songs such as "Blue Devil Blues" and "Squabblin'," with rhythmic flow, riff settings, and solo chord sequences, highlighted a sweet rather than hot style, and in future years, characterized Count Basie's own band.

After the Blue Devils disintegrated, bassist Page became a member of Count Basie's rhythm section and worked around Oklahoma in El Reno, Chickasha, the Riverside Club in Shawnee, and Japanese Gardens in Oklahoma City.

Troy Floyd

Troy Floyd organized a nine-piece jazz combo in the early twenties, playing in such spots as Ozarks Night Club and Shadowland Club, both in San Antonio, Texas. Claude "Benno" Kennedy was a solo trumpeter in the band, and later, Buddy Tate, alto saxophonist, joined the group. The band broadcast frequently over Radio Station HTSA from San Antonio's Plaza hotel. "Wabash Blues" and "Shadowland Blues" were among the favorite songs associated with Floyd. The band broke up during the depression years in 1932.

Jazz Places and Other Notables on the Jazz Scene in the Twenties and Thirties

Following Floyd's group, San Antonio boasted trumpeter Don

Albert and his Ten Happy Pals, who played at Shadowland and at the Chicken Plantation Nightclub. Good solos were heard in swing rhythm by tenor saxophonist Jimmie Forrest. Albert played at The New Orleans Jazz Festival much later in 1969 and is remembered for "Liza" and "Deep Blue Melody." Clifford "Boots" Douglas, a drummer, came to San Antonio in the early thirties with a group known as Boots and His Buddies. "How Long Blues" and "The Sad Ain't Misbehavin'" were sung by their vocalist, Al Hibbler.

Still other places and groups highlighted jazz in the West. Tulsa, Oklahoma was the home of the Southern Serenaders; Andy Kirk and Band played in Crystal Lake Park, Oklahoma; Oklahoma City's Aldridge Hotel helped spread jazz and swing. In Houston, Milton Larkin's Band battled Nat Towles at Harlem Square and at the Aragon Ballroom. Larkin had Eddie Vinson on alto sax and vocal, and the featured guitarist/pianist Bill Davis. Houston also had the American Hotel for performers such as Johnson's Joymakers. Dallas's Log Cabin Club was popular and Terrence Holder's Band, with Carl "Tatti" Smith on trumpet and Lloyd Glenn at the piano, entertained here. The Blue Moon Chasers were a Dallas specialty at the Simovar Club.

El Paso welcomed Ben Smith's Blue Syncopaters; Greenville, the Dixie Stompers; Austin boasted the Deluxe Melody Boys and Royal Aces. Hotel Tyler in Tyler, Texas, hosted the Coy Band and other big bands traveling through the West.

Omaha, Nebraska had a top group in the thirties, bass player Nat Towles's Band, which had originally been formed in Texas. They played at Omaha's favorite nightspot, Dreamland Ballroom. The Omaha Night Owls, a jazz combo, performed at the Century Room; the Grotto Club featured Red Perkins, vocalist. Elaborate floor shows were offered in addition to the music, in much the same fashion as the Cotton Club revues in New York. Murphy's Egyptian Club was a favorite dancing place in Omaha.

Denver, Colorado's Albany Hotel recognized one of the first jazzmen to play for dancing, a violinist by the name of George Morrison. Morrison provided the start for Jimmie Lunceford, who rose to fame in later years with a swing band. The Dome in Bismarck, North Dakota, and the Gladstone Hotel in Casper, Wyoming offered opportunity to innovative jazz guitarist, Charlie Christian, who had worked originally with Alphonso Trent in Dallas. Christian recorded a famous single string solo on electric guitar, "I Found a New Baby," which was musically characteristic of later be-bop guitarists.

Concurrent with these jazz events was the development of another offshoot of popular music, which claimed equally large audiences and was significant in the West—Western swing.

Western Swing

The great western region gave rise to a variety of popular music branching from the country music base. Beginning in the 1920s, fading away in the late forties and fifties, and revived in the sixties was the regional trend that mixed jazz with original country-Western, producing western swing, the counterpart of big band sounds in the Northeast.

Western swing, the western equivalent of the big band sound in the Northeast, developed at the same time that the big bands of Benny Goodman and Tommy Dorsey were developing. Western swing was targeted for large dance halls and was heard in the band of Bob Wills, a major western musical figure until the end of World War II.

Wills, a fiddler and singer, was born in Limestone County, Texas, in 1906. He formed the Wills Fiddle Band with Herman Arnspiger, a guitarist, in Fort Worth, Texas, in 1929, and they played in such dancehalls as Crystal Springs, a place frequented by the notorious Bonnie and Clyde. After appearing on a Fort Worth radio show, the band changed its name to that of the sponsor's, the Light Crust Doughboys. From there, Wills and his band moved on to Waco, Oklahoma City, and finally to Tulsa, where they settled, playing such tunes as "Cotton-Eyed Joe" and "Take Me Back to Tulsa" for large audiences.

From 1934 to 1942 Wills experienced a heyday in Western swing, improvising and experimenting with music sounds. He added trumpet, trombone, saxophone, and clarinet to a heavily-bowed fiddle, banjo, piano, and steel guitar. Thus he made a swing band, augmenting strings with brass and reeds, playing in dance rhythm, and adding lyrics to tunes. Further innovative was Wills's technique of gaily and loudly exhorting names of his musicians and their instruments at solo time, while he moved up and down the stage, singing part of the chorus: for example, "Jerry on sax . . . let's hear it . . . dum dum." Steel guitarist Leon McAuliffe was noted for his swing renditions of future classics such as "Steel Guitar Rag" and "San Antonio Rose." Evident in these recordings was a reminder of yesterday's characteristic southern twang and whine of hillbilly music. It was Bob Wills's band which put Western swing on the map.

Honky-tonk

In the 1930s, people migrating to Texas and Oklahoma from the northern and southern regions brought with them strains of folk and hillbilly music, which soon assumed characteristics of cowboy, Mexican, and other regional influences. The image of the cowboy denoted freedom, open land of the Great Plains, cattle trails, blue skies, roaming, no ties, individualism, and occasional loneliness. This almost mythical vision supplanted musically that of the poor rural Southern hillbilly, with its plaintive cries and quiet, stoic resignation. (Traditional cowboy music of the early twentieth century is discussed in the Midwest Section.)

The West adapted country music to its own milieu. Heavy drinking, gambling, guns, jails, loose morals, and wild outpouring of emotion in raucous saloons nurtured a style of loud, blaring, steady-beat music called honky-tonk. Farmers, laborers, and oilmen made merry in such favorite East Texas places as Reo Palm Isle Ballroom, Danceland, Roundup Club and Horseshoe Lounge. A popular dance was the Cotton-Eyed Joe, in which four to eight people slung their arms around one another's shoulders and danced in a line. Most often, a dress code accompanied country-Western music. It consisted of blue denims, leather boots, cowboy hats, ornate belt buckles, and glittering accessories. Indeed, this attire became an almost unwritten requirement as the uniform for performers.

Several names identified with the honky-tonk style in Texas were Ernest Tubb and later Willie Nelson.

Ernest Tubb

Tubb was born in Crisp, Texas, just south of Dallas, in 1914. He idolized country music pioneer Jimmie Rodgers. Tubb formed a band, the Troubadours, using electric guitar, and recorded "I'll Get Along Somehow" and "Walking the Floor Over You" in San Antonio. His deliberate and unique phrasing, pauses, heavy slurs, and slides brought the honky-tonk sound to country music. Tubb eventually went to Nashville with his fused style and made history at the Grand Ole Opry. Over the years, Tubb was responsible for many hits, including "Rainbow at Midnight," "Pistol Packin' Mama," and "Headin' Down the Wrong Highway." In 1965, he was elected to the Country Music Hall of Fame in Nashville.

Willie Nelson

Willie Nelson followed Tubb in the fifties and sixties, promoting honky-tonk. Sometimes referred to as the "outlaw," Nelson actively rebelled against the smooth inflections of pure country, offering instead a raw, cutting, untamed sound. He performed in Forth Worth dancehalls with distinctive musical phrasing, somewhat similar to Tubb's pauses, slurs, and sustained notes, and even more dramatically inclined toward the abrasive. A master of honky-tonk style, Nelson dressed provocatively, like a long-haired hippie and became known as "Wild Willie." He influenced artists who followed in his tradition, namely Waylon Jen-

"Country rebel" Jerry Jeff Walker (Courtesy Variety Artists International, Minneapolis)

nings, Kris Kristofferson, and Jerry Jeff Walker, performers known as country's rebels.

Commercial cowboy songs, another branch of country-Western, which became popular after the traditional cowboy songs of the early twentieth century (see the Midwest Section) found their way into music as folklore, augmented heavily by the radio and film industry. Among the singing cowboys representing music and myth were Gene Autry and Tex Ritter.

Gene Autry

Autry was one of the most colorful singing cowboys in history because of his fame in Hollywood films beginning in the 1930s. He was born on a farm in Tioga Springs, Texas, in 1907. As a young man, he bought a guitar and began writing tunes such as "My Old Pal of Yesterday." He sang on Radio Station KVOO in Tulsa, Oklahoma, then later in Chicago, on WLS's "National Barn Dance."

In 1934, Autry went to Republic Studios in Hollywood and began to appear in films ("Mexicali Rose," "Tumbling Tumbleweeds," and "The Last Roundup"), helping to establish country-Western music as a pillar of the American dream. Other songs with cowboy images ("Back in the Saddle Again," and "Tears on My Pillow") written by Autry and used in films, became country-Western clasics. In 1969, he was elected to the Country Music Hall of Fame.

Tex Ritter

Another singing cowboy was Woodward Maurice "Tex" Ritter, born in Murvaul, Texas. Ritter attended the University of Texas and had decided to study law when he changed direction and decided upon a career in music. He started singing on Radio Station KPRC in Houston in 1929. Following that he traveled and made many recordings, among which the best known are "Have I Stayed Away Too Long," "Jingle Jangle, Jingle," and "Hillbilly Heaven."

In 1936, he followed Gene Autry to Hollywood and enjoyed commercial success as a singing cowboy. Ritter appeared in many films for Republic and Columbia Studios, among which were "Trouble in Texas," with Rita Hayworth, and "Ridin' the Cherokee Trail." No one can ever forget his rich baritone rendition of the theme song in *High Noon*. Plush Hollywood was actively portraying the singing cowboy.

Ritter went to Nashville in the sixties, appearing at Grand Ole Opry, and becoming president of the Country Music Association. In 1964, he was elected to the Country Music Hall of Fame.

Rock

The mid-fifties rock scene in the West, notably in Texas, was defined in large part by the "Tex-Mex Sound," a blend of country-Western and rock. It was characterized by a steady rhythmic pulse in lieu of a hard-driven beat. It actually resembled Western swing, and showed little of the black influence found in the rock music of the other regions. Western rock was exemplified in the music of Buddy Holly, a young artist who influenced the Beatles, the Rolling Stones, Bob Dylan, and many other stars in later years.

Buddy Holly

Charles Hardin (Buddy) Holly was born in Lubbock, Texas, in 1936. At age thirteen he started to work at the local spots with friends, singing and playing guitar in Western bop style. The Lubbock Youth Center, at 2025 North Akron, was a place where Holly appeared on numerous occasions. (One can visit it today.) The Cotton Club on Slaton Highway was another early place that welcomed Holly. Also, KDAV, a Lubbock, Texas, radio station produced a Sunday afternoon radio program that helped popularize the singer. At a rock and roll show, after Holly performed for Bill Haley and the Comets, Decca records signed him up to record, but with little success. Shortly afterwards, Holly met Norman Petty, a pianist/organist who had a recording studio in Clovis, New Mexico. Petty invited Holly and his group, the Crickets, (consisting of a second guitarist, a bass player, and a drummer) to record some songs. Their first release, "That'll Be the Day," established Holly's unique vocal style, evident as well in his following hit, "Peggy Sue."

His unique vocal style largely subordinated lyrics in favor of stretching syllables, changing a tone suddenly from bass to falsetto in nervous excitement, and adding hiccups for effect. Although an admirer of Elvis Presley with his sex appeal, Holly himself was playful, childlike, and wholesome, wearing traditional dark-rimmed glasses, short curly hair, and straightforward clothes. He liked to sing songs telling of true love: "Words of Love," "I'm Gonna Love You Too," and "True Love Ways."

Occasionally the Crickets used a back-up vocal group called The Roses, embellishing the sound with amplified electric guitars and nasal high-pitched voices. Rhythm was still pulsating, though not piercing, representative of the Tex-Mex Sound.

After leaving the Crickets and Petty in the West, in 1958, Holly traveled to New York and made his home in Greenwich Village. His singing became more subdued, and he was the first rock star to experiment with strings in "It Doesn't Matter Anymore" (a tune written by pop star Paul Anka), and in his own composition, "Raining in My Heart." The Beatles would utilize this technique several years later.

As with so many artists, Holly's creativity ended abruptly. An airplane crash in 1959 took his life at the age of twenty-three, and the day, February third, is remembered as "the day the music died." Don McLean, singing "American Pie," sings the line in exactly that context. Buddy Holly has become a legend, as seen in the "I Remember Buddy" album, in the film *The Buddy Holly Story*, and in the many remakes being made of Holly's songs today.

Las Vegas

No heyday in rock would be complete without mention of the posh "strip" in downtown Las Vegas, Nevada. Rock was strong throughout the sixties, and although music was incidental to gambling in Las Vegas, top entertainers and high quality shows were available at almost all the big hotels. Hotels are still opulent, spectacular, and full of glitter with neon lighting producing a fairy-tale quality. Blue-black mountains frame the background of the super-luxury hotels, and no clocks are in evidence anywhere. Popular music and gambling turn day into night and back into day at the gold and white Caesar's Palace, the bluish Tropicana, the deep red MGM, and the chandeliered Hilton. One must of course walk through the casinos in order to get to the music.

The following pages list places where one can find jazz, country-Western, or rock music in the west.

ARIZONA
Payson
The Payson Rodeo Grounds has hosted a Fiddler's Contest and Festival since 1970. It takes place in September. There is seating for three-hundred and more room on the lawn. This is a particularly lovely area in the center of Arizona, five-thousand feet high amidst tall pine trees, lakes, and streams.
Phoenix
The Veteran's Memorial Coliseum, 1826 West McDowell, hosts country-Western and rock events on its Plaza stage. Johnny Cash, Waylon

Pure Prairie League, one of the many groups that have performed at the Veteran's Memorial Coliseum in Phoenix. (Courtesy Variety Artists International, Minneapolis)

Jennings, Dionne Warwick, and The Beach Boys have entertained here.
The Center for Performing Arts Sundome (Sun City West), 19403 R. H.
Johnson Boulevard, features artists such as Tony Bennett.
Gammage Center at Arizona State University (Tempe), a building de-
signed by Frank Lloyd Wright in pinks and sandy desert colors, has an
active music calendar that has featured Chuck Mangione, Gordon Light-
foot, the Inkspots, and the Newport Jazz Festival group.
Sun Devil Stadium, Arizona State University, has welcomed The Who.
Graham Central Station, Thirty-third Avenue and Indian School Road,
features country music, rock, and disco on a large dance floor.
Chuy's Choo Choo, 396 Mill Avenue (Tempe), presents blues, jazz and
rock in an informal setting.
Dooley's, 1216 East Apache Boulevard (Tempe), is a good spot for nation-
ally known country and rock bands.
The Mesa Amphitheater presents such rock stars as Bobby and The
Midnights.
Different Points of View, 11111 North Seventh Street, offers country-
Western and popular music as well as a breathtaking view of the city.
Glenn Yarborough was here recently.

Scottsdale

Scottsdale Center for the Arts, 383 Scottsdale Mall, is a multipurpose
facility hosting all musical events, including a jazz series.
Mt. Shadows, 5641 East Lincoln Drive, offers after dinner jazz.

Springerville

An old-time Fiddler's Contest is held here in October.

Tombstone

May brings fiddlers' contests to the streets.
The restored Crystal Palace Saloon, Fifth and Allen Streets, is worth
seeing for yesteryear flavor as well as honky-tonk country-Western music.
The Bird Cage Theater, Sixth and Allen Streets, is now a museum, but it
was a frontier cabaret in the 1880s. Upstairs are "cages" where pretty
girls worked at their trade and inspired the lyrics for the song "Only a
Bird in a Gilded Cage." The original furnishings and fixtures are still
here.

Tucson

After the Gold Rush, 144 West Lester, is a popular disco.
The Night Train, 424 North Fourth Avenue, presents rock bands.
Hotel Fray Marcos de Niza hosts country-Western music and dancing in
its Sky Room.
The Southern Arizona Square and Round Dance Festival takes place in
January.
Gold Rush Days, featuring country-Western music takes place in Febru-
ary.

The Tucson Festival takes place throughout the city in April.
Yuma
The Square and Round Dance Festival takes place in March.
Wichenburg
The Bluegrass Music Festival, a throwback to country music, takes place in November.

COLORADO
Aspen
An addition to the Aspen Music Festival from late June to August, there are performances by a jazz/rock ensemble. Concerts are held in a large tent which has additional seating space on the lawn.
The Paragon Parlour, in a high-ceilinged Victorian building at 419 East Hyman, offers disco.
Chisholm's, 404 South Galena, presents country-Western music in an informal setting.
Boulder
The Blue Note, 1116 Pearl Street, offers jazz.
The Wallstreet Jazz Cellar, just up the block at 1136 Pearl, also offers jazz.
The Olympic Saloon and Dance Hall, 1720 Thirtieth Street, has music and ambience in a country-Western flavor.
Breckenridge
Town Park hosts a Folk Festival and music week with country music in July.
A Fiddlers' contest takes place in September.
Canon City
The Blosson and Music Festival in May offers all kinds of music.
Denver
Many places are available in Denver for jazz, country-Western, and rock.
Taylor's Supper Club, 7000 West Colfax.
Ebbet's Fields, 1445 Curtis Street.
Turn of the Century, 7300 East Hampden.
Oxford Hotel, Seventeenth and Wazee Street.
The Paramount Theater, Sixteenth Street Mall, has welcomed Kai Winding and Billy Butterfield.
El Chapultepec Lounge, 1962 Market, has hosted Billy Tolles, and Express. There are neon-lit, wooden booths, facing a red-lit stage.
The Denver Coliseum East Forty-sixth Street and Humboldt, offers jazz, country-Western, and rock concerts.
Red Rocks Amphitheater offers jazz, country-Western, and rock concerts under the stars. Red Rocks is located on Interstate 70, south of US 6, overlooking the city, and is carved into red sandstone.
The Denver Center for the Performing Arts, Twelfth and Fourteenth

Streets, between Stout and Arapahoe Streets, has four theaters that house musical events of all kinds.

Swallow Hill Music Hall presents blues and country-Western music.

The Guild Theater, 1028 South Gaylord presents blues and country-Western music.

Country Opry, 4842 Morrison Road, features country and country-rock.

Zeno's, in Larimer Square, offers Dixieland.

Café Nepenthes, 1416 Market Street, offers blues and country music.

Mr. Lucky's, 555 South Cherry, offers rock and roll.

Durango

The Fairgrounds hosts La Plata County Fair in August.

The Golden Slipper, 645 Main Street, offers rock.

Diamond Belle, 699 Main Street, offers country-Western music in a Victorian decor.

Farquarts, 725 Main Street, offers country-Western music.

Glenwood Springs

The Strawberry Days Festival and Rodeo, with square dancing and lively country-Western music, takes place in June.

Pueblo

The Bandshell at Mineral Palace Park presents band concerts of popular music in the summer.

The Fairgrounds hosts the Colorado State Fair in August, with country-Western music abounding.

Telluride

A country-Western Coonskin Carnival takes place in January.

Town Park hosts a Bluegrass Festival in June and a Jazz Festival in August.

Trinidad

The Cokedale Mining Days Festival, in July, offers bluegrass and square dancing. It's loud and merry.

IDAHO

Boise

Boise Music Week takes place in May.

Fiddling contests go on all year.

The Western Idaho State Fair takes place in August.

Some of the entertainment spots are:

The Jolly King Restaurant, 1115 North Curtis.

Rodeway Inn, Twenty-ninth and Chinden Boulevard.

The Owyhee Plaza Hotel, Eleventh and Main.

Jerome

There is a country fair and rodeo in August, with an emphasis on country-Western music.

Montpelier

Bear Lake County Fair and Rodeo takes place in August.

Pocatello
Frontier Rodeo Days, in August, provides country-Western music.
Cotton Tree Inn, 1415 Bench Road, has colorful entertainment.
Holiday Inn, on Bench Road.
Shoshone
An Old-time Fiddlers' Jamboree takes place in July.
The Lincoln County Fair takes place in August.
Twin Falls
Twin Falls County Fairgrounds, on US-30, is the site of the Twin Falls
County Fair and Rodeo in September.
The Alley, 121 Fourth Avenue South, is a lively place.
Weiser
The Historical Museum, 44 West Commercial Street, has memorabilia
of fiddling and folk music. It's open in the summer.
The main event in Weiser is the National Old-time Fiddler's Contest,
held in June in the High School gym, which has twenty-five-hundred
seats.
Worley
Leo Worley's club offers country-Western and rock music, and dancing.

MONTANA
Deer Lodge
The Tri-County Fair and Rodeo take place in August.
Glasgow
The Northeast Montana Fair and Rodeo, at the Fairgrounds in August,
provides cowboy and country-Western music galore.
Red Lodge
The Music Festival, in June, is comprised of students who make merry
with all forms of music.

NEVADA
Las Vegas
The strip along Las Vegas Boulevard is *the* place for jazz, country, and
rock music, offered by numerous hotels and nightclubs. You can't escape
the music if you're here; it goes on until dawn. Three typical spots are:
Caesar's Palace, 3570 Las Vegas Boulevard; Sands Hotel, 3355 Las Vegas
Boulevard; and Desert Inn, 3145 Las Vegas Boulevard. There are dozens
of others, and the decor runs from tasteful to tasteless.
The University of Nevada, Las Vegas, at 4505 South Maryland Parkway,
features festivals of contemporary music in Artemus West Ham Concert
Hall. Jazz and popular music are frequently on the program. The Univer-
sity also hosts a Music Festival in September.
The Helldorado Festival in May has country-Western music.
Union Plaza, downtown, is somewhat quieter, with live bands especially

at the Treasury Hotel, 115 East Tropicana, just off the Strip.
Reno
Reno, too, has its Strip with entertainment spots, such as: Eldora Hotel, Fourth and Virginia Streets; Ponderosa Hotel, 515 South Virginia; and MGM Grand Hotel, Reno, 2500 East Second Street.
The Nevada State Fair comes to town in September.
The Reno Rodeo, which takes place in June, is said to be the best country-Western show.
Wells
The Wells Rodeo, filled with country-Western, takes place in May.

NEW MEXICO
Albuquerque
Chelsea Street Pub, in Coronado Center, offers rowdy country-Western music
Another Graham Central Station is here, at 3301 Juan Tabo NE. It's said to be the world's largest disco with over twenty-two-thousand square feet of dance floor, holding over a thousand people. A cowboy hat is sometimes required to be worn by its patrons.
The Best Western Hotel features lively country-Western and rock music,
The University of New Mexico Fiestas, in early May, offer country-Western and rock music.
Albuquerque's State Fair and Rodeo, in September, feature many top stars.
The University of New Mexico presents regular musical events year round.
Clovis
A place of early rock recording, Clovis presents an RCA Rodeo in June with rock and country-Western music, and a County Fair in September.
Portales
Eastern New Mexico University Theater presents jazz events.
The Roosevelt County Fair takes place in August.
Santa Fe
The Old Cienega Village Museum, off I-25, hosts a Folk Art Festival in April and October, with country-Western music and dancing.
Silver City
Frontier Days, complete with Western attire, rings out in July, for the best in country-Western music.
Taos
A rodeo comes to Taos in June, with country–Western music.

NORTH DAKOTA
Devils Lake
Hosts Fort Totten Days in July.

Fort Totten Fairgrounds, on ND-57. Country-Western music prevails.
Grand Forks
The Fairgrounds hosts a big, impressive, musical country-Western Fair in June.
University Park hosts Summerthing Festival in June. All kinds of music can be heard here.
Minot
Festival in the Parks is held in July.
Winterfest, offering jazz, is presented in October.

OKLAHOMA
Claremore
The Will Rogers County Free Fair in September is always full of country-Western music and dance.
Enid
Phillips University, on Maine Street, hosts the Tri-State Music Festival in the spring.
Eufala
A country-Western Fair takes place in August.
Hugo.
Salt Creek Park hosts Grant's Bluegrass and Old-time Music Festival. There are contests for the audience as well as performances.
Oklahoma City
The Festival of the Arts takes place in April, with country music and dancing. Lloyd Noble Center, 2900 South Jenkins, houses thousands for country-Western shows. Recently Willie Nelson starred here.
The Hilton Inn West, I-40 at Meridian, offers quality country-Western music and dance.
Pryor
Pryor Creek Western Days and Rodeo on the Rodeo Grounds, OK-20, in May, provides country-Western music.
Tulsa
The Northeast Oklahoma Square Dance Festival takes place in the early spring.
Duke's Country hosts country-Western bands in its enormous barroom.
The Oklahoma Theater Center, 400 West Sheridan Avenue, hosts musical events, including country-Western music.

SOUTH DAKOTA
Belle Fourche
The Black Hills Round-up Rodeo takes place in July. It is known all over the West for its authentic cowboy flavor.
Mitchell
John Philip Sousa and his Band played here in 1904. Today, name bands

and popular entertainers perform here in September.

Rapid City

The annual Square Dance Festival, in July, features folk and country music.

The Band Festival, in May and June, during Dakota Days, features folk and country music.

The Circle B, on SD-44, offers authentic country-Western.

Yankton

An Old-time Fiddlers' Contest takes place in October.

TEXAS

Abilene

Old Abilene Town, on I-20, welcomes the lively Frontier Festival in May. Country-Western music, costumes and square dancing are featured.

Perini Ranch hosts the Buffalo Gap Bluegrass Jamboree in June.

Amarillo

The Greater Southwest Music Festival takes place in April.

The Tri-State Fair, one of the largest in Texas, takes place in September.

Athens

An Old Fiddlers' Reunion takes place in May.

A Black-Eyed Pea Jamboree takes place in July.

Needless to say, both of the above events feature country-Western music.

Austin

Austin has honky-tonk and rock places, two of which are Soap Creek Saloon, 11306 North Lamar; and The Broken Spoke, 3201 South Lamar, a lively dance hall.

The Austin Opry House, 200 Academy Drive, offers top entertainment. It is owned by Willie Nelson.

Lock, Stock, and Barrel, 200 West Anderson, has welcomed progressive country-Western groups. A fireplace adds ambience to the music.

Texas Tumbleweed, on FM Road, is a favorite spot for country music.

Corpus Christi

Cantina Santa Fe, 1011 Santa Fe, hosts jazz bands.

Inza's Lonesome Coyote, 5550 Kostoryz, is noted for progressive country-Western and rock music.

The Yellow Rose of Texas, 2001 Saratoga Boulevard, is a large dance hall for cowboys and would-be cowboys (and cowgirls).

An old-Texas Jazz Festival takes place in July, with name performers.

Dallas/Fort Worth

Dallas/Fort Worth abounds in nightspots. Below is a partial listing.

Belle Star, 7724 North Central, is a dance hall for good country music.

Cotton-Eyed Joe's, Northwest Highway and Harry Hines Boulevard, offers disco.

Doubletree Inn, in Campbell Center, is noted for its jazz presentations.

Diamond Jim's, 5601 Greenville, specializes in jazz and country-Western music. Two dance floors are available.

Four Seasons, 4930 Military Parkway, features big band sounds.

Longhorn Ballroom, with impressive cactus pillars, 216 Corinth, offers quality country-Western music.

Billy Bob's of Texas, 2520 Commerce Street, Fort Worth, is said to be the world's largest honky-tonk place. It looks somewhat like Las Vegas, with endless pinball machines, bars, and neon lights. Country-Western music goes on non-stop.

London House, in Fort Worth, is a quieter place, with guitar music and cool jazz.

Clancy's Saloon and Dance Hall, 2101 Stemmons, is another honky-tonk place. San Francisco Rose, 3024 Greenville Avenue, also offers honky-tonk.

The Greenville Avenue Bar, just up the street from San Francisco Rose at 2821 Greenville, features jazz performances.

Whiskey River, 5421 Greenville, has featured Wendell Atkins and Hank Williams.

The Fairmont Hotel offers something in a quieter vein. Lola Falana has entertained here.

The historic Adolphus Hotel, 1321 Commerce Street.

Pantheon Stadium, 503 East Freeman, has welcomed rock star Jerry Lee Lewis.

Ganny's, 205 Coit Road, has also featured Jerry Lee Lewis.

Some favorite rock spots are: Nick's Uptown, 3606 Greenville; Hot Klub, 4350 Maple Avenue, where the Blasters have entertained; Cardi's, 500 Medallion Center; Reunion Arena, 777 Fourth Street, and Little Gus, 1916 Greenville.

Poor David's Pub, 2900 McKinney, offers a mixed-bag. Folk and rock stars have entertained here. Tom Paxton, Uncle Walt's Band, and Shake Russell are among those who have performed.

Dallas Agora, a broad, squat building at Abrams and Northwest Highway, features disc jockeys between band sets. Audiences listen to Chick Corea, Cheap Trick, and Johnny Winter.

El Paso

Chamizal National Memorial hosts the Border Folk Festival in October, with country-Western square dancing galore.

Galveston

Menard Park, Twenty-seventh Street and Seawall Boulevard, presents band concerts during the summer months.

The Strand Street Festival takes place in June, with folk and country music.

Houston

Rockabilly Club, originally Cotton-Eyed Joe's, 2745 Gessner, has country-Western music.

Fitzgerald's, 2706 White Oak, features artists such as Joe Ely and Bruce Springsteen.

Mums Jazz Place, 2016 Main Street.

Melody Lane Ballroom, 3027 Crossview, offers a big-band sound and a large dance floor.

Gilley's (Pasadena), 4500 Spencer Highway, of *Urban Cowboy* fame, is a crowded honky-tonk place.

Countryland, 24639 North I-45, also features honky-tonk music.

Birdwatchers, 907 Westheimer, is an interesting place for jazz, with its sunken stage and bird-decked walls.

The Astrodome, 610 Kirby Drive, holds a jazz festival in July.

March brings arts festivals and fairs.

Miller Outdoor Theater, 100 Concert Drive, hosts all varieties of music in the summer.

The Avis Center, 615 Louisiana, hosts a gala Houston Festival in March. The emphasis is on folk music.

St. Michel, 2150 Richmond, offers jazz. You can enjoy the music from a balcony.

Cooters, 5164 Richmond, offers disco.

The Hyatt Regency Hotel, 1200 Louisiana, offers all kinds of music.

Nickel's, 1399 Voss, features disco on a spacious dance floor.

The Texas State prison, in Huntsville, northwest of Houston, presents the "wildest rodeo behind bars" on Sunday afternoons in October. Top country-Western artists like Buck Owen and Merle Haggard have entertained here, with the proceeds going to the prison's programs for rehabilitation.

Juarez

Julio's Cafe Corona, 2200 Avenue 16 de Septiembre, is a honky-tonk night club with popular entertainers.

Lubbock

Lubbock Memorial Civic Center, on Main Street, hosts the Lubbock Arts Festival in May. Folk and country music ring out. The Fairgrounds, on Ninth Street, hosts the Panhandle South Plains Fair in September.

The Cotton Club, on Slaton Highway, is a well-populated honky-tonk.

San Antonio

The Farmer's Daughter Dancehall, 542 North West White Road, is a place where one can dance the Cotton-Eyed Joe. There are numerous photos on the walls that portray the history of country-Western music.

The Cowboy, 5607 Kenwick, features disco on a small dance floor.

Burgundy Woods, 2379 North East IH, also features disco on a small dance floor.

The Landing, 522 River Walk, offers jazz, presenting music from the 1920s.

Mendiola's Ballroom, 16490 U.S. South Highway 81, has a large dance floor.

La Louisiane, 2632 Broadway, has dancing and jazz.

Villita Assembly Hall, 401 Villita Street, hosts Dixieland jazz during Fun-tier Nights in the summer.

Texarkana

The Fairgrounds at Spring Lake Park hosts the Four States Fair and Rodeo in October.

UTAH

Heber City

This mountain-ringed valley holds the Wasatch County Fair each August, packed with country-Western music.

Moab

The Canyonland Festival and Rodeo takes place in June.

Mi Vida, on North Highway 163, is a nightspot that presents country-Western and popular entertainment. Enjoyment is enhanced by a spectacular view of the Colorado River at the foot of La Sal Mountains.

Ogden

Weber State College, off UT-104, hosts a National Old-time Fiddler's Contest in June.

Panguitch

To celebrate historic Forty-niners Day, there is a country-Western dance in May.

In May and September, there's a country rodeo, just east of Bryce Canyon, off UT-12.

Provo

Jedediah's, 1292 South University Avenue, is the locally popular spot for music and dancing.

St. George

The Dixie Roundup offers folk and country-Western music in September.

WYOMING

Buffalo

The Johnson County Fair and Rodeo takes place in August. It's colorful, exciting, and packed with country-Western.

Cheyenne

The Hitching Post, 1600 West Lincoln Way, makes merry with traditional and progressive country-Western music.

The Frontier Park area hosts Frontier Days in July, one of the nation's most famous rodeos since 1897.

Cody

Cody Nite Rodeo is authentic as well as being a musical earful.

King's Castle, on Old Airport Road, is noted for popular entertainment. Local color is added by a drawbridge connecting to the front door.

Jackson

Excellent entertainment can be found at the Virginian, 740 Broadway, Silver Dollar Bar in the Wort Hotel, 50 West Deloney, the Cowboy Bar, 25 North Cache Drive, and the Rancher, 20 East Broadway.

Two theaters where one can sing along with the musical presentations are the Pink Garter Theater, at the Plaza, on Broadway, and Dirty Jack's Wild West Theater on Cache Drive.

Torrington

The Goshen County Fair and Rodeo takes place in August.

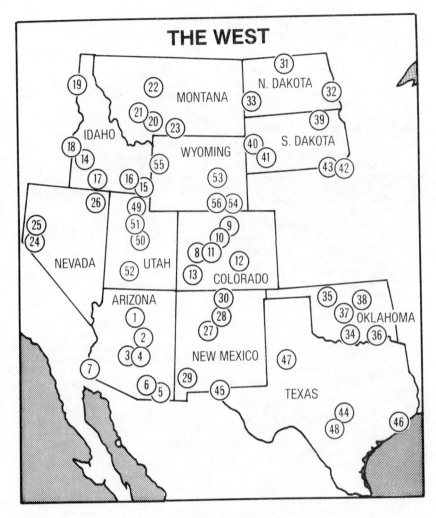

THE WEST

The West

1. *Flagstaff, AZ—Northern Arizona State University has Flagstaff Festival of the Arts in summer with symphonic and chamber music, and dance*

2. *Payson, AZ—The Rodeo Grounds host fiddlers' contests and festivals*

3. *Phoenix, AZ—Country-Western, jazz, and rock at Veterans' Memorial Coliseum, 1826 W. McDowell, at Graham Central Station, Thirty-third Avenue and Indian School Road. and at Different Points of View, 11111 N. Seventh Street. Arizona State University, Tempe, just south of Phoenix, hosts musical*

events in Gammage Auditorium. Kerr Cultural Center, 6110 N. Scottsdale Road, is a place for symphonic, chamber, and choral music. The Phoenix Art Museum, 1625 N. Central Avenue hosts chamber groups. Civic Plaza Symphony Hall, N. First Avenue and Van Buren, is home to the Phoenix Symphony. Sun City Dome in Sun City, slightly west of Phoenix at 19403 R. H. Johnson Boulevard, features much varied music

4. *Scottsdale, AZ—Scottsdale Center for the Arts, 383 Scottsdale Mall, holds*

musical events of all kinds. Mt. Shadows, 5641 E. Lincoln Drive, has jazz and rock

5. Tombstone, AZ—Fiddlers' contests regularly. Crystal Palace Saloon, Fifth and Allen streets, for country-Western. Bird Cage Theater, Sixth and Allen streets, is a former 19th century cabaret

6. Tucson, AZ—After the Gold Rush, 144 W. Lester, for disco. Rock at The Night Train, 424 N. Fourth Avenue. Festivals and square dances. The Tucson Symphony performs in Community Center Music Hall, 260 S. Church Street

7. Yuma, AZ—Square Dance Festivals year-round

8. Aspen, CO—Aspen Music Festival features symphonic and chamber music plus jazz. courtesy of its Music School. Aspen High School Performing Center, Castle Creek Road, for Utah's Ballet West in summer. Country-Western at Chisholm's, 404 S. Galena, and disco at Paragon Parlour, 419 E. Hyman

9. Boulder, CO—Jazz at The Blue Note, 1116 Pearl Street, and Wallstreet Jazz Cellar, 1136 Pearl. Country-Western at Olympic Saloon and Dance Hall, 1720 Thirtieth Street. Chautauqua Park, 900 Baseline Road, for concerts and opera

10. Central City, CO—Opera at Old Central City Opera House on Eureka Street

11. Leadville, CO—Former Tabor Opera House, 308 Harrison Avenue, connected with opera, The Ballad of Baby Doe, by Douglas Moore

12. Pueblo, CO—Memorial Hall, Union and Grand avenues, is home to the Pueblo Symphony. Mineral Palace Park has Bandshell for summer concerts

13. Telluride, CO—Country-Western, Bluegrass, and jazz at Tour Park

14. Boise, ID—For popular music there's the Owyhee Plaza Hotel, Eleventh and Main, Rodeway Inn, 29th and Chinden Boulevard, and Jolly King, 1115 N. Curtis. Northwest Nazarene College, 623 Holly Street, has a madrigal choir. Boise State College has a community orchestra

15. Montpelier, ID—Bear Lake County Fair for country-Western

16. Pocatello, ID—Cotton Tree Inn, 1415 Bench Road, for popular music. Idaho State University, 714 S. Seventh Avenue, for year-round concerts. Davis Park, Boise Park, and Ross Park for summer concerts

17. Twin Falls, ID—Country-Western at The Alley, 121 Fourth Avenue S.

18. Weiser, ID—Historical Museum, 44 W. Commercial Street, for folk music memorabilia. Weiser High School for famous old-time fiddlers' contests

19. Worley, ID—Leo Worley's Club for country-Western and rock

20. Bozeman, MT—The Loft Theater offers musical productions

21. Deer Lodge, MT—Fairs and rodeos bring country-Western

22. Great Falls, MT—Seasonal concerts throughout Great Falls

23. Red Lodge, MT—Music festivals given by students

24. Carson City, NV—Brewery Arts Center, 449 W. King Street, for musical groups

25. Reno, NV—Pioneer Theater, 100 S. Virginia, for Reno Philharmonic. Masonic Theater for chamber music. The University of Nevada-Reno has musical groups. Eldora Hotel, Fourth and Virginia streets, Ponderosa Hotel, 515 S. Virginia, and MGM Grand Hotel, 2500 E. Second Street for popular music. Many state fairs and rodeos

26. Wells, NV—Country-Western and rodeos

27. Albuquerque, NM—Popejoy Hall, University of New Mexico, Central Avenue, is home of Albuquerque Symphony. Chelsea Street Pub, Coronado Center, for country-Western. Disco at Graham Central Station, 3301 Juan Tabo NE. State fairs and rodeos. Best Western for rock and country-Western

28. Santa Fe, NM—Home of the Santa Fe Opera, off US-84. Orchestra of Santa Fe performs at St. Francis Cathedral, 275 E. Alameda, in Museum of Fine Arts, 113 Lincoln, and at St. John's College, Camino de Cruz Blanca. Country-Western at festivals in Old Cienega Village Museum, off I-25

29. Silver City, NM—Country-Western at country fairs

30. Taos, NM—Taos Community Auditorium on N. Pueblo Road holds musical events by many groups including the Taos School of Music Rodeos and fairs in summer

31. Bottineau, ND—International Music Camp near Canadian border presents concerts and dance

32. Fargo, ND—Seasonal music festivals

33. Medora, ND—Gold Seal Amphitheater presents concerts

34. *Ardmore, OK—Charles B. Goddard Center, First Avenue and D Street SW, for symphonic music and ballet*
35. *Enid, OK—Phillips University on Maine Street hosts musical events*
36. *Hugo, OK—Salt Creek Park for country and Bluegrass*
37. *Oklahoma City, OK—Civic Center Music Hall, 201 N. Dewey, is home to Oklahoma City Symphony, Oklahoma City Opera, and Oklahoma City Ballet. Lyric Theater, 2501 N. Blackwelder Avenue, has musical events*
38. *Tulsa, OK—Tulsa Theater, 1511 S. Delaware Avenue, for musical fare. The Performing Arts Center, Second and Cincinnati, is home to the Tulsa Philharmonic, Tulsa Opera, and Tulsa Ballet. Country-Western at Oklahoma Theater Center, 400 W. Sheridan Avenue, and at Duke's Country on East Admiral Place*
39. *Aberdeen, SD—Northern State College on S. Joy Street has an active music department*
40. *Lead, SD—The restored Homestake Opera House is located at 309 W. Main Street*
41. *Rapid City, SD—Circle B on SD-44 for country-Western*
42. *Vermillion, SD—Shrine to Music Museum at the University of South Dakota, Clark and Yale streets has an unusual display of instruments*
43. *Yankton, SD—Old-time fiddlers' contests seasonally*
44. *Austin, TX—Zilker Park Hillside Theater, 2000 Barton Springs Road, for concerts. Palmer Auditorium, 51st and W. Riverside, hosts Austin Symphony. Country-Western and rock at Soap Creek Saloon, 11306 N. Lamar. Lock, Stock, and Barrel at 200 W. Anderson, and Texas Tumbleweed, FM Road*
45. *El Paso, TX—Civic Center hosts El Paso Symphony, square dancing, festivals and many musical events*
46. *Galveston, TX—Menard Park, Twenty-seventh Street and Seawall Boulevard, hosts concerts. The Amphitheater in Galveston Island State Park has many musical programs*

47. *Lubbock, TX—Lubbock Memorial Civic Center on Main Street holds many musical events. Country-Western at the Cotton Club, Slaton Highway*
48. *San Antonio, TX—Theater for the Performing Arts, HemisFair Plaza, S. Alamo, houses San Antonio Symphony. The Cowboy, 5607 Kenwick, features country-Western, rock and disco. Jazz at The Landing, 522 River Walk, and La Louisiane, 2632 Broadway*
49. *Ogden, UT—Old-time fiddlers' contests at Weber State College, off UT-104*
50. *Provo, UT—Brigham Young University, University Hill, offers many classical music programs. Jedediah's, 1292 S. University Avenue, for popular music*
51. *Salt Lake City, UT—Salt Palace, W. Temple and S. Temple streets, is home of the Utah Symphony. The Tabernacle on Temple Square is home of the Mormon Tabernacle Choir. Ballet West performs at the University of Utah, University Street, and 300 S. Capital Theater at 50 W. 200 S. is a place for dance groups*
52. *Panguitch, UT—Country-Western dances and rodeos, east of Bryce Canyon, off UT-12*
53. *Casper, WY—Casper Events Center, Events Drive, for Casper Symphony and Casper Comic Opera*
54. *Cheyenne, WY—Cheyenne Civic Center, 510 W. 20th Street for symphonic music and ballet. Country-Western at Hitching Post, 1600 W. Lincoln Way. Rodeos and country-Western in Frontier Park*
55. *Jackson, WY—Country-Western and rock at the Virginian, 740 Broadway, at the Rancher, 20 E. Broadway, and at Cowboy Bar, 25 N. Cache Drive. Teton Village holds the Grand Teton Music Festival with classical and choral music*
56. *Laramie, WY—Fine Arts Center in the University of Wyoming hosts year-round musical events*

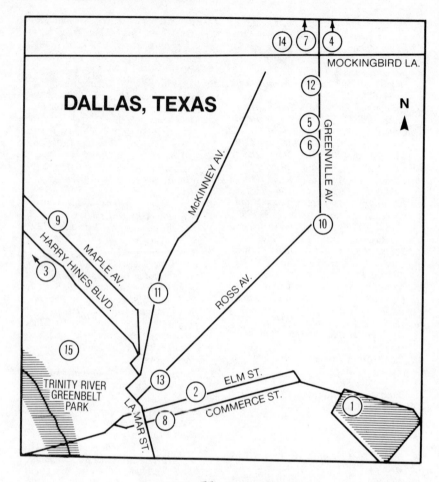

Dallas, TX

1. Music Hall in Fair Park, off I-30, hosts the Dallas Symphony, Dallas Ballet, and Dallas Civic Opera

2. Majestic Theater, 1925 Elm Street, for dance groups

3. Cotton-Eyed Joe's, famous for disco at Northwest Highway and Harry Hines Boulevard

4. Diamond Jim's, for jazz, rock, and country-Western, is at 5601 Greenville Avenue

5. San Francisco Rose, 3024 Greenville Avenue, honky-tonk and country-Western

6. Greenville Ave. Bar plays jazz at 2821 Greenville

7. Whiskey River, 5421 Greenville, for country-Western

8. Adolphus Hotel, famous jazz site at 1321 Commerce Street

9. Hot Club, for rock at 4350 Maple Avenue

10. Little Gus, for rock at 1916 Greenville

11. Poor David's Pub, 2900 McKinney, has rock and country-Western

12. Nick's Uptown, 3606 Greenville, plays rock

13. Fairmont Hotel, Ross Avenue and Akard Street, for all popular music

14. Belle Starr, 7724 North Central, for country-Western

15. Clancy's Saloon and Dance Hall, 2101 Stemmons, for country-Western

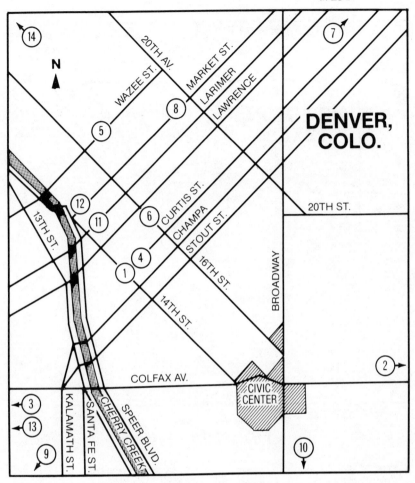

Denver, CO

1. Boettcher Hall, one of four theaters for music and dance in the Denver Center for the Performing Arts, is located at Fourteenth and Curtis streets and is home to the Denver Symphony as well as host to numerous musical groups including Central City Opera
2. Bonfils Theater, E. Colfax and Elizabeth streets, hosts the Colorado Concert Ballet and other dance groups
3. Taylor's Supper Club, 7000 W. Colfax, for jazz, rock, and country-Western
4. Ebbet's Fields, 1446 Curtis Street, for jazz, rock and country-Western
5. Oxford Hotel, Seventeenth and Wazee streets, jazz, rock, and country-Western
6. Paramount Theater, Sixteenth Street Mall, for jazz and popular music
7. Denver Coliseum, E. Forty-sixth and Humboldt streets, concerts of all kinds
8. El Chapultepec Lounge, 1962 Market Street, for rock
9. Red Rocks Park on I-70 is a site for many musical performances
10. Turn of the Century, 7300 E. Hampden, for popular music
11. Zeno's at Larimer Square, for Dixieland jazz
12. Café Nepenthes, 1416 Market Street, plays blues, jazz, and country
13. Country Opry features country-rock groups at 4842 Morrison Road
14. Arvada Center for the Arts, 6901 Wadsworth Boulevard

299

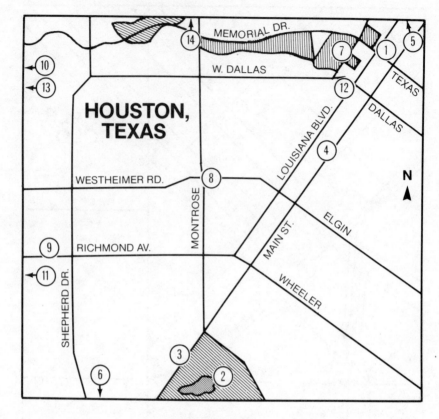

Houston, TX

1. *Jones Hall for the Performing Arts, 615 Louisiana Boulevard, is home to the Houston Symphony, Houston Grand Opera, and the Houston Ballet*

2. *Miller Outdoor Theater in Hermann Park is the summer home of many performing groups*

3. *Shamrock Hilton Hotel, 6900 Main Street, hosts dance groups*

4. *Mums Jazz Place, 2016 Main Street, for all popular music*

5. *Countryland, 24639 N. I-45, has honkytonk and country-Western*

6. *Astrodome holds jazz and rock festi-*
vals at 610 Kirby Drive

7. *Music Hall, 810 Bagby Street, for dance groups*

8. *Birdwatchers at 907 Westheimer, for jazz*

9. *St. Michel, 2150 Richmond, for jazz*

10. *Disco at Nickel's, 1399 Voss Road. Country-Western too*

11. *Cooters, 5164 Richmond, for rock and disco*

12. *Hyatt Regency Hotel, 1200 Louisiana, for popular music*

13. *Rockabilly Club, 2745 Gessner, for country-Western*

14. *Fitzgerald's, 2706 White Oak, for rock*

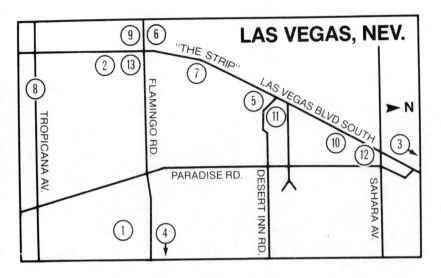

Las Vegas, NV

1. University of Nevada, 4505 S. Maryland Parkway, presents musical programs of symphonic and choral music, and dance
2. Aladdin Theater for the Performing Arts has a concert hall on Las Vegas Boulevard S.
3. Whipple Cultural Center, 821 Las Vegas Boulevard N., presents chamber music
4. The Library at 1401 E. Flamingo Road is a site for chamber music
5. Desert Inn, 3145 Las Vegas Boulevard, for rock and country-Western
6. Caesar's Palace, 3570 Las Vegas Boulevard, for rock and country-Western
7. Sands Hotel, 3355 Las Vegas Boulevard, for rock and country-Western
8. Treasury Hotel, 115 E. Tropicana, off the Strip, for popular music
9. Dunes Hotel on Flamingo Road, for rock and all popular music
10. Silverbird Hotel, Las Vegas Boulevard, for rock and country-Western
11. Royal Las Vegas, Las Vegas Boulevard, for rock and country-Western
12. Sahara Hotel on Sahara Avenue, for all popular music
13. MGM Grand Hotel, Las Vegas Boulevard, for all popular music

W·E·S·T- C·O·A·S·T

INTRODUCTION

The West Coast, much like the Northeast, was a commercial area for popular music. Further impetus was given to country-Western music because of the proximity of Hollywood and the film industry, which disseminated musical styles, discovered new talent, and exploited commercialism.

To the north, boasting a congenial, benign climate, and tolerant of varied social behavior, was San Francisco, a prominent location for the rock and roll explosion in mid-century, which served to give a sense of purpose to restless groups with ambiguous yearnings. The center for this counterculture was Haight/Ashbury in the North Beach section of San Francisco. Adolescents professing "flower power" represented the love generation who overturned the Puritan work ethic by "blowing their minds" and transcending horizons through drugs and music.

In addition to eclecticism, the Coast was noted for the initiation of a Wagnerian Festival in Seattle, Washington, the first city in the United States to produce *Der Ring des Nibelungen* in both German and English. The wide-open, natural outdoor beauty of Seattle was chosen to parallel the mythical paradise of the *Ring,* with its heroes and gods. Today, the Festival attracts music lovers from all over the world and most closely approximates the original Bayreuth setting of Wagner's Germany.

SYMPHONIC MUSIC, OPERA, DANCE

On the West Coast one finds the San Francisco Symphony Orchestra and the Los Angeles Philharmonic. They are two of the West Coast's major cultural attractions.

The San Francisco Symphony Orchestra

Several sporadic attempts were made between 1854 and 1911 (when the San Francisco Symphony Orchestra came into existence) to establish local instrumental ensembles. Rudolf Herold was among the first to offer concerts intermittently during the late nineteenth century. Herold is commonly referred to as the "father" of San Francisco's orchestral music. Louis Homeier organized a group of forty men in 1880, and following that, Gustave Hinricks and Fritz Scheel made efforts to create an early Philharmonic Orchestra.

By 1910, a budding Philharmonic had been directed by various conductors and was fortunate enough to be supported by wealthy patrons. Visiting conductors Theodore Thomas from Chicago and Walter Damrosch from New York added an occasional touch of professional elegance. Feelings ran high for plans to establish a permanent symphony orchestra, especially since the historic earthquake and fire, several years before, in 1906, had destroyed all the theaters and cultural sites, and the Grand Opera House.

In 1911, the Mutual Association of San Francisco, together with American composer and conductor Henry Hadley, created a permanent orchestra, with a season of six subscription concerts. The new Cort Theater, later to be the Curran, with a seating capacity of almost two-thousand, hosted the first performance of the San Francisco Symphony Orchestra under the baton of Henry Hadley. The program consisted of music by Haydn, Liszt, Tchaikovsky, and Wagner, and musicians were gathered from all over the country. Hadley incorporated the music of Saint-Saëns and Dvořák into succeeding programs as well as several of his own works (including an overture *In Bohemia*), which he composed during his term as conductor.

Shortly thereafter, Alfred Hertz, a conductor of German opera from New York, came to San Francisco to assume leadership and remained for over a decade, during which time he expanded the Orches-

305

tra's horizons. He increased the players from sixty-five to eighty, strengthened discipline and formality, and introduced "pop" concerts to the West Coast. The pop concerts were performed in Civic Auditorium, which had a seating capacity of ten-thousand. Repertory was heavily German with the addition of works by Sibelius, Debussy, and several Bay Area contemporary composers, including Ernest Bloch, who was the director of the San Francisco Conservatory of Music in 1925. After a somewhat stormy reign, Hertz resigned in 1930, and the orchestra was caught in the throes of the depression.

In 1935, an Art Commission was appointed to help with financing for the Orchestra. An interesting feature was a charter amendment that decreed a percentage of taxes to go toward financing the Orchestra. In return, the Orchestra played pop concerts for the city in the summer. The Curran, Tivoli, and Capital Theaters were alive with symphonic music. Then the Municipal Auditorium and the War Memorial Opera House in Civic Center (the first municipally owned opera house in the nation), with seating for over three-thousand, provided space for the Orchestra and for the San Francisco Opera. (The Opera performs in the War Memorial Opera House today, which has a large shell with a deep stage.)

The following year, 1936, brought Pierre Monteux to conduct. Having achieved a reputation in Boston (see Section I. Chapter 5), and as a guest conductor for many other major orchestras, he revitalized the West Coast with the sophisticated repertory of Chabrier, Berlioz, Chausson, Ravel, and Milhaud.

An affiliation was established between the San Francisco Symphony Orchestra and students in Bay Area colleges in 1938, at which time an entire subscription series was devoted exclusively to student audiences. The programs were highly successful and this concept gained recognition throughout the country.

The San Francisco Symphony is an opera orchestra as well as a symphony orchestra, playing for the San Francisco Opera Company, and frequently for the San Francisco Ballet. Its present home is Davies Hall.

The Los Angeles Philharmonic

In 1893, a group of thirty-five musicians assembled to perform works of Wagner, Rossini and Mendelssohn. The group's concertmaster, Harley Hamilton, then organized his own group, the Los Angeles Symphony Society, and in 1898, they gave their first public concert in a converted music hall on Spring Street. They continued performing for several years, playing the repertory of Handel, Brahms, and Dvorák, among others. Hamilton retired soon afterwards and Adolf Tandler from Vienna assumed leadership of the Los Angeles Symphony. Tandler and

Davies Symphony Hall, home of the San Francisco Symphony Orchestra (Courtesy San Francisco Symphony Orchestra)

the Symphony performed at the Alexandria Hotel beginning in 1900 with ninety musicians.

Coincident with this development, one William Andrews Clark, Jr., an amateur violinist and mining heir, was organizing a professional orchestra for which he enjoyed the services of Englishman Walter Henry Rothwell, former assistant to Gustav Mahler in Hamburg, and former conductor of the St. Paul Symphony Orchestra. Rothwell opened a series of concerts with a ninety-piece orchestra at Trinity Auditorium in 1919, which caused the old Los Angeles Symphony Orchestra to lose its members and collapse. The Orchestra was reorganized as the Los Angeles Philharmonic Orchestra and became part of community life, with Clark's financing behind it.

Trinity Auditorium was abandoned in favor of the old Clune Auditorium, later known as Philharmonic Auditorium, seating twenty-five-hundred. Rothwell's repertory was mostly traditional with strains of Liszt and Mahler. Summer concerts were given at the famous Hollywood Bowl.

Rothwell died in 1927, and after several unsuccessful replacements, Artur Rodzinski took over until 1933, playing surprisingly little Austro/German music, but stressing French and Russian repertory. Guest conductors Bruno Walter, Alfred Wallenstein, and Sir John Barbirolli followed Rodzinski on the podium. Wallenstein, a cellist, assumed directorship for a time, playing standard and modern works, and avoiding experimentation. In late years, Zubin Mehta reversed the pattern by offering experimental works, something he does today with the New York Philharmonic. At present, the Los Angeles Philharmonic performs in the Music Center's Dorothy Chandler Pavilion.

Opera

The Seattle Opera and Wagner's "Ring" at the Pacific Northwest Festival

The Seattle Opera, established in 1964, has grown from a small company producing two operas during the first year to a leading cultural force.

In addition to featuring such traditional fare as Verdi's *A Masked Ball,* with Richard Tucker, and Offenbach's *Tales of Hoffmann,* with Joan Sutherland, the Seattle Opera has been innovative in offering opera in English since 1966, with American singers in leading roles: Robert Moulson has sung *Of Mice and Men,* by Carlisle Floyd; Joanna Simon has sung *Black Widow,* by the American composer Thomas Pasatieri.

A scene from *Das Rheingold,* part of Wagner's *Der Ring des Nibelungen,* presented by the Seattle Opera at the Pacific Northwest Wagner Festival. (Courtesy Seattle Opera Association)

Experimental productions are frequent too: the rock opera *Tommy*, by The Who, was given, as was Stravinsky's *The Story of a Soldier*, with Stravinsky himself conducting in 1967.

The Seattle Opera Company is perhaps best known for its heroic endeavors during the last decade in presenting the summer Pacific Northwest Festival and Wagner's *Der Ring des Nibelungen* (The Ring of the Nibelung). Commonly referred to as "The Ring," the event consists of epic tales of gods, mortals, dragons, giants, love, and hate in four different operas: *Das Rheingold, Die Walküre, Siegfried*, and *Götterdämmerung*. The operas are sung in both an English and a German series.

The force behind the Festival is Glynn Ross, the general director of the Seattle Opera. The operas are performed in the three-thousand-seat Seattle Opera House, formerly the Civic Auditorium, which was built for the 1962 World's Fair. A monorail offers a two minute ride from downtown Seattle to the Opera House. A preview of each opera of the Ring is presented in Symphony Room on the loge level of the Opera House an hour and fifteen minutes before curtain time. Tickets are inexpensive.

In the *Ring*, Wagner created the mythical land of Valhalla, a city high up in the clouds where gods and heroes live. Although mortals live in Seattle, the terrain is filled with mountains, gorges, forests, rivers, and wilderness to accommodate the dragons, armor, pomp and myth. The orchestra is augmented in true Wagnerian style and the sets are traditionally romantic. The Festival is usually booked in advance with 20 percent of its orders filled from countries other than the United States. Wagner's music is simple, yet majestic. Such singers as Anthony Raffel portraying Wotan, Janice Yoes as Brünnhilde, and Edward Sooter as Siegfried have performed here. This Festival is the closest to the production's in Bayreuth, Germany that one can find without traveling there. Subscribers attend anticipating a peak experience and leave satisfied.

Dance

San Francisco Ballet

The present San Francisco Ballet, the oldest ballet company in the United States, was founded originally as the San Francisco Opera Ballet, in 1933. It was primarily engaged in training dancers for operatic productions through the San Francisco Ballet School. Gradually, the Ballet School achieved some autonomy and sought additional direction, other than in the opera. Adolph Bolm, of Ballets Russes fame (see Section

I. Chapter 5), became the San Francisco Ballet's first choreographer. He was succeeded by Serge Oukrainsky, in 1936, and then by première danseur, William Christensen. It was Christensen and other members of his family who broadened the artistic horizons of the Ballet by adding a more varied repertory and enlarging the audience in its tours of the United States.

Brother Harold Christensen assumed directorship of the Ballet School in 1944 and continued to expand the School and the Company. Still a third brother, Lew Christensen, became choreographer and Artistic Director in 1951, having been a dancer in the Ballet for several years, and having had previous experience as one of Balanchine's principal dancers with the New York City Ballet. Christensen was one of America's first choreographers of note. A favorable reciprocal agreement was established between the New York City Ballet and San Francisco Ballet, whereby dancers and repertory were exchanged. This arrangement did much to further enrich the West Coast group.

The Ballet continued its growth throughout the fifties and sixties, touring the United States and other continents. Several principal dancers, however, began to leave the company to pursue careers with New York ballets that offered greater opportunities. One who left, and returned in 1973 to become Assistant Artistic Director with Lew Christensen, was Michael Smuin. A few others, who had left for New York, joined Smuin in his return to the West Coast. They were Paula Tracy, Vane Vest, and Betsy Erickson.

A financial crisis darkened prospects in 1974, and a most unusual and interesting effort took place to keep the company solvent. Dancers, directors, stagehands, and local citizens engaged in all-out fundraising drives in the streets. Dancers danced on street corners, as they solicited funds. A local park was used for a benefit production, in which *Beauty and the Beast* was danced with real animals (monkeys, birds, and an elephant for sheer naturalism). The Oakland Symphony Orchestra volunteered its services and the merry event proved to be financially successful.

The following season in 1975 hosted many guest artists, among whom were Cynthia Gregory, Judith Jamison, and the Russian-born Panovs. The San Francisco Ballet was established as a major company on the West Coast. Today, performances are given at the Opera House.

The West Coast has much to offer travelers seeking symphonic music, opera, and dance. The following pages list some.

CALIFORNIA
Aptos
The Cabrillo Festival takes place in August, presenting the experimental music of Ives, Harrison, John Cage, and Barati.

Berkeley
The University of California, Berkeley, opposite the Golden Gate Bridge, has an active music department that offers symphonic and dance programs. Martha Graham's company appeared here recently.

The Greek Theater, off University Drive, a gift of William Randolph Hearst, has musical performances regularly.

Carmel
Scandia, Ocean Avenue between Lincoln and Monte Verde Streets, offers symphonic music.

Sunset Center, San Carlos and Ninth Street, hosts the famed Carmel Bach Festival in July. Although the music of Bach predominates, works by Handel, Vivaldi, Mozart and Telemann are frequently on the program.

Concord
Concord Pavilion, 2000 Kirker Pass Road, hosts music and dance performances from April through October.

Clayton Valley, in the Mt. Diablo foothills about thirty miles east of San Francisco, hosts the San Francisco Symphony Orchestra in their Summer Series of classical and pop music. The programs take place in August.

Idyllwild
Idyllwild School of Music and the Arts, on Tollgate Road, is a summer division of the University of Southern California. It is nestled on a scenic, mile-high, 250-acre mountain campus. A gala Festival Concert is presented here in late August.

Hollywood/Los Angeles Area
The Los Angeles Memorial Coliseum, 3911 South Figueroa Street, presents classical music concerts and dance programs.

The Hollywood Bowl, 2301 North Highland Avenue, in Hollywood, is a seventeen-thousand-seat hillside amphitheater with an acoustical shell designed by Frank Lloyd Wright. Classical music concerts and dance programs are presented here. The Los Angeles Philharmonic Orchestra has its summer season at the Hollywood Bowl.

The Music Center has three theaters: The 3,250-seat Dorothy Chandler Pavilion, where the Los Angeles Philharmonic Orchestra performs during its regular season; the Mark Taper Forum; the Ahmanson Theater. Dance companies and the Los Angeles Civic Light Opera perform at the latter two theaters.

In 1982, after a fourteen-year opera respite, Verdi's *Falstaff* was performed in the Dorothy Chandler Pavilion, with the Los Angeles Philharmonic conducted by Carl Maria Giulini. It was a gala event, with artists Katia Ricciarelli, Michael Sells, and Leo Nucci performing. In 1983, the Joffrey Ballet became the resident dance company of the Music Center, and currently, plans are being considered to double the size of the Music

Center, so that its annual audiences of two million would become four million.

The Greek Theater, 2700 Vermont Avenue, hosts top classical and popular artists in a lovely open-air setting.

The Performing Arts and Convention Center, 300 East Ocean Blvd., Long Beach, includes two theaters and a large auditorium. The Long Beach Civic Light Opera performs here.

The Country Museum of Art presents concerts.

The Pasadena Center Auditorium, 300 East Green Street, Pasadena, presents concerts.

Wilshire Ebell Theater, 4401 West Eighth Street, offers dance and chamber music.

The Pilgrimage Theater, 2580 Cahuenga Boulevard in Hollywood.

The Shubert Theater, 2020 Avenue of the Stars, Century City.

The Ivar Theater, 1605 North Ivar Street, Hollywood.

The Mayfair Music Hall, 214 Santa Monica Boulevard, in Santa Monica, is reminiscent of nineteenth-century music halls. Formerly the Santa Monica Opera House, it glitters with crystal chandeliers, polished brass, and stained glass.

The Santa Monica Civic Auditorium is home base for the Santa Monica Symphony Orchestra.

Oakland

The Paramount Theater, 2025 Broadway, home of the Oakland Ballet and Oakland Symphony, was made a National Historic Landmark in 1977.

Lakeside Park, in downtown Lakeland, features bandstand concerts.

Joaquin Miller Park, on Warren Freeway, has an Amphitheater for summer concerts.

Creative Arts Center, 2267 Telegraph, offers dance programs.

Sacramento

Community Center Theater has produced the Opera *Carmen*.

A Sacramento Festival of the Arts takes place in October.

Music Circus is held under a tent at Fifteenth and H Streets in the summer. Many kinds of music are performed.

San Diego

The Open Air Theater, San Diego University, hosts the San Diego Symphony Orchestra during the summer. Among its guest conductors have been André Kostelanetz and Arthur Fiedler.

Organ Pavilion, in the fourteen-hundred-acre Balboa Park, offers outdoor organ concerts. The Spreckels outdoor organ has five-thousand pipes.

Civic Theater, at Civic Concourse, hosts the San Diego Opera.

Sherwood Hall, 700 Prospect Street, in La Jolla, is home to the La Jolla Symphony.

The popular Verdi Festival takes place in June in many places around the city. Among the operas performed are *Aida, La Traviata,* and one of Verdi's earliest operas, *I' Lombardi.*

San Francisco

Davies Symphony Hall, Civic Center, Van Ness and Grove Street, hosts the San Francisco Symphony Orchestra. There are three-thousand seats in this thirty-million-dollar concert hall, which was built in 1980. The orchestra gives "pops" concerts in summer.

The War Memorial Opera House, Civic Center, hosts the San Francisco Opera. The Opera company has two seasons—one beginning in September; the other in June. This is the first civic-owned opera house in the United States. It has hosted such artists as Luciano Pavarotti, Joan Sutherland, and Placido Domingo. The San Francisco Ballet also performs here.

Many modern dance groups, including the Margaret Jenkins Dance Co., the Oberlin Dance Collective, and the San Francisco Moving Company experiment with abstract movement.

Sigmund Stein Grove, a thirty-five-acre park at Nineteenth and Sloat Boulevard, offers opera, ballet, and symphony concert series. Carlos Montoya has appeared here.

The Herbst Theater, Van Ness and McAllister Street, Civic Center, hosts an annual July Midsummer Mozart Festival.

The Alcazar Theater, 650 Geary Street, hosts the Pocket Opera. Most of the operas are sung in English.

Community Music Center, 544 Capp Street, offers opera.

Hillman Hall, Nineteenth and Ortega, offers chamber music, featuring such groups as the Empire Brass Quintet.

The Curran Theatre, 445 Geary Street, offers opera on a stage that extends over the orchestra and provides contact between the singers and the audience. Frederica Von Stade has sung here.

The Orpheum Theatre, 1192 Market Street, hosts the San Francisco Light Opera.

The Masonic Auditorium, 1111 California Street, offers concerts by such groups as the Berkeley Symphony Orchestra.

Golden Gate Park holds many concerts in a delightful, relaxed setting.

The San Francisco Conservatory of Music, 120 Ortega Street, presents a June Festival of chamber music.

San José

The San José Symphony performs at 170 Park Center Plaza.

San Luis Obispo

California State Polytechnic College presents a Mozart Festival on its 3,500-acre campus in August. One can hear choral works, symphonic music, and recitals.

Saratoga

The old Paul Masson mountain winery offers "Music at the Vineyards" in the summer. Concerts and recitals by such groups as Beaux Arts String Quartet, the Lenox Quartet, and the Opera Comique of San Francisco are presented. Champagne is served during intermission. There's a lovely view of the Santa Clara Valley below.

The Merola Opera comes to Saratoga in August.

The Villa Montalvo, a cultural center off CA-9, hosts concerts and recitals, and has musical artists-in-residence. Festivals are held here during the summer.

St. Helena

The Charles Krug Winery, 2800 Main Street, hosts August Moon Concerts. Programs of classical music are augmented with wine tours.

OREGON

Eugene

The Hult Performing Arts Center, One Eugene Center, hosts many music and dance groups. Silva Concert Hall opened here in 1982. It is an electroacoustic multi-purpose hall with twenty-five-hundred seats. It houses the Eugene Symphony.

Jacksonville

Britt Music Pavilion, 46 North Front Street, Medford, hosts the Peter Britt Gardens Music and Arts Festival in August. Orchestral concerts, choral programs, and recitals are presented amidst contemporary design on beautiful grassy slopes à la Tanglewood, by such groups as the Philadelphia String Quartet.

Portland

Reed College, 3203 SE Woodstock Boulevard, holds a series of summer chamber music concerts called Chamber Music Northwest.

Civic Auditorium, 222 SW Clay Street, hosts the Oregon Symphony Orchestra and the Portland Opera.

Washington Park has been the site for "Music by Moonlight" since 1949. These summer events include ballet performances.

WASHINGTON

Cheney

Eastern Washington University has a recital hall which hosts recitals, chamber music programs, and some concerts featuring choral works.

Seattle

The Opera House, in the Seattle Center Opera House Building, hosts both the Seattle Symphony Orchestra and the Seattle Opera. The Pacific Northwest Festival is presented in the summer with Wagner's *Ring* taking over the city's musical attention, presented in German and in English. Pacific Northwest Dance is the resident ballet company, and the Philadelphia (sic) String Quartet performs regularly. The Gilbert and Sullivan Society offers their particular musical fare. The Coliseum at

Interior of the Civic Auditorium, Portland, Oregon, home of the Portland Opera (Courtesy Portland Opera Association)

Fifth and Pike Street, and the Seattle Arena offer concerts.

Spokane

The twenty-seven-hundred-seat Opera House, West 334 Spokane Falls Boulevard, hosts performances by the Spokane Symphony Orchestra, with regular guest artists. Dance is also performed here.

Riverfront Park hosts Celebration of the Arts in July.

The Fox Theater, West 1005 Sprague.

Tacoma

A major attraction in Tacoma is its Symphony Orchestra. Two unusual musical treats are an organ at St. Peter's Church, 2910 North Starr Street, and a half-ton bell mounted on a tower.

JAZZ AND SWING, COUNTRY-WESTERN, ROCK

Jazz and the development of big bands on the West Coast in the 1920s and 1930s took place predominantly in the Los Angeles area. There were several jazz/swing events worthy of note.

The Spikes Brothers

The Spikes Brothers, Benjamin "Reb" and Johnny, are generally referred to as pioneers in the growth of jazz and swing movements. The brothers were talented all-around musicians who began working with the original So-Different Orchestra at Bill Brown's Cabaret on Central Avenue. The band traveled along the West Coast for a while, performing at such nightspots as the Alhambra in Seattle, Washington, and then returned to their home base in Los Angeles. Les Hite, on saxophone (who later formed his own group), George Orendorff on trumpet, Johnny Strong on clarinet, and for a brief time in 1929, Lionel Hampton on vibes, were members of the group, which peaked in popularity throughout the 1920s.

The band reorganized into Reb Spikes's Majors and Minors Orchestra and played for several years at Main Street's Follies Theater. Further changes occurred as the Spikeses formed the Legion Club 45s, with Leon White on trombone, Bill Perkins on guitar, and Eugene Wright at the piano. "My Mammy's Blues" was their hit in 1927.

Ever expanding, Johnny and Reb Spike established a music and record store on Central Avenue in Los Angeles, close to Hollywood residents. The shop rapidly became a focus for musical activity in the area, and grew into a large business enterprise and booking agency. Shortly afterwards, the Spikes formed their own recording company on the Sunshine label. They entered the businesses of music publishing and arranging and turned out their biggest hit, "Someday Sweetheart." In addition, they taught popular music and involved themselves in all aspects of jazz promotion. Only the depression caused them to fade from the music scene.

Paul Howard

Another West Coast jazz figure was Paul Howard, a saxophonist and clarinetist, who decided to pursue jazz as a career after he heard Freddie Keppard and the Original Creole Orchestra perform in New Orleans in the early 1900s. Howard started by taking a job playing with Wood Wilson's Syncopaters; then he joined a brass band, the Black and Tan Orchestra, originally from Texas. Howard reorganized the Black and Tans in Los Angeles. James "Tuba Jack" played piano and Harry Southard played the trombone. The group performed at the Cadillac Café. Howard left the Black and Tan group in 1923 to form the Quality Serenaders, playing in such nightspots as the Nightingale Club in 1926. Lionel Hampton came to Los Angeles at that time to join the Serenaders on drums. Later that year, the band moved to the New Cotton Club, where they entertained for more than two years. The New Cotton Club was expensive and posh, with lavish floor shows that attracted Hollywood audiences.

On the move again, Howard and his group changed their musical residence several years later to the Kentucky Club on Central Avenue, and, in 1930, they moved to Montmartre in Hollywood. The guitar came into prominence and some memorable tunes associated with Howard's Serenaders were "Moonlight Blues," "Overnight Blues," "Harlem," and "California Swing."

Les Hite

A third California-based band in the thirties was that of Les Hite, who had formerly been with Reb Spike. Hite formed the California Syncopaters and performed at the New Cotton Club, frequently featuring soloists like Louis Armstrong and Fats Waller. Hite and his group also worked for Hollywood studios, recording soundtracks for films and appearing in "Sing, Sinners, Sing," in 1933.

The Syncopaters played at Los Angeles's Paramount Theater in 1935 and shortly thereafter, the thirteen-piece band again provided background music for films, including the Marx Brothers' *A Day at the Races*. Hollywood films did much to sustain the band during the depression.

Hite wrote the arrangements for the band and played clarinet and alto and tenor saxophone. Some songs that were associated with his band are "That's the Lick," and "It Must Have Been a Dream." During World War II, Dizzy Gillespie joined the band and recorded "Jersey Bounce," an instant hit. The band collapsed in 1945.

In addition to places of a bygone era that have already been mentioned, there were others that welcomed jazz and swing bands. Within the Los Angeles area, you might have visited the Vernon Country Club, Lincoln Gardens, Club Alabam, Solomon's Dance Pavilion De Luxe, the Little Cotton Club, and Papkie's Club. To the north, San Francisco had Hartford Ballroom and Long Beach Dance Hall. To the south, Creole

Palace was located in San Diego. Many bands passed through these places, including those of Johnny Otis, Ed Garland, Floyd Ray, and Vernon Elkins.

Music in Hollywood

Movies lagged behind radio in catching onto jazz and swing until the invention of the sound track in the early thirties. This led to special film music with imaginative settings, scenery, and big bands. Millions of moviegoers were dazzled by the creation of original musical films.

Film companies hired musicians, singers, and live orchestras to provide quality entertainment for a nation of moviegoers. Studios built up large music departments, with conductors, vocal teachers, arrangers, and choral groups. And these musicians brought jazz and swing, as well as all forms of music into the film industry, located eight miles northwest of the center of Los Angeles in Hollywood.

In 1913, Cecil B. DeMille, Jesse Lasky, and Samuel Goldwyn combined forces to produce *The Squaw Man* in a barn at the intersection of Hollywood Boulevard and Vine. The barn was moved to Paramount Studios, which, together with Universal, Twentieth-Century Fox, Warner Bros., RKO, and MGM, and under such men as William Fox, Louis B. Mayer, and Adolph Zukor, were to become legendary giants. Hollywood pushed out its boundaries from Cahuenga Pass into the San Fernando Valley and across Beverly Hills to Culver City. Songwriters and their staffs moved from Broadway to Hollywood.

Paul Whiteman and his orchestra were among the first musicians to make music in Hollywood. In 1930, the *King of Jazz* had Whiteman and his Rhythm Boys in fancy sets, rising out of a piano. Bing Crosby sang "So the Bluebirds and Blackbirds Got Together."

Jeannette MacDonald and Nelson Eddy, coloratura soprano and baritone, sang in *Naughty Marietta.* Eleanor Powell and Nelson Eddy sang Cole Porter's "Spring Love is in the Air" in the famous *Rosalie,* in 1937. *Babes in Arms* in 1939 filmed Judy Garland and Mickey Rooney singing "Where or When." The same year produced *The Wizard of Oz,* one of the most memorable musicals ever to be made in Hollywood. Several years later, in 1948, Fred Astaire and Ginger Rogers sang and danced their way through *Barkleys of Broadway* with "They Can't Take That Away from Me."

The big bands also enjoyed a film heyday in the 1930s and 1940s. Benny Goodman starred in *Big Broadcast of 1937.* Artie Shaw and his band made *Dancing Coed* with Lana Turner dancing to "Jungle Drums." Gene Krupa and his band made *Some Like it Hot* with Marilyn

Monroe.Glenn Miller had two movie hits: *Orchestra Wives*, in which he played "Serenade in Blue;" and *Sun Valley Serenade*, in which he played "Chattanooga Choo-Choo." Harry James and his band starred with Betty Grable in *Springtime in the Rockies*, and Tommy Dorsey played in *Dubarry was a Lady*, along with Buddy Rich on drums.

The beat continues today with whatever style of music is popular. A visitor can enjoy a tour of the Hollywood studios and see a musical being made. A typical Hollywood studio consists of several hundred acres of land, surrounded by high gates, thick walls, sentry posts, and private roads. One can join a tour through special entrances and be accompanied by multilingual guides. Shootings on sound stages can be observed. Large and lavish production techniques, an infinite variety of props, scenery and sets, make-up and wardrobes are there, all lending pomp, glitter, and a touch of fantasy to the pulsating town of Hollywood.

Country-Western Music

In the 1960s, Bakersfield, California, became the Nashville of the West. Country music was born in the South, in Nashville, traveled up through Texas and Oklahoma in the West, and finally reached California, its last frontier of development.

Bakersfield, situated up in the hills of the lower San Joaquin Valley, with its orange groves, cotton fields, oil wells, roadhouses, and fundamentalist churches, recalled the early Southern Appalachian setting to a certain extent. Popularized by Steinbeck's novel, *The Grapes of Wrath*, California became the destination for large numbers of migrants coming from the dustbowls of Oklahoma, Texas, and Arkansas, to seek a better life. They brought banjos, guitars, fiddles, and scanty household furnishings in dilapidated trucks.

Bakersfield had wide, flat streets and bleached white buildings, which made for lazy, hot summers. Relief came in the spring with melting snow from mountains and occasional swelling rivers. Entertainment was sought and provided largely by television which helped propel country-western music to its final geographic destruction.

Bob Wills's band, originally from Fort Worth, Texas, and Tulsa, Oklahoma (see Section IV Chapter 3), played regular engagements on the West Coast and performed in the flat, arid, agricultural and oil valley town of Bakersfield. In Beardsley Garden, on Edison Highway, Wills's Western swing proved to be enormously popular and attracted listeners from all the neighboring towns. Other dance halls, barrooms, and clubs sprang up: Rhythm Rancho on South Union and the Blackboard on Chester Street offered country-Western music; Lucky Spot and

319

Clover Spot on Edison Highway, Trout's, and Tex's Barrel House all offered music in the loud, honky-tonk style. Of all these places mentioned above, only Trout's and Tex's Barrel House can be seen today. Hank Williams, Pee Wee King, Tex Butler's Band, and a favorite neighboring group, the Billy Woods Band appeared in these local spots.

But it was the television era that helped popularize country-Western music.

Country-Western on Radio and Television

Radio and television played all-important roles in promoting country-Western music. The first country music radio program in Bakersfield, even before the sixties, was the quarter-hour "Bob Wills's Show," in 1946, on Station KGEE. Following Wills, the "Billy Woods Band and Orange Blossom Show" was broadcast, later moving to Station KBIS, where Woods became a disc jockey. The fifties ushered television into Bakersfield and country-Western music was offered by the local TV personality, Cousin Herb Henson. Henson organized the Trading Post Gang, which included Fuzzy Owen, Roy Nichols, and the Farmer Boys. Trading Post Gang became Bakersfield's favorite group, entertaining locally, as well as in Oakwood Park, near Fresno, to audiences of more than ten thousand. The guitarist, Alvis Edgar "Buck" Owens, Jr., was in this group. He and Merle Haggard were significant figures in West Coast's country music history.

Buck Owens

Owens was born in 1929 in Sherman, Texas, near the Oklahoma border. His family moved to Tempe, Arizona, where Owens learned to play electric guitar, emulating the sounds of Bob Wills, Red Foley, and Roy Acuff, whom he had heard on radio. By the age of sixteen, he was playing at rough and sleazy honky-tonks in Arizona. In 1951, he headed for Bakersfield, California, where he was booked into the Blackboard Club, a tough drinking spot, with Bill Woods's Band.

Owens started traveling to Hollywood for recording engagements at Capitol Towers with the stars Tennessee Ernie Ford, Gene Vincent, and Tommy Sands. Some of the songs he wrote and sang for Capitol ("Under Your Spell Again" and "Act Naturally," with heavy drum rhythm) were hits in the late fifties. He formed Buck Owens Enterprises in 1963, a Bakersfield booking agency that discovered Merle Haggard and Wynn Stewart, among other artists. Buck Owens Radio and Television Productions was established next, followed by the Buck Owens Ranch

Show on radio stations KUZZ-KZIN in Bakersfield, and KTUF-KNIX in Phoenix, Arizona.

Producer of The Brass in the seventies, discoverer of Susan Raye, who had hits in "Wheel of Fortune" and "Pitty, Pitty Patter," Owens, with his Buckaroos Band, is known as the man who put Bakersfield on the music map.

Merle Haggard

Merle Haggard, another West Coast figure in country-Western history, was born in a railroad car in a Southern Pacific railroad yard in Bakersfield. His parents were among the migrant "Okies" who had fled Oklahoma earlier. Haggard spent time in reform school, escaped to Eugene, Oregon, then returned to jail in Bakersfield on counts of theft. In 1958 he found himself in San Quentin Prison. His songs, "Branded Man" and "Sing Me Back Home," told of prison life. In 1972, Ronald Reagan, then Governor of California, pardoned Haggard, who, by then, had been named by the Country Music Association as "entertainer of the year."

Music was an emotional release for Haggard. Restlessness, disappointment, loneliness, and isolation combined with feelings of family and patriotism in his songs, "Okie from Muskogee" and "Fightin' Side of Me." The theme song for the TV series "Movin' On" won artistic recognition for him and established Haggard as a foremost artist in country-Western music. "White Line Fever," written in 1969, expressed the scope of Haggard's feelings as he sang of a sickness deep in his soul.

In 1982, entertaining in "Performances at the White House," Haggard offered "Are the Good Times Really Over" to President Reagan, and sang out for the American flag and the liberty bell.

Rock

The San Francisco Scene

San Francisco, city of tradition and culture, was ripe for the rock revolution fostered by the Haight-Ashbury/Berkeley "flower children," who challenged conventional and artistic values.

Two historic places where live rock concerts took place in the early 1960s were the old Fillmore Auditorium and the Avalon Ballroom. Both sites featured three different bands, a large dance floor, and an interesting light show that provided unique visual elements. It was more than a psychedelic show. Slides of paintings and colored posters were projected on the walls in arrays of lights, a technique thought to be the pictorial representation of rock. Posters combined pop, op, and folk art subjects, and contributed to new sophisticated expression in a total rock experience. The Matrix was one of the popular folk-rock clubs presenting a lively light show.

The San Francisco scene was extreme in its use of drugs; it was also influenced by the occult (Far Eastern): the drugs at first caused shrieking, piercing sounds in "acid" rock performers, which then gave way to mental stupor, sometimes accompanied by Eastern Indian music, which is droning, repetitive, and tranquilizing.

Haight–Ashbury

The North Beach section of San Francisco, running along Columbus Avenue and Broadway, encompassed Haight and Ashbury Streets. This slightly decadent, large urban area was a mecca for the flower children of the sixties, and the West Coast center for the counterculture.

Today there are only remnants of that era, but in the sixties, flower power was the password in Haight–Ashbury. Young people were in motion everywhere: in love-ins, hippie tribes, and selfless communes. Barefoot, bearded, long and shaggy-haired, flowered, beaded, booted, middle- and upper-class adolescents rejected the establishment, did their "own thing," and demanded acid rock, which could be heard coming from the frame houses on the streets. The odor of pot was prevalent as these teen-agers sat on pavements playing guitars, begging money occasionally, and espousing the messages of peace, love, and joy.

1967 was Haight-Ashbury's heyday. The number of psychedelic groups in the Bay area exceeded a thousand. Before rock collapsed in the 1970s, some stars had risen to national prominence with cult followings. Among them were The Grateful Dead, Jefferson Airplane, and Janis Joplin.

The Grateful Dead and Country Joe and the Fish

This group of five, sometimes called the Crazies, performed under the influence of LSD and developed a heavy electrified sound called acid rock, heard in "In the Midnight House." The massive instrumental sounds were produced with the assistance of what seemed like tons of sound equipment that created special effects of fervor and ecstasy. Additional people were required to transport, assemble, disassemble, and maintain the accessories, which often took hours. Youth cult groups followed the Grateful Dead, who, after performing in Haight–Ashbury, disbanded briefly, then regrouped in the late seventies to resume their career.

At the same time, another acid group, Country Joe and the Fish, were performing in the Berkeley area. They too derived effects from using LSD, and made efforts to appeal to hippies and flower children and involve them in the intensely emotional framework that surrounded their music.

Jefferson Airplane

This acid rock group of five young men and a woman claimed to represent the voice of the love generation. Their style was a mixture of folk-rock and blues with jazz overtones as heard in such songs as "Today" and "Somebody to Love."

The female singer was Grace Slick, a hard, cutting soprano who wrote provocative songs. She articulated the drug experience in lyrics that told of a circus tent where she could pay her rent.

Concerts by the Jefferson Airplane were almost tribal in nature, urging a sense of oneness, with zeal reminiscent of a revivalist meeting, as in "Let's Get Together." The Airplane landed when the members of the group went their separate ways in the seventies.

Janis Joplin

Born in 1943 in Port Arthur, Texas, Joplin came to San Francisco in 1966 to join Big Brother and the Holding Company. The following year she performed at the Monterey Pop Festival with the group and established a name. Shortly thereafter she left Big Brother to pursue her own career.

Joplin's style was solidly grounded in the black blues style: wailing, moaning, protesting, hoping. Women's liberation appealed to her in its fight against sexual stereotyping. She spewed out frenzy and despair in "Ball and Chain" and "Piece of My Heart."

Drugs were part of her high-keyed lifestyle. She was driven to sing hard, lose herself in oblivion, and pursue pleasure relentlessly. Joplin performed at Woodstock in 1969, with other rock artists, and perhaps is best remembered for "Me and Bobby McGee," the lyrics of which describe the essence of the counterculture community to which she was committed. She died in 1970 of an overdose of drugs.

Southern California: The Surfing Scene

The special locale of southern California served the needs of the rock culture in the early sixties, beckoning the pursuit of an endless, carefree summer in sun, beach, and water. This was a natural setting for the surfing scene, a phenomenon of the sixties, exemplified in the music of the Beach Boys ("Surfin' USA," "Surfer Girl," "Warmth of the Sun").

The Beach Boys, with their leader Brian Wilson, had clean-cut, high-pitched, stylistic voices, with a delicate sound that was carried forward by a pulsating beat. Five voices accompanied by three electric guitars projected a refined sound with images of leisure and fun. Their style was characterized by a falsetto, nasal drone, counterpoint, and occasionally solemn violins. Social and political comment was left to others as the Beach Boys made the charts with "Don't Worry," and "Fun, Fun, Fun."

Their entrance into the psychedelic scene came with "Good Vibrations," in which they used an organ, a harpsichord, a theramin and even sleigh-bells.

The group's popularity climaxed with "Wild Honey" in the late sixties, and as cheerful values faded from the scene, so did they. A comeback surfaced with an album entitled *The Beach Boys Love You,* but the Beach Boys are mainly identified today with their hits from the early sixties.

The West Coast has much to offer the traveler in the way of popular music. Country-Western, blues, jazz, swing, and rock have all left indelible traces in the musical arena. The following pages list some of the places where one might hear this music.

CALIFORNIA

Azusa

Golden Days Celebration takes place in October with country–Western music and dance.

Bakersfield

Trout's, 805 North Chester Avenue, and Tex's Barrel House, 1524 Golden State Highway, are still in existence and offer country rock as well as honky-tonk.

Maison Jaussard, 1001 South Union Avenue, is a quieter place, locally popular for its dancing and entertainment. Original paintings are displayed on the walls.

The Kern County Fair takes place in September.

Barstow

A Calico Spring Festival takes over in the old mining town of Barstow, with fiddle and banjo contests and square dancing. The location is off I-15, then north on Ghostown Road.

Berkeley

The Keystone, 2119 University Avenue, has hosted the Grateful Dead, and jazz groups.

The University of California at Berkeley has presented Bill Monroe and the Bluegrass Boys.

Larry Blake's, 2367 Telegraph Avenue, has jazz and blues.

Dock of the Bay, Berkeley Marina, foot of University Avenue, offer jazz and blues.

Beverly Hills

The Beverly Hilton Hotel, 9876 Wilshire Boulevard, is lovely and expensive, with quality entertainment and a window view of the city. Ye Little Club, 555 North Canon Drive.

Concord

Concord Summer Jazz Festival, at the Concord Pavilion, 2000 Kirker Pass Road, in July. This Festival has been an annual event since 1969. Woody Herman, Mel Tormé, and Pearl Bailey have entertained in these Mt. Diable foothills in Clayton Valley. The Pavilion is sometimes referred to as "the house that jazz built."

Del Mar

The Southern California Exposition, in June, presents name entertainers.

Escondido

The Lawrence Welk Theater-Museum, 8975 Champagne Boulevard, has one-hour musical presentations and memorabilia of Welk's big-band career.

Grass Valley

The Fairgrounds, McCourtney Road, hosts a Bluegrass Festival in June.

Guerneville

A Russian River Jazz Festival is presented in September at Johnson's Beach.

Kelseyville

Whiskey Flat Days, in February, bring back the Gold Rush era and honky-tonk.

Los Angeles and Hollywood

The Lighthouse, 30 Pier Avenue, Hermosa Beach, is said to be the world's oldest jazz club. It's small and somewhat run down, but it features top jazz performers. Bus-style seats adorn the interior.

The Parisian Room, 4906 West Washington Boulevard, is a serious jazz club. There are tiny tables and they are close together, but the music is good.

One Hundred Fisherman's Wharf, Redondo Beach, hosts a jazz Concert by the Sea.

Blue Moon Saloon, 207 North Harbor Drive, Redondo Beach, offers popular entertainment and dancing.

Clarke's Turn of the Century Saloon, 239 North Harbor Drive, Redondo Beach.

Doug Weston's Troubadour, 9081 Santa Monica Boulevard, in West Hollywood, is the former stomping grounds of Linda Ronstadt, Blood, Sweat and Tears, Joni Mitchell, and Miles Davis. It features rock, country-Western, and jazz.

The Roxy, 9000 Sunset Boulevard, West Hollywood, is an elegant spot in art deco style.

Womphoppers, Lankershim at Hollywood Freeway, has a full Western-style saloon and honky-tonk country-Western music.

Folk-rock singer John Prine, who performs at the Greek Theater in Los Angeles. (Courtesy Variety Artists International, Minneapolis)

The Palomino, 6907 Lankershim Boulevard, offers country-Western and rock music.

Universal Amphitheater offers country-Western and rock music in the summer.

The Greek Theater, 2700 North Vermont Avenue, offers country-Western and rock music.

Donte's, 4269 Lankershim, is a popular entertainment spot.

Backflat, at Studio One, 652 North La Peer Drive, North Hollywood, offers rock, jazz, and country-Western music.

Whiskey a Go-Go, 8901 Sunset, has rock, jazz, and country-Western music.

The Forum, Civic Auditorium, Inglewood and South M Street, has rock, jazz, and country-Western music.

The Los Angeles County Fairgrounds, 1101 West McKinley Avenue, in Pomona, hosts the Los Angeles County Fair every September. It is probably the largest fair in the nation.

The Variety Arts Roof Garden Restaurant, 940 South Figueroa Street, has quality musical entertainment amidst Old-World charm.

The Palladium Ballroom, 6215 West Sunset Boulevard, has room for sixty-five hundred people.

The Hollywood Bowl, 2301 North Highland Avenue, offers all varieties of music in its outdoor amphitheater which seats 17,000 people. The Bowl rests against a hillside and overlooks beautiful sagebrush.

The Hollywood Roosevelt Garden Room Lounge, 7000 Hollywood Boulevard, features jazz and disco.

Scandals, 1635 North La Brea Avenue.

Pasquale's, Pacific Coast Highway, in Malibu, presents mainstream jazz artists.

Monterey

The famous Monterey Jazz Festival has been delighting thousands since 1958. Dizzy Gillespie, Janis Joplin, Pee Wee Russell, and Carmen McRae are some of the stars who have appeared here. It takes place in September.

The Fairgrounds hosts the Monterey County Fair in August. It is something of a preview of the Monterey Jazz Festival.

Napa

The Town and Country Fair in August.

Norco

A Golden West Bluegrass Festival is held in February.

Oakland

Eli's Mile High Club, 3629 Grove Street, offers rock and country–Western music. Troyce Key and the Rhythm Rockers have performed here.

Lucky Lion, 4100 Redwood Road, has featured Rock Candy.

The Hotel Claremont, Domingo and Ashby Avenues, offers more formal entertainment.

Redding

Anderson River Park hosts summer jazz concerts.

Redwood City

The San Mateo County Fair takes place in August.

Sacramento

Since 1974, the 4500-seat Amphitheater, First and I Streets, has presented a Dixieland Jazz Festival in May. Billy Butterfield and Connie Haines have performed here.

The Sacramento Inn, 1401 Arden Way, offers a lovely view of the courtyard and wood carvings of Gold Rush days to enjoy along with the music.

Salinas

The California Rodeo, Rodeo Grounds, 1034 North Main Street, takes place in July. It has a hoedown and square dancing to country–Western music.

San Diego

The Roxy Theater, 4642 Cass Street, presents top rock entertainment.

Rasputin's, 4230 West Point Loma Street, has two dance floors for disco dancing.

Crystal T's, 500 Hotel Circle, has a large disco floor.

The Fox Theater, 720 B Street, hosts country-Western stars, such as Hoyt Axton, as well as the Duke Ellington Orchestra.

The San Diego Stadium presents rock and roll stars, including Chuck Berry, Joan Jett and the Blackhearts.

Spirit, 1130 Buenos Avenue, has welcomed Country Dick and the Snuggle Bunnies.

Tacey's Chopping Block, 1740 East Vista Way, Vista, specializes in rock.

Belly Up, 143 South Cedras, Solana Beach, has presented John Lee Hooker.

The Educational Cultural Complex has hosted the West Coast Jazz All Stars.

The Bacchanal, 8022 Clairemont Mesa Boulevard, has presented Jerry Jeff Walker and Moving Targets.

Mom's Saloon, 945 Garnet, has rock.

Greenhouse, Camino del Rio South, Mission Valley, offers rock.

The Alamo, 3093 Clairmont Drive.

Windrose, 1935 Quivira Way, has hosted the New Dallas Collins Band.

The Jolly Roger, 1900 Harbor Drive North, Oceanside, offers dancing.

Saska's, 4520 West Point Loma Boulevard.

Tradewinds, 1775 East Mission Bay Drive, offers music and dancing.

Bodie's, 6149 University Avenue and Blue Parrot, 1298 Prospect, La Jolla offer jazz.

Old-Town San Diego State Historic Park, 2725 Congress Street, hosts a fiddle and banjo contest in May.

Santa Barbara

Baudelaire's, 435 State Street.

The Shack, 5796 Dawson.

Peppers, 27 West Canon Perdido, has a disc jockey who plays New Wave rock and disco.

San Francisco

Several hotels are noteworthy for popular music: The Mark Hopkins, One Nob Hill; the Fairmont, California and Mason Streets, top of Nob Hill; and the Sir Francis Drake, Powell and Sutter Streets.

Keystone Corner, 750 Vallejo Street, offers jazz and rock, with John Lee Hooker, Bonnie Hayes, and the Wild Combo as performers.

The Great American Music Hall, 859 O'Farrell Street, the Boarding Hosue, 901 Columbus, and Earthquake McGoon's, 128 Embarcadero offer jazz and rock.

The Hyatt Union Square, Ripples at Embarcadero Center, posh Mumms on Powell Street, Epaminondas at Bay and Kearny Streets all offer disco.

Brooks Hall in the San Francisco Civic Center, Fulton and Hyde Streets, presents country–Western music with such artists as Quickstep Band.

Songwriter and performer Norton Buffalo, a favorite at the Great American Music Hall in San Francisco. (Courtesy Variety Artists International, Minneapolis)

Last Day Saloon, 406 Clement, has featured Counterpoint.

Holy City, is next door to Last Day Saloon at 408 Clement. The building is over eighty years old with an old barn and a balcony made of wood that should last several more years.

Major Pond's, 2801 California Street, has billed Hot Links.

Heaven's Gate, 1821 Haight Street, offers straight rock, with performers such as Mental Floss and Holy War.

Off Union, 2511 Van Ness Avenue, offers straight rock with Peer Pressure and Northern Rockers.

Bajones, 1062 Valencia, offers good jazz groups, for example, Moment's Notice.

Barnaby's, Embarcadero Center, offers jazz with groups such as Pretty Face.

Enzo's, 3 Embarcadero Center.

Jackson's, 2237 Powell Street.

Players' Saloon, 3920 Geary Street, has hosted the White Rose Band.

Jolly Friars, 950 Clement, is known for big-band sounds. Golden Gate Swing and Mr. Music have appeared here.

Kabuki, 1881 Post Street, has featured Psychedelic Furs.

329

Punch Line, 444A Battery Street, and The Stone, 412 Broadway, have presented performers such as Bonnie Hayes, Humans, and Soul Agents. Stern Grove, Nineteenth Avenue and Sloat Boulevard, occasionally holds popular programs such as "Back in the Saddle" concert and Preservation Hall Jazz Band.

Kabballah Koffee House, 3200 California Street, offers African style jazz, blues, folk, and bluegrass.

Santa Monica

An Arts Festival is held in August, with folk music and dancing in the main streets.

South Lake Tahoe

Caesar's Tahoe and Sahara Tahoe, both off US-50, are two expensive places offering entertainment and dancing.

Yreka

The Fairgrounds, on Fairland Road, hosts the Siskiyou Golden Fair, which offers authentic country–Western.

OREGON

Canyonville

Pioneer Days takes place in August, bringing back the flavor of the old West.

Eugene

The Lane County Fair is a big event in August.

The Left Bank Dining Room, Valley River Way is a local favorite. One can dance while enjoying a window view of the Willamette River.

Newberg

The St. Paul Rodeo takes place in July, with country–Western music.

Portland

The Melody Lane Ballroom, 615 Southeast Alder, offers dancing to big bands such as Chuck Bradford's Orchestra.

The Thunderbird, 1401 North Hayden Island Drive, overlooking the Columbia River, is popular with the local citizens.

Jazz de Opus, 33 Northwest Second Avenue, is informal and experimental.

The following places offer jazz, rock and disco:

Up the Down Staircase, 424 Southwest Fourth Street.

Prima Donna, 2015 Southwest Fourth Avenue.

Opening Night, 2270 Southeast Hawthorne.

The two places listed below offer country–Western music:

Toni's Lounge, 9843 Northeast Sandy Boulevard.

Flower Drum, 14542 Southeast Division.

Washington Park and Civic Auditorium present summer concerts.

A "Music by Moonlight Festival" has been presented since 1949 in the city parks. The Festival offers musical variety.

Exposition Center hosts the Multnomah County Fair in the summer. Country–Western music is performed at the Fair.

Last Hurrah, 555 Southwest Alder, is a famous place.

Peppertree, at Holiday Inn, 8349 Northeast Columbia Boulevard, is a popular place.

The Boiler Room in the Rodeway Inn, 8247 Northeast Sandy Boulevard, offers disco.

Roseburg
The Douglas County Fair takes place in August.

Salem
The Fairgrounds, Seventeenth Street NE, hosts the Oregon State Fair in August.

Yachats
Silver Smelt Festival, in July, has a fiddler's contest with much music.

WASHINGTON

Centralia
The Southwest Washington Fair, off I-5, is a large country–Western event which takes place in August. It was held for the first time in 1909.

Cheney
Rodeo Days take over in July.

Dayton
Dayton Fairgrounds hosts the Columbia County Fair in September.

Friday Harbor
Café Harry, 35 First Street, offers jazz and rock.

Electric Company, 175 First Street South, offers swing.

Kelso
The Hilander Summer Festival takes place in June.

Mt. Vernon
Max Dale's, 2030 Riverside Drive, offers dancing and popular entertainment.

Olympia
Vance Tyee, 500 Tyee Drive, has Indian décor. It offers country–Western music and dancing.

Pasco
Columbia Basin College has hosted the Jazz Unlimited Series.

Puyallup
The County Arts Fair takes place in August. All styles of music are performed.

Seattle
The Elks Club, 2040 Westlake North, Rocking Chair, and Black and Tan have hosted Ray Charles.

Maxi's, 18740 Pacific Highway South, offers good popular entertainment and dancing.

The Trojan Horse, 415 Lenora, Doc Maynard's, 610 First Avenue, and Jack McGovern's Music Hall, Seventh and Olive, all offer quality jazz. Seattle Center presents many musical events, including the Northwest and Regional Folklife Festival in May.

Spokane

Spokane House, West 4301 Sunset Highway, offers good popular entertainment and dancing. There is a beautiful view of the city.

The Bing Crosby Library at Gonzaga University, 502 Boone Avenue. Located in the center of the campus, the Crosbyana Room contains Bing's numerous memorabilia.

Interstate Fairgrounds, Broadway and Havana Streets, hosts the Spokane Interstate Fair in September.

Vancouver

The Thunderbird Inn at the Quay, Columbia Street, offers pleasant popular music and dancing amidst nautical decor.

Walla Walla

The Orchard Street Fairgrounds hosts the Southeastern Washington Fair in September. The Fair features band concerts and rodeo shows with country–Western music.

Westport

Sourdough Lil's, 1202 Dock Street, offers banjo music, honky-tonk piano, and country–Western sing-alongs. The place is decorated in late nineteenth-century style.

Yakima

Sunfair, which hosts square dancing and country–Western music, takes place in September.

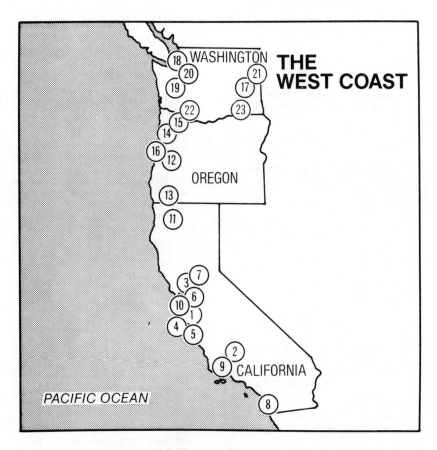

West Coast

1. Aptos, CA—Cabrillo Festival, annually with experimental music

2. Bakersfield, CA—Country-Western at Trout's, 805 N. Chester, and at Tex's Barrel House, 1524 Golden State Highway

3. Berkeley, CA—The University of California, Berkeley, has an active music department with regular presentations. The Keystone at 2119 University Avenue has rock. Jazz and blues at Larry Blake's, 2367 Telegraph Avenue and at Dock of the Bay, Berkeley Marina, foot of University Avenue

4. Carmel, CA—Sunset Center on San Carlos and Ninth streets hosts a famous Bach Festival

5. Monterey, CA—Place of Monterey Jazz Festival and Monterey County Fair

6. Oakland, CA—Paramount Theater,

2025 Broadway, houses the Oakland Symphony and Oakland Ballet. Rock and country-Western can be found at Eli's Mile High Club, 3629 Grove Street and at the Lucky Lion, 4100 Redwood Road

7. Sacramento, CA—Amphitheater at First and I streets has Dixieland Jazz Festivals. Popular music at Sacramento Inn, 1401 Arden Way. Community Center Theater presents opera

8. San Diego, CA—Open Air Theater at San Diego University hosts San Diego Symphony. San Diego Opera at Civic Theater at Civic Concourse. San Diego Stadium for rock concerts. More rock at Tacey's Chopping Block, 1740 E. Vista Way, Vista, Mom's Saloon, 945 Garnet, and Saska's, 4520 Point Loma Boulevard. Jazz at Bodie's, 6149 University

Avenue. Fiddle and banjo contests in Old-Town San Diego State Historic Park, 2725 Congress Street

9. Santa Barbara, CA—Popular music at Baudelaire's, 435 State Street and at The Shack, 5796 Dawson

10. Saratoga, CA—Villa Montalvo, off CA-9, hosts concerts and recitals as does Paul Masson winery

11. Yreka, CA—The Fairgrounds hold country fairs with much country-Western

12. Eugene, OR—Hult Performing Arts Center, 1 Eugene Center, is a site for many music and dance groups including the Eugene Symphony. Folk festivals and county fairs

13. Jacksonville, OR—Britt Music Pavilion at 46 N. Front Street, Medford, hosts music festivals

14. Newberg, OR—Site of rodeos with country-Western

15. Portland, OR—Civic Auditorium, 222 SW Clay Street, is home to the Oregon Symphony and the Portland Opera. Washington Park holds concerts and ballet performances. Melody Lane Ballroom at 615 SE Alder is for popular music as is the Thunderbird, 1401 N. Hayden Island Dr. Jazz at Jazz de Opus, 33 NW Second Avenue. Rock and disco at Up the Down Staircase, 424 SW Fourth Street and at Opening Night, 2270 SE Hawthorne. Country-Western at Toni's Lounge, 9843 NE Sandy Boulevard and at Flower Drum, 14542 SE Division. Exposition Center holds county fairs.

16. Yachats, OR—Fiddlers' contests and country-Western here

17. Cheney, WA—Rodeos, fairs here. Recitals, chamber music, and choral works at Eastern Washington University

18. Friday Harbor, WA—Jazz, swing, and rock at Café Harry, 35 First Street and at Electric Company, 175 First Street S.

19. Olympia, WA—Country-Western is at Vance Tyee, 500 Tyee Drive

20. Seattle, WA—The Seattle Center Opera House Building hosts the Seattle Symphony and Seattle Opera. The Coliseum at Fifth and Pike streets offers concerts. The Pacific Northwest Festival takes place in summer. Rock can be found at the Elks Club, 2040 Westlake North. Maxi's, 18740 Pacific Highway S., for popular music, in addition to The Trojan Horse, 415 Lenora, Doc Maynard's, 610 First Avenue, and Jack McGovern's Music Hall, Seventh and Olive streets

21. Spokane, WA—The Opera House, W. 334 Spokane Falls Boulevard, is home to the Spokane Symphony. Fox Theater, W. 1005 Sprague, hosts musical fare as does Riverfront Park. Bing Crosby Library is at Gonzaga University, 502 Boone Avenue. Popular music at Spokane House, W. 4301 Sunset Highway. Interstate Fairgrounds holds country fairs at Broadway and Havana streets

22. Vancouver, WA—Thunderbird Inn at the Quay, Columbia Street, features popular music

23. Walla Walla, WA—Orchard Street Fairgrounds hold concerts and rodeos with country-Western

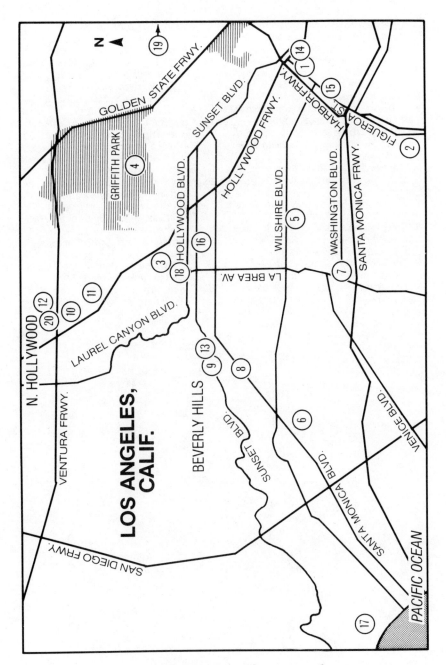

Los Angeles/Hollywood, CA

1. Music Center, 135 N. Grand Avenue, is home of the Los Angeles Philharmonic in the Dorothy Chandler Pavilion, and host to numerous opera and dance groups in the Mark Taper Forum and Ahmanson Theater

335

2. Los Angeles Memorial Coliseum, 3911 S. Figueroa Street, for concerts and dance

3. Hollywood Bowl, 2301 N. Highland Avenue, is summer home of Los Angeles Philharmonic and site of many musical events

4. Greek Theater, 2700 Vermont Avenue, for symphonic and popular music

5. Wilshire Ebell Theater, 4401 W. Eighth Street, hosts chamber music and dance groups

6. Shubert Theater, 2020 Avenue of the Stars, Century City, features musical events

7. The Parisian Room, 4906 W. Washington Boulevard, for jazz

8. Doug Weston's Troubadoor, 9081 Santa Monica Boulevard, W. Hollywood, for jazz, rock, and country-Western

9. The Roxy, 9000 Sunset Boulevard, W. Hollywood, for popular music

10. Womphoppers, Lankershim Boulevard at Hollywood Freeway, has honky-tonk and country-Western as does The Pal-omino, 6907 Lankershim

11. Rock and country-Western at Universal Amphitheater

12. Backflat at Studio One, 652 N. Lapeer Drive, N. Hollywood, for jazz, rock, and country-Western

13. Whiskey à Go-Go, 8901 Sunset Boulevard, has all popular music

14. Civic Auditorium in Civic Center, Inglewood and S. M Street, holds regular musical programs

15. Variety Arts Roof Garden, 940 S. Figueroa Street, for all popular music

16. Hollywood Palladium Ballroom, located at 6215 W. Sunset Boulevard, features popular music

17. Jazz at Pasquale's, Pacific Coast Highway, Malibu

18. Scandals, 1635 N. La Brea Avenue, for jazz and disco

19. The Pomona Fairgrounds holds the famous Los Angeles County Fair

20. Lankershim Boulevard has numerous rock, country-Western, honky-tonk and rock places

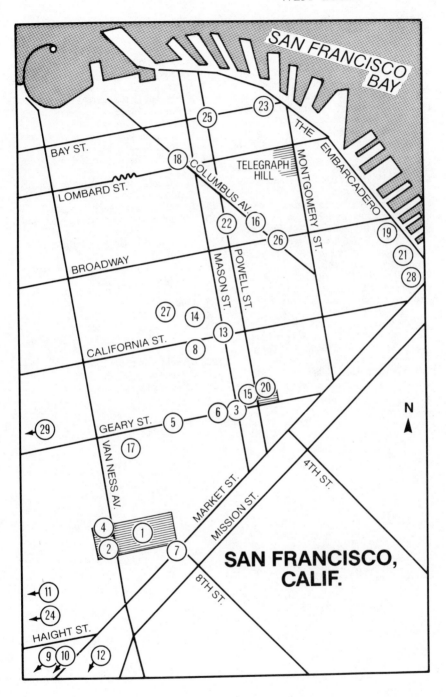

SAN FRANCISCO BAY

THE EMBARCADERO

BAY ST.

LOMBARD ST.

TELEGRAPH HILL

COLUMBUS AV.

MONTGOMERY ST.

BROADWAY

MASON ST.

POWELL ST.

CALIFORNIA ST.

GEARY ST.

VAN NESS AV.

MARKET ST.

MISSION ST.

4TH ST.

8TH ST.

HAIGHT ST.

N

SAN FRANCISCO, CALIF.

San Francisco, CA

1. Davies Symphony Hall in Civic Center, Van Ness and Grove streets, home of the San Francisco Symphony
2. War Memorial Opera House, Civic Center, home of the San Francisco Opera and San Francisco Ballet
3. Geary Theater, Geary and Mason streets, summer home of the San Francisco Ballet
4. Herbst Theater, Civic Center, Van Ness and McAllister streets, presents chamber music groups
5. Alcazar Theater, 650 Geary, for opera
6. Curran Theater, 445 Geary, for opera
7. Orpheum Theater, 1192 Market Street, has the San Francisco Light Opera
8. Masonic Auditorium, 1111 California Street, features concerts
9. Hillman Hall, Ninteenth and Ortega streets, for chamber music groups
10. San Francisco Conservatory of Music, 120 Ortega Street
11. Golden Gate Park, site for concerts
12. Sigmund Stern Grove, Nineteenth Street and Sloat Boulevard, for symphonic music, opera, and ballet
13. Fairmont Hotel, California and Mason streets, for popular music
14. Mark Hopkins Hotel on Nob Hill presents popular music
15. Sir Francis Drake Hotel, Powell and Sutter streets, is a popular nightspot
16. Keystone Corner, 750 Vallejo Street, jazz, rock and disco
17. Great American Music Hall, 859 O'Farrell Street, for rock
18. Boarding House, 901 Columbus, for rock
19. Earthquake McGoon's, 128 Embarcadero, for rock
20. Hyatt Union Square, rock and disco
21. Ripples, Embarcadero Center, jazz and rock
22. Mumms, Powell Street, for jazz, rock, and disco
23. Epaminondas, Bay and Kearny streets, for jazz and rock
24. Heaven's Gate, 1821 Haight Street, rock
25. Country-Western and honky-tonk at Jackson's, 2237 Powell Street
26. The Stone, 412 Broadway, rock
27. Nob Hill, for popular music at the hotels
28. Barnaby's and Enzo's, at Embarcadero Center, for jazz
29. Kabuki, 1881 Post Street, for rock

SOURCES FOR FURTHER READING

Balanchine, George, and Mason, Francis. *Balanchine's Complete Stories of the Great Ballets*. Garden City, NY: Doubleday, 1977.

Balliett, Whitney. *New York Notes: A Journal of Jazz in the Seventies*. New York: Da Capo Press, 1977.

Bauer, Marion, and Peyser, E. R. *Music through the Ages: An Introduction to Music History*. 3d ed., rev. by Elizabeth E. Rogers. New York: G. P. Putnam's Sons, 1967.

Blum, Daniel C. *A Pictorial Treasury of Opera in America*. New York: Greenberg, 1954.

Chase, Gilbert. *America's Music, from the Pilgrims to the Present*. 2d rev. ed. New York: McGraw-Hill, 1966. Reprint. Westport, CT: Greenwood Press, 1981.

Clark, Dick, and Robinson, Richard. *Rock, Roll and Remember*. New York: Thomas Y. Crowell, 1976.

Cornfield, Robert, and Fallwell, Marshall. *Just Country: Country People, Stories, Music*. New York: McGraw-Hill, 1976.

Davis, Ronald L. *Opera in Chicago*. 1966. Reprint. New York: Irvington Publications, 1982.

DeMille, Agnes. *The Book of the Dance*. New York: Golden Press, 1963.

Doeser, Linda. *Ballet and Dance*. New York: St. Martin's Press, 1978.

Engel, Lehman. *The American Musical Theater*. Rev. ed. New York: Macmillan, 1975.

Ewen, David. *All the Years of American Popular Music*. Englewood Cliffs, NJ: Prentice-Hall, 1977.

Gaillard, Frye. *Watermelon Wine: The Spirit of Country Music*. New York: St. Martin's Press, 1978.

Green, Douglas B. *Country Roots: The Origins of Country Music*. New York: Hawthorn Books, 1976.

Gregory, Neal, and Gregory, Janice. *When Elvis Died*. New York: Washington Square Press, 1982.

Harris, Stacy, and Krishef, Robert K. *The Carter Family*. Minneapolis, MN: Lerner Publications, 1978.

Hart, Philip. *Orpheus in the New World*. New York: W. W. Norton, 1973.

Haskins, James. *The Cotton Club.* New York: Random House, 1977.

Heilbut, Tony. *The Gospel Sound: Good News and Bad Times.* New York: Simon & Schuster, 1971.

Henderson, Mary C. *The City and the Theater: New York Playhouses from Bowling Green to Times Square.* Clifton, NJ: James T. White & Co., 1973.

Hentoff, Nat, and McCarthy, Albert. *Jazz: New Perspectives on the History of Jazz.* New York: Rinehart, 1959. Reprint. New York: Da Capo Press, 1974.

Howard, John Tasker. *Our American Music: A Comprehensive History from 1620 to the Present.* 4th ed. New York: Thomas Y. Crowell, 1965.

Kolodin, Irving. *The Metropolitan Opera: 1883-1966; a Candid History.* 4th ed. rev. New York: Knopf, 1966.

Krishef, Robert K. *Grand Ole Opry.* Minneapolis, MN: Lerner Publications, 1978.

Leatherman, Leroy. *Martha Graham: Portrait of the Lady as an Artist.* New York: Knopf, 1966.

Lowens, Irving. *Music and Musicians in Early America.* New York: W. W. Norton, 1964.

Marrocco, William Thomas, and Gleason, Harold. *Music in America: An Anthology from the Landing of the Pilgrims to the Close of the Civil War, 1620-1865.* New York: W. W. Norton, 1974.

McCarthy, Albert. *Big Band Jazz.* New York: Berkely, 1977.

McGregor, Craig, ed. *Bob Dylan: A Retrospective.* New York: William Morrow, 1972.

Oakley, Giles. *The Devil's Music: A History of the Blues.* New York: Harcourt Brace Jovanovich, 1978.

Ostransky, Leroy. *Jazz City: The Impact of Our Cities on the Development of Jazz.* New York: Prentice-Hall, 1978.

Peltz, Mary Ellis. *The Magic of the Opera: A Picture Memoir of the Metropolitan.* New York: Praeger, 1960.

Peyser, Ethel Rose, and Bauer, Marion. *How Opera Grew: From Ancient Greece to the Present Day.* New York: G. P. Putnam's Sons, 1956.

Price, Steven D. *Take Me Home: The Rise of Country and Western Music.* New York: Praeger, 1974.

Rabin, Carol Price. *Music Festivals in America.* Rev. ed. Stockbridge, MA: Berkshire Traveller Press, 1983.

Rolling Stone Press. *The Rolling Stone Illustrated History of Rock & Roll, 1950-1980.* Edited by Jim Miller. New York: Random House, 1980.

Schonberg, Harold C. *The Great Conductors.* New York: Simon & Schuster, 1970.

Shapiro, Nat, and Hentoff, Nat, eds. *Hear Me Talkin' to Ya: The Story of Jazz by the Men Who Made It.* New York: Dover, 1966.

Shaw, Arnold. *Honkers and Shouters: The Golden Years of Rhythm and Blues.* New York: Macmillan, 1978.

Shelton, Robert. *The Country Music Story: A Picture History of Country and Western Music.* Indianapolis: Bobbs Merrill Co., 1966.

Simon, George T. *The Big Bands.* Rev., enl. ed. New York: Macmillan, 1975.

Tassin, Myron. *Fifty Years at the Grand Ole' Opry.* Gretna, LA: Pelican, 1975.

Ulanov, Barry. *A Handbook of Jazz.* 1957. Reprint. Westport, CT: Greenwood Press, 1975.

Waldo, Terry. *This Is Ragtime.* New York: Hawthorn Books, 1976.

Work, John, ed. *American Negro Songs and Spirituals.* Reprint. New York: Crown, 1942.

INDEX

DATE DUE

GAYLORD			PRINTED IN U.S.A